The Truth in Hell and Other Essays on Politics and Culture, 1935–1987

The Truth in Hell
and Other Essays
on Politics and Culture,
1935–1987

HANS SPEIER

New York   Oxford
OXFORD UNIVERSITY PRESS
1989

HM
101
.S7695
1989

Oxford University Press

Oxford   New York   Toronto
Delhi   Bombay   Calcutta   Madras   Karachi
Petaling Jaya   Singapore   Hong Kong   Tokyo
Nairobi   Dar es Salaam   Cape Town
Melbourne   Auckland

and associated companies in
Berlin   Ibadan

Copyright © 1989 by Oxford University Press, Inc.

Published by Oxford University Press, Inc.,
200 Madison Avenue, New York, New York 10016

Oxford is a registered trademark of Oxford University Press.

Library of Congress Cataloging-in-Publication Data
Speier, Hans.
The truth in Hell and other essays on politics and culture,
1935-1987 / Hans Speier.   p.   cm.
Two essays translated from the German.   Includes index.
ISBN 0-19-505875-5
1. Culture.   2. Communication — Social aspects.
3. Propaganda.   4. War and society.   5. Peace.
I. Title.   HM 101.S7695   1989   306 — dc19   88-37158   CIP

9   8   7   6   5   4   3   2   1

Printed in the United States of America
on acid-free paper

For Rebecca and Julie

Preface

The papers collected in this book were written during different periods of my life while residing in the United States. I have not included anything published prior to 1933, the year in which I left my native Germany. The subjects of the essays point to different interests: sociology, foreign affairs, and the history of war; communication and propaganda; literature and the history of ideas. Only two essays, the Introduction and chapter 1, were originally written in German. In preparing the English version of the Introduction, I was grateful to receive helpful suggestions from Robert Jackall and Tom Dickey. I am also indebted to Robert Jackall for his translation of chapter 1. Differences in dates of composition and written style, as well as the wide range of themes to be found in this book, perhaps justify the autobiographical Introduction, which tries to relate at least some of my intellectual interests to experiences in my life.

All of the remaining essays were previously published, many in books that are now out of print or hard to locate. If the reader feels so inclined, he may attribute this collection either to an author's vanity in trying to prove the enduring relevance of his thought or to his wish to test its coherence.

Hartsdale, N. Y.   H.S.
December 1988

Contents

Prologue

by Arthur J. Vidich

This volume includes essays spanning more than fifty years of Hans Speier's work. Reflecting the range of his intellectual concerns, the essays reprinted here are embedded in both his personal biography and the significant political events of the twentieth century. They provide us access to a selected but panoramic portrait of this century, comparable to that provided by the classical sociologists and political economists of the past century. Just as we rely for our understanding of modern capitalism on the economic, social, cultural, and historical specificity of the works of Marx, Simmel, and Weber, so future scholars will turn to those of Speier for a sound and comprehensive interpretation of our age.

Speier was twenty-eight years old in 1933, when he arrived in the United States. He had made the decision to leave parents and homeland because he understood that Hitler and the National Socialists would not be stopped in their quest for total power. As an emigré to the United States he helped Alvin Johnson recruit the first faculty of the "University in Exile" (later called the Graduate Faculty of Political and Social Science) at the New School for Social Research in New York City. Along with other scholars recruited to that faculty, Speier examined the origins and causes of totalitarianism and the conditions under which democracy and freedom might prevail. The work of that faculty went almost unnoticed in the United States, which at that time was more concerned with its own internal problems than those of European totalitarianism. Only later was that faculty's work given notice by Hannah Arendt, whose studies on the same subjects reached a wider audience. Nonetheless, the work of these scholars remains an unjustly

neglected and voluminous body of seminal literature on political justice, democracy, the masses and classes, bureaucracy, constitutional-
ism, and the modern state.[1]

When, on December 7, 1941, the United States entered World War
II, the Graduate Faculty was recognized as a pool of talent, from
which agencies in Washington began to draw. Speier, whose studies of
public opinion and propaganda were already known, was recruited to
analyze German propaganda. As part of America's war effort, his
work gave him the opportunity to study the techniques, methods, and
mind of Joseph Goebbels, with whom he developed a deep adversarial
relationship. Speier respected Goebbels's intellect but disdained his
misuse of it in the service of National Socialism. As Speier puts it, "In
peacetime and without Hitler [Goebbels] would have been a minister
of postal service in a country without letter writers!"

Speier's wartime experience, as well as his interest in the fate of his
birthplace, led him to continue in governmental service during the
postwar occupation of Germany. Until 1947 he concerned himself
exclusively with studies of the political and social psychology of the
defeated Germans. His autobiographical account of this period poignantly reveals his state of mind when confronting fellow Germans who
neither emigrated nor opposed Hitler. In particular, the excerpts in this
volume from his book *From the Ashes of Disgrace* and his stinging
review of Karl Jaspers's book, *The Future of Germany,* also in this
volume, capture the social and political psychology of both the vanquished Germans and the young emigré whose life had been so fundamentally affected by National Socialism.

By 1947 he had completed his participation in the American occupation of Germany. He returned to the Graduate Faculty but found the
weekly routine of teaching dull; it lacked the excitement of public life
in Washington and Germany. When offered a position as director of
the Social Science Division of the Rand Corporation, he accepted;
Speier remained as director for twenty-one years. Those years provided
Speier with an unusual opportunity to observe the inner workings of
American political and military affairs and the occasion to write some
of the scholarly essays appearing in this volume.

Speier's worldview has been guided by three axiological propositions. First, he rejects all Enlightenment conceptions of progress, utopianism, and human perfectability. Living after the optimism of the
nineteenth century began to fade and through the brutality and irrationality of two twentieth-century world wars, Speier abandoned the
once sanguine idea of humankind's inevitable march into a more radi-

ant future. Having experienced, at first hand, the collapse of the Weimar Republic and Hitler's resort to force, Speier turned his attention to subjects often left untreated by more conventional sociologists, who committed to the path of enlightened progress. His outlook set him apart from those American sociologists who perceived that their nation's prosperity and emerging world dominance had given renewed impetus to Enlightenment optimism. By contrast, Speier took up such topics as militarism, total warfare, propaganda, political and diplomatic treachery, class structure, status distinctions, and the hatreds generated by ethnic, racial, and religious ideologies. This focus on the darker side of Western civilization offends the sensibilities of those who believe we live in the best of all possible worlds, or will soon achieve that exalted state of perfection. Certainly Speier's political realism did not resonate with the surge of idealism and moralism that affected the generation of sociologists who came of age in the United States during the sixties and seventies. Imagine how youthful protestors against racial injustice, unjust war, and the machinations of the military industrial complex might respond to Speier's treatment of political morality:

> Strong moral convictions, however, lead to neglect of time and circumstances, since good and evil are not subject to change. And yet, regard for time and circumstances are of the essence of politics, as they inevitably affect whatever relevance certain good or evil actions assume for taking or justifying a particular political course. Nazi Germany, as a living menace, presented the same moral problem yesterday which she presents today as a haunting memory. Politically, however, there is a difference between Germany to be conquered and Germany vanquished. A peculiarly modern type of man, usually referred to as a "moralist," tends to overlook this difference.

One should not assume from this statement that Speier is a relativist; rather, he is concerned to point out that absolute values applied to politics may produce more evil than good. Indeed, the complexities of political moralities is the deepest and most pervasive theme in all of Speier's work.[2]

Recognizing the crimes committed in the name of, or in powerful opposition to, the Enlightenment, Speier grounds his political ethic in a conception of a universal human nature. This second axis of Speier's work recognizes the full range of humanity in human nature, that is, the inevitable presence of good and evil, truth and falsehood, love and hatred, greed and generosity, loyalty and betrayal—in short, all human qualities intrinsic to men and women in all societies, times, and places. That men and women can and do commit acts of barbarity against one another is, for Speier, morally deplorable. It is, however, a still fundamental fact of life that must be recognized and accounted for when studying the social world. That they can also express and enact the highest values of civilized life is similarly embraced as part of his sociological worldview. The sociological attitude requires that the most elevated as well as the lowest and meanest features of men's and women's nature be accepted on their own terms, an attitude that, for purposes of analysis, requires that one set aside personal ethical and moral values. One cannot grasp the character of Speier's work without at the same time recognizing his fundamental respect for the dignity of the individual, his rigorous ethical standards, his deep and profound political morality, and also his unflinching realism.

Theories that appeal to an enlightened humankind's elimination of prejudice, hatred, ignorance, inequality, arbitrary government, and war overlook the persistently irrational dimensions of human nature and conduct. Treating such ideas as ideologies, Speier emancipated his intellectual perspective from the ever-hopeful and religiously or irreligiously salvational fantasies about a coming perfectability of human nature that had been espoused by such Enlightenment thinkers as Montesquieu, Rousseau, and Marx.

A fine example of Speier's perspective is found in his commentary on Maurice Joly's construction of a dialogue between Montesquieu and Machiavelli.[3]

> Joly sympathized with Montesquieu's view on liberty, but through Machiavelli refuted Montesquieu's belief in progress toward perfection of man and his social order. In the dialogue Montesquieu holds that institutional inventions of the modern enlightened age have erected a bulwark against repressive political forces of the past. To the extent that the principles of enlightenment have spread in Europe and the principles of modern political science become known, law has replaced force in theory as well as in practice. Machiavelli counters with what he regards as an "eternal truth": Man's "evil instinct" is more potent than are his good intentions, and force, fear and greed hold sway over him.

In this dialogue, Speier clearly identifies his own perception of reality with that of Machiavelli. He could hardly do otherwise. Considering the scale and ferocity of modern wars, the magnitude and extent of twentieth-century rebellions, revolutions, and genocides, and the self-righteousness with which the leaders and the followers of these wars and revolutions have convinced themselves that they are on the side of God and history, Speier shows how culturally sanctioned rhetorics provide justifications for some of the greatest horrors committed by humankind against itself. A benign hope for a brighter future is dangerously naive. Having observed some of the most atrocious of these events, Speier writes only *as if* he stood outside of them; he does this to understand them. His stance demands personal values that, although informing his particular analysis, are anchored in a universal philosophical spirit. That spirit takes justice, morals, politics, power, love, compassion, and the pursuit of truth as its basic concerns.

Clearly the political disorder, internecine treachery, and use of murder as a political weapon in the Germany of his youth left a lasting mark on Speier's character and strongly influenced his intellectual perspective. The headiness of confronting such momentous and monstrous events when so young would not permit the prolongation of late adolescent idealism. The generation of German youth who came of age in the midst of their society's moral collapse wondered where to turn for hope, let alone for personal survival. In Speier's case, the answer to this question provided the foundation for the third axis of his work, leading him to reasoned political engagement and to an intellectual attempt to understand German society. In the German intellectual tradition, in contrast to that of the United States, a sociologist does not forfeit his disciplinary identity by engaging in political activity or becoming a party member. Speier was both a political sociologist and a Social Democrat; he quickly took a stand against National Socialism.

From his earliest investigations of the new middle classes in Germany, Speier concluded that Marx's doctrine of class struggle provided neither an understanding of the modern world nor a solution for its most pressing problems. In its place he perceived that Max Weber's tripartite analysis of the relations between class, status, and political party provided an empirically powerful perspective on both the new middle classes and the new social order. He also came to see that Weber's concept of charisma — about which so much has been written in the past fifty years — all too easily becomes a catch-all term for all modern forms of hero worship. Given Weber's penchant for finding charisma as an active force in the deference shown to would-be saviors, prophets, heroes, magicians, great judges, shamans, and kings, Speier warned against a too ready use of this concept: "One suspects that Weber found charisma too often." Although Speier drew on Weber's insights on charisma, he did not accept Weber's conclusion that the social recognition of charismatic qualities "is a devout, wholly personal surrender psychologically born out of misery and hope." Speier does not believe "misery and hope" to be a sufficient explanation for an understanding of modern hero worship:

> His [Weber's] notion of charisma which has been applied to modern totalitarian leaders like Mussolini and Hitler (though less often to bolshevik chieftains) does not help us to understand why "misery and hope" may lead to frenzied political mass support of tyrants in modern civilized society, i.e., a society we like to regard as moderately rational, since it has been exposed to enlightenment and industrialization.

For Speier the problem was how to understand the heroization of modern political leaders, since clearly more than charisma is involved in the ability of modern leaders to enthrall and move the masses. Speier considered this issue in his effort to comprehend the rise and acceptance of Hitler as a German hero, and his work deepens our understanding of social and political hero worship and of personality cults. Still, the example of Hitler notwithstanding, modern civilization has not been liberated from political and other forms of irrationality. Indeed, it has even bred new forms of its own. Thus, the point at which a population might opt for a totalitarian solution, at the cost of legality and freedom, remains as central to social science today as it was for Speier. His work provides a fundamental starting point for anyone who would take up this issue today.

Having witnessed how industrialized warfare facilitated the moral depravity of both victors and vanquished in World War II, Speier could not be expected to adhere to the ethics of the Sermon on the Mount. Speier had, of course, read Max Weber's essay "Politics as a Vocation," written after the defeat of Germany in World War I, but he disagreed with what Weber had to say about ethics. Contrasting a political ethic of responsibility with one of absolute values, Weber considered which values political leaders might rely on when they decide to go to war, to bomb cities, to order the annihilation of the enemy, and to ask for superhuman sacrifices from their own followers. Weber had no answers to these questions apart from placing his faith in the decency and humanity of the political leaders whom he insisted should both examine and be held accountable for the consequences of their actions. In retrospect, this faith did not apply to the modern totalitarian leader whose political dogmatism disregarded the human consequences of his actions. The generations that came of age in Germany in the 1920s and 1930s needed moral reference points divorced from the dogmatism of religious faith and grounded in something other than nationalism. All of Speier's writings may be seen as an effort to find just such a civilized moral standard in a world all too corruptible and uncivilized. For example, how might someone from the nineteenth century, such as Marx or Weber, grasp the horrors of the twentieth as reported by Speier in a conversation with a German general:

> Then the general spoke about the firestorms, but he did not dwell on the scenes of horror described in the literature: suffocation in the shelters, people burning like torches, their feet sunk in the molten pavement. He spoke of something else. In a toneless voice he said, "The storm is so strong, it tears the clothes off so that in the face of death, the people are — naked!" To the general this was unsurpassed human degradation and horror, and it left an indelible mark of anxiety in his heart: people in the street swaying in a storm of fire, undressed before they die. I was silent. After the shadow of doomsday had passed, he continued. He said that the air attacks did not win the war and the morale of the people was not adversely affected by them, nor was production until the last phase of the war. All this is correct.
>
> Later I thought of political decisions that degraded human beings in a measure comparable to that caused by a firestorm. Jews were sent naked to the ovens to be gassed, and participants in the abortive attempt to kill and overthrow Hitler on July 20, 1944, were hanged on piano wire — naked. Such was the fate of Admiral Canaris.

Even in the twentieth century it is difficult for us to imagine a phenomenon like a firestorm, or the nuclear destruction of a city, not to mention the degradation of human dignity that occurs at the moment of a death during these or similar horrors. It was thought that the enlightened world had overcome the barbarities of the past and that irrational barbarism was now associated only with our contemporary primitives. For many "moderns" the barbarity of primitives conveniently sanctioned an assumption of their own moral superiority, blinding them to the depravity of their own civilization. Speier rejected such ethnocentrism and the smug nationalism it can engender. His own metaphor for this rejection is his memory of his father thrice "making the sign of the cross with a knife before cutting a new loaf of bread," indicating the close association between the cross and the weapon — or religion and war — in European history. When the cross, the flag, and the military crusade had once again come to dominate Europe, Speier taught himself to stand outside the values associated with those icons, assuming instead a stance of cultural marginality, provided by a deep historical awareness and a mordant sociological consciousness.

For reasons that perhaps cannot be explained, Speier's intellectual and emotional instincts led him to study the seventeenth century, particularly the thirty years of religious wars in Europe, as depicted by Grimmelshausen in *The Adventurous Simplicissimus* and the Simplician cycle of novels as a whole. Although Speier cultivated literary interests throughout his life, Grimmelshausen left an especially strong imprint on his view of the world. Once during a conversation, he told me he had encountered an old review (1838) of a new edition of *Simplicissimus* in a Berlin library when he was preparing his dissertation. The review argued that *Simplicissimus* was a satire on Parzival, the pure fool. The observation intrigued Speier at the time, but not until thirty years later, while he was a fellow at the Center for Advanced Study in the Behavioral Sciences in 1956–57, did he reread Grimmelshausen. Returning to the Rand Corporation after that year and dissatisfied with a book he was writing on German rearmament, he began translating Grimmelshausen into English, at the same time apparently reopening a source that had helped shape his own attitude to the world. It is my impression that Speier's renewed acquaintance with Grimmelshausen led to a rediscovery of himself and his sociological and historical attitude. His first reading of the work, when he was a youth, had left a deep impression on his world view and helped to shape his image of human nature. Now he had discovered the source of his own philosophy of life.

In his introduction to *"Courage, the Adventuress" and "The False Messiah,"* Speier notes the universal themes guiding Grimmelshausen's world view: "If any three motifs of universal human concern were to be singled out for the poignancy with which Grimmelshausen treats them, they could be either folly, inconstancy and laughter; adventure, evil and despair; or war, sex and religion. Consideration of any of these triads leads to the center of Grimmelshausen's world." So, I would add, do these triads lead to the center of Speier's work. Witness, in this volume, his writings on militarism, war, honor, risk, security, hero worship, laughter, fools and folly, the truth in hell, and the critique of Mannheim as a sociologist of knowledge — all Grimmelshausen in their profundity and each comprehensive in conceptions of human nature. While interpreting Grimmelshausen, Speier also reveals his own psychology of human nature; for him such a psychology includes dissimulation, masking, duplicity, the doublesidedness of good and evil, and human pretensions to godliness — all framed by the enigmas and ironies of life. To give only one illustration of how Speier reveals his own attitude, I quote from his interpretation of life presented in *The Enchanted Bird's-Nest,*

> according to which appearances cannot be trusted, because behind the facade of reasonableness, politeness, and morally impeccable behavior lie boundless evil and folly.
>
> Folly and evil are rooted in the passions: in lust and greed, in the desire to excel others and the will to dominate them, in envy and vengefulness, miserliness and sloth. Man is evil, and evil grows in the company of evil men. What rules should govern the conduct of wise men? The moral precepts which the hermit gives shortly before his death to the child Simplicius are, interestingly enough, not specifically Christian in character, a fact to which critics of Grimmelshausen have paid no attention. The dying hermit says nothing about loving one's neighbor, turning one's cheek, or trusting in God's will. *Instead he urges the child to observe three rules of conduct: know thyself, avoid bad company and be steadfast.* (emphasis added).

The advice given to the child is not as simple as might appear at first glance. The three rules of conduct would require deep introspection and a philosophical attitude toward oneself and those through whom one is revealed to oneself; an ability to select those others through whom one would wish to be led to the ethical and moral norms appropriate to a civilized life; and holding to one's values in the face of social pressure, threats, and opportunities for illicit gain. This package of advice represents an ideal that few of us are capable of fulfilling, yet it is a moral and ethical standard by which we might judge our own conduct in the world. It assumes a personal strength of character to live with as much dignity as one can muster in a world where others' shameless pursuits of their self-interests may tempt one to compromise one's own morality. Nowhere in this formula is it assumed that the good life is easily attained; yet for all the profound seriousness of life and the difficulty of knowing our own limits, all of us at times are fools. The irrationality of fate and the stupidity of the choices we sometimes make are continuous reminders of the foibles and follies of human beings. Speier makes this point in his essay "The Fool and the Social Order":

> The social order is a mold into which nature has been pressed with a crippling effect. The licentious fool disregards this order as though this was the easiest and most natural thing to do. In the process he not only exposes hypocrisy and dissimulation and pricks the bubble of pretension,

but he also robs the social order of its claim to sanctity and permanence. The fool does so without pleading a cause; he is no rebel wanting to do away with rulers, nor does he seek to establish a better rule. He is simply unruly. He seems to make no sense, but he acts as though in the light of nature everything that we think makes sense is in fact nonsense. When laughing at the fool we share this carefree disregard of the rules that we sometimes wish, and almost never dare, to break. If we never felt that order fettered our natural appetites, we would not laugh, but punish the fool who indulges his appetites and permits us to indulge vicariously our own. Through laughter we become the fool's passive accomplices.

However, the fool is only a would-be redeemer of our own foolishness, for he provides only temporary surcease, at best a small safety-valve releasing some of the burdens of living up to our own prized self-images. Speier suggests the limits of this unspiritual solution in his essay on Karl Mannheim. Modern men and women can overcome their spiritual void only by an act of commitment to a higher value. "The crisis of modern consciousness does not consist in the total suspicion of ideologies, but in the claim of politicians, sociologists, and psychologists to do away with philosophy. An allegedly socially free floating intelligentsia is not going to show us the way out of the crisis. Rather, this task belongs to the spiritually free man who cherishes spiritual freedom."

It might be added that this task belongs to the spiritually strong and the intellectually courageous, for they alone can offer us a glimpse of the world that includes irony and ambiguity unsanitized by ideological purification. This is the example that Hans Speier's work gives to us.

NOTES

1. Hans Speier's work has been known to a small group of cognescenti for many years. Best known among them in the United States was C. Wright Mills. His book, *White Collar,* was inspired by Speier's 1932 study of the German middle classes, a monograph that had been suppressed by the Nazis and was first published in Germany in 1977 under the title *Die Angestellten vor dem Nationalsozialismus: Ein Beitrag zum Verständnis der deutschen Sozialstruktur, 1918–1933* (Göttingen, 1977). A German paperback edition of the work appeared in 1989. The book was republished in English in 1986 under the title *German White-Collar Workers and the Rise of Hitler,* New Haven. C. Wright Mills had access to some chapters of this work that had been translated and reproduced in mimeograph form at Columbia University under a Works Progress Administration project in 1937.

2. This complexity of political morality was not seen by moralistic young radicals in the 1960s and 1970s, who indiscriminately assaulted government-sponsored research institutes, failing to understand that intellectual integrity is sustained by both personal conviction and artful practice, and not by institutional affiliation. One young radical, in fact, opened his anonymous review of one of Speier's books in the *Yale Review* (Spring 1969) with the statement that "for those who have been busily engaged in protesting the American military-industrial complex, the book presents a rare opportunity to confront the enemy head-on, at least in a literary way. The author [is] . . . a long time member of the *Rand Corporation*." This attempt to prove guilt by association relieved that generation from confronting Speier's work on its own terms. Some may wish to believe that mere membership in the academy bestows moral virtuosity, but such claims cannot be sustained if one recognizes that corruptability and corruption are possible anywhere, including the halls of academia. In 1968 when naive but not so innocent youthful radical students, and sometimes their not so youthful professors, laid claim to political self-righteousness, Speier's historical sociology and complex moral understanding of Western civilization probed complexities beyond their reach. One hopes that generation might now be prepared to read and understand Speier's practical and political philosophy of life.

3. See "The Truth in Hell: Maurice Joly and *The Protocols of the Wise Men of Zion*," in this volume.

*The Truth in Hell and Other Essays
on Politics and Culture, 1935–1987*

Introduction:
Autobiographical Notes

Parents and Childhood

My mother came from Anklam in Pomerania. The Persons, my mother's family, were originally from Sweden. As a Lutheran my mother had anti-Catholic prejudices. She believed that all Catholics were held in servitude by their priest, and she wrote in my diary: "Be no one's master and no one's man."

My father had the habit of making the sign of the cross with a knife three times before cutting a new loaf of bread. He was born in Berlin, as far as I know. His mother was widowed early and he left school at age fifteen to support her. He was bright and active, learned English, and in the course of time worked himself up to a fairly prominent position. Eventually, he became a director in a life insurance company. While my mother had a brother and many sisters, I knew no relatives on my father's side. When I grew up, his mother was no longer alive. He was a modest, kindly man, a good husband and father, though irascible at times.

I was born in 1905 in Berlin-Friedenau, a western suburb of the city bordering on fields where wheat and barley were grown at the beginning of the century. The modest walk-up apartment of my parents still had a tiled stove in every room, but during World War I only the small dining room was heated. The kitchen had no stove, but during the war my father built a cooking box to save gas; the box was padded inside with wood shavings. The balcony, which one entered from the dining room, was so small that only a tiny table and two chairs could be placed on it, the third chair stood half inside. When I sat on it as a child, I saw only geraniums and the sky above them, through the foliage of a tree.

I heard singing first at our neighbors, who were friends of my parents. Their name was Schlesinger. Leo Schlesinger, a salesman for a shoe factory, was the brother of Bruno Walter, the famous conductor. In his leisure time Uncle Leo sang ballads by Löwe, as well as Schubert's songs. His wife accompanied him on the piano. His old mother was my first piano teacher. She did not tolerate the slightest lack of attention and insisted on regular exercises. To her, finger exercises were the first step on the almost infinitely long way to a church in which Bach's cantata "Sleepers Awake" was being sung.

My parents favored my musical education, whereas they paid hardly any attention to my literary inclinations. Nor do I owe the awakening of my interest in the visual arts to them. It was aroused by Kurt Roesch, a friend at school who later became a master student of Karl Hofer. Kurt Roesch was a Calvinist who, like me, emigrated in 1933 to the United States because the Nazis considered his paintings "degenerate art." We remained close friends until his death in 1984.

I recall many events from my childhood, but only when I remember something I read can I report what happened in my youth in Berlin, in Germany, in the world. Nor can I fully realize that I was born during the war between Russia and Japan. As a matter of fact, even my recollections of World War I are confined to events in which I was personally involved. It was, for instance, the season of purism, in which everyone tried to replace foreign words in daily speech with German words. I collected a penny in my little bank for every *trottoir* instead of "sidewalk" (*Bürgersteig*) or *Adieu* instead of *Auf Wiedersehen* that my parents or their guests used at home. For children the war was the time of "extras" loudly announced by news vendors. One day, while playing in the street, I heard that a British ship had been sunk. I ran home breathlessly to tell my mother the news. As a reward she gave me a candy. Even at that time, the reward struck me as strange and inappropriate, and probably for this reason I still remember it.

In the summer, I went to school barefoot. In the winter I wore shoes with wooden soles. I found it strange that my father weighed the slices of bread on letter scales before distributing them. A few years later the city of Berlin sent me, as a hungry child, to an East Prussian farm. In storms and under the sun, I suddenly discovered that I was alive and felt myself to be part of nature. This was far more important to me than what followed soon: the revolution in Germany.

At School

The Helmholtz Realgymnasium in Berlin-Friedenau, where I went to school for nine years (not including the first three years of elementary instruction), was a very reactionary institution. The principal referred to the top form as his "First Battalion of the Guarda," and students who denounced a comrade to the teacher for some infraction of the rules were rewarded. The highest distinction consisted of the Helmholtz-Emblem, a kind of school medal.

At age fifteen I shocked my parents and teachers with my sudden refusal to be confirmed. I would have had the whole world against me if the Lutheran minister had not come to my help. After a close examination, he concluded that the imminent ceremony had lost its lustre in my eyes since other youngsters had openly expressed their expectations to receive many presents from parents and relatives on the occasion. Perhaps the minister understood my rebelliousness as a token of hidden awe. He visited my parents to tell them that one should not attempt to undo a conscientious decision. My parents followed his advice, but a few mothers visited the school and threatened to cancel the membership of their sons in school associations to which I belonged.

At this time a teacher beat me so violently in the face that my father noticed the traces of the punishment when he came home in the evening. Secretly he requested moderation the next time, but the teacher showed me my father's letter to him — "apparently you had to cry your eyes out at home" — and this humiliation was much worse than the punishment.

After the flight of the emperor, the collapse of the monarchy, and the end of the war, the school appeared even more reactionary to me. Almost all teachers openly showed their joy at the armed rising led by Wolfgang Kapp in 1920 and hoped for the restoration of the monarchy. Many of the students, mostly sons of civil servants and white-collar workers, were also nationalistic, whereas I visited public meetings about reforming the schools, and in my last years at school I read Ibsen and Wedekind, Gerhart Hauptmann and Ernst Toller, Georg Forster, Georg Büchner, and the new Russian literature. While I was still at school, I argued against the legend of the "stab in the back," according to which the civilians at home, not the armies at the front, had been responsible for losing the war. Nor did I ever use words like "the lie about war guilt," "November criminals," "the dictate of Versailles" — political slogans that rapidly became popular.

After my final examination in January 1923, I hoped to study at a university, but my father told me I would first have to learn something "practical"; the inflation was upsetting him. Thus, without grumbling and with poetry in my heart, I became an apprentice at a banking firm where I served first at the Berlin stock exchange as a telephone boy. It was very boring. I had barely time at noon to attend a one-hour lecture at the university. After the currency was stabilized, the bank, like many other financial institutions, was placed under temporary receivership and I was dismissed, having been employed for a little more than a year. To escape from another similar job, I became a tutor in mathematics to seventeen-year-old boys. This increased my income and left the mornings free for study at the university. It was only in 1925 that I succeeded with the help of an older friend in persuading my father to let me study in Heidelberg.

Heidelberg, 1925–1928

My major fields of study were economic theory and sociology, and I chose philosophy and modern history as minors. Because of my father's ominously progressing illness, his doctor had urged me to complete my studies as soon as possible. In 1928 I passed the doctoral examination summa cum laude with a dissertation on "Lassalle's Philosophy of History." Although I had been an assistant to the economist Emil Lederer,[1] I was especially influenced in the beginning by the sociologist Karl Mannheim and became his first doctoral student.

In Heidelberg the students lived in strictly separated circles whose boundaries could be crossed only in extraordinary circumstances, for example, because of a love affair. I had relations with students of medicine because, at a mardi gras dance in the house of the psychiatrist Hans Gruhle, I had fallen in love with Lisa Griesbach, a medical student through whom I met other students of medicine. I married Lisa in Berlin in 1929, at the time of her special training in pediatrics.

Politically more important than the separation of students by fields of study was that between the hermetically closed worlds of ordinary and of fraternity students, which resembled the civilian dress versus uniform division in the former German Empire. All my friends considered the duelling fraternity students to be ridiculous; yet they had no desire to examine the validity of this prejudice through closer association.

In my militancy I went to see the former Social Democratic Minister of Justice, Professor Gustav Radbruch. In the name of the socialist students, I told him that the university's scheduled annual festivity in honor of Bismarck would have to be canceled because the founder of the Reich had been responsible for both the antisocialist law against the workers and the so-called cultural struggle against the Catholics. Radbruch tried to calm me down, probably attributing my zeal to my youth.

There was a group of students who admired Lederer and Mannheim and felt intellectually indebted to them. They had little in common with the students of other sociologists such as Carl Brinkmann or even Alfred Weber. I did attend a seminar by Brinkmann, however, in which I happened to meet Talcott Parsons, who was studying in Heidelberg at the time.

The students who were particularly close to me included Gerhard Münzner, who later pursued an important political career in Israel; Hans Gerth (d. 1978), who probably deserves more praise than any other German immigrant for familiarizing American students with Max Weber; Svend Riemer, my old schoolmate in Berlin, who taught at the University of California, Los Angeles, until his death; Werner Falk, who went to Australia later; Ruth Ludwig (née Neuberg), whom I still visit regularly in Zurich; and several sociologists and economists from Budapest. I also knew Norbert Elias, who became Mannheim's assistant in Frankfurt and attained an impressive international reputation in exile. Only as I write these lines does it occur to me that *all* the German students who were close to me in the twenties at Heidelberg emigrated after Hitler's ascent to power. I did not think much of other sociologists, like Hans Freyer and Leopold von Wiese, but all my friends and I read Max Weber most attentively.

The students around Karl Jaspers at the time included Dolf Sternberger and Hannah Arendt. Like them I attended Jaspers's seminar, since I had to write my doctoral dissertation on the "Young Hegelians." Jaspers was very reserved, and I considered him to be "professorial." Only once did he seem interested in me personally. He put his signature next to his name, which I had entered on the registration form, and appeared to note a startling similarity of our handwritings. He said nothing, but for once looked at me for a moment. Later, at the doctoral oral examination at his house, he was reserved, as always, but friendly. In October 1945 I visited Jaspers again in Heidelberg[2] and as late as 1964 I wrote a critical paper on the development of his political views (see chap. 18).

Berlin, 1929–1933

Even before I received my doctorate, Lederer told me to see his old friend Rudolf Hilferding in Berlin, then Minister of Finance, who was later murdered by the Nazis. To him I owe a position in the book department of the Ullstein publishing house. They were preparing a huge encyclopedia, and I was engaged as editor of social science materials.

I did not regard the change from the life of a student to that of a salaried employee as a loss of freedom, for my attitude toward academic life had been ambivalent. The university simultaneously made me anxious and aroused my admiration, but it seemed to me that dependence on the dignitaries in the academic hierarchy subtly corrupted many assistants and lecturers: they tried too hard to gain the favor of their superiors and sometimes of their superiors' wives. Each of them was in danger of becoming "somebody's man." Only with increasing experience did I realize that intellectuals can be corrupted as consultants in business or advisers to statesmen, as ecclesiastical dignitaries or academic luminaries, as recipients of salaries, stipends, or grants.

My impression of the restraints of academic life was also influenced by the dream to become a free writer. In Berlin I continued to write occasional poems and short stories. Even several years after receiving my Ph.D degree I vainly tried to finish a novel, and as late as 1952 Alvin Johnson described me in his autobiography as "a sociologist with passionate literary interests."[3]

In 1929 I began to write articles for *Die Gesellschaft*, edited by Rudolf Hilferding and—while he was preoccupied with his ministerial duties—by Albert Salomon. The *Zeitschrift für Sozialforschung* of the Frankfurt Institute published many of my book reviews. I was especially proud of a magnanimous letter by Thomas Mann in which he praised an article of mine that attacked his political views. Possibly my joy was even greater when *Die Neue Rundschau*, at that time the leading literary monthly, published one of my essays in 1932.

In Berlin I at first kept as much company with writers, painters, musicians, and—thanks to my wife—physicians as with social scientists. This changed slowly only as a consequence of my work at the Deutsche Hochschule für Politik, where I began to teach political sociology in 1931, and of my participation in the Labor Education of the Social Democratic Party. I had an opportunity to meet young employed and unemployed workers and to learn more about their views, worries, and wishes than could be found in books. In preparing a seminar on unemployment, I accompanied a social worker for several weeks on home visits to families with unemployed members. This had been arranged by my wife, who had become a municipal pediatrician in Wedding, a proletarian district of the city.

Perhaps because of my contacts with workers, it now seemed to me that Mannheim had neglected real social life in his research and studied only writings. Later, when his book *Ideology and Utopia* appeared in English, I spent two painstaking months writing a long, basic criticism of his work. I said that Mannheim's sociology of knowledge was only a sociology of opinion. I had read with admiration Leo Strauss's book on Hobbes, in 1937 when this critique was published, and this had influenced my criticism of Mannheim.

I had met Strauss in 1929 in Berlin; in the thirties we became colleagues and friends at the New School in New York. Miriam, his wife, and Lisa had been good friends since childhood: they had gone to the same school in Erfurt. We met again later, when Strauss taught in Chicago and still later when he lived in California. Concerning Mannheim, let me add that I am glad to have seen him again in London in 1945, not long before his untimely death. As late as 1970 I gave an academic course on Mannheim and at that time wrote a lecture on his sociology of knowledge for the Austrian broadcasting station in Salzburg (see chap. 1).

Yet in the years 1929 through 1933 in Berlin, I was occupied not only with the sociology of knowledge and the political tasks of the intellectuals but, increasingly, with the structure of German society. I wrote a book on white-collar workers, their economic conditions, and their life-style, organizations, and political views.

The publication of this book was announced in 1932, but in 1933 the publisher refused to publish it on the advice of a National Socialist editor whom he had speedily engaged. A few chapters appeared in an English translation as a mimeographed edition in 1937, but the book as whole, revised and enlarged in German, saw the light of day only forty years later, and in an English translation only in the winter of 1986.

Since 1929, unemployment in Germany had increased in a measure that is today unimaginable, while real wages had declined. In the summer of 1933, there were about 6 million unemployed and about 3 million part-time workers, while the number of employed persons (health insurance members) amounted to less than 11.5 million. In the last years of the Weimar Republic, many new governments were formed, and their measures were based not on parliamentary decisions but on emergency legislation. Private armies—Nazi Storm Troops, communist Red Front, the Iron Front, the Steel Helmet, the republican Reichsbanner—were more visible in the streets than the police. Each organization had its own uniform, flag, heroes, slogans, and songs. They battled one another on the streets and in assembly halls.

I began to take the political danger of National Socialism seriously only in 1931, when the so-called Harzburg Front was founded through an agreement between Hugenberg, the reactionary, and Hitler, the rabble rouser. From then on I considered it possible that a coalition government with Hitler as chancellor would be formed, and I feared the influence of Hindenburg's son on his old father. I learned of the illegal removal of the Prussian government by Chancellor von Papen while I was lecturing at the Hochschule für Politik. Assuming that a general strike would be the immediate response to that act, I expected the lights to go out at any moment. But everything remained bright.

Then, on the evening of January 30, 1933, from the upper deck of a motor bus, I saw the triumphant torchlight parade of the SA in the inner city. It ushered in a period of new political delusions among those Germans who were not Nazis. Many observers believed that in due time Hitler would be tamed or dominated by the reactionaries in his government, a view that was shared by communists. Many Jews and other Germans believed Hitler's anti-Semitism would no longer be important once it had served its purpose in getting him into power.

I had read *Mein Kampf* and other Nazi literature only after my student days. I was shocked most by Hitler's telegram, in August 1932, publicly expressing his loyalty to the five SA men in the Silesian village of Potempa who had been sentenced to death (and were later pardoned) for having dragged a communist out of his bed at night to trample him to death in the presence of his mother. I could not understand why, after this telegram, Hindenburg appointed this man Chancellor of the Reich, he had found collaborators outside his party, and millions of Germans had voted for him.

Soon after Hitler assumed power, the Deutsche Hochschule für Politik was closed and taken over by the Ministry of Propaganda. I lost my position, and Lisa was dismissed by the city because she was Jewish. I did not accept an offer to work in Belgium because, in case of war, Belgium was too close to Germany. From the beginning I considered it probable that Hitler would drag Europe into war and his rule would end only with Germany's military defeat. My opinion was not shaken by the foreign-policy support Stalin and the pope quickly gave Hitler. Predictions of a short-term dictatorship supported by economic arguments did not impress me. Economists, I thought, did not adequately understand phenomena of power, and they underestimated the strength of Hitler's will to power because they considered the will to power for its own sake impermissible — an irrational violation, as it were, of the neatly predictable motives of *homo economicus.*

New York, 1933–1942

In August 1933 I met Alvin Johnson in London. He was the director of the New School for Social Research in New York, a school for adult education established during World War I.

When the first lists of the German scholars dismissed by the Nazis were published in April 1933, Johnson wanted to add a "University in Exile" to his school to permit a group of German scholars to continue their work as free men. In London, he consulted Lederer, whom he had met in Germany on earlier travel to Europe, about the composition of a new graduate department at the New School. A few of the ousted professors who had reached England preferred to remain there, but a few other projected members of the new faculty were still in Germany. Lederer had asked me to come to London so that I might return to the Third Reich armed with contracts of employment and establish contact with the chosen academicians, who were entirely unaware of their luck. Before I departed from London, Johnson told me he hoped that I, too, would agree to teach at the University-in-Exile. I was, of course, happy to do so and thus became the youngest member of the group. The lectures began on October 2. In early September, two weeks after the birth of my daughter, I traveled on a German ship to New York; my wife came with the baby in October. In the first faculty meeting, Lederer was voted to be Dean and I secretary of the new faculty.

My recent experiences deeply influenced my scientific interests; the most important of these was not my own emigration but Hitler's triumph, which appeared to me as the last fatal step in a decivilization of life. In the nineteenth century, certain artists who had grown tired of Europe fled middle-class civilization as a solution for personal problems. Richard Wagner made such flight a recreational cult in his *Ring of the Nibelungen*. The Dadaists celebrated this flight in an eccentric manner in Zurich during World War I and later in Europe and the United States. Finally, it was praised and recommended to the youth by political writers such as Ernst Jünger.

I considered Hitler a pathological case; but why did this man have so many adherents? In my studies of the structure of German society, I believed that I had discovered certain relevant facts: the traditionally popular tendencies toward antifeminism, antiparliamentarism, anti-Semitism, and jingoism; the traditional contempt for the workers as "men without a fatherland," a widely shared educational conceit in the middle classes that went hand-in-hand with growing numbers of half-educated people; and an equally widespread ignorance in the middle classes about the life of the lower classes. All of these defects, which had helped the Nazis, I found to be prominent in the so-called new middle classes, especially among those white-collar workers who were organized in the most successful German National Association of Clerks (DHV).

In addition, the middle classes had a special predisposition for Nazism that may perhaps be dubbed aggressive stupidity. For example, on April 2, 1913 a member of the high bourgeoisie spoke in the Prussian Diet about modern art on the occasion of a special exhibition in Cologne. Utterly outraged, he showed reproductions of paintings by Franz Marc. Then, uncannily adumbrating Nazi lingo, he urged the Ministry of Culture "not to support this *sick* art (bravo!), i.e., especially no acquisitions for museums (laughter)! For, gentlemen, we have here a trend which from my layman's point of view amounts to *degeneration*, one of the symptoms of these *sick* times."[4] Of the 443 deputies, none rose to contradict the man.

In addition to such predispositions in the middle classes, the special vulnerability of the young to Hitler's temptations also puzzled me. How could this phenomenon be explained? It seemed to me that in modern society, unemployment and other "passive" imposed risks of life were coupled with a withering away of self-chosen "active" dangers. Perhaps young people, in the darkness of tedious lives punctuated only by imposed risk, yearned for the adventurously flickering light of active, self-chosen dangers. The attractiveness of such danger was certainly celebrated before them by excited writers and propagandists. In 1940 I presented an elaborate paper on this point for discussion in two sessions of a seminar conducted jointly by Max Wertheimer, Kurt Riezler, Karen Horney, and myself (see chap. 5).

Regarding immigration, I reflected on its influence on intellectual work. At the fourth anniversary of the Graduate Faculty of the New School, I participated with others, including Thomas Mann, in a celebration. There I presented a paper on the intellectuals in exile, citing many historical precedents. Somewhat defiantly I referred to Hugo Grotius, who had said that if his country did not miss him he could live without it.

It had not been easy for me to leave Germany, my morally sullied homeland, for I was deeply worried about my parents. Both of them were very ill and virtually paralyzed. I had no brothers or sisters who could have looked after them. Before I left, I went to see the physician who treated my father and was well acquainted with the whole family. In my anguish, I asked for his advice. He replied seriously and calmly that in the case of such a grave conflict, wife and child must be given more consideration than parents. I have often asked myself what turn my life would have taken had I not been married in 1933. Probably I would have stayed in Germany because of my parents. My parents died in Berlin, fortunately prior to the outbreak of war. The house in which they lived all their married life was demolished in an air raid. I visited my father once more for three days after my mother's death in 1936. He was sitting in a wheelchair, unable to speak or to write. A nurse took care of him. She prevailed upon him to change his last will in her favor. After his death I learned from a legal document that in the presence of the nurse and two lawyers he had agreed to this change by lowering his eyelids.

While writing my book on white-collar workers I had learned a great deal from de Tocqueville's and Max Weber's reflections on honor and social esteem. Demanding and conveying esteem appeared to be social phenomena crucial for the functioning of German society. In the United States I continued to reflect on the nature of social prestige and in this connection studied the French moralists in the Ancien Régime; finally, I wrote a paper on "Honor and Social Structure" (see chap. 2). In addition, I read many books on war and militarism at that time. Militarism I understood as the adoption of military values by civilians — a characteristic phenomenon in modern pre-Hitler German society.

I may have been the first social scientist in the United States, prior to World War II, to offer a lecture course on the sociology of war. At the time, I planned to write a book on this subject but finished only certain preparatory studies: papers on the social types of war, class stratification and war, militarism in the eighteenth century (see chap. 3), Ludendorff and the German concept of "total war" (see chap. 4), the "fifth column" and its historical precursors, maps as instruments of propaganda, and a few other studies. Shortly after Chamberlain returned from Munich to London with the announcement of "Peace in Our Time," I chose *War in Our Time* as the title of symposium papers that I was editing with Alfred Kähler. It contained contributions by various faculty members; I wrote the introduction and the chapter on "Morale and Propaganda." The book was published in 1939.

Emil Lederer, who contributed two chapters to this volume, died suddenly that year. He left an unfinished book-length manuscript on National Socialism, which I edited for publication in 1940. Titled

State of the Masses: The Threat of the Classless Society, it was re-published in 1967.

Studies of propaganda had been conducted in the United States since the end of World War I, especially under the influence of Harold D. Lasswell, whom I met in 1935 in Chicago. Not very much later Paul Lazarsfeld's market research attracted wide attention, as did many studies on methods and techniques of opinion polls. The growth of this literature was not an unmixed blessing for the social sciences. Certain analytical methods were refined, but the substantive questions that were being asked became shallower. Interest in the structure of modern society faded along with interest in the fate of man in that society. As the techniques of *interviewing* became increasingly standardized, the art of *conversation*, which also provides civilized access to the life of the mind, deteriorated.

My efforts began from the proposition that political propaganda is a secondary phenomenon. Facts and measures are the primary phenomena and the existence of these cannot be denied effectively by propaganda, nor can evident meaning be reversed forever. When the price of food is rising, housewives do not believe propagandists who say food prices are stable. Propaganda can only report or try to cover with silence; it can evaluate and interpret, magnify or belittle, and so on. In foreign affairs, the points of reference and the limits of propaganda are set by diplomacy and political decisions, and in wartime especially by military events. Later, Goebbels had no cure for Stalingrad, and in peacetime without Hitler he would have been a minister of postal service in a country without letter writers. Mass propaganda is as little capable of winning a war as are aerial bombardments of civilians: in general, only the government or the military leaders can call a halt to fighting.

About a year after the beginning of World War II in Europe, I became acquainted with Ernst Kris, a Viennese art historian and psychoanalyst. He emigrated first to London and showed up in New York only in 1940. When war broke out in Europe, the British Broadcasting Corporation (BBC) listened in on German domestic radio broadcasts and made up "monitoring reports" that were distributed to British government offices. Kris came to the United States with a promise from the BBC to put these confidential reports at the disposal of researchers. He suggested that we propose to the Rockefeller Foundation the funding of a research project on totalitarian communication to be directed jointly by us. The project would analyze the voluminous BBC material. The Rockefeller Foundation realized that such a project would give young social scientists an opportunity to be trained in propaganda analysis. These specialists would have useful skills and experiences in the event the United States entered the war. For this reason, Kris and I received the means to employ some assistants and students. There was at that time no better opportunity in the United States for closely examining the Nazi mentality while trying out new methods of content analysis. Participation in the project also offered opportunities to observe the connection between politics, warfare, and propaganda and to study the organizational preconditions for molding public opinion. Kris, I, and some of our collaborators published a few papers, and in 1944 a book entitled *German Radio Propaganda* concluded our research in this area.

Washington, D.C., 1942–1947

Shortly after Hitler's declaration of war with the United States, I received an offer from the Federal Communications Commission (FCC) in Washington to work in the analysis division of its Foreign Broadcast Intelligence Service. At first I was in charge of the German section, and later of the entire division. Kris stayed in New York, but several members of our group followed me. For about a year I continued work on our project in New York on weekends.

The analysis division produced weekly publications on the propaganda of many governments. These periodic publications were supplemented by special reports on so-called black (i.e., camouflaged) broadcasting stations that spread propaganda allegedly originating in resistance groups, or on important speeches by German leaders and other topics. Work in the FCC was strenuous, but we were rewarded by intimate knowledge of the material we worked on. In addition, we formed a group of gifted sociologists, psychologists, anthropologists, and political scientists. A few of my colleagues became lifelong friends: Alexander George,[5] today an internationally recognized authority on foreign affairs; Henry Kellermann, later a colleague of mine in the Department of State; and Nathan Leites, an unusually gifted interpreter of bolshevism. Edward A. Shils, the Chicago-based sociologist, was also personally close to me at that time.

In 1944 my work changed. I went from the FCC to the Overseas Branch of the Office of War Information (OWI). There I wrote the directives for the broadcasts to Germany. The European department was headed by Wallace Carroll, a highly regarded journalist.[6] Eventually my grandiose title was "propaganda policy adviser." My work

required close contact with specialists in the State Department, representatives of the War Department in the OWI, and a few Englishmen
stationed in Washington for liaison purposes, especially Geoffrey
Gorer, the author of a book on the Marquis de Sade.

My assignment gave me an opportunity to observe the connections
between political measures, military events, and propaganda. Under-
standably, the war aim of unconditional surrender was heatedly discussed in the office, as in the whole country. We knew Goebbels used
this demand, enunciated at the Conference of Casablanca at the beginning of 1943, to spur the fighting spirit of his compatriots. I did not
find it hard to accept the unconditional surrender of the enemy as our
war aim. I understood the proclamation of Casablanca as an effort to
sustain and strengthen the hope of liberation in the countries occupied
and exploited by the Germans. At the same time I regarded the blunt
demand as a rhetorical contribution to the war at a time when hundreds of thousands of Russians were killed fighting the Wehrmacht,
with more than one and a half years still to pass before a second front
was established. Finally, the declaration of Casablanca served to assure Stalin that the Western powers would not conclude a separate
peace with Hitler and at the same time disabuse Stalin of his ominous
declaration of November 6, 1942, according to which it was not only
"impossible" but "inadvisable" to destroy Germany's military power.[7]
This declaration did not exclude the possibility of a separate peace
between the Soviet Union and Germany. Stalin did not repeat himself
on this point after Casablanca but left repetitions to the captured
German officers who conducted anti-Nazi propaganda with Russian
support.

What did we in the OWI think about the events of July 20, 1944?
The attempt of the conspirators to get rid of Hitler by force came
rather late, and I considered it inappropriate to glorify a failure at that
time. In addition, no doubt, Goebbels eagerly awaited an opportunity
to cite American comments, using them in calumniating the German
resistance. I was not surprised when on November 11, 1944, the Berlin
correspondent of *Aftonbladet* reported that Dr. Ley, the leader of the
Labor Front, had declared in Goebbels' paper *Der Angriff* that responsibility for the military setbacks of the Wehrmacht since Stalingrad — in Russia, Africa, Sicily, and Italy — was exclusively that of the
traitors Victor Emmanuel III and Pietro Badoglio. Dr. Ley then added
that all these traitorious actions had reached their acme in the attempted assassination on July 20.

In late summer of 1945, the Department of State assumed the responsibility for American information policy abroad, and in September I returned to Europe for two months to establish personal contact for the State Department with General Robert McClure in the U.S. military government and with personnel in the Information Control Division under his command. On this trip I met William Benton, the later senator from Connecticut, who had just been appointed Assistant Secretary of State for Information Policy. On his journey to Europe he was detained by fog in Bad Homburg and spent a few unplanned hours behind barbed wire in General McClure's headquarters. I was asked to talk with him. After the conversation, he cabled Washington, praising my familiarity with the German situation in an excessively generous way. Thereupon the State Department sent a cable offering me a position on its planning staff. I did not accept this offer but asked for an extension of my leave from the New School to become the acting chief of the Division for Occupied Areas. I was responsible to Benton. In 1946, accompanied by the nominal chief of the division and two engineers, I traveled again to Europe; the group was to recommend the technically and politically best location for a European broadcasting station that could relay programs originating with the Voice of America to the East. After consultation in London, Paris, and Luxemburg we recommended Munich as the best location. General Clay did not wish the State Department to curtail his authority and use "his" zone of occupation to do anything against "our allies." He did not prevail.

Before giving an account of my first return to Germany, I want to comment on another subject. After Pearl Harbor, U.S. government agencies tried to obtain the services of German-born anti-Nazis who had sought refuge in the United States, become citizens, and possessed useful area knowledge. Nevertheless, I expected to encounter occasional distrust or at least reserve in government service, but I was wrong. My German origin led to difficulties only once, and this unimportant episode occurred in Europe after the fighting had ceased.[8] In this connection I recall two other relevant incidents.

Toward the end of hostilities in Europe all activities of the occupation authorities had to be planned. The question arose: What kind of music ought to be broadcast in Germany? The required recordings had to be procured in time. Geoffrey Gorer wanted to prohibit not only military music and Nazi tunes but also German classical music. The Germans had heard enough Bach and Beethoven, he said, and they ought to listen for once to Purcell, Tchaikovsky, and Sibelius. I thought that he might have at least suggested a list of more distinguished composers, such as Purcell, Monteverdi, and Rameau, and I did not hide my anger.

Much worse than this absurd incident was a speech in Washington made by a prominent official in the OWI after his return from a trip to Germany in the spring of 1944. He had been to Aachen. Describing the destruction of the city, he concluded, "Facing such devastation, one only wishes to see all German cities in this condition." It was a civilian who spoke in this way. Perhaps I should have considered that this outburst of hatred occurred after the last German offensive in the Ardennes (where more American soldiers were killed than in Vietnam). Perhaps the speaker had lost a son or a brother in the war. But I did not think of that at the time. I shuddered, faced with Hitler's power over the feelings of this man and faced with his unrestrained thirst for revenge.

After terminating my work in Washington in 1947 (except for consultative services), I published a systematic study of psychological warfare (see chap. 8). I also gave a series of lectures on this subject in the school for diplomats of the State Department and in various military academies.

Sojourns in Germany

Since 1945 I have spent about two months in Europe almost every year (without ever being tempted to change my permanent residence). Many of my impressions of Europe derive from these late, long visits. Thus, my reading of the Nibelungenlied as a boy in Berlin is connected in my mind with a visit from Wiesbaden to the imperial cathedral at Worms in 1952 and with an excursion from Vienna to the Wachau, the Nibelung district, in 1969. I also visited Austria for the first time in my life only in 1945, when I traveled to many German cities in a military vehicle. I discovered Germany when its cities were in ashes. In Berlin, where I had lived for many years, I lost my way. I tried to capture the crushing impressions of misery and destruction on my first visits in 1945 and 1946 in letters to my wife.[9]

In the first years after the war urban Germany was not only physically devastated, but the social order was tottering as well. Moreover, the moral deterioration in consequence of Nazi rule, war and occupation was not confined to the Germans. At the time, I often thought of Grimmelshausen's descriptions of the unspeakable cruelties the peasants perpetrated on the marauders and the marauders in turn on the peasants during the Thirty Years' War. Despite the arrival of the large masses of German refugees from the East, it was perhaps not as terrible this time as it had been in the seventeenth century. However, under Hitler's rule it had been more atrocious than at the time of Gustav Adolf and Wallenstein. But then they had been civilized.

When I arrived in Germany in September 1945, the first American official reports on the concentration camps had just been published. In Frankfurt I attended the first public test-showing of the documentary film *The Mills of Death*, on conditions in the camps; immediately thereafter in the backroom of a pub, I conducted a discussion with Germans who had been asked to attend the showing by the military government (see chap. 15). After that day I have never asked a German—neither in 1945 nor later on, during more than thirty trips to Germany—whether or not he or a member of his family had been a Nazi. At first I feared being lied to or receiving an evasive and possibly even cynical answer. At the time I believed—after the murder of Jews, Gypsies, political dissenters, Jehovah's Witnesses, homosexuals, sick people, foreigners of all sorts, men and women, children and old people—that the Germans would never be able to lead a quiet life.

At the same time, I soon noticed that those Germans who did live with a sense of guilt had not been fanatical Nazis and, conversely, that those who had been fanatical Nazis felt the least remorse about their political and moral depravity. In addition, misery in Germany was so grave and the ability to reflect quietly so rare that it appeared vain and unproductive to me to discuss the past with Germans.

Disorientation was widespread. For example, there soon emerged so-called inner emigrants, who boasted not to have emigrated, although they were (or claimed to have been) anti-Nazis. In 1945 Frank Thiess justified his decision to stay in Germany with the argument that he had not wished to leave his sick mother (viz., Germany) to watch "the German tragedy from the boxes and orchestra seats abroad."[10] And Arnold Bergsträsser, who had come to the United States only in 1937, wrote as early as 1942 about the intellectuals who remained in the Third Reich: "Their difficulties were incomparably greater than those of a refugee who enjoyed the accommodating hospitality of a free country."[11] Evidently, during five years in the United States Bergsträsser had never met a single immigrant who had to struggle with misery.

Neither in 1945 nor later did Germans inquire of me about the lives of former friends or acquaintances who had emigrated after 1933. The only exception was the theologian Rudolf Bultmann, who, when I visited him in Marburg, inquired about Leo Strauss. By contrast, Karl

Jaspers did not ask about Emil Lederer, one of his former colleagues, nor about any other emigrated German academician. Perhaps he was well informed in any event, or perhaps the end of 1945 did not yet permit even simple friendliness.

Later, Germans spoke often about their miserable life under Hitler. In fact, they were so preoccupied with their own experiences that the lives of their listeners grew pale for them. Even as late as the 1970s, my second wife, Margit (Lisa had died in 1965) interrupted the endless monologue of an old friend by saying; "We know you went through hard times, but at least you are alive. . . . " She did not add that her own brother and father had been killed by the Nazis, and that she herself had spent two years in prison. As it happens, all this was known to the loquacious lady. She had, indeed, suffered. Toward the end of the war, her family had been bombed out in Berlin, and after the war she had been raped by a Soviet officer. But she had never inquired what had happened in our lives in the years from 1933 to 1945 or 1972. She connected our presence with our earlier, pre-1933 past, with which she was familiar. Perhaps it was embarrassment or some vague guilt feelings that prompted her not to inquire about later events that were unknown to her, and the flood of words about her own miserable life offered her a refuge from her own confusion.

In the first years after the war, I was not happy with all aspects of the American policy toward Germany. I regarded the thesis of the collective guilt of the Germans as faulty and regrettable. It was effective primarily with those Germans who were least responsible for the moral collapse of their nation. Moreover, it attributed to every citizen of the victorious powers a moral superiority that, had fates been reversed under the coercion of a totalitarian regime, might have proved untenable. Related reasons prompted me to oppose the talk about "reeducation," which seemed to make Americans the guardians and teachers of political civility, quite apart from the fact that adults cannot be taught such civility as children can be taught to read and write. While I was still working in the State Department, I wrote a paper on this subject (see chap. 17).

Furthermore, in the first years of the occupation period I was disappointed that American policy offered so little support to the noncommunist left. The Christian Democrats were closer to the authorities than the Social Democrats, which disquieted me for two reasons. In the initial period after the war had ended, I feared a revival of German nationalism once the economy was revived, and I expected such neonationalism to be resisted by the socialists. In addition, I felt closer to the

Social Democrats than to the Christian Democrats because in the Nazi period the former had suffered more and offered more resistance than the latter. Indeed, even in the fifties, the percentage of Social Democratic deputies in the Bundestag who had been arrested or had suffered economic disadvantages during the rule of the Nazis was much higher than the corresponding percentage of Christian Democrats.[12] At the time, I underestimated the possibility of a gradually increasing neutralist orientation, which gained importance rather soon, after 1950, and eventually (in 1987) led to a "humanistic" fraternization between Social Democrats in western Germany and the Socialist Unity Party in East Germany.

In 1947 I left government service, but I remained a consultant to the State Department until 1952. Thus, in 1950 I traveled with Wallace Carroll to Europe, and the two of us, at the behest of John McCloy, the first American ambassador in Bonn, wrote recommendations for American policy and propaganda toward East Germany.[13]

After leaving the government, I returned to the New School. However, the graduate faculty seemed sleepy compared with Washington — indeed, almost provincial — and in any event it was a strange oasis of exile. Many of my old friends in the faculty had died or found other work. Thus, in 1948 I accepted an offer to establish a social science division in the Rand Corporation.

Santa Monica, California, 1948–1969

Rand — a contraction of *R*esearch *an*d *D*evelopment — is a nonprofit organization. It has nothing to do with a British motion picture firm, as General Gehlen, the head of German counterintelligence, assumed when I visited him for the first time. Rather, Rand researched questions in the area of national security and other problems of public interest. Founded shortly after the conclusion of World War II by General "Hap" Arnold, the commander of the U.S. Air Force, Rand was at first supported exclusively by public funds. Later its income was derived increasingly from sources of civilian government agencies and by grants from municipalities and foundations. In its initial phase Rand had only three divisions — mathematics, nuclear physics, and technology — but very soon two new divisions, economics and social science, were added. The staff of my division represented many academic disciplines: history, psychology, philosophy, anthropology, political science, and statistics. In addition, almost every member was especially familiar with a particular country. The number of languages that could be spoken and written in the division was greater than the number of persons. At the beginning, I also saw to it that every staff member had been active at some time in a government office, for I feared the naiveté and conceit of academicians who had no experience in Washington.

I enjoyed complete freedom in selecting personnel, setting initial remunerations, and developing the research program; none of my suggestions was vetoed. I advocated not confining the research program to the interests of the Strategic Air Force but extending it to NATO, Soviet foreign policy and military doctrine, and other areas. A listing of the various titles of a few of the books produced by members of this division in the first years of my association with Rand reflects the multifaceted nature of this research (see p. 32). We set out to work on the interrelations of foreign policy and military power. We tried to develop personal contacts with foreign leaders in various walks of life. In allied countries we had close contacts with politicians, civil servants, military personnel, scientists, business leaders, journalists, and publishers. Often foreign acquaintances were invited to visit Rand, present lectures, and participate in discussions. For my part, I arranged for the visits to Rand of many members of the German Bundestag, along with German diplomats and scientists. Also, members of the government in Bonn, high civil servants, and ecclesiastical dignitaries came to Santa Monica, the main headquarters of Rand.

Contact with the universities was close and extended beyond professors. Occasionally we offered positions at Rand to postgraduate students. They could finish studies Rand was interested in and submit them as doctoral dissertations to specified universities with which we had made arrangements. Also Rand gave grants to selected universities to support research by graduate students as they saw fit. The Freie Universität in Berlin was the only foreign university to receive such annual stipends for several years.

Only a few mathematicians, physicists, or engineers had an adequate understanding of the contribution social scientists could make in working on problems of national security. Either they believed in the omnipotence of social scientists, expecting that they could build castles in the air the way one builds bridges across a river, or they held the equally inappropriate view that social scientists were not concerned with anything scientific at all and the solution of political problems could therefore just as well be left to astrologers, charlatans, or poets. Seldom did one encounter the opinion that it was perhaps possible to enhance the scientific character of work in the social sciences. Even then, however, physical scientists usually expected such an improvement to come not from more precise knowledge of the subject matter but from simplification of the question and increased mathematization of the answer. These and related prejudices occasionally demanded much from my limited skill in dealing with people.

Once two engineers came to see me with the following suggestion. The United States had great difficulties with de Gaulle and other allies, a harmful situation for the West. In contrast, the Soviet Union was always supported by its satellites. Shouldn't Rand study the alliance behavior of the East, reduce it to maxims, and recommend to the State Department or the president the application of these maxims to our policy vis-à-vis NATO? I did not begin my reply with praise of freedom but with the assumption of a conflict between different divisions at Rand. What was to be done about it? admonishments? a discussion? arbitration by an ombudsman? firing those who quarreled? shooting them? At the same time this incident illustrates what made Rand a great place to work. Any question could be raised; no question was absurd on the face of it, only answers might be.

Outside the social science division life at Rand had futuristic features. The past, however, had no value except as a steppingstone on the way to the present. The futuristic character of thinking in Rand expressed itself, among other things, in the fact that many bright people believed the future could be planned and "made." There was even talk of "futures"—that is, future in the plural form. Little, if anything, was to be left to chance. Chance was considered a disturbance, an irregularity, a blemish. In a conversation with a mathematician, I once mentioned that Napoleon, when choosing a man for promotion to the position of general, always inquired whether the man had been favored by luck in important moments of his life. I shall never forget the complete lack of comprehension on the face of my colleague.

Rand has often been attacked, from both the left for alleged war mongering and the right for alleged defeatist views. In 1958, when a book by Paul Kecskemeti on strategic surrender was published, a storm of indignation was unleashed from the right. It raged in Senate debates, and involved even the White House in utterly meaningless excitement. Prominent people who had never read the book accused the author and Rand of advocating surrender of the United States in a future war! The author had only expressed the view that unconditional surrender was not a reasonable war aim.

Conversely, during the war in Vietnam, Daniel Ellsberg committed an act of sensational insubordination: as an employee of Rand he was obligated to observe the rules of secrecy, but he photocopied a voluminous secret document concerned with the war and put it at the disposal of the New York *Times*. The ensuing public scandal led to the resignation of the president of Rand, and for years Air Force officers were stationed at Rand to supervise the handling of classified documents.

Of course, everybody considered for employment by Rand was investigated before he was hired and gained access to classified documents. I had to wait an unusually long time for the so-called Q-clearance required for access to nuclear installations and documents. Eventually I learned the delay was caused by the fact that Lisa and I knew Gerhard Colm's wife. Hannah Colm, a psychologist, had given a personal check in the amount of ten dollars to a cooperative bookstore in Washington without realizing that the store distributed communist propaganda.

In the course of the more than twenty years that I worked at Rand (without any written contract, by the way), I lectured occasionally at the Air Academy, the Air War College, other military schools, and various universities. I visited not only military command posts in the United States but also U.S. and allied military headquarters in Europe, especially Paris, Wiesbaden, and Heidelberg. In Paris and Santa Monica I talked with General Lauris Norstad about the Atlantic alliance; in my own work I was occupied, though not exclusively, with NATO and American policy toward Germany.

On my travels I visited Germans in many walks of life, but especially politicians of all parties and many higher officers who had played important roles in the past war or were in some way participating in the rearmament effort after 1950, as advisers, in active service, or as critics.

I prepared with special care my encounters with these former officers by reading memoirs, diaries, and the rapidly growing historical literature on World War II. In the course of time I learned much not only about the ideas of the former German military elite, to which I had never had any prior access, but also about their manners and ethos.

It was relatively easy after the war to gain access to higher officers in the former Wehrmacht. Through defeat, the war crimes trials, and the political upheaval that followed the war, they had lost status. Contacts with American visitors who were not overbearing or ignorant, or simply curious, strengthened their impaired self-esteem.

Twice — each time after a seven-year period of work — Rand arranged for a sabbatical so that I could work without administrative diversions. In 1956–57 I was a Fellow of the Center for Advanced Study in the Behavioral Sciences in Stanford and finished my previously mentioned book on German rearmament. I also edited, with W. Phillips Davison, symposium papers on the political views of the civilian German elites (*West German Leadership and Foreign Policy*, 1957). I spent 1964 in New York as senior fellow of the Council on Foreign Relations. I concerned myself again with U.S. policy toward Germany, but only a few chapters of a new book were published as articles in American and British journals.

On November 27, 1958, Khrushchev's ultimatum was published, with which he initiated the second Berlin crisis. I followed the subsequent events closely and wrote a report on the Soviet tactic of intimidation and blackmail. The expanded version of this report was published in 1961 as a book, *Divided Berlin*, with simultaneous publication in German and soon thereafter in Spanish and Japanese. While the book was at the printer, the walls were built in and around Berlin.

In addition to Germany and NATO, I worked at Rand on the techniques of nuclear blackmail and the development of a political "game," namely, the simulation of international conflict. In these games or exercises, for the development of which my colleague Herbert Goldhamer deserves major credit, the players simulated the governments of countries locked in an assumed conflict. They made the decisions of their respective "governments." The umpires played god, providing nongovernmental input into the game (e.g., a poor harvest, a strike, the death of a leader, leaks of [possibly distorted] intelligence, and so forth). Rand was an organization almost made for developing such an exercise, for it disposed of many scientific, military and technical specialists, and the social science division offered good area knowledge. Our efforts became known in Washington and the request reached us to admit personnel from the State Department and the Pentagon as observers. We agreed with the provision that the visitors would actively participate in the game. It was a pathbreaking success. The techniques developed in Rand were also tried out at various universities for purposes of instruction.[14]

After the Berlin wall was erected, I continued to travel frequently to Germany. For many years I participated in the so-called Wehrkunde conferences in Munich, at which prominent politicians and military experts from all NATO countries (and from Switzerland) discussed the prevailing military and political situation of the alliance.

In the spring of 1966 I spoke at the University of Texas in a lecture series on the Atlantic Alliance and American Interests. The other participants were Henry A. Kissinger, André Philip, Fritz Erler, and John J. McCloy.

During the long years of my work at Rand, a few other books of mine were published. In 1952 a collection of selected papers and essays covering the years 1929–51 was published under the title *Social Order and the Risks of War*. I included in it a few previously unpublished papers, among them an essay, especially dear to me, on Shakespeare's *The Tempest*, which I had written in 1942 for my students in conjunction with a seminar on the sociology of literature (see chap. 10).

Beginning in the early fifties, I devoted my leisure time to an intensive study of Grimmelshausen, who had participated in the penultimate total war in Europe (1618–48) and described the then prevailing conditions of life in a cycle of picaresque novels. Only in 1963 did I write, as a contribution to the Leo Strauss-Festschrift, a paper on Grimmelshausen's last novella, which concludes *The Wondrous Bird's Nest, Part II*. I translated this astonishing tale as "The False Messiah"; it was published together with my translation of *Courage, the Adventuress*, the sixth book in the cycle.[15] I introduced these translations with a long statement in which I presented the view, based on my research (see chaps. 11 and 12), that Grimmelshausen's work is replete with blasphemous double meanings.

In 1969, a second volume of selected essays was published: *Force and Folly*. Part I contained papers in the field of international affairs; Part II consisted of papers in literary history and a related essay, "The Fool and the Social Order," which was an enlarged version of a paper presented at the 1967 meeting of the American Sociological Society in San Francisco (see chap. 13).

**Amherst, Massachusetts, 1969–1973, and
Hartsdale, New York, 1973**

In 1970 I would have reached retirement age at Rand, but I had resigned a year earlier. While I was active at Rand, several universities had inquired whether I might want to resume my academic career. In the early fifties a prestigious university had approached Rand and suggested moving the whole social science division to their campus and offering faculty positions to the senior personnel. Over a period of time I had rejected eight offers of academic and administrative positions, including one at the Ford Foundation, where in 1950 I had consulted with Rowan Gaither, who later served as the president of the foundation, on a new program in the social sciences.[16]

However, I accepted the offer I received in 1969 from the University of Massachusetts at Amherst. As the Robert M. MacIver Professor of Sociology and Political Science, I belonged to two departments and could avoid narrow intellectual confinement. Furthermore, Amherst, a small village in the charming Connecticut River Valley, was only a few hours by car from the beautiful old farmhouse in New Hampshire I had acquired in a dilapidated condition in 1936 and where my family had spent many happy summer months. Kurt Roesch owned the nearest house, a mile down the road. My children learned almost everything they know about nature and rural America in New Hampshire.

The University of Massachusetts at Amherst had a respected department of German, and I expected more frequent opportunities for conversations on literary history than I had had at Rand. Unfortunately, the compartmentalization of intellectual life found at many universities confined such exchanges to cocktail parties. I was astonished that few people spoke about their work or their plans of work, and I have only a few recollections of interesting tabletalk.I was either unwilling or unable to change this deplorable situation and tried instead to compensate for this failure with my teaching activities. In my lecture course on communication, I spoke initially about silence and gestures. I asked the students to jot down quickly what they thought could be expressed by silence — rejection, agreement, irresolution, mourning, etc. — and then read to them the poem by Edgar Lee Masters on this subject ("Silence"). I illustrated my comments on gestures with pictures of gestures and body postures that have opposite meanings in different cultures and others whose meaning is culturally and historically unchanging, like genuflection (for which parallels can be found in submissive animal behavior), or raised hands, as in Grünewald's Isenheim Altarpiece in Colmar, and of Buddhist sculptures with the symbolic finger signs (Mudrā).

The members of my seminar on Mannheim's sociology of knowledge read contemporary books by Jaspers and other authors on the intellectual crisis of Germany in the twenties; I informed them about the economic and social situation and finally invited them in the evening to my house, where they listened to the 1958 German-language production of *The Threepenny Opera*. With the help of an English translation, they were able to follow the recording. The evening did not begin with Brecht and Weil, however, but with an aria from Handel's *Rodelinda*. I told the listeners to imagine that in Handel's time the heroic tenor arias were sung by castrated singers with soprano voices. The parts of Cesare and Tamerlano were given to Italian eunuchs, and

Handel's early opera *Teseo* had no role requiring a voice deeper than contralto. The aristocratic public favored mythological and ancient historical subjects in operas and regarded outstanding castrati as highly as later generations admired Caruso and Tagliavini. I mentioned that the psychoanalysts had neglected to study the life of famous castrati, possibly to unearth relevant material on the so-called castration anxiety.

But Handel's style of opera suddenly became unpopular. The public went wild over *The Beggar's Opera* with which John Gay and John Christoffer Pepusch scored such a sensational success in London in 1728. Two hundred years later, Brecht borrowed the characters and the cynical insolence of the text for his *Threepenny Opera*. The music of *The Beggar's Opera* was not high art: it was borrowed, in part, from English and French folk songs, although one of the finest melodies came from Handel's concert for the harp.

Finally, after some selections from *The Beggar's Opera*, Weil's music was performed, while the students made themselves comfortable on the rug and listened to Brecht's impudent words. Their astonishment waxed when I told them that more than forty years ago (1928) this aggressive opera was a great success in free Berlin, not long before Hitler was appointed chancellor. I also mentioned that the "Ballad of Sexual Dependency," sung by Trude Hesterberg, could be heard only in this version, for in the first New York performance of *The Threepenny Opera* (1954) it was timidly toned down; it was even announced as the "Ballad of Dependency." I had to translate this ballad for the students more accurately than Marc Blitzstein had rendered it. This was followed by questions and answers on censorship and the complicated connections between middle-class political freedom and lack of sexual freedom, on the one hand, and sexual openness and lack of political freedom in premodern times, on the other.

I left Amherst in 1973, again one year before attaining the retirement age for employment at the university. I moved to Hartsdale, a village in the vicinity of New York City. A year after the move, the university held an international conference in my honor on the subject "Intellectuals, Knowledge, and the Public Arena."[17] In my concluding speech I spoke about agonies and triumphs in the life of intellectuals. The most trying humiliation of intellectually creative persons is perhaps not the consequence of tyrannical demands to deny their convictions: again and again good writers have successfully evaded such constraint by learning how to write between the lines. The worst blackening was rather the perverted use and praise of ideas that an author has presented but condemned. As a model case I referred to Maurice Joly's *Dialogue aux Enfers entre Montesquieu et Machiavel*, a book published in 1864 with a barely disguised message against Napoleon III and his government practices. Later it served Russian anti-Semitic forgers as a source for the so-called Protocols of the Wise Men of Zion, which, like the scriptures, were translated into all languages to become the bible of fanaticism. With the views he attributed to Machiavelli, Joly wanted to chastise Napoleon III, but the forgers put them into the mouths of alleged Jewish conspirators (see chap. 14).

In the next few years I worked on several unfinished projects. I published in German a small book entitled *Wit and Politics*, an expanded version of a lecture presented at the University of Freiburg. I revised and enlarged my early book on white-collar workers in the Weimar republic and translated it several years later for the English-language edition of 1986. I wrote several contributions to the three-volume *Propaganda and Communication in World History* (see chaps. 6, 7, and 9). One of them, "The Communication of Secret Meaning," had been in the making for more than ten years. Finally, I put together letters, reports, and notes on my impressions and conversations during the first ten postwar years in Germany. This was published in 1976 as *From the Ashes of Disgrace* (see chaps. 15 and 16). In 1976 I was visiting professor for one semester on the graduate faculty of the New School. The same year I presented the opening address on "The Chances for Peace" (see chap. 19) at an international conference in Bad Godesberg in honor of Gustav Heinemann, president of the Federal Republic of Germany.

Finally, I wrote a paper, in both German and English, on Emil Lederer's "Life and Work." In honor of Lederer's hundredth birthday, both Heidelberg University (1982) and the New School (1983) held memorial celebrations. On both occasions I spoke about my old and unforgettable teacher.

Postscript

Thinking back on my life, I consider the influence of my immigration rather unimportant. Not so that of National Socialism: Hitlerism has strengthened my moral and political convictions. True, the immigration experience gave me opportunities for interesting and perhaps useful work, but this was partly because I was young when I arrived in America, standing at the threshold of my career. I had no reason to mourn something I had lost. Nor did I miss the familiar, since I was captivated by the unfamiliar in the new country, and I was fully occupied.

Through my children I was able to catch up with many early experiences which contribute, in the first school years and even earlier, to the process of Americanization. Older immigrants do not have this advantage. My daughter, Sybil, who was born in Germany, was not even two months old when she arrived in New York. Later, during her first school years, I drove her to school in the morning so that she would not have to cross a major thoroughfare on foot. Often we were late. On one occasion Sybil noticed that I was restless for this reason. She only said, "It's not bad. I'll tell the teacher I overslept." Suddenly I realized I still had the fear of teachers in my bones, although I now was a grownup American. Since that time I have noticed only rarely any conscious sense of being an "exile." When this does occur, it is usually prompted by matters of taste and occasionally by Germans asking me stupid questions that I could not answer the way I would have had I still been a German. About three years ago, for instance, a well-educated German lady asked me which side I had hoped would win the war while I was in government service: the Germans or the Americans. Fortunately, the alienating effect of such questions spares the Germans, past and present, who are dear to me.

My son, Steven, was born in the United States in 1939. He speaks no German. His wife, Nancy, and he have two adopted children. The elder boy is half-Chinese and the younger is Korean by birth. A few years ago, when I vainly tried to find out something about my father's family, Steven asked me why I was interested in that. I laughed, replying that possibly I was of Jewish origin. He countered, "I did not know that the Nazis influenced you after all." I think he was wrong, but I liked his response.

NOTES

1. "Emil Lederer (1882–1939): Life and Work" in M. Lewis and J. L. Miller (eds.), *Research in Social Problems and Public Policy*, Vol. 3, Greenwich, Conn., 1984, pp. 1–20.
2. In a letter from Germany to Lisa Speier, my first wife, I described my visit to Jaspers in October 1945; see Hans Speier, *From the Ashes of Disgrace: A Journal from Germany, 1945–1955*, Amherst, Mass., 1981, pp. 35–40.
3. Alvin Johnson, *Pioneer's Progress*, New York, 1952, p. 343.
4. Quoted by Jürgen Klaus, "Dokumentation," in *Entartete Kunst-Bildersturm vor 25 Jahren* (catalogue of exhibition held at Haus der Kunst, Munich, October 25 to December 16, 1962).

5. Alexander L. George later analyzed the wartime work of the German section in his book *Propaganda Analysis*, Chicago, 1959.
6. Wallace Carroll published an account of American wartime propaganda directed at Germany in *Persuade or Perish*, New York, 1948.
7. Stalin made this remark on November 6, 1942. See *Soviet War Documents*, Embassy of the USSR, Washington, D.C., Information Bulletin, Special Supplement, December 31, 1943, p. 41.
8. See Speier, *From the Ashes of Disgrace*, pp. 3–4.
9. Ibid., pp. 17–73.
10. Frank Thiess in *Frankfurter Rundschau*, August 25, 1945 (rpt. from the *Hessische Post*).
11. Cited by Claus-Dieter Crohn, "Der Fall Bergsträsser in Amerika," in *Exilforschung, Ein internationales Jahrbuch* (Munich), vol. 4, 1986, p. 266.
12. See Hans Speier, *German Rearmament and Atomic War*, Evanston, Ill., 1957, pp. 176–77.
13. Speier, *From the Ashes of Disgrace*, pp. 90–106.
14. See Herbert Goldhamer and Hans Speier, "Some Observations on Political Gaming," in Hans Speier, *Force and Folly*, Cambridge, Mass., and London, 1969, pp. 163–79.
15. H. J. C. von Grimmelshausen, *"Courage, the Adventuress" and "The False Messiah,"* Translation and Introduction by Hans Speier, Princeton, N.J., 1964.
16. See Arnold Thackray, "CASBS: Notes Toward a History," in Center for Advanced Study in the Behavioral Sciences. Annual Report, 1984, pp. 59–71.
17. For an account of this conference, see Charles H. Page, *Fifty Years in the Sociological Enterprise*, Amherst, Mass., 1982, pp. 254–56.

AUTHORED WORKS

German Radio Propaganda (with Ernst Kris et al.). New York, 1944.
Social Order and the Risks of War, New York, 1952. Cambridge, Mass., 1969.
German Rearmament and Atomic War. Glencoe, Ill., 1957.
Divided Berlin, New York, 1964.
J. C. Grimmelshausen's *Courage/The False Messiah*. Translation and Introduction by Hans Speier. Princeton, N.J., 1964.
Force and Folly. Cambridge, Mass., 1969.
Witz und Politik. Zurich, 1975.
From the Ashes of Disgrace: A Journal from Germany 1945–1955. Amherst, Mass., 1981.
German White-Collar Workers and the Rise of Hitler. New Haven, Conn., 1986; English translation of *Die Angestellten vor dem Nationalsozialismus*. Göttingen, 1977.

EDITED WORKS

War in Our Time (with Alfred Kähler). New York, 1939.
Emil Lederer, State of the Masses. New York, 1940.
West German Leadership and Foreign Policy (with W. Phillips Davison). Glencoe, Ill., 1957.
Propaganda and Communication in World History, (with H. D. Lasswell and D. Lerner). Honolulu, 1979 (Vol. 1); 1980 (Vols. 2 and 3).

SELECTED PUBLICATIONS OF THE RAND SOCIAL SCIENCE DIVISION, 1952-1963

P. Selznick, *The Organizational Weapon: A Study of Bolshevik Strategy and Tactics*, 1952

H. Goldhamer and A. W. Marshall, *Psychosis and Civilization*, 1953

N. Leites, *A Study of Bolshevism*, 1953

R. L. Garthoff, *Soviet Military Doctrine*, 1953

N. Leites and E. Bernaut, *Ritual of Liquidation: The Case of the Moscow Trials*, 1954

B. L. Smith and C. M. Smith, *International Communication and Political Opinion: A Guide to the Literature*, 1956

H. Speier, *German Rearmament and Nuclear War*, 1957

M. Rush, *The Rise of Khrushchev*, 1958

W. P. Davison, *The Berlin Blockade*, 1958

P. Kecskemeti, *Strategic Surrender: The Politics of Victory and Defeat*, 1958

A. George, *Propaganda-Analysis: A Study of Inferences Made from Nazi-Propaganda in World War II*, 1959

N. Leites, *On the Game of Politics in France*, 1959

F. N. Trager, ed., *Marxism in Southeast Asia*, 1959

B. Brodie, *Strategy in the Missile Age*, 1959

H. S. Dinerstein, *War and the Soviet Union: Nuclear Weapons and the Revolution in Soviet Military and Political Thinking*, 1959

A. S. Whiting, *China Crosses the Yalu: The Decision to Enter the Korean War*, 1960

J. J. Johnson, ed., *The Role of the Military in Underdeveloped Countries*, 1960

P. Kecskemeti, *The Unexpected Revolution: Social Forces in the Hungarian Uprising*, 1961

G. K. Tanham, *Communist Revolutionary Warfare: The Vietnim in Indo-China*, 1961

H. L. Hsieh, *Communist China's Strategy in the Nuclear Era*, 1962

L. Gouré, *Civil Defense in the Soviet Union*, 1962

L. Gouré, *The Siege of Leningrad*, 1962

J. M. Goldsen, ed., *Outer Space in World Politics*, 1963

PART ONE

Society in Peace and War

1

Karl Mannheim as
a Sociologist of Knowledge

When one speaks of Karl Mannheim as a sociologist of knowledge, one must confine oneself to his middle period, which may be dated with some precision as the years from 1925 to 1933. His writings before 1925 deal especially with epistemological problems and with questions about the interpretation of visual art.

Except for some preparatory essays, it was the book *Ideology and Utopia* that first established Karl Mannheim's reputation as a sociologist of knowledge. It appeared in 1929, just as the Weimar Republic had reached the high point of its intellectual productivity. Mannheim taught in Germany only for a few years. He began in the Winter semester of 1926 as a lecturer in sociology in Heidelberg. I attended his inaugural lecture and decided afterwards to ask him during his office hours for permission to join his seminar. He inquired which of his writings I had already read. I was disconcerted, since I had not registered for a single course in sociology, nor had I read any of his writings. I told him that I had heard his lecture the day before and was now firmly resolved to study sociology as my main subject. Mannheim laughed. A little more than two years later, I was his first Ph.D. candidate.

This essay was originally written in German in 1969 and revised in 1988. English translation by Robert Jackall first published in the *International Journal of Politics, Culture, and Society*, 2, no. 1 (Fall 1988), 81–94. Reprinted by permission of Human Sciences Press, Inc.

Soon after that, Mannheim was appointed full professor at Frankfurt, but in 1933 he became one of the first prominent academic victims of the Nazi regime. Mannheim was a Jew and his sociology was considered a destructive science. Even before Hitler assumed power, the outstanding Romanist Ernst Robert Curtius (1886–1956) had written about Mannheim that his publications were an "interlacing of German Jewry with socialist or marxist or 'submarxist' teachings about society." Such vulgarities, even in German academic circles, preceded the establishment of the concentration camps. The German mind was endangered, wrote Curtius. This was indeed the case, and even distinguished scholars like Curtius contributed their part to it.

Mannheim emigrated to London but there he did not pursue his interests in the sociology of knowledge but turned rather to other things, especially to macrosociological structural analyses and to questions about education and social planning. Evidently, England was not a fertile soil for further research in the field of studies about ideology and the so-called existential determination of thought.

During the twelve years of Nazi domination, the seats of learning in German sociology were occupied by half-educated careerists or by tedious pedants; the works of Mannheim on the sociology of knowledge were read only in foreign lands. The translation into English of *Ideology and Utopia* by Louis Wirth and Edward A. Shils was of seminal importance, and this appeared in New York in 1936. A long series of critical essays and monographs followed in different languages. After the war, German social scientists began to focus attention on Mannheim once again. Unfortunately, many of these new works centered continually on the sterile topic of whether Mannheim was a Marxist or not — a question which had already been amply discussed in 1928 at the German Sociological Society in Zurich. In this debate, Alfred Weber contended that Mannheim was influenced by Karl Marx and that was bad; Werner Sombart (1863–1960) said that Mannheim was not influenced by Marx and that was good. Then Professor Alfred Meusel (1896–1960), who taught sociology at Aachen, said that Mannheim was influenced by Marx, something he considered good, but Meusel went on to say that he had to object to the particular presentation of Marxist views on the sociology of thought that Mannheim had given. Meusel was entirely right in his objection and the postwar German discussion has added nothing essential to the Zurich debate. Generally speaking, the epistemological questions which Mannheim raised still seem to arouse greater interest in Germany today than the possibility of undertaking empirical research in the sociology of knowledge.

The best overview of the international literature on Karl Mannheim's sociology of knowledge comes from Kurt H. Wolff, one of his former students, who has been teaching in the United States since 1935. His book,[1] a collection of essays in which Mannheim and his early German and later American critics are treated fully, is basically a scholastic exegesis of social scientific theories; it offers no advance beyond Mannheim in the empirical investigation of events in the history of thought. We are indebted to Kurt H. Wolff for publishing in his book a long letter that Mannheim had written shortly before his death responding to a critical analysis of his work in a seminar arranged by Wolff. The letter, Mannheim's last comment on the sociology of knowledge, permits no doubt that right up to his death Mannheim regarded the epistemological implications of his sociology of knowledge as a pathbreaking accomplishment. He wrote that he wished "to break through the old epistemology in a radical way," that it seemed to him that "he had not entirely succeeded" in this, and that he "believed our whole generation must work on it." But I am getting ahead of my story.

When Mannheim began to teach at Heidelberg, the university was for students of social science the place where Max Weber, the most important sociologist of this century, had taught. Of course, in 1926 Max Weber was no longer alive, but students were still concerned with his methodology, argued about his typology of domination, and discussed his teaching on the relationship between capitalism and the Protestant ethic. They admired Weber's comparative sociology of religion and fought over his interpretation of politics, but above all, they learned from him the most important thing that students can learn: high standards of scientific work.

Max Weber's well-known brother Alfred, who lived in the shadow of his older sibling, lectured on cultural sociology in Heidelberg. Max Weber's methodological views were influenced by the philosopher Heinrich Rickert, who still lectured in Heidelberg in 1926. The students heard him in the same auditorium in which Hegel had taught. Hegel's phenomenology was the subject of a seminar by Karl Jaspers. Among economists, Mannheim's friend Emil Lederer exercised the greatest power of attraction. In conjunction with Joseph Schumpeter and Alfred Weber, he edited the *Archiv für Sozialwissenschaft und Sozialpolitik* that had been founded by Werner Sombart, Max Weber, and Edgar Jaffé. It was the most important German periodical in the field of social science. It was also in this *Archiv* that Mannheim's first essays on the sociology of knowledge appeared. Naturally, in 1933 the journal ceased publication. Among the many other professors of social science at Heidelberg of rank and name, the legal scholar Gustav Radbruch, a former Minister of Justice, especially deserves to be mentioned. Also the George circle was represented in the faculty of philosophy among others. But above all the distinguished historian of German literature, Friedrich Gundolf, taught in Heidelberg without giving a hint of the eloquence of his writing or the charm of his personality in his lifeless lectures. One occasionally encountered the master himself on the street. Stefan George did not saunter, however; rather, he strode — a white-haired, inaccessible actor of the cultural role that he had created and was performing.

In Heidelberg, the train station stood on the edge of the city away from the university, as if the world and its traffic were unconnected to the spiritual home of the students. When this observation was being made, one shrugged and remarked ironically that there were two mountains [*Berge*] in Germany, the Magic Mountain [*Der Zauberberg*] and Heidelberg. In any event, one spoke in such a way among the ordinary students. They had scarcely any contact with the members of the dueling fraternities. These two groups of students lived in separate worlds. The students who belonged to fraternities had more money, ate better, and were almost never seen at the cheap "mensa." They also read less and did not seem to seek out the same lectures. In the years from 1926 till 1928, I don't remember seeing even a single fraternity student in a seminar by Jaspers, Lederer, or Mannheim.

From 1926 to 1928, Karl Mannheim lectured and gave seminars about conservative thought, about Max Weber, and he also gave, if I remember correctly, together with Emil Lederer, a seminar on imperialism. But these topics do not explain his power of attraction and his following, which grew from semester to semester to the satisfaction of his admirers and to the dismay of some of his colleagues who regretted or envied his influence with students. He was a good pedagogue. Free of any professorial haughtiness, he expected solid intellectual exertion, without demanding it. Criticism did not make him impatient. He gave the independent efforts of his students praise and even open admiration. But even his talents as a teacher do not really account for the fascination which Mannheim exerted. Much more, it impressed those who listened to him or read his works that he seemed to be concerned in everything that he said or wrote with the diagnosis of the deep spiritual crisis of the time. And like many other cultural critics before him and after him he seemed also to point to a way of resolving the crisis. No wonder that only a few who heard him or read him remained indifferent! There were those who thought his diagnosis to be false or who took offense at his teachings which boldly called into question the competence of philosophy. There were others who succumbed to the magic of his words or felt his deep passion and great seriousness. So it happened that in the last years of the Weimar Republic, the sociology of knowledge became almost a fashionable school of thought. It is astonishing how many then and later well-known scholars and publicists were seriously engaged with Mannheim's sociology of knowledge. Among only some names to note: Herbert Marcuse (1898-1979), Hans Zehrer, editor of *Die Tat*, the historian and sociologist Alfred von Martin, the philosopher Eduard Spranger (1812-1963), Karl August Wittvogel (1896-1988), Max Horkheimer (1895-1973), the Viennese positivist Otto Neurath (1882-1945), Hannah Arendt (1906-1975), Siegfried Marck (1889-1957), Alexander von Schelting (1894-1963), and the theologian Paul Tillich — they all published articles about Mannheim in the years before 1933.[2]

Mannheim's teaching is easily understood, if one does not burden the description with the arguable definitions of ideology and utopia, as the title of his major work might suggest, but rather starts with the commonplace observations which exemplify the asserted perspectivism of thought. I will confine myself to three examples.

Some years ago, I found myself in the difficult position of having to explain to a child who was five years old the difference between "concrete" and "abstract." I said to her that all things are concrete that one can touch, for example, the chair, the table, and the bread on the table. Many other words, like "dream" or "the day after tomorrow" or "joy" signify something abstract, which one can not even touch. The child was reflectively still for a moment and then said: "I understand." Somewhat disconcerted, I asked what then might be truly abstract. The answer: "God, Santa Claus, and poison ivy." The child had not only understood my faulty descriptions, but she had also misunderstood them in a way appropriate for her age. Of course, unlike adults, little children do not differentiate between "can" and "may," so that poison ivy, Santa Claus, and God belong in the same category, for one neither can nor may take any of the three things in one's hand. The child sees the world from the perspective of a child. Just as there is a standpoint of a child, there is also that of an adult, and that of a sick person. There are many such natural perspectives of both feeling and thought.

In a similar way, one can speak of particular historical perspectives. By way of example, epilepsy was considered for many hundreds of years to be a holy exception among people. It was believed that epileptics were divinely inspired. Today, epileptics are treated as sick people who need medical help.

A third example from an entirely different area: Frederick the Great once said that the wars he waged should not concern his peasants. This viewpoint might seem strange to us today, but it was justified in the eighteenth century when wars were universally carried on with armies who got their weapons from arsenals. The wear and tear of war was not replaced from the production of new weapons. Food provisions came from warehouses and military operations were confined to certain seasons of the year and to certain times of the day. The peasants were illiterate; they tilled the land and paid taxes. Society was not mobilized for war as in the industrial age and the vital risk of war, that is, of a violent death, was run only by officers and soldiers, not by civilians. In short, Frederick the Great was a child of his age and spoke about war from the perspective of his historical experience.

This perspectivism of outlook and thought becomes especially meaningful in conflict, that is, it is not only a natural or historical reality as is the perspective of a child or that of the Prussian king, but it is also a socially important phenomenon. If employers and employees are embroiled in wage disputes, their views split apart chiefly along the lines of their interests; the employer ordinarily prefers to pay a lower wage than the worker wishes to get. But beyond that the parties in this conflict also have different ideas about a just wage and probably about justice in general.

Each party has its own standpoint. From it, it sees in a characteristic and particular way the nature of the struggle, the distribution of power, the desirable order of social life, and how to get from the present into the future, that is, politics. And from this standpoint, each party forms an opinion of the arguments of the opponent, perceiving the opponent's prejudices without necessarily recognizing its own. All of this holds fundamentally true in every social conflict, no matter whether it concerns political parties, or families that have fallen out, or social classes, age groups, religious communities, ethnically divided peoples, or states.

Occasionally, Mannheim differentiated the area of perspectivist, existentially determined thought from that which constitutes the exact natural sciences. Not all thought is existentially determined. Mathematics, physics, biology, and the other natural sciences are not ostensibly perspectivist. He remarked once that one cannot tell who thought that the sum of $2+2=4$. But it is different in thinking about history, or politics, or spiritual matters, or social science, and even in everyday thinking. In all of these modes of thought — to borrow a phrase from Dilthey — it is "the whole man" who thinks. But the whole man is inextricably caught up in historical change and in social circumstances.

For Mannheim, thought is, before all else, related to particular social classes at a particular stage of historical development. Because of the perspectivism of thought, one can speak of certain styles of thought and these styles of thought may be attributed to the known wishes or the unknown motivations of social classes. Clearly, Mannheim's sociology of knowledge grew out of the ground of Marxist teachings on ideologies, although one can easily note differences between Marx and Mannheim. Undoubtedly, during the 1920s, Mannheim stood under the influence of Georg Lukács, especially of his book *History and Class Consciousness*. Probably, he was also indebted to Lukács for his interest in the idea of so-called false consciousness.

Some critics used to assert that Mannheim's sociology of knowledge was a consequence of the struggle between political parties in the Weimar Republic. I consider this explanation questionable. From the standpoint of the history of ideas, Mannheim saw his sociology of knowledge as a final phase of a development that led from Kant continuing through Hegel and Marx into the present. It is the way of "consciousness in general," leading to the Hegelian "folk mind" as the expression of the historized consciousness, and further to Marx's notion of social classes as carriers of ideologies (in the case of bourgeois or other class interests destined to perish in history) and as the basis of the proletariat's program of action that is historically destined to be victorious. Mannheim claimed for himself to have developed a total notion of ideology in all of its "perilously radical meaning." With this he thought that he could show "the radical disquiet of our whole spiritual condition but also its ultimate fruitfulness." It was the ominous but at the same time extremely hopeful tone of such formulations that thrilled the students.

What did he mean when he spoke of ideology as a *total* and *general* phenomenon? He had a double contrast in mind. He did not mean to suggest that only a few *particular* statements that somebody made were ideological, but rather *all* of his statements. Nor did ideology in Mannheim's sense refer only to the thinking of certain *special* groups, for example, the bourgeoisie, but not the proletariat; instead, the term characterized the thinking of *all* groups. To put it differently, formerly one might accuse somebody of being unable to do justice to a given subject and thus either consciously or unwittingly falsifying it. Today, by contrast, one denies his ability to think correctly at all by

discrediting the whole structure of his thinking as ideological. Second, when one spoke formerly of ideology, one meant basically only the ideas of the *opponent*, while today even one's own thoughts are seen to be existentially determined.

Since 1925, Mannheim had argued that "the emergence of the 'unveiling' consciousness" and the societal relativization not only of one's own thought but of the "totality" of the mental world were two of the essential conditions of the sociology of knowledge. All thought, that of the philosophers no less than that of the propagandists, is existentially determined; not only all moral teachings but also epistemologies are ideological. Philosophical inquiries about being and time, or about the nature of man, can be attributed to social interests in just the same way as can political claims.

It is in an atmosphere of such a total suspicion of ideology to which all thinking is exposed that the crisis of modern consciousness takes shape. Briefly put, the sociology of erroneous ideas, of opinions, and of prejudice is extended by Mannheim to a sociology of truth, so that the sociology of knowledge, one might say, dislodges philosophy.

Mannheim's notion of social class is expressed broadly and inexactly, which makes it, unfortunately, impossible to prove adequately the theory of existential determination. Also, the method recommended by Mannheim for "attribution," that is, the assignment of certain ideas to certain social classes, class interests, or class needs, encounters insuperable difficulties if one is not satisfied with apodictic though vague formulations, but prefers unambiguous language. These difficulties become intensified still further insofar as Mannheim occasionally brought notions borrowed from psychoanalysis into his teachings. He spoke, for instance, of "unconscious motivations" of the social classes. Now clearly it is hard enough to grasp adequately the known interest of social groups simply because these interests often get articulated not by the group itself but by intellectuals who don't belong to the class for which they speak. It was Marx and Engels, not workers, who put forth the idea that the proletariat had a class interest in overthrowing capitalism. Other intellectuals, like Lenin, for example, have stated just the opposite, namely that workers had an interest solely in bettering their situation within capitalist society as the trade unions had already in fact done and are still doing where they have the political possibility to act collectively. Only radical intellectuals and organizations truly designed for struggle want to alter society in a revolutionary way. This gap between intellectuals and workers has accompanied the political history of the working class from the beginning.

The sociologist of knowledge must therefore be clear about these matters. That is, does he want to describe the interests of a class on the basis of the *practice* of this class or does he rather want to rely on the *theories* of intellectuals? In my opinion, only practice is a firm ground for such constructions while other treatments lead to speculative distinctions like those between "correct" and "false" consciousness. Radical intellectuals who are not workers regularly claim to know what the right consciousness of workers should be. In the history of the workers' movement, radical intellectuals have often charged workers with not pursuing their own proper interests, with acting falsely, and with having a "false consciousness." When Mannheim speaks of the *unconscious* motivations of social classes, not only is he raising the difficulty of how to ascertain these unconscious collective processes, but also the possibility of having to distinguish the false and correct contents of the collective unconscious. All of this is, of course, fantastic. Nowhere in Mannheim's work can one find a clue of how one can advance from these notions to empirical investigations. Nowhere in his work has Mannheim tried to authenticate the existence of any unconscious motivations of social classes. And never has he undertaken the task of showing which specific social interests or unconscious motivations corresponded to different programs of class goals or class actions. Who had the correct or false consciousness: Karl Marx the intellectual, the radical journeyman Wilhelm Weitling, or the socialist organizer Ferdinand Lassalle? Which unconscious motivations of the working class were expressed by the reformist theoretician Eduard Bernstein? Which other motivations by the orthodox Karl Kautsky? Which social class needs did Stalin satisfy, but not Trotsky? Stalin, but not Bukharin? Stalin, but not Tito? Khruschev, but not Malenkov? Breshnev, but not Khruschev? In all of these and many other similar cases, political struggles for power and ideological programs for action were at stake but the social class bases of these struggles and programs — no matter whether one understands them as interests, needs, or unconscious motivations — lose their shape in a thick fog of unprovable hypotheses.

Of course, it is somewhat oversimplifying matters to assert that Mannheim regarded only social classes as carriers of distinctive ways of thought. Occasionally, he spoke of other carriers, for example, sects, the diocese, parishes (as distinguished from the church), and of other "circles of everyday life," in which, as he said, certain human feelings, longings of the soul and ways of thought originated. Mannheim never doubted that emotions and thought were governed by the same laws of change and that a change in the interests and motivations of the social carrier meant a change in emotions and thoughts. But he seldom offers us, along with his observations about the existential determination of ideas and feelings, the results of social research. The poverty of social experience in *Ideology and Utopia* is astonishing. The only exception to this is in his study of conservative thought, although, even in this significant work, the textual interpretation of the political writings of German conservatives is more important to the author than the social circumstances which produced political views with a conservative stamp. In all his other investigations in the sociology of knowledge, the relevant social facts to which Mannheim referred were entirely second hand. For example, he owed Ernst Bloch[3] insights into the utopias of the anabaptists, and he borrowed from Max Weber observations about social structure. Nowhere in his main work on the sociology of knowledge does one find concrete, detailed investigations of the social facts that, according to his theory, are crucial for the sociological understanding of particular ideologies and utopias. Nothing about the friendship pacts at the time of the Romantics, nothing about the salons, political clubs, language societies, coffee houses, lending libraries, moral weeklies which marked the beginning of middle-class culture in Germany; very little about universities or academies and their significance for the diffusion of modern scientific thought; nothing about the elimination of illiteracy as the precondition for the participation of large masses of people in politics; nothing about exile as the fertile social ground of the contentiousness and invective-filled style of early Marxism. Nothing about craftmen's associations and worker organizations in conjunction with the development of socialist doctrines. Similarly, Mannheim's larger study about the problem of generations is almost wholly unsociological. He said nothing about the rich history of political movements in which students played a role and his dry conceptual distinctions and theoretical assessments do not rest on historical research. One comes to the paradoxical conclusion that this sociologist had no burning desire to study closely the diversity of social life. He was interested in the logic of understanding, in epistemological problems, in ontology, in the structure of thought and meaning, in the conscious and allegedly unconscious intentions of writers and in the existential adequacy of their perspectives. But when he dealt with this last theme, the definition of existential adequacy was more important to him than were the patient understanding and meaningful description of the social phenomena to which he attributed the ideologies and utopias of the writers.

A change in the right direction can be detected only in the posthumously published *Essays on the Sociology of Culture*,* particularly in the second essay. There Mannheim adduces a few works on the social history of the "intellectuals" and their forerunners. He mentions the salon, the language societies, the coffeehouses, political clubs, and a few other social institutions that were important in the emergence of the modern intelligentsia. But again, if in *Ideology and Utopia* sweeping attributions of styles of thought to conscious and subconscious motivations of social classes took the place of empirical social research, so in the posthumous work do certain psychological observations arrest the attention of the reader. However brilliant they are, they do not amount to more than intriguing hunches which are illustrated but not verified.

Today, it is almost unintelligible that Mannheim gave virtually no indication in his writings before 1933 that National Socialism and Fascism arrested his attention. Neither the ways in which the black and brown shirts fought their battles, nor the social origin of the men who in the 1920s succumbed to increasing political and human savagery; neither the sources of financial help the Nazis received nor the moral support given to them by half-educated intellectuals and politically uneducated scholars; neither the Nazi ideology nor its social breeding grounds — none of these became a subject for Mannheim's research. In his writings before 1933, we find almost no statements about the important political and social events of his time.

A second example that suggests that Mannheim was much more concerned with the construction of theories than with empirical research on historical constellations is taken from one of his early and

---

*Edited by Ernest Manheim, in cooperation with Paul Kecskemeti (London, 1956). According to an editorial note by Adolph Lowe, confirmed by Ernest Manheim in his interesting introduction, Mannheim wrote the three essays collected in the volume "in the early thirties shortly before the advent of Nazism put an end to Mannheim's work in Germany." However, the essay on the intellengentsia, that is, Part II of the volume, contains many references to works published between 1936 and 1953. Karl Mannheim died in 1947. Ernest Manheim, the translator of this essay, must have added many of the references bearing on various aspects of the development of the modern intellengentsia. It is possible, however, that Mannheim continued to work on the essay in London from 1933 to 1947.

best works. On the basis of the encouragement and the direct invitation of the art historian Max Dvorák to demonstrate the relationship of art history with the study of ideas, Mannheim wrote a large treatise which was published in 1923 by the Art Historical Institute of the Federal Office for Monuments in Vienna.[4] In this work, Mannheim distinguished, in the most instructive manner, the contents of a work of art from the expressive meaning of this content and showed, in fact, that the expression could change historically while the contents remained constant. In order to make this clear by an example, he remarked among other things that in "medieval drama the blind and the halt play a comic role."[5] In Mannheim's later work, this observation was not taken further. The possibility of extending it to other related issues was never pursued; nor was it followed into the past or into modern times, and thus he never examined whether the change of attitude toward human infirmities should be understood in relationship to shifts in religious, social, or technical aspects of life. All of this might have been done relatively easily and might have led to some significant result in cultural history. Clearly, Mannheim had devoted himself to epistemology, to the process of understanding, to the theory of history, and to psychology, but much less to the analysis of historical and social facts. He lived in a realm of speculation, but was sociologically anaemic.

It is not entirely correct to assert that Mannheim left no following, as Professor Edward Shils has stated in the new edition of the *Encyclopedia of the Social Sciences*. Shils says that only three of Mannheim's pupils had worked further in the tradition of their teacher, namely Hans Gerth in his dissertation about German liberalism,[6] Kohn-Bramstedt in a study of the sociology of literature,[7] and I myself in an early study of Lassalle's philosophy of history.[8] Shils disregarded the fact that many works about Mannheim's sociology were done in exile during the years of Nazi rule, and that, as already mentioned, the interest in Mannheim is recently growing again in Germany and elsewhere. But he is correct insofar as the numerous expository and critical books about Mannheim are concerned exclusively with his concepts and his theories. It is simply easier to point to the mistakes, or the omissions, or the vagueness in Mannheim's teaching, than to do real sociological investigations of political meanings, literary products, and the development of thought, things that Mannheim had recommended, but which he himself had pursued only seldom and then inadequately. So it happens that many new monographs in the area of literature and art history, about the beginning and development of

modern science, or about the role of intellectuals in social development are indebted to Mannheim's sociological way of thinking for
many insights, but not properly to his methodology.

I will not go into Mannheim's distinction between ideology and
utopia nor will I discuss his methods of attributing ideas to styles of
thought and social classes. Instead, I would rather close with some
remarks about the role that Mannheim assigned in his main work to
intellectuals. If all thought is perspectivist, there is as a result no truth,
but rather, at the most, along with lies, erroneous ideas, propaganda,
and flattery, various partial views of truth, all of which are attained
from different historical-social standpoints. The teaching of the existential determination of thought leads inexorably to relativism. Mannheim had sought to go beyond this relativism in two ways. First, he
neatly turned aside from it in a terminological way by speaking of
relationism instead of relativism; but that of course does not lead out
of the blind alley. Second, he asserted that the intellectuals are in a
position to knit together different points of view to achieve an optimal
synthesis and that this synthesis has a measure of truth which exceeds
that attained from each single vantage point.

Mannheim taught therefore that thinking men are in a position to
overcome the existential determination of thought. But he gave this
entirely correct viewpoint a sociological stamp which is not correct.
Following Alfred Weber, he considered the modern intellectuals to be a
"socially free floating" group in order to make sociologically understandable, as it were, his notion that the universal existential determination of thought could not be invalidated through a direct approach
to truth. For he asserted that it was again only a certain social stratum,
namely the intelligentsia, that had access to the synthesis. And he
asserted that truth stemmed not from inspecting something closely,
but rather from a synthesis of perspectivist partial truths.

Now the notion of a socially free floating intelligentsia is false because the intellectuals, like all other social strata, must work and,
barring inherited wealth, depend for their livelihood on patrons or on
a generous public. They are also placed in a certain power relationship
no matter whether as advisers, functionaries, critics, syncophants, or
victims. And, just like other occupational groups, they have a certain
social prestige which can be high or low.

Conversely, it is of course entirely possible for intellectuals to alter
their social milieu willingly or unwillingly without their intellectual
work being affected thereby in any decisive way. There are men and
women whose homeland is the universe and not the land of their

fathers. Patriotism and class loyalty have nothing to do with the life of the mind and with truth. The uneducated or half-educated person is more firmly bound to the traditions and prejudices of his surroundings than the intellectual who, precisely because of this, is often designated by the glorifiers of blood and soil as "rootless." The mind has its roots in the mind. It is therefore not surprising that the social situation and the social descent of a thinking man in no way always match his views. For example, many advocates of middle-class interests in the eighteenth and nineteenth centuries came from aristocratic families and many advocates of revolutionary causes, including Marx and Engels, came in the nineteenth century from bourgeois circles. There is a certain analogy to all of this in the political jumble of our own time when old men can be the spokesmen of radical anarchist youth.

Political ideologues are very often social deserters, that is, spiritually free men. Besides they can, although they may be conservative, understand even liberal or revolutionary ideologies and vice versa. The intellectual can search out the society that he will join and also that in which he feels happy. Although he lives in the twentieth century, Aristotle can stand closer to him than Mao. He is free to choose and change his convictions.

How then will he choose them? Unfortunately, Mannheim is not of much help here. The person dedicated to the life of the mind strives to find the truth. He is not socially free floating, but he is free to do this. Even though he can fall into error, he does not seek error, but rather tries to shun it. He doe not seek a perspectivist unencumbered fragment of the truth; he also does not seek a synthesis of perspectives. He is spiritually free to seek the truth itself.

The crisis of modern consciousness does not consist in the total suspicion of ideologies, but in the claim of politicians, sociologists, and psychologists to do away with philosophy. An allegedly socially free floating intelligentsia is not going to show us the way out of the crisis. Rather, this task belongs to the spiritually free man who cherishes spiritual freedom.

NOTES

1. Kurt H. Wolff, *Versuch zu einer Wissenssoziologie*, Berlin and Neuwied, 1968.
2. All of these articles, and many more, were republished in Volker Meja and Nico Stehr, *Der Streit um die Wissenssoziologie*, vol. 2, Frankfurt, 1982.
3. Ernst Bloch, *Thomas Münzer als Theologe der Revolution*, Munich, 1922.

4. Karl Mannheim, "On the Interpretation of *Weltanschauung*," first published in German in *Jahrbuch für Kunstgeschichte*, 1921–22, Vienna, 1923.

5. Cited from the English translation by Paul Kecskemeti, in Karl Mannheim, *Essays on the Sociology of Knowledge*, ed. Paul Kecskemeti, New York, 1952, p. 49.

6. Hans Gerth, "Die sozialgeschichtliche Lage der bürgerlichen Intelligenz um die Wende des 18. Jahrhunderts." Ph.D. diss., Heidelberg University, 1935. Published as *Bürgerliche Intelligenz um 1800*, Göttingen, 1973.

7. Ernst Kohn-Bramstedt, *Aristocracy and Middle Classes in Germany: Social Types in German Literature, 1830–1950*, 2nd ed., Chicago, 1964.

8. Hans Speier, "Die Geschichtspilosophie Lassalles," in *Archiv für Sozialwissenschaft und Sozialpolitik*, vol. 61 (1929), 103–27 and 360–88. For a condensed translation, see Hans Speier, *Social Order and the Risks of War*, 2nd ed., Cambridge, Mass., 1969, chaps. 11 and 12.

2

Honor and Social Structure

The life of the king Ahasuerus had been saved by Mordecai, uncle and guardian of Esther. The king permitted him to be dressed in the royal robe and to wear the royal crown. On one of the king's horses Mordecai rode through the streets of the capital, conducted by a prince who announced, "Thus shall it be done to the man whom the king delighteth to honor." (Esther, VI). By another king, or perhaps even by Ahasuerus himself at another time, it was granted to another man to wear the royal robe, but the king added, "You shall do so as my fool." Thus, in a form very similar to the honoring of Mordecai, the second man was dishonored. These two stories lay bare, in a lucid, simple fashion, the origin and nature of honor.

A man's honor neither springs from his personality nor clings to his deeds. It depends upon other men who have the power to bestow honor on him and a will to pay it. Mordecai did not immediately rise to honors by virtue of his having saved the king's life. The Bible relates that his deed remained unrewarded for a time and obtained its recognition only by chance. Ahasuerus had forgotten Mordecai until a certain day when the chronicles were read before the king. He inquired then what distinction had been given to Mordecai, and the servants an-

First published in *Social Research*, vol. 2, 1935. Reprinted by permission of *Social Research*.

swered that he had not been rewarded. It was only after this accidental mention that King Ahasuerus decided to honor his subject.

Even before Mordecai was honored, his rescue of Ahasuerus may have become known in the capital and may have been praised as prudent or good. Both the man and his deed may have been already famous — perhaps the place, too, where he had discovered the plot. For fame can attach to anything, to men, things, events, places, ideas. But honor is paid only to a man, or to God.

Ahasuerus' will to honor Mordecai did not suffice for the creation of honor. The king bestowed honor, it is true, but this act did not assure general homage. For that it was necessary that the king's will and intention be proclaimed to the people. Honor would not have been brought into social existence had its bestowal been known only to Ahasuerus and Mordecai. The relationship would have remained private. The king would have entered it in gratitude, or perhaps in friendliness, and possibly the private distance between the two would have been shortened, but the king would have been acting as a man, not as sovereign. In that situation it would have been impossible to express his gratitude by bestowing honor on his friend. If Ahasuerus as a friend had lent his crown and robe to Mordecai, for Mordecai to array himself in them only in private, it would have been a senseless act, conceivable only in one whose kingship had deprived him of the qualities he should possess as a man. The relations of private distance require other forms of expression than those of vertical public distance.[1]

Ahasuerus' act, which raised Mordecai above the other subjects, shortened the vertical public distance between the two men without necessarily touching their private relations. Ahasuerus may have been more intimate with his lowest servant. The meaning of Mordecai's ride through the streets, and of the proclamation in the king's name, was that this subject should be honored, not that he was Ahasuerus' friend.

Thus for honor to arise it is essential that there be bearers, bestowers, and observers of honor. The observers, who are to be understood as those who pay honor, may on occasion perform the same function as the bestowers of honor, but theoretically they must be distinguished. The problem of the relationship between personal honor and honor in the sense in which it has been used here will be discussed in section V.

II

The extent of the circle in which honor is paid is determined by two factors: the number of persons familiar with the claim that honor is to be done, and, more directly, the number of those who are willing to pay it. At first Mordecai was honored only in the city; as the news spread into the many provinces of the kingdom, the circle of honor extended. Correspondingly, with the shrinking of the circle, honor is threatened. It is lost by the statesman *incognito*, the explorer cut off from his country among a primitive tribe. Possibly the explorer gains new distinction, say by his ability to light a match, but this new honor is subject to the same law: its extent shrinks in proportion as the knowledge about it diminishes, and if there is complete ignorance of this prowess he has neither honor nor fame.

In the first quarter of the nineteenth century Chaca, the chieftain of the Zulus, was famous and highly feared in Africa. During the two years that followed his accession he is said to have deprived more than two hundred communities of their independence, by means of his perfectly disciplined army, and to have brought under his sway half a million people. His fame and his honor spread far beyond the limits of his realm.[2] But very few white men know of Chaca.

The dependence of honor, fame, and glory upon some kind of proclamation can be exemplified in various cultures and in many forms. Every social structure has its special proclaimers of fame, individuals or institutions that perform the function of spreading fame to the wider public. Edgar Zilsel, who studied the origin of the concept of genius in Greek and Roman antiquity and in the Renaissance, arrived at the conclusion that with the growth of an urban money economy intensified needs for fame and immortality assert themselves, unless religious interests exercise a diverting influence. Under these circumstances a class of literati arises, proud of its knowledge and technique, whose professional function is the spreading of fame.[3]

Professional proclamation of fame is not limited, however, to urban cultures. In pagan Arabia, for example, men whose ancestors were not distinguished, or who were unable to speak the Arabian language, were exposed to contempt. In both war and peace, a factor of decisive importance for the prestige of a tribe was the poems sung about it. A fight in poetry between two tribes meant the beginning of war; when this defamation by songs had ceased, the war had come to an end. Thus the poets exerted a sometimes portentous influence upon the Arabian tribes by spreading their good or bad fame. Mohammed's disapproval of poetry as an agency for fostering rivalry among the tribes was closely connected with his attempt to substitute for tribal organization a brotherly and disciplined community.[4]

In modern society, press, film, radio, and the other agencies for expressing and controlling public opinion are the chief instruments with which fame and honor are spread.

The second factor determining the extent of the circle in which honor is paid is the number of those who are willing to pay it. King Ahasuerus' power to honor and to dishonor is not as unlimited as it appears, for it depends upon the recognition of those who are to be subjected to his will. This holds not only for the ruler's order that honor be paid, but for all his orders. It holds not only in democracies but in all kinds of governments, even in dictatorships. In a word, it holds for all relationships of authority, whether they rest upon persuasion, slavery, discipline or any other basis.

The test of authority is always its power of obtaining obedience. Accordingly the very existence of authority presupposes a certain freedom of choice on the part of the subject.[5] There is profound wisdom hidden in Hegel's paradox that "the essence of authority is the reverse of that which it wishes to be."[6] Only in the case of actual physical compulsion does the last vestige of freedom disappear.

Since the payment of honor to Mordecai contains a recognition of the royal bestowal of honor, it might be supposed that Mordecai's honor is based on the king's power. In connection with this same Biblical tale Thomas Hobbes, for example, has declared " . . . of Civill Honour, the Fountain is in the person of the Common-wealth, and dependeth on the Will of the Soveraigne . . . "[7] But this judgment is open to question. Suppose Ahasuerus had been a crowned rascal whom his subjects obeyed but who was in privacy the object of their deepest hatred. In that case his rescue would probably have been followed by the people's secret maledictions. The bestowal of honor upon Mordecai would have had only their apparent approval. Honor would have been paid him, possibly even in the same form, but it would have been feigned. There is no difference between genuine and feigned observation of honor. But honor itself does not permit of counterfeit. The function of one who pays it is not performed by acts alone, as is the case with obedience. Honor requires valuations, and valuations lie outside the political realm in which authority remains and is satisfied. The degree of freedom that enters the relationship of authority does not touch the essence of authority, nor do the motives of the one who obeys: only the actual obedience matters. In contrast to obedience the payment of honor, however, depends on the intention of the act rather than on the act itself. If those who seem to be paying a man honor do not approve the valuation included in its bestowal, the essential quality of honor is denied; their obedience signifies not the payment of honor but merely their submission to power. It is evident that the bestowal of honor can be performed by persons other than the observers only if there is agreement on what deserves to be honored.

III

The subjects of honor are many—strength or beauty, cruelty or sorcery, virtue even though it be impotent. Its content is relative, or, as Hobbes says, "temporary." There are no activities which are honorable in themselves and are held excellent in all social structures. In some primitive societies physical strength is honored, in others, age; in some the possessor of wealth, in others the magician. More highly developed societies often accord honor to the wealthy, but many instances are known in which wealth receives no more honor than poverty. In old Japan the rich rice dealer ranked below the poor craftsman he employed.[8] The Prussian Junker, even when he was impoverished, maintained his superiority in social esteem to the bourgeois rich. In Germany the soldier enjoys conspicuous honor, but the soldier's prestige is relatively low not only in countries so unaccustomed to war as Holland but also in France, whose history has been by no means peaceful. As to the artist, he has not been honored in all cultures. Even in Greece, where art was a very important part of life, little prestige was granted the artists. Plato put them on a level with the ship builders and the other craftsmen, and Plutarch compared artists and poets with perfumers and dyers; of all of them, he said, it remains true that "we enjoy their work and despise the master."[9] In short, whatever activity is examined reveals the greatest variety in the valuations attached to it.

It is very tempting to try to stabilize this historical relativity of honor by finding a general formula which will define its contents. But the search is hazardous. Fahlbeck's opinion that those whose concern is with the religious, ethical, intellectual, and aesthetic aspects of life are "usually" highly esteemed[10] does not answer the question. "Usual" is but a seemingly neutral term for "normal"; the quest is for the contents of honor not as we would like them to be, but as they are.

The theory has also been offered that the social order of ranks corresponds to the social utility of the classes.* Those who satisfy the most urgent needs in a given society are the most highly esteemed, those who supply the least important demands rank lowest. But it can

---

*For the sake of the argument the possibility is disregarded that the order of rank in terms of honor is obscured by the order of rank in terms of power.

be proved that to those who provide society with the same social utilities different values are attached in different social structures. Under Japanese feudalism the farmer ranked relatively higher than the farmer in feudal Europe, though no conspicuous difference can be discovered in their respective social utility. In different cultures the utility of the physician may vary, but scarcely enough to explain his extremely low rank in the Indian caste system, where the majority of the Brahmans prefer for ritual reasons the lowest service in the house to the ministrations of a physician.[11]

Since no correlation can be established between the social utility of a function and the honor it receives, it might be contended that the evaluations which determine the content of honor depend on the relative importance which society attaches to its various needs. Mitgau has incorporated in the system of needs themselves the historical factors making for the relativity of honor. Instead of positing a fixed hierarchy of needs, he assumes that the urgency of needs is in itself subject to change. The religious need, for example, can be strong or weak, and thus with any other need. Then in a certain society the high rank, say, of the priest, is attributable to the urgency of the religious need, and other differences in rank can be similarly explained.[12] But it is obvious that this analysis cannot lead very far, because it is based on a circular conclusion. Rank is explained according to urgency of need, while the degree of urgency is recognized in relative rank.

Thus the essence of honor cannot be derived from the contents of the honorable, and there remains only the formal determination that honor always attaches to what is held to be excellent. What specific excellence is meant derives not from honor itself but from its bestowers and its observers. There is pungency and conviction in two concurring opinions to be found in French literature. Vauvenargues has declared that "esteem is an inner approval of the merit of something; respect is the *sentiment* of someone's superiority."[13] And the Jansenist, Pierre Nicole, is even more precise: "What is generally called honor has almost no certain object. Men place it where they want, according to their fantasy, and there are few honorable things which could not become ignominious by another turn of imagination; therefore although honor does not depend upon our inclination to love honor, nor on the belief that this attitude is natural, it depends nevertheless upon the inclination to attach it more to something than to something else."[14]

From the fact that honor is derived from a concept of excellence it is inevitable that the process of honoring creates hierarchical distinctions. The order of ranks which it sets up determines the image of the right life. He who honors regards the bearers of honor as ideals, be they gentlemanly or violent, be they addressed "Your Reverence" or, as Chaca was, "Sigidi," which means "thousand" in reference to the number of men he had slain.

Fame does not establish distinctions of rank. In contrast to honor it is not bestowed and observed, but only spread. Fame grows with the number of those who are conscious of it. Some one may be more famous than another who excels him in honor, for honor does not increase with the number of the observers. Its greatness depends rather upon the distance of the man who is honored from the bearer of highest honors, that is, it is determined by the extent to which the man lived up to the image of excellence.

IV

Montesquieu declares that there is no honor under despotism and in many cases not even a word for it. The life and death of his subjects are at the arbitrary disposal of the despot, and if a subject imposes his own death in defense of his honor, then death imposed by the despot is no longer effective as an instrument of tyranny and thus tyranny and honor are irreconcilable.[15]

But Montesquieu's opinion is based on the untenable assumption that an integral part of honor is the conviction that death is preferable to a life devoid of honor. The honor of a craftsman is strict and precise in its requirements, but it does not necessarily demand death as the penalty for its violation. Even the code of the samurai, which imposes suicide if allegiance to an immediate superior entails the violation of allegiance to the highest superior, cannot be considered irreconcilable with a despotic regime, because the samurai in inflicting his own death may be conforming with the will of the tyrant. His code, in other words, constitutes honor for him but merely convenience for the tyrant.

There is more validity in Montesquieu's further contention that honor has no place in tyranny because the arbitrariness of the tyrant is irreconcilable with rules established by honor. The perfect tyrant has a monopoly of bestowing honor, but he cannot use it. His tyranny would be diminished if he did. If his rule is entirely arbitrary, all ranks are leveled,[16] not only because he cannot permit one to be less dominated than another but also because the obedience of all is concentrated in himself. And he cannot himself be honored, because his rule admits no certainty. In Plato's description the perfect tyrant is a man who, like a dreamer, is driven by wild and uncontrolled urges.[17] He cannot be honored because, as La Bruyère has said, "a man of unsteady mood is not one man, but several."[18] The tyrant's unpredictable whim can change the forms of paying honor into forms of disrespect. Thus if honor is paid to him he ceases to be the perfect tyrant, for the possibility of doing honor to him is a contradiction of his nature. The closer tyranny approaches perfection the less honor can it receive.

Honor is incompatible with tyranny in another, more important, respect. It establishes, as has already been mentioned, definite rules about the conduct of life. The one who pays honor expects the bearer to conduct his life in accordance with certain rules, which constitute the code of honor. These rules consist in definite prohibitions and duties which refer primarily to activities of vital importance, such as the public relations with the opposite sex and the circle with whom social intercourse, especially at meals, is permitted. Intermarriage, commensalism and social intercourse with persons of lesser honor are prohibited. Except in the caste system, all these rules pertain to public relations. In private relations honor is concerned only if infractions become known, that is, if the private character is lost. The circle of honor extends also to occupational activities; frequently all occupations are taboo for the bearers of highest honor, always a few are considered ignominious, and between these two extremes they receive gradually differing valuations.[19] The Greek nobleman was considered base if he himself sailed the ships which he financed. In the Middle Ages social contempt of the minstrels was so great that they were even excluded from the sacrament of the communion. Sometimes their derogation was given a scornful implication, as for example in the old Swabian *Landrecht*, where it was declared, "minstrels and all those who take goods for honor, to those one gives a man's sun-shadow; that is, he who has done them harm, and shall atone for it, shall step before a wall shone upon by the sun and the minstrel shall go to him and beat the shadow on the wall at its neck. With this revenge penance shall be done."[20]

In this or that way honor sets up boundaries; it disciplines life. As a result of its hierarchical nature it not only determines the realm of the taboo but also sets up a scale of excellence in the realm of that which is permitted. A perfect illustration is afforded by the system of knightly virtues in the European Middle Ages. On the basis of the four ancient virtues of wisdom *(prudentia)*, fortitude *(fortitudo)*, temperance *(temperantia)*, and justice *(justitia)*, the honorable *(honestum)* was determined precisely, so that every detail of behavior would be referred to one of the four cardinal virtues. Under fortitude, for example, was subsumed *magnanimitas*, that is, an ennobled vitality; under temperance, restraint in behavior *(modestia)*; under *justitia*, the Christian virtue of *misericordia*; under *prudentia*, the rule to speak neither too much nor too little *(circumspectio)*.[21] Thus honor establishes a specific kind of order in life, based on implicit duties and prohibitions. But tyranny lacks order and cannot tolerate its imposition.

V

To the excellence required by honor there always corresponds a specific form of behavior, which may be called dignity, varying according to the concrete content of honor. Dignity, be it that of a prince or of a thief, always serves to demonstrate that the distinction between high and low contained in honor, and more specifically the code of honor itself, are as compelling for the bearer as he expects them to be for the observers. This compelling force manifests itself in "personal honor," which determines a man's moral integrity, and through which the code becomes a part of his personality. In other words, honor has a double aspect. From the point of view of the observers it displays its relativity as a social phenomenon; for it is time-bound and dependent on valuations. From the point of view of the bearer, however, honor is absolute, for in the integrity of the man of honor there can be no suggestion of relativity. Personal honor obliges him to orient his behavior toward definite rules, which are to him absolute. Sir William Segar, who wrote a valuable book on honor in 1602, noticed this double aspect of the problem. Attempting to reconcile his opinion with the idea of Aristotle, so frequently quoted through the Middle Ages and the Renaissance, that honor does not depend on him who receives it, Segar suggested: "reverence is only the first motive to honour, which after becommeth honour absolute. The like difference is between honour and praise, for honour [i.e. "personal honor"] is of it selfe; but praise tendeth to a further end."[22]

Since to the bearer honor is absolute, a man's loyalty to his own standards must be independent of the opinion of others. His personal honor is violated if even in privacy he fails to meet its requirements. When a man of honor is faced with a difficult decision he is in danger of losing his honor as long as he is uncertain as to whether he should follow its demands of him. Since he is divided into two parts, he represents two persons: as the man whose personal honor demands that he do *this*, he is to himself the image of the right life; as he whose convenience, or safety, or comfort, suggests that he do *that*, even though it violate his honor, he is a potential apostate from that image. His moral monologue is in reality a dialogue, which corresponds to the relation existing in public honor between the observers and the bearers, where the two are different persons.

The double aspect of honor explains the striking contrast between those theories in which the social origin is made the point of departure for the analysis of honor and those in which the absolute character of personal honor is the focus of the examination.[23] Both points of view are seen to be tenable, provided that neither excludes the other.

It can still be objected that "personal honor" is the result of a man's personal valuations, independent of the bestowal and observation of social distinction, so that its absolute character derives from the fact that it has no connection at all with public honors. But such an autonomy of personal honor presupposes a social situation in which no agreement exists concerning what is excellent. It can be demonstrated by a historical analysis that the modern individualistic notion of "personal honor," as independent from any other's opinion, is a polemic conception which served the middle classes in their struggle to overthrow the feudal conception of honor. One of the most important aspects of this struggle was the finally successful attempt of the middle classes to make the soul and the mind rather than acts and deeds the fountainhead of honor. The conspicuously honorable behavior of the nobility was devaluated to mere gestures, irrelevant politeness, symbols of an insignificant order, against which was set up a realm of "natural" inner quality accessible to everyone alike. For France this historical development, which included several transformations of the conception of the *honnête homme*, has been studied with enough care to permit relatively concrete statements. Magendie, for example, discovered that in the first half of the seventeenth century the writers who belonged to the middle classes or to the lower nobility (*petite noblesse de robe*) held chiefly those qualities of the soul in high esteem which they called solid and permanent. It was to these qualities that they attached the honor and dignity of man.[24] They protested against the "abuse" of the term *honnête homme* in its application to persons who lacked "moral quality."

The rise of autonomous honor was much more complicated than is frequently assumed. It was by no means an achievement of the Enlightenment alone. Christian theologians in France, especially the Jansenists, were instrumental in its development; Nicole and Pascal were especially important figures.[25] But the Jesuits also contributed to the overthrow of the feudal honor, a fact which is not sufficiently taken into account in Max Weber's sociology of religion. The Jesuit, Louis Bourdaloue (1632–1704), court preacher of Louis XIV, combined a disapproval of idleness, whether of the noble or of the miserable, with a high esteem for merchants, craftsmen, and all men of the middle classes who obtained their livelihood by work (*médiocres états de vie qui subsistent par le travail*); and in accordance with this he declared that the true basis of respect is the devotion to one's duty.[26]

This short discussion must suffice to suggest that it was only under special social conditions that the modern notion of autonomous personal honor arose. Personal honor, it is true, is always absolute to the bearer; by the very fact that he decides a moral question man disregards the relativity of honor. But this relativity is revealed when man himself, as he exists in a time-bound society, is made the subject of consideration. And the idea that personal honor is independent of social valuations, because the individual sets up his own code of honor, presupposes a social situation in which representative behavior is devaluated and is considered to be no more than empty forms which are perhaps either pleasant or ridiculous, but in any case utterly insignificant when compared with the inner moral quality of man. In the struggle against the nobility this quality was called true, just, real, natural, universal. It was made the basis of "independent personal honor," but it was held to be independent only because immaterial sources of honor were mobilized against the socially conspicuous status in which feudal honors resulted. The independence of personal honor from public valuations was but an illusion; a public that considered itself totally reducible to autonomous individuals substituted for a moribund kind of honor new valuations in which precisely the moral autonomy of the individual was made a point of honor. In this tremendous spiritual revolution it was forgotten that the autonomy of the individual was related to his aspiration to a higher status.

VI

Since the order which honor creates is hierarchical, honor is no less incompatible with equality than with tyranny. This does not preclude the possibility that equals may confer honor; but it should be noted that in so doing they create inequality. The incongruity between equality and honor results necessarily from the analysis, but it deserves further consideration.

The Romans denied that slaves possessed honor. A loss of freedom was followed not only by a diminution of honor (*minutio existimationis*, or *infamia*), but even by its entire disappearance (*consumtio existimationis*, or *turpitudo*). The lack of honor, according to the legal theory, was based on the notion that the slave was not a person but a thing; similarly in Japan the intentional killing of a *hinin* ("not human being") was not regarded as murder, and was punished only with a small fine. R. von Ihering[27] concluded from the slave's lack of honor that honor embodies the legal value of the person as such. Honor, he said, must be considered a legal concept, the corresponding sociological concept being respect; consequently, *infamia* and *turpitudo* have to be sharply distinguished, and the modern distinction between *infamia juris* and *infamia facti* must be rejected.

Von Ihering was not aware of the fact that his analysis was conditioned here by his juridical point of view. The difference between honor and respect does not correspond to that between law and society. Respect is rather the specific attitude of the observer of honor toward the bearer. In Roman law, it is true, legal honor was restricted to those who were free; freedom, however, was determined not by liberty alone but by this liberty in relation to slavery. The group of the free was socially superior to the group of the slaves. This legal honor was but a privilege, a legally guaranteed claim to receive, as the highest group, the respect of those who formed the lower group. If the contrast between the two groups is eliminated, by abolition of slavery, the origin and significance of the honor guaranteed by law are veiled, since legally everyone then bears honor equally; but man's honor still rises within a hierarchy.

Before examining this hierarchy it must be admitted, of course, that the tendency of honor to maintain social stratification, a tendency which is always conspicuous when individuals or specific subgroups within a group are honored, has entirely vanished when honor is legally universal and equal. But the loss of this tendency cannot be explained in terms of the difference between general honor and honor limited to a specific group. Rather it results from a sociological law according to which honor is socially the less effective the more frequently it is bestowed. The discriminating force of honor grows with the exclusiveness of its bearers. The smaller the circle of the honored, the greater the distinction to belong to it. Accordingly, inflations of honor may occur. The German iron cross, for example, was held in high esteem before 1914, since only a few men possessed it. In the course of World War I, however, it was so frequently bestowed that its value was greatly decreased. The same law holds true with respect to dishonoring. Cesare Beccaria, the famous Italian legal philosopher, has observed, "If we declare those actions infamous which are in themselves indifferent, we lessen the infamy of those which are really infamous. The punishment of infamy should not be too frequent, for the power of opinion grows weaker by repetition; nor should it be inflicted on a number of persons at the same time, for the infamy of many resolves itself into the infamy of none."[28]

It must still be explained why honor is based on distinctions, even when there is no legal stratification of society. The notion of equality tends, it is true, to level differences, but not necessarily the differences arising from vertical public distance. The medieval dance macabre, in which the mundane distinctions of status and rank were suspended, since death seized the emperor as well as the beggar, did not touch the foundations of the social order of ranks; rather it demonstrated the relative insignificance of social order as compared with the supersocial order. It is obvious that a will to abolish secular ranks presupposes precisely the opposite notion that a final significance attaches to secular status.

But apart from that, if the distinctions which establish honor do not consist in arbitrary distinctions between man and man, they must be sought in man's nature itself. Obviously man is honored not because he is equal to everything that exists, but because he is different from and superior to something. He is not honored as a work of nature, as a mere creature of the animal world. His honor arises from something specifically human, by means of which he excels nature; it may be reason and free will, or it may be, all inclusively, the belief that man is created *ad imaginem et similitudinem Dei*. In the latter case his honor belongs to his primary natural rights and is derived, like all rights of this kind, from man's duty to pay honor to God; his honor, then, is good if its principle is charity (*caritas*).

It is unnecessary to raise the question as to whether either theology or philosophy recognizes the superiority of man over nature as something objective, or merely imputes it to him.[29] The only consideration that is relevant here is the fact that a hierarchical character of human existence is an essential condition of human honor, and that man's respect, honor, and dignity can arise only in a culture in which the higher and lower in man is precisely distinguished.[30]

If such a distinction is made, and is socially valid, the command to pay honor to animals or things implies an insult to human dignity.

When in war horses are regarded more highly than men, the preference is a sign of monstrous inhumanity and of man's degradation only on the assumption that man should be valued more highly than horses. Only on the same assumption can it be inferred that in the Swiss legend of Wilhelm Tell the *Landvogt*, Gessler, meant to humiliate and degrade the peasants when he commanded that his hat, fixed on a stick, be greeted by the populace. And again, only the assumption that man is superior to animals can justify the deduction that Caligula's order to pay to his favorite horse the honor of a consul was an act not of honor to an animal but of dishonor to men.[31]

Even if man were dishonored it could only be because the emperor was adjudged to have the ability to dishonor him. For just as honor contains an evaluation of the bearer by the payers of honor, violation of honor rests upon the bearer's assumption that the violator is able to violate. Thus children and fools are forgiven when they do not pay homage to the king, and the dolt violates the honor of the philosopher only if the philosopher enables him to do so.[32] These mutual evaluations as bases of the violation of honor were institutionalized in the test of ancestors prescribed in the Middle Ages for establishing a warrior's ability to engage in a tournament. Such evaluations are necessary for every violation of honor, no matter how small or large the circle of bearers may be; they are indispensable even in the case of national honor, where the circle is very large and lacks the criteria of general human honor. In this connection Schopenhauer was moved to remark that every pitiable fool who has nothing to be proud of snatches at the last straw of being proud of the nation to which he accidentally belongs.[33]

VII

In static structures the principle underlying the distribution of honor is not questioned; thus the claims to highest honor are not advanced in the name of various kinds of honor, because in such societies there is only one basis for highest distinction. The various noble families in medieval cities who fought among themselves for highest rank adhered to the same principle of honor; their struggles were for power alone. But if different principles of honor are launched by those striving for highest honor, the struggle assumes another character; the social structure has become dynamic. The position of highest honor is then claimed by various honors, even though the actual power may be still undivided in the hands of one group, defending its power or its honor or both. Thus dynamic social structures are characterized by a pluralism of honors.

Since the highest honor can never be bestowed, a fact which follows from definition and is self-evident in the attributes accorded to God, a pluralism of honors means disintegration of the homogeneous hierarchy characteristic of the static system. The rising groups, refusing to renounce, for the sake of their new honor, the claim to power allied with the old, and refusing also to allow the old honor to be bestowed upon them, try to establish new hierarchies by usurpation. The usurpation of honor corresponds, in dynamic social structures, to the bestowal of honor in static systems. An historic example of the latter is the absorption of the English middle class in a relatively fixed hierarchy; instances of usurpation are the French and Russian revolutions. But just as "dynamic" and "static" social structures are not necessarily defined by their economic organizations, the usurpation of honor does not exclusively manifest itself in political revolution. At the end of the eighteenth century, for example, the German nobility began "to study with middle class seriousness; thereby it put a one before its cipher of birth."[34] The polemical formulation of this contemporary statement indicates a struggle between the principles of honor based respectively on birth and education. But education, the new middle-class principle of honor, was asserted without a political revolution.

It is possible that a pluralism of honor includes a specific kind of impotent honor, known only to a very small group. Such an isolated honor would be found, for example, in an esoteric circle of men who in the midst of capitalism, by continuing to distinguish men according to their endeavor to obtain profit or "honor" on the basis of the four cardinal virtues, remained loyal to the old code of honor which had fallen into disrespect through the degeneration of the nobility and the rise of the bourgeoisie. Similarly isolated is the position of intellectuals who within a closed circle refuse to measure a spiritual achievement according to its utility, even though the social structure in which they live favors the confusion of utility with value. Thus while there is no current recognition of any distinction between the ideas representing partisan interests and those demanded by a search for truth, the small group holds fast to the distinction, preserving its value in solitude and making this value a basis of isolated honor.

Pluralism of honor has a highly important bearing on the practical conduct of life in dynamic social structures, for it means that several images of the right life compete with one another. The individual image loses its representative force, because the realms in which the various images are recognized as valid are usually not separated according to groups formed by economic or political interest, but rather along the lines of demarcation between the various spheres of life, such as politics, art, economics. In other words the different images are valid not for different groups, but for different activities of men; various codes of honor overlap in the same individual. Thus, with pluralism of honor, life threatens to dissolve into relativity.

As an illustration, let there be assumed a "capitalistic society" in which labor is strongly socialistic, and in which the capitalists are not only powerful but also observe a certain code of honor. This assumption is not unrealistic. Under these conditions it would be reasonable to find that the workers do not pay honor to the capitalists, because as socialists they attempt to assert another honor, different from that of the capitalists which they deny and despise.

It would be reasonable, in other words, to find two kinds of honor precisely corresponding to two different groups. In reality, however, the situation is more complex. Every day, though perhaps unconsciously, the workers observe the honor of the capitalists as superior to their own; they do so by recognizing the capitalist's life as an ideal. For example they are willing, if not as a group then as individuals, to rise in the social scale and become capitalists themselves, if this is possible. In this respect the capitalist represents for the worker an image of the right life. In aesthetic taste or in particular moral matters, such as honesty, or in educating their children, the workers imitate traits of the capitalist's conduct of life. Thus their apparently fundamental disagreement concerning the capitalist's honor is not complete; they oppose it in some but not in all respects,[35] so that their life is oriented toward two images. The fact that in certain respects capitalists and workers observe the same code of honor does not abolish the essential relativity and the historical pluralism of honor. It means only that both groups belong to the same culture, a heritage which is broader than the particular status within it. But the culture represented by the capitalists is itself subject to change. In other words, the images which are valid for the various spheres of life change more slowly in some spheres than in others.

The social importance of imitation of ways of life by strata which rank lower than those who present the [models] was discussed even before Tarde by many sociologists and psychologists, very trenchantly, for example, by Mandeville. The phenomenology of honor emphasizes the important role of emulation and imitation, since imitation is but the counterpart of the [model] which is set up in the process of honoring.

VIII

The social model, or when there is a pluralism of honor, the several social models indicate the special character of a social structure. The difference between social structures can thus be understood by comparing the images which are typically valid. The difference between the social structures of England and Germany in the last third of the nineteenth century, for example, can be clarified by a comparative analysis of the contemporary "gentleman" on the one hand, and the "military officer" on the other, and the extent of the circles in which these images were imitated. Such an analysis leads farther than a comparison of the class stratifications in the Marxian sense of the term.[36] Since both countries were capitalistic the Marxian inquiry would emphasize only the homogeneity of the two social structures, and the distinctive conceptions of honor, which in this case are not apparent from criteria of economic power, would remain unintelligible. In the frame of the Marxian theory the social model represented in England by the gentleman is as "irrational" as the plurality of social models represented in Germany by the business man, the civil servant and the worker, a plurality in which the military officer nevertheless asserted in many respects the predominance of his honor. Nor can the Marxian theory distinguish between social structures in which the ruling group lacks honor and those in which its power is as honorable as its honor is powerful. But there is a striking difference between the two kinds of structure. The theory of honor which has been suggested here does not, like the Marxian theory, presuppose a decision about the causes of social rank, but its scope is broad enough for these causes, economic or otherwise, to be incorporated in its analysis.[37]

The concept of class compatible with this theory of honor cannot be found in Marx; rather its formulation must follow the line suggested by Eugène Dupréel: "A social class is a group placed in a hierarchy in a position above or below that of another group comparable to it, another class. The inequality of two classes or their hierarchical order does not result directly from any advantage or prerogative of either of them, such as wealth. It results only indirectly: it is necessary that one of the two classes be recognized by itself and by the other class, as advantageous and superior. This recognition is explicit or implicit."[38]

Honor, implicitly or explicitly paid, is a basic phenomenon of man's social existence. It cannot exist under complete tyranny, because life is then arbitrary and unpredictable; nor can it exist under complete equality, because honor is essentially hierarchical. But complete tyranny and complete equality are only abstract extremes, which serve to demonstrate that man's social existence is put into an approved order by honor.

NOTES

1. I cannot justify here my preference for the terms "private distance" and "public distance" to the distinction between the concepts "horizontal" and "vertical," "subjective," and "objective" social distance; in my opinion every social distance can be traced to a vertical relationship. But I shall mention the most important discussions of the concept of social distance, indispensable for an analysis of social stratification. The references given by Earle Edward Eubank, who introduced the concept of "lateral distance," in *The Concepts of Sociology*, New York, 1931, pp. 453–54, include the studies by P. E. Park, E. S. Bogardus, W. C. Poole, Jr., P. Sorokin, and L. von Wiese. Sorokin, in *Social Mobility*, New York and London, 1927, pp. 3ff. and 9f., mentions the earlier writers who dealt with the problem, but not Hume. Reference should also be made to Andreas Walther, "Soziale Distanz" in *Kölner Vierteljahrshefte für Soziologie*, vol. 9, 1931. Cf. also the studies by Günther Müller, the German historian of literature, "Gradualismus. Eine Vorstudie zur altdeutschen Literaturgeschichte" in *Deutsche Vierteljahreschrift für Literaturwissenschaft und Geistesgeschichte*, vol. 2, 1924, pp. 681–720; "Höfische Kultur der Barockzeit" in Hans Naumann and Günther Müller, *Höfische Kultur*, Halle, 1929. In his *Geschichte des deutschen Liedes vom Zeitalter des Barock bis zur Gegenwart*, Munich, 1925, Müller employs the concept of *Distanzhaltung*.
2. Kimball Young, *Source Book of Social Psychology*, New York, 1926, p. 590.
3. Edgar Zilsel, *Die Entstehung des Geniebegriffs*, Tübingen, 1926.
4. Ignaz Goldziher, *Muhammedanische Studien*, Part I, Halle, 1889, p. 49ff.
5. Cf. the analysis of superordination and subordination in Georg Simmel, *Soziologie*, 2nd ed., Leipzig, 1922, pp. 101–85. Cf. also G. L. Duprat, "La sociologie des hiérarchies sociales" in *Annales de l'Institut International de Sociologie*, vol. 15, 1928, pp. 173–316.
6. G. W. F. Hegel, *Phänomenologie des Geistes*, ed. by Georg Lasson, 2nd ed., Leipzig, 1921, p. 129. Cf. the philosophical discussion of the relation between master and servant, pp. 123–31.
7. Thomas Hobbes, *Leviathan*, Everyman's Library, pp. 45–46.
8. Lafcadio Hearn, *Japan, An Attempt at Interpretation*, New York, 1924, p. 270.
9. Quoted by Zilsel, op. cit., p. 28.
10. Pontus M. Fahlbeck, *Die Klassen und die Gesellschaft*, Jena, 1922, p. 101.
11. Max Weber, *Gesammelte Aufsätze zur Religionssoziologie*, vol. 2, Tübingen, 1923, p. 59.
12. J. H. Mitgau, *Familienschicksal und soziale Rangordnung*, Leipzig, 1926.
13. Vauvenargues, *Introduction à la connaissance de l'esprit humain*, chap. 40, "De l'estime, du respect, et du mépris."

14. P. Nicole, "Honneur," in *Pensées de Pascal suivies d'un choix des pensées de Nicole*, Librairie de Paris, p. 365.
15. Montesquieu, *L'esprit des lois*, book 3.
16. Cf. the examples in Simmel, op. cit., p. 112ff.
17. Plato's *Republic*, book 9.
18. La Bruyère, *Les Charactères*, chap. 11, "De l'homme."
19. Cf. Thorstein Veblen, *The Theory of the Leisure Class*.
20. Quoted by Theodor Hampe, *Die Fahrenden Leute in der deutschen Vergangenheit*, 2nd ed., Jena, 1924, p. 19. For the legal significance of honor in German history cf. the survey in Otto Gierke, *Deutsches Privatrecht*, vol. 1, Leipzig, 1895, pp. 416–33.
21. Cf. Hans Naumann, "Ritterliche Standeskultur um 1200," in Naumann and Müller, op. cit.; Frederick Tupper, *Types of Society in Medieval Literature*, New York, 1926; Ruth Mohl, *The Three Estates in Medieval and Renaissance Literature*, New York, 1933.
22. Sir William Segar, *Honor*, London, 1602, pp. 209–10.
23. For a careful discussion of some theories of honor from the second point of view, cf. the chapter on sociology of honor in Arthur Salz, *Das Wesen des Imperialismus*, Leipzig and Berlin, 1931, pp. 103–73.
24. M. Magendie, *La Politesse mondaine et les théories de l'honnêteté en France au XVII siècle, de 1600 à 1660*, Paris, 1925, p. 896.
25. Cf. Pascal's distinction between *estimer* and *saluer*, between *grandeurs d'etablissement* and *grandeurs naturelles*. "I do not need to hold you in esteem because you are Duke; but it is necessary that I salute you." Cf. Pascal's "Sur les conditions des grands" in his *Pensées*.
26. Louis Bourdaloue, *Oeuvres de . . .* , Paris, Didot Frères, 1865, vol. 1, p. 561 and vol. 3, p. 391. Cf. *"Illusions et grandeur d'une grande réputation,"* in vol. 3, pp. 445–50, and *"Sermon pour le dimanche de la Septuagésime. Sur l'oisiveté,"* in vol. 1, pp. 556–65. It was Bernhard Groethuysen, in his *Origines de l'esprit bourgeois en France*, Paris, 1927, who first called particular attention to Bourdaloue in this respect. For England, cf. W. Lee Ustick, "Changing Ideals of Aristocratic Character and Conduct in Seventeenth Century England," in *Modern Philology*, vol. 30, 1932–33, pp. 147–66.
27. R. von Ihering, *Der Zweck im Recht*, 4th ed., Leipzig, 1905, vol. 2, p. 388ff. This book deserves more attention from the students of social distance.
28. Cesare Beccaria, *An Essay on Crimes and Punishments, with a Commentary by M. de Voltaire*, new ed., Albany, 1872, p. 83. Montaigne also recognized the connection between honor and exclusiveness; cf. his *Essays*, book 2, chap. 7. Balthasar Gracian in *The Art of Prudence*, translated by Savage, London, 1702, p. 266, advises "to make absence an expedient for being both respected, or esteemed."
29. This problem surpasses both the interest and the competence of sociology.
30. Cf. Friedrich Schiller, *Über die ästhetische Erziehung des Menschen*, 24th letter.
31. The last two examples are mentioned by von Ihering, op. cit., p. 389n.
32. Cf. the collection of amusing examples mentioned with grim satisfaction by Arthur Schopenhauer in his *"Aphorismen zur Lebensweisheit,"* in *Sämtliche Werke*, ed. by Frischeisen-Köhler, Berlin, vol. 6, pp. 341–89.
34. August Ludwig Schlözer, *Theorie der Statistik, nebst Ideen über das Studium der Politik überhaupt*, Göttingen, 1804, p. 136.
35. An easily accessible field of research which would throw more light on this phenomenon of overlapping codes of honor can be found in a comparison of the fashions

and political ideas of revolutionary groups with the fashions and opinions prevailing in the ruling groups.

36. Cf. Max Weber, *Gesammelte politische Schriften*, Munich, 1921.

37. The attempt made by Georg Lukács, in *Geschichte und Klassenbewusstsein*, Berlin, 1923, pp. 229–60, to show that historical materialism permits the recognition of different "bases" of the historical process in different epochs is highly interesting but not in accordance with the anthropological presuppositions which are found in Marx's early writings. For a more comprehensive critique of the Marxian class concept in its applicability to present social structures, cf. Hans Speier, "Bemerkungen zur Erfassung des sozialen Struktur," in *Archiv für Sozialwissenschaft und Sozialpolitik*, vol. 68, 1933, pp. 705–25.

38. Eugène Dupréel, *Traité de Morale*, Brussels, 1932, p. 310. As one of the ways of implicit recognition Dupréel mentions imitation, p. 311. Cf. also Edmond Goblot, *La barrière et le niveau. Etude sociologique de la bourgeoisie française*, Paris, 1930. For a similar definition of class, cf. Albert G. Keller, *Societal Evolution*, New York, 1915, p. 86.

3

Militarism in the Eighteenth Century

Social structures in which political power and social esteem are distributed in favor of the military class may be taken as the most general type of militarism.[1] In this very broad sense militarism has been frequent in societies with a differentiation of military and nonmilitary functions and with a coordinated setup of social classes. For a more specific understanding of the different historical types of militarism it is necessary to analyze militaristic social structures with reference to both the particular organization of political power and the extent to which the evaluations inherent in the social esteem of the military class are shared by other classes. Such analysis will show that what may be called the most extreme form of militarism exists when the distribution of power and esteem assumes the form of centralization of control, an attendant state monopoly of raising, controlling, and equipping armies, and a universality of military mores. Societies which have not these characteristics are not wholly militaristic, regardless of the frequency with which they resort to war. Without these systematic distinctions militarism becomes, as in Spencer's use, a conglomerate term, equally applicable to primitive tribes of warriors, to feudalism and to the regime of the absolute state.

In feudalism power and esteem were distributed in favor of the

First published in *Social Research*, vol. 3, 1936. Reprinted by permission of *Social Research*.

military class but the other salient features of militarism in its more specific meaning were lacking. The military estate was socially superior to the other strata and more powerful. Yet these strata were expected to respect rather than to participate in the honor of the military estate. Nor did they attempt anything else. They had social functions, corresponding codes of honor and social images of their own; as a rule they did not emulate the nobles. The social structure was thus pluralistic. It lacked centralization and uniformity. Its absence of centralization was evident in the military domain in the self-equipment of the fighter and the prevalence of individual combat in battle. Its lack of uniformity in activities and patterns of behavior was reflected in the variety of coordinated but not rival mores.

Even further removed from extreme militarism are societies with religious or racial control of social differentiation. In caste systems, for example, any encroachment of nonmilitary castes upon the activities and conduct of the military caste assumes the character of religious offense. For this reason where caste systems have come in contact with scientific civilization the establishment of modern armies has encountered the same obstacles as the establishment of capitalistic enterprises. The rationalistic principles of military or economic organization, based upon impersonal discipline which increases efficiency, are incompatible with any social system of this kind. A Brahman who conforms to the prescriptions of his caste can not enter a modern army, as he might become the subordinate of someone of inferior status. Conversely, the rise of the Sikhs in India toward the end of the eighteenth century was partly a consequence of the fact that many of the Sikh leaders, being of low status, were prevented from becoming leaders in the hierarchy of caste. An efficient national army can exist only in a society which is not divided by differences of race, kinship, religion, caste or social estate. For extreme militarism to exist these differences must be absent or culturally irrelevant, so that they do not preclude universal acquiescence in rational discipline and uniformity of mores.

What I have called the extreme form of militarism is evident in modern society. It originated in the French Revolution, with the moral participation of the masses in politics and war, and is being brought to perfection in contemporary dictatorships under which every civilian, whether or not a potential soldier, is urged to discard nonmilitary patterns of behavior and thought. It is integrally related to bourgeois civilization, and thus represents a new type of militaristic society.

Modern militarism depends in many ways upon the political heritage of the absolute state—a bureaucratic and centralized organization of political power and a bureaucratic organization of a disciplined army. In order to build up these institutions absolutism had to destroy the forces in its own inheritance from feudalism which stood in the way of this development.

The complex endeavors of the absolute state to disintegrate feudal liberties and to achieve control of the armed forces fill several centuries. It was necessary to transform the armies from private enterprises of speculators and military entrepreneurs into public organizations financed, controlled, and equipped by the state and commanded by a reliable nobility. Imperative in this development was the establishment of a central administration. At first it lacked a legal basis, since the content and extent of its functions were determined not by law but by monarchical order and confined to the persons to whom the commissions were given. These extraordinary functionaries, the nucleus of modern bureaucracy, were appointed in contrast to and in conflict with the old legal administration. Thus their origin was revolutionary, their task primarily military and financial in character, their purpose the destruction of liberties in the interest of centralization. The contrast between the ordinary legal administration ("office") and the extraordinary new one ("commission") was typical of absolutism in general. It existed not only in France but also in Spain, Sweden, Prussia, and other states, with the important exception of England, which was fortunate enough to have her militaristic experience early, at a time when officers held prayer-meetings and Cromwell could address his parliament only as "My Lords and Gentlemen."

The most important contribution of the absolute state to modern militarism was its rationalization of political life. To accomplish this it was necessary to break the power of the independent nobles and to transform them into a hierarchy of officers, with the monarch as its peak. Richelieu did not hesitate to have the first representatives of the obstinate nobility beheaded by a royal executioner in a public square in Paris. Even in the eighteenth century superiority in social status still impeded military subordination among officers.[2] Prussian noblemen were far from pleased at becoming officers of the king. Not a few of them, in order to escape service, tried to prove that they were not Prussian, and the *règlement* of 1726 obliged the officers to obey their superiors only if their honor was not violated by discipline.

In order to discipline the rank and file the state had to take upon itself, among other tasks, the centralized equipment of its armies with food. Only by this device could it succeed both in restricting pillage

and devastation of the country and in imposing a check upon desertion, from which armies of the ancien régime suffered hardly less than
from actual loss of men in battle. In France the beginnings of the
famous magazine system can be found even in the time of Henry IV; it
rose to eminence under Louvois and was soon adopted by other countries. Grain and flour were stored in magazines to be used for supply-
ing the troops in war and, if need be, for regulating prices in times of
peace. These magazines were indispensable in the "armament for
war."[3]

Before the establishment of the military magazine system many European countries had provided for the collective storage of grain. The
storehouses were operated by communities, parishes, local associations of farmers, or the like, but they did not suffice to prevent either
famine or considerable waste of parts of the crop in years of abun-
dance. The most efficient storehouses of this cooperative type existed
in Amsterdam, the center of the grain trade in the ancien régime.
Dutch economists of the seventeenth and eighteenth centuries, who
were related to the rich merchants of the trading city, approved of them
for the reason that they helped to maintain social stability.[4] The merchants did not need to fear hunger revolts of the poor urban workers;
when prices rose they opened the storehouses. It should be noted that
the objective of maintaining social peace in a highly stratified urban
community in times of emergency is comparable to the objective of
disciplining an army. German writers at the beginning of the eighteenth century referred to the Dutch experience when they proposed the
establishment of magazines for the poor. They did not succeed, however; state magazines were erected in Prussia only when the increasing
army demanded them—under Frederick William I and Frederick the
Great. This development was typical of economic policy in general
during the seventeenth and eighteenth centuries; economic policy was
dictated by military considerations and, until the middle of the eighteenth century, this was true even of England.

From 1748 on the Prussian king distinguished between "war magazines" and "land magazines," the former filled preferably with flour
ready for use, the latter mostly with grain. The distinction was not
quite tenable, however, since the land magazines too were under the
control of the military administration, and the stores of the war magazines were used when prices went up in times of peace not only for
soldiers but also for the poorer classes of the population. The location
of the war magazines was determined by strategic considerations. In
Prussia they lay at the important water communications. Much of the

food supply of the armies had to be bought from foreign markets. Dutch merchants provided Louis XIV's armies with grain for the conquest of Flanders,[5] and of the grain which the Prussian state purchased for its magazines from 1764 to 1788 only one third was obtained in Prussia, most of the foreign purchases being made in Poland, where grain was cheap.[6]

The economic significance of these storehouses and the opportunities they afforded for corruption may be realized from the fact that in the middle of the eighteenth century, when Prussia had about five million inhabitants, the magazines could provide an army of 100,000 men with food for a year and a half. Toward the end of his reign, in 1784, Frederick the Great had collected grain for three campaigns, and money for three more lay ready in the public treasury. Thus war could be waged for six years without increasing the taxes.

Eighteenth century militarism thus bears a resemblance to modern militarism: it was bureaucratic and centralized and subordinated national economy to military considerations. Any attempt, however, to understand militarism as a social order cannot fail to realize the decisive difference between absolutistic and postabsolutistic militarism. This difference lies in the fact that the bellicose absolute state, in contrast to the modern state, kept its armed forces outside of productive society. There was a clear distinction between military and nonmilitary activities, a distinction which was closely related to the social stratification of society.

The Social Composition of the Armies

The most obvious evidence of this separation is the social composition of the armies. The corps of officers consisted of noblemen, the rank and file was recruited from the dregs of the people. Both classes were exempt from productive activities, while conversely the middle classes were prevented from participating in war and military action. La Rochefoucauld has said "L'air bourgeois se perd quelquefois à l'armée; mais il ne se perd pas à la cour."[7] Yet even in his time there were not many bourgeois in the army. During the Seven Years War the sons of the French bourgeoisie had again been allowed to purchase commissions in the army, but this practice was invalidated in 1781 by the notorious reforms of the Comte de Ségur. He restored the prerogatives of the poorer nobility of the sword at the expense of both the nobility of the robe and the nouveaux riches. Public opinion, governed by the philosophes, bitterly resented this measure which evaluated birth more highly than merit. It did not realize that the decree was to give to the poorer ranks of the nobility of the sword a compensation for their being barred from all profitable occupations in the productive sector of society.

At the end of the ancien régime the French corps of officers belonged to various groups, and because of the different economic and social positions of its members was far from being solidary: great nobles and aristocrats who were presentable to the king; country noblemen with the required number of proper ancestors but without the fortune requisite for acceptance at court; officers of bourgeois origin who had purchased commissions before the decree of 1781; finally the limited number of soldiers of fortune. The common officers could hardly rise above the rank of lieutenant, since the noblemen of superior social status were privileged as to both pay and promotion.

The columns were filled with men who lived outside productive society, that is, below it. They were recruited either from abroad or from the economically useless population within France. Enlistment in the regular army as distinguished from the militarily insignificant militia was "voluntary." The recruiting officers, however, were called "sellers of human flesh," a designation which indicates the desperate kind of freedom that made people enlist. The Comte de Saint Germain, who became war minister in 1775 and succeeded in doubling the army without increase in cost, wrote in his memoirs: "It would undoubtedly be desirable if we could create an army of dependable and specially selected men of the best type. But in order to make an army we must not destroy the nation; it would be destruction to a nation if it were deprived of its best elements. As things are, the army must inevitably consist of the scum of the people and of all those for whom society has no use."[8] Frederick the Great expressed himself to much the same effect in his *Anti-Machiavelli*.

In England the army was much smaller. The social composition of its rank and file, however, was the same. Recruits were drawn from the scum of the earth. The practices of the English press gangs paralleled those of the continental recruiting agents. Kidnapping was customary. Insolvent debtors and criminals under sentence could escape punishment if they enlisted in the army. These devices were surpassed only by the habit of a Hessian Landgraf, an opponent of capital punishment, who was accustomed to send to his regiment criminals under sentence of death; there they were gladly put into the ranks, their chains replaced by arms. The British navy, too, was supplied with men by violent means. Sailors preferred to serve in the merchant marine, which offered higher wages and paid with greater regularity; nor was the discipline so cruel and the absence from home so long as on the warships. The English had hated soldiering and despised soldiers ever since the military dictatorship under Cromwell. This attitude, coupled with the greater stake of the English ruling classes in commercial interests, accounts for the difference between France and England in regard to the social descent of officers. The patents of officers had to be purchased often through "commission brokers," and were thus controlled by the wealthy classes. Moreover, since 1689 the raising and keeping of a standing army in times of peace had been against the law "unless it be with the consent of Parliament," that is, of the classes which controlled parliament. The militia, too, was under the control of the leading classes, in this case the country gentlemen. Promotion was regulated along the same lines. Even at the time of the Peninsular War impecunious officers after twenty-five years of service and many campaigns were not promoted, whereas wealthy and socially influential officers paid off those who had a chance for promotion, or managed to exchange their positions in unhealthy or unpopular stations with ruined officers in more favorably located regiments. In a way Wellington, who rose from ensign in 1787 to lieutenant-colonel in 1793 — "five steps in seven years, during which he had been moved through as many regiments" — is a notable case in point.[9]

In Prussia conditions differed in correspondence with the different social structure of its agricultural economy. The peasants lived in villages around the manors, paying no rent but in return for their land rendering services to the landlord, who sold their produce at the market. The captains of the regiments preferred Prussian peasants as recruits; they were cheaper, if only because they did not desert so often as foreigners, and they could be used during the harvest on the estates of their military commanders. The so-called cantonal system, introduced in 1733, legalized this practice and at the same time rationalized it. "Since there has hitherto been so much disorder and no *égalité* among those enrolled"[10] special districts (*cantons*) were assigned to the regiments for recruitment and universal enrollment at an early age was prescribed for the economically dispensable classes. Thus the state claimed its subjects for military service; therefore, it could not help restricting certain prerogatives of the landlords. The law was a compromise. It created something like a nationalized militia in a political structure that was undergoing a process of centralization and equalization but was still determined by the institution of agricultural servitude. It was an attempt at as comprehensive a utilization of the population for military purposes as the economy could bear and the privileged estate would tolerate. As has been often remarked, it foreshadowed the universal military service of the nineteenth century which postulated and eventually brought about the liberation of the peasants. The imperative demands of economy and the unequalitarian social structure, however, did not yet permit universality of service. In 1742 an instruction of Frederick the Great to the infantry reversed the proportions of foreign and national recruits. Two thirds of the whole strength was to be obtained from abroad. The important *réglement* of February 12, 1792, postulated again, it is true, the principle of universal conscription. But actually the exemptions necessary "for the prosperity of the state" were greater than ever before. They included practically all of the urban middle classes and the agrarian upper class. At the close of the century Leopold Krug, an able statistician, gave an estimate of all exceptions to the rule. He assumed a total population of about 8,700,000 persons. About 1,170,000 men were exempt because of local privileges, granted to certain towns and centers of industrial activity, about 530,000 for reasons of status, denomination, wealth or occupation—a total of 1,700,000 persons.[11] Under these conditions and in view of the fact that two fifths of Prussia was Polish provinces, to which for political reasons the cantonal system could not be applied, it was an amazing accomplishment of the state to have in the ranks of its army at the end of the century more subjects than foreigners. Yet it must be understood that this extraordinary military strength of so small a state as Prussia was possible because after their first year of service the native recruits were actual soldiers only during the two months of the great maneuvers; for the rest of the year they were on furlough and worked as peasants. This combination of agricultural and military activities, which gave to great parts of the Prussian army the character of a militia, accounts for the relative numerical superiority of Prussia to the other military states of the ancien régime.

The officers, taken as a class, were superiors of the privates also in civil life. It was the landed aristocracy which composed the corps of officers. The king considered them as vassals[12] who, unlike the civil servants of the state, were bound to him by personal ties of fealty. If a long war thinned their lines so much that militarily distinguished rankers had to be entrusted with higher commands, after the war the king at once restored the order which he deemed desirable and which was required by the social structure; officers of common birth were ruthlessly replaced. The urban middle classes were slowly becoming richer and more educated, but they had, according to the king, no *point d'honneur*. The aristocracy, on the other hand, was barred from commerce and industry. Nor could it, as in southern Germany, the Rhineland and the Hapsburgian monarchy, serve at court or in the Catholic church. To the impoverished elements of the Prussian nobility military service was thus, as in France, an economic necessity.

The Prussian officers were ordered not to mix with middle-class elements, and Frederick the Great even refused to give his consent to marriages between noblemen and bourgeois ladies. In 1806 as many as 9 percent of the Prussian officers were of middle-class origin, but they were to be found almost exclusively in troops which stood in low esteem, such as the artillery or the engineering corps. Many of them were half-disabled veterans, unfit for service in the field, who had been promoted with their assignment to garrison companies.

In south Germany matters were somewhat different. The percentage of middle-class officers appears to have been higher than in Prussia.[13] The poor middle-class officers whose career was limited considered their occupation merely as a way of making a living, since the noble officers did not set any standards of military honor. There was hardly any comradeship between the noble and the middle-class officer;[14] even hatred was not rare, as many of the noble officers were "intruders" from France, Hungary, and other countries. In Bavaria it was the court and not the army, luxury and the arts rather than military prowess, which set the pace of civilization and attracted those who could afford to distinguish themselves. On the other hand, the gulf between officers and civilians was, for the same reason, not so deep as in the north. They came in contact with each other and the conduct of the officers was unassuming.[15] Conflicts between the soldier and the civilian were confined to the lower strata. Since privates were poorly paid they had to add to their income through clandestine trade and manufacture; their officers tolerated this practice, although throughout the century the urban population complained at the unfair competition which it entailed.[16]

In short, the guiding principle of eighteenth century military organization was to have a strong army without injuring the productive forces of society, without destroying the nation. Economy needed to be strengthened by all means of governmental planning. Technique was still much more attached to persons than to machines, and although beggary was widespread in all of Europe the number of skilled workers was inadequate to the needs of the expanding economy. Thus governments tried to prevent their emigration and by every possible means, legal or illegal, tried to obtain workers from abroad.

The transformation of the armies into national militias, as proposed by Machiavelli, Leibniz, Spinoza, the Landgraf Moriz of Hesse, and, in the eighteenth century, men like the Marshal of Saxe or Justus Möser, was for economic and political reasons unfeasible. Most of these suggestions were far from being anticipations of the system of universal conscription, as was not infrequently assumed by nineteenth-century military historians. Rather they were reversions to degenerated preabsolutistic liberties as expressed in local militias composed of free burghers or peasants. Möser, for example, clearly realized the close connection between the *esprit de fabrique* and the centralization of politics, both of which he held responsible for the enforced alienation of townsmen from military life and for the universal decline of the soldier's prestige.[17] His analysis, so suggestive also for an understanding of the high repute of soldiering in Switzerland, was sound. Yet the political structure of eighteenth century militarism no less than economic necessities demanded recruitment from the dregs of society. Enlistment of foreigners was preferable because of the incidental increase of the population which it entailed. Despite the high ratio of deserters there were foreign mercenaries who married and settled down as economically valuable craftsmen.

The low social origin of the privates was frequently considered justification for the severe and cruel discipline in the armies of the ancien régime. Yet there were national differences in severity of drill which must be ascribed to other factors. In Catholic countries discipline was more liberal, less efficient and not so pitiless as in Prussia. Also, in France and in Austria, where many noblemen were subject to the civilizing influence of the court, the socially required behavior of the officer was that of the *honnête homme* who did not tolerate personal brutalities. Prussian soldiers were taught to fear their officers more than the enemy. The troops took on the character of machines and their efficiency caused the adoption of Prussian methods by other countries.

A contemporary of Frederick the Great attributed the preference of fire to bayonet in the Prussian infantry to the fact that the troops were "animated neither by a spirit of patriotism nor by loyalty to their prince." They were "composed of men of every nation and of every religion in Europe." It is alleged that at the instant the general ordered them "to charge with the bayonet a great part of them would go over to the enemy."[18] This description is not very judicious in detail but it hits the point with which we are here concerned: the lack of middle-class loyalties and of artificial emotions in the army. And this was typical of other European troops as well. It contributed to the contempt in which the soldier was held by public opinion and would alone suffice for an explanation of the wholesale desertion that the commanders had to cope with. Even of the American Revolution it has been said that the combatants had so little zeal for the struggle that the British and American armies were composed of each other's deserters. Frederick the Great issued decree after decree against desertion, including orders to pay rewards to deserters who returned within six months. This method was less expensive than paying the earnest to a new recruit. The danger of desertion affected strategy and tactics. Marching during the night and camping in a forest had to be avoided. Troops which advanced in an attack were commanded to stop and to proceed after a rearrangement of the lines, as prescribed and practiced in maneuvers. The social composition of the armies was responsible also for the preference of closed formations and the open field as battle ground. Ranged battles were still customary, and therefore the general who wished to avoid a decisive combat could always do so.

The limitations of eighteenth-century warfare arose also from the system of political coalitions. It was in diplomatic negotiations from cabinet to cabinet that the plan of a campaign was determined. The interest of belligerents to spare soldiers paid by subsidies of economically advanced allies was strong, stronger sometimes than military logic. Delegates of the court accompanied the generals, as did the later commissioners of the French Convention, and the result was a restriction in the freedom of military action.

Thus the well-known indecisiveness of campaigns and the relative rareness of battles in eighteenth century warfare must not be attributed only to the strength of fortresses, to the poor roads which hindered rapid movements and to the "increased humanity" which "helped to increase the independence of armies upon magazines."[19] These specific conditions which made for the predominance of the defensive in war and refined the art of maneuvering must be understood in the light of the general social, political, and economic forces of the time. All forms of warfare and militarism reveal this functional dependence upon the social structure as whole.

All these social, economic, and political forces operating interdependently brought about a type of war which was completely the product of the period. In many countries the military elite was hardly less penetrated by the ideas of rationalism than were the philosophers.

War seemed to offer chiefly mechanical and calculable problems. Topography appeared as the basic element of warfare. The predominance of the defensive to the offensive seemed to testify to the superiority of reason to the unformed passions, of human faculties to nature. The emotional and intellectual resources of the rank and file were not exploited as in the nineteenth century; they were neglected and despised.

There were military writers who derived from this increasing rationality of war the prediction of its end. If war is reducible to scientific elements and if the function of reason is all-comprehensive, it does not indeed seem paradoxical that the Prince of Ligne suggested the establishment of an "International Academy of Military Science" (1780). A German writer who analyzed the new spirit of the "system of war" arrived at the conclusion that with the irresistible advancement of reason, witnessed and celebrated in so many other domains of modern civilization, military science will put an end to war. "If the true principles of this science were equally known everywhere, one could soon renounce war as futile, since the armies trained and commanded with equal skill could not gain from each other, and thus the inexpediency of war would induce an uninterrupted peace which probably will not so soon result from the benevolent opinions of the men of our earth."[20] Behrenhorst, the important German critic of eighteenth-century warfare, was also inclined to believe in eternal peace. No book, said a contemporary, was so much read as Behrenhorst's *Considerations of the Art of War* (1797), in which the "science of strangling according to rules" was denounced in a Voltairian manner.

The attitudes of the strategists who preferred the mechanical, precise, and rational in the art of war to its imponderable and chaotic chances were later, in the nineteenth century, much despised and derided. Yet the hesitation to call upon the forces of nature, sentiment and unrestricted violence did not indicate merely a lack of imagination. In the eighteenth century the leading classes did not share the sentimental and enthusiastic attitudes toward nature which spread in the nineteenth century under the influence of Rousseauists and romantics. Their rationalism was a cultural trait to be found in conversation and art, in parks and music as well as in warfare. A new nature was discovered by those who were eager to substitute for the "artificial forms" and "mechanical forces" of rigid and limited eighteenth-century warfare the "moral" participation of masses in war: that is, by the prophets and apostles of the *bürgerliche Krieg*, the "citizens' war," by philosophers like Guibert in France and Clausewitz in Germany.[21]

They and the political forces which they expressed promoted militarism in its modern form, the first great exponent of which was Napoleon.

Society Versus the State

The social structure of the armies and the corresponding political system of the ancien régime must again be taken into account in order to understand the relations between civilians and soldiers, the attitudes of society toward the state. Society was connected with the state primarily by taxes. Expenditures for war purposes were exceedingly high; soldiers had to be fed, clothed, armed, paid, and administered by the state. In Necker's budget for 1784 the expenditure for military purposes amounted to about two thirds of the total budget. Prussia spent 86 percent of its budget in 1739–40 for this purpose, 76 percent in the last three years of Frederick the Great's regime, 71 percent of 1797–98, and 75 percent in 1805–06. If we include the service for military debts England in 1781 used for military purposes no less than 94 percent of all her expenditures.[22] In so far as these sums could not be obtained from rich countries as subsidies they had to be raised by means of loans and taxation. Thus the gap between the state and society was systematically entrenched by the conflict between creditor and debtor. Yet it should be noted that the tax burden pressed less on the classes which were decisive for the formation of a critical opinion concerning the military state than on the peasants. The percentage of the urban population was small and only its upper strata were effective in an explicit formation of attitudes toward the military system. This elite consisted by no means exclusively of bourgeois. In France, which is most interesting for an analysis of the relations between society and state, it included many aristocrats. When we speak of public opinion, which as Necker put it in 1784 had become a king without visible attributes, dictating alike to town and court and even in the palace of kings, we must bear in mind that the public of this time was small and not without aristocratic traits.[23] It consisted primarily not of economically interested groups but rather of persons who assumed intellectual responsibilities.

The attitude toward the soldier was one of open contempt. In France, a military career for anyone but a nobleman was considered degrading. Up to the revolution one could read on many public buildings or garden walls, "No dogs, servants or soldiers allowed."[24] Fortescue says of England, "There was no idea in those days of making a hero of the soldier, not even for a day. When he had served his purpose he was cast aside and went back to his status of a plague of the nation."[25] As to Prussia, it sheds full light on both the army and the backward development of public opinion in that country that cabinet order was issued in 1780 according to which "unauthorized writing" and mutinous activities were to be punished by military service in case the convict could not prove that he was able to earn his living honestly. In 1787 this regulation, which affords a fair illustration of the disgrace in which the soldier was held even by the state, was extended to those who had taken part in crimes against the authorities by advice, encouragement, pernicious insinuations, and the like.

European economists, moralists, and publicists vied with one another in denouncing the profession of the soldier. Physiocrats proved that he was unproductive, political philosophers that he was a mere instrument of dynastic ambitions and despotism, moralists that he was barbaric. Fichte held that soldiers, forming a state within the state, were "almost as dreadful as Jews."[26] A whole literature arose against standing armies.[27] Wars, it was said and repeated, were unreasonably expensive; they increased prices and taxes, retarded economic progress, and pressed upon the poor. The argument that wars ruin both victor and vanquished was very familiar to the time. If it be true, wrote Herder, that the system of military conquest is the unshakable foundation of Europe, what else could one say than that Europe declines for the benefit of the world. The opponents of war counted the most distinguished minds in their midst: Hume in England, Voltaire in France, Kant in Prussia. Pamphlets and magazines disseminated the ideas in a cruder form.

The opposition to war was most effectively buttressed by the theory of progress, according to which the development of commerce and trade meant civilization and peace, whereas war, characteristic of the earlier, less enlightened, and more prejudiced stages of human development, had now become an atavism. This idea of progress found possibly its most naive presentation in the book of a Swiss writer whose optimism knew no bounds. A decline of Europe, he suggested, need not be feared since art, science, and gentle convictions have been too well entrenched by the art of printing.[28]

It has already been mentioned that even military writers contemplated the end of war in the course of human development. Yet it took an antimilitary writer to elaborate the idea that only the private person belongs to a permanent society whereas the ruler, living in a *non-société*, should for his safety and economic profit enter a new international society of equals. The Abbé de Saint-Pierre "was indeed terribly at ease in confronting the deepest and most complex problems,"[29] and his utilitarian suggestions as to how to establish permanent peace were not the ideas of the age. Yet his conspicuous aptitude for confusing political categories with economic ones was shared to varying degrees by many progressive thinkers of the period.

The conflict between society and the military state, which indicates the limitation of absolutistic militarism from the point of view of modern militarism, is most impressively reflected in a specific trait of the antimilitaristic philosophy of the period: in the critique of heroism. In comparison with the state society was unheroic in character. There were French philosophes who did not hesitate to declare that they were not willing to sacrifice themselves for their convictions since any need for sacrifice merely proved that unfortunately their ideas still lacked recognition. Meanwhile they busied themselves in collecting evidence of the fragility of heroism, with the intention of disintegrating the moral basis of war and of undermining the philosophy of those, that is the privileged nobility, who had a chance to distinguish themselves in war through courage. This antiheroism is conspicuous in all kinds of literary activity, in the writing of history as well as in philosophy, in weeklies and in novels;[30] the heroes and heroines of fiction were rather unheroic characters. Historians belittled the function of the conqueror in history. Pope in his *Essay on Man* spoke of the boring similarity of all conquerors from Alexander on; all of them, he said, have been "badly mad."[31] Hume held that most of mankind considers heroism "the most sublime kind of merit," yet "men of cool reflection are not so sanguine in their praises of it." They notice that there are infinite "confusions and disorders" caused by this "supposed virtue." Military glory is followed by "the subversion of empires, the devastation of provinces, the sack of cities."[32] Also Herder in his *Briefe zur Beförderung der Humanität* called the heroic spirit the "destroying angel of mankind," and he pleaded to withdraw from it the glory which it had received and the esteem in which it had been held since the ancients.[33] In an attempt to evaluate the comparative merit of the conqueror, the soldier, the saint, the "great man," the writer, the artist, Thomas Abbt expressed only a common opinion when he said that the hero who is nothing but a hero is not worth anything. If he had "virtues" Abbt was willing to pity him because of the consequences of his heroism and was even generous enough to admire his "unheroic" qualities.[34]

These critical attitudes must be understood as special aspects of a general process in which the social [models] of the privileged classes were being transformed in accordance with the new moral convictions that were developing in the urban public. In England, which was economically most advanced, the ideal of the gentleman was democratized in favor of the business classes climbing to respectability. Periodicals corroborated and diffused the opinion that "men should be esteemed according to the wealth they bring their country, and trade be accounted of all professions the most honorable."[35] In France the interpretation of the *honnête homme* underwent similar changes, although the innovations were not so stolidly practical. Colbert, referring to the urban and commercial spirit of the Italian and English nobilities, had already criticized the notion, detrimental to economic progress, that aristocrats must not engage in trade and industry. In the eighteenth century this attitude increased in strength and turned against the state.[36]

With the rise of a literary public which included the upper strata of the middle classes, especially their women, the man of letters began to form a secular profession. He gained social distinction and economic independence, since he could live on the anonymous collective public, whereas formerly the writers depended on rents or the financial support of a patron, and did not produce ideas in order to make a living. Even in Germany the number of writers doubled within the last thirty years of the century, and a contemporary publicist declared that reading had become a need of the German public which could doubtless be put in the same class with the need of food. Most of what the public read did not precisely strengthen military mores. In this limited form of militarism it was society which conducted the propaganda, not the state. The intellectuals were not all radical, and even in France, where more of them were so disposed, they adopted many traits of the aristocratic tradition.[37] Yet they certainly did not represent a military social type. They developed a dignity based on reason, wit, and literary merit rather than on birthright or courage. "A man of letters," wrote d'Alembert, "forced by singular circumstances to spend his days near a minister of state, said one day, with much truth and delicacy, 'he would be familiar with me, but I push him from me with respect.'"[38] The quotation indicates how with the assertion of the potentially equalitarian principles of intelligence and reason as new bases of social esteem the technique of expressing the old deferences was reversed in its meaning. Minor evidence of these egalitarian implications in the new attitude is the fact that in the French plays which propagandized the new philosophy in a milder form the philosophe did not regularly belong to a particular social class. In these plays aristocrats and peasants, wealthy bourgeois and innkeepers appeared as philosophes, although in the majority of the plays they were members of the upper and lower bourgeoisie.[39] In the second half of the eighteenth century the *homme de lettres* of common origin entered the French salons, those glamorous institutions where literary fame was acquired and the seats for the French Academy distributed.

In Germany the egalitarian implications of reason, or rather the antidespotic implications of the philosophy of enlightenment, were recognized long before they became politically effective. According to Thomasius it was due only to differences of social status that not everyone arrived at knowledge and wisdom.[40] At the time when Fichte expounded his ideal of the scholar as the educator of mankind, the greater part of the European public knew that mankind did not live in the state but in society, which, as a glance at the contemporary programs of progressive education reveals, was an antiheroic society. In that society education was to realize the ideal of "classlessness."

The Devaluation of Courage

Since the intrinsically unheroic character of industrial society must be borne in mind in order to understand militarism in its most recent forms, it may be helpful to outline some of the arguments, varying of course according to the particular philosophical schools to which the writers belong, that were used in devaluating courage, the cardinal virtue of the hero.

The most elementary argument consisted in distinguishing between "true" courage and its distorted forms, with the implication that the courage of the nobleman was not the true one. The history of philosophy affords fair illustrations that this technique of devaluating the arguments of an opponent is a favored device of polemics in general, and many a fatal deadlock in contemporary political debates results from its indiscriminate application. It should be noted incidentally that inasmuch as the argument indicates a certain remnant of agreement it is not radical. In eighteenth-century discussion of courage this technique was often used, especially by the Baron d'Holbach, who always took comfort in acknowledging the terminology of his opponents in order to declare that they simply did not understand "le vrai courage," "la politique véritable," "le grandeur d'une âme véritable," "l'honneur véritable," and the like.

Yet eventually Holbach did not fail to indicate what he meant by true courage: "une disposition utile, louable et vertueuse si l'on désigne sous ce nom, ce courage, cette énergie, cette magnanimité, qui portent un bon citoyen à défendre et servir sa Patrie."[41] The definition is fairly typical of a popular trend of radical thought in this time. Not courage as such, it seems to suggest, but courage under the prevailing political and social conditions, courage in "despotism," lacks moral character. To be a real virtue courage thus had to be useful, an idea which led many writers to entangle themselves in the politically useful inconsistency of finally depriving courage altogether of the character of a virtue. Useful was productive society. Useless was the nobility and, broadly speaking, the state. The nobility was held to be courageous at the expense of society. It cherished notions of virtue which contradicted the rationale of society. Its uselessness, then, revealed the ultimately vicious character of its prowess.

It should be noted that this argumentation, so admirably fit for discrediting both the social prerogatives and the predominant activities of the higher nobility, presupposes the acceptance of economic utility as the criterion of virtue. It neglects the political aspect of social life and waives the question of personal perfection. Its reasoning is far from being self-evident. Rather it indicates an imposition of the economic principles vital to commercial and industrial society upon ethical problems, and thus it testifies to the modern reversal of the old relationship between the *utile*, the *honestum*, and the *summum bonum*.

The confrontation of productive work and useless upper classes is as old as the contrast between the moral philosophies of Homer and Hesiod. Its history accompanies that of social inequality, with the upper classes devoted to military pursuits and contemptuously looking down upon those who labor. This history includes, during the period of European chivalry, the revolutionary figure of Dinadan who in the prose version of Tristan vigorously attacked the knightly conceptions of duty and fortitude. In the Renaissance, it produced attempts to determine the relative status of the soldier and the jurist — from the fourteenth century on it had been debated whether those who taught or those who fought were to be superior — by analyzing their respective usefulness for the state. But not until the eighteenth century did these discussions assume a general character and refer to an alleged contrast between society and state.

One of the earliest writers who insisted that peace can be secured on the basis of a redistribution of social esteem in favor of the commercial classes was Emeric Crucé, a monk. He wrote at a time when, as he said, there was "hardly a way to acquire a modest fortune by any honest means,"[42] but he declared that "there is no occupation to compare in utility with that of the merchant who legitimately increases his resources by the expenditure of his labor and often at the peril of his life, without injuring or offending anyone: in which he is more worthy of praise than the soldier whose advancement depends upon the spoil and destruction of others."[43] Consequently Crucé proposed that the princes should invite "indifferently the great and the small to trade." The most interesting aspect of his ideas is the suggestion that the problem of social esteem must be considered in any attempt to plan a more peaceful society. Thus he did not think of depriving the nobility of its position of honor but proposed that more beneficial activities be substituted for the pursuits which the nobility followed at the time. He mentioned the chase; it is noble, he said, and "becoming to men at arms." He contemplated the transformation of the noble fighters into a police force which should wipe out piracy and brigandage, much to the benefit of a peaceful society engaged primarily in agriculture, commerce, and the arts. Saint-Pierre, who did not admit any debts to Crucé, his greater predecessor, hinted at the same point when he declared that the nobility of the sword need not suffer any loss of honor in the new peaceful order to be established, since the gradations of offices would offer ample opportunities for distinction on the grounds of justice, goodness, talent, and diligence. He added that noblemen could even count on pensions and thus acquire greater wealth, since the state would save money if it did not wage war. Crucé also anticipated the proposals made by many eighteenth-century critics of the military system that soldiers be employed in useful public works like draining marshes and building canals.[44]

Crucé differs from many eighteenth-century promoters of peace in that his writings show no idea of moral progress as a law governing history. Hence he presented no evolutionary hypothesis which would enable his successors to transform courage from a moral to a historical problem. Crucé's casual critique of courage stands rather in the Catholic tradition, which had very early, with St. Ambrose's Christianization of Cicero's ethics, succeeded in substituting for the pagan hero the image of the heroic saint and which had later civilized barbaric knighthood by introducing into its moral code the ideas of justice, protection of the weak and gentleness. Crucé distinguished the "ordinary bravery which has no other foundation or support than force . . . from that magnanimity which consists in a firm courage, and disdain of all adversity. The effects of real bravery are to repel injury and not to cause it; to bear generously death and all other accidents when they present themselves and not to seek for them."[45] Here, then, courage as courage is not removed from the picture of the moral world; it is regarded from a Christian point of view.

The philosophy of progress, however, made it possible to dissolve the problem into one of circumstantial relevance. the uselessness of courage in a productive society sufficed to deprive it of its moral value. Again from Holbach: "At the origin of society man was exclusively attached to courage, because courage was then the virtue par excellence, that is, the most useful quality in wholly warlike nations. In modern and civilized nations which for their interest must be more peaceable, it becomes necessary to attach the idea of man to qualities which are more peaceful and more advantageous to a society whose wants have changed."[46]

The relativistic idea that the moral qualities of man change with time and space was indeed common to many moralists of the period. Yet only few thinkers succeeded in combining the maintenance of absolute values with a penetrating understanding of moral relavism, which was so powerfully suggested by the discrepancy between state and society, the history of manners and accounts of travelers. The writers who developed and at the same time overcame the "sociology of moral knowledge" before the name was coined include, in this period, Montesquieu, Christian Garve, and Adam Ferguson. It was not incidental that it was they who retained their enthusiasm about the moral character of industrial society; nor did they dissolve courage as a virtue.

Without attempting completeness two other tendencies should be mentioned in the arguments used to devaluate courage. There was the possibility to explain on aesthetic grounds the undeniable admiration which courage evokes. Its ethical relevance could be more easily discarded if its aesthetic importance were admitted. Hume had already moved in this direction when he said of the hero that "there is something so dazzling in his character, the mere contemplation of it so elevates the mind" that the inclination to hate rather than to admire is at first overpowered by a more immediate sympathy.[47] Also Kant, who otherwise agreed with Hume on the detestable character of war and on its incompatibility with a commercial society, expressed the opinion that from the aesthetic point of view the superiority of the military leader to the statesman cannot be doubted.[48] It should be noted that this separation of the aesthetic from the moral was utterly inadequate for understanding the conduct of a leisure class, although it was effective as the basis of an invidious critique. A leisure class always tends to develop standards which combine inseparably the good and the beautiful. Prince Eugen reminded his noble officers before a battle that their only right to live consisted in their readiness to give an example, even in the greatest danger, but to do it with such grace and composure that no one could reproach them. One would inevitably be led astray who tried to separate the moral from the aesthetic in the Prince's code.[49]

Another, perhaps more important, attack on courage was its reduction to vanity and physical strength. The argument from usefulness meant a sociological disintegration of the metaphysical problem which courage represents. The separation of the aesthetic from the moral permitted of a more definitely rationalistic approach. But the argument from pride and force meant a psychological destruction of courage. It assumed its most extreme form in the writings of two physicians, Helvétius and Mandeville. They could conveniently borrow from the observations of numerous great moralists such as Gracian, La Rochefoucauld, Saint Evremond, and others, whose detachment from society had helped them to recognize the role of ambition and flattery, vanity and pride in social life. The modern cynics differed from their predecessors by the sweeping application they gave their convictions, which thus freed from all limitations, produced nothing but brilliance in the void.

Mandeville's account of courage, contained in his *Fable of the Bees*, is especially noteworthy because it offers ideas on the propaganda of courage which supply a theory for modern practice. He drew a distinction between true valor and artificial valor. The former is based on rage, which since it results from an appropriate physical condition, can be aroused by intoxicating drugs; it presupposes ignorance and vanishes with it. In modern warfare, conducted by means of strategy, this sort of courage is useless because it permits of neither advice nor discipline. Statesmen have therefore sought a psychological substitute for true valor which would not have its deficiencies but would serve the same purpose of overcoming the fear of death. Since all ethical conduct is rooted in flattery and pride this end is achieved by drawing upon the intrinsic weakness of human nature: man is persuaded that he possesses a special principle of courage apart from rage and other affects, and that a perfect performance of this artificial courage merits the highest praise. By means of this propaganda man is brought to confuse with courage his induced pride in not fearing death. His pride, carefully cultivated by proper rewards and flattery, will increase until his fear of disgrace will eventually outstrip his fear of death.

Thus Mandeville transformed the moral problem of courage into one of political and military expediency. Once courage becomes of primary concern to propagandists there is no more suggestion that it was once called one of the two excellences of the irrational part of soul. What remains is but the shrewd hypocrisy of the propagandist and a useful but empty display of pride on the part of the brave. It has become proof and product of man's fear of disgrace; thus its origin is fabricated opinion, and instead of giving testimony to the greatness of man it proves only that he is vain and foolish.

The Devaluation of Honor

The changing interpretations of courage are corroborated by the attitudes of public opinion toward the honor of noblemen. It suffices to read the comments of Helvétius and Destutt de Tracy on Montesquieu's discussion of honor (in the fourth book of his *Esprit des lois*, dealing with the modes and functions of education under the different forms of government) in order to realize how violently the philosophers waged a fight against honor.

Montesquieu was still aware of the values of the civilization destined to pass and yet not unaware of the values of that to come. His critics were blind to the former and understood only the new society. When Montesquieu declared that under a monarchical government which has honor as its principle the actions of men are judged not as good but as beautiful, not as just but as grand, not as reasonable but as extraordinary, Helvétius replied that this describes courtiers rather than the nation. When Montesquieu declared that the education for honor blends virtue with noblesse, conduct with candor, manners with politeness, Destutt de Tracy interpreted the idea polemically as the royal concern for rendering minds light and superficial. In this connection even Voltaire spoke of Montesquieu's empty phrases which had nothing to do with what mattered: the laws. But we have neither his nor any other critic's comment on Montesquieu's third "higher rule" of honor, according to which matters not allowed by honor are more strictly prohibited if the laws do *not* forbid them, and likewise matters commanded by honor are more urgently required if no law imposes them. As in the case of courage it was "nature" and the virtues of honesty, order, diligence, and justice which were being proposed by society as substitutes for the rules of honor.[50]

It should be noted that most of the arguments used by eighteenth-century atheists and materialists in the fight against honor and courage could be conveniently derived from earlier writers, from Molinists and Jansenists, even from Jesuits. Baron d'Holbach in his verdict on courage quoted the Jansenist Nicole. In Diderot's and d'Alembert's *Encyclopédie* the individual self was proclaimed as the source of honor; Pascal had held that only Christianity, that is, not high status in the social order, confers *honnêteté*. He had also anticipated the argument on the basis of the circumstantial relativity of esteem, which rendered the hero an assassin when he crosses a border. Crucé, who foreshadowed Saint-Pierre's ideas on the organization of peace, was a Catholic monk who still insisted on the cautious distinction between just and unjust war. Bossuet's Catholic denunciation of honor in his first sermon on the subject written in 1660 was repeated in the "natural light" of reason and wit in Moliére's *Le misanthrope*.[51] This similarity of arguments in the devaluation of courage and honor is striking. It does not mean, of course, that the points of reference necessary for this devaluation were also similar or identical. The Christian writers referred to the self, that is, the Christian self; its supreme value made the worldly realm of inequality and ambition appear relative and irrelevant. Eighteenth-century critics of honor and courage, war and militarism, emphasized the superiority of the natural, reasonable, virtuous individual to the unnatural, irrational, and unjust inequalities of the existing social order. Yet the conspicuous similarity of arguments remains and indicates a more profound transformation of culture during the period of absolutism than an analysis in terms of economic causation would suggest.

There are various traits of eighteenth-century militarism which have not been included in this paper. One major problem, in particular, which arrests the attention of the sociologist who attempts to understand militarism as a social order, could not be taken into account within the frame of this essay — the problem of the self-esteem of the nobility. Obviously it underwent a transformation with the decline of feudal liberties and the integration of the leading class into the absolutistic regime. Voltaire realized the significance of this question when he emphasized, or rather overemphasized, the fact that because of the policy of Louis XIV birth had given way to merit as a principle of promotion in the army. He added, "The new principles of government inspired a new courage."[52] The character of this "new" heroism would have to be analyzed if an attempt were made to understand the peculiarity of eighteenth-century militarism more comprehensively.

The nobility and its conception of heroism were affected not only by spiritual changes and transformations in the economic set-up of society but also by the bureaucratization of military life which, as has been indicated, accompanied the rise of absolutism to power. The court was another important influence in affecting the self-esteem of the nobility, especially in those countries where it was not a mere resort for officers, but assumed a social significance of its own. In France the court gave rise to new ideas of glory and triumph — a word introduced in the French language only in the seventeenth century. It offered new opportunities for intimate psychological observation and it laid bare the wheels of favor and failure, ambition and grandeur in the machinery of human affairs; the court was truly a sociopsychological laboratory of the first class which left its mark of refinement even on the style of those who despised and depicted its vices.

The significance of these forces which worked upon the self-esteem of the aristocracy varies from country to country and also according to the social status of the noblemen within the aristocracy.

Summary

Thus, in short, eighteenth-century militarism differs as a social order from preceding forms of militarism and also from the form we are familiar with today. It was built on an economy that did not tolerate the removal of its useful members for military purposes. The big armies were composed of economically exempt classes, and the rank and file were free of loyalties. To the nobility, in exchange for political submission, the state offered privileged posts in the bureaucratized army and professional careers as officers; the recruits were obtained by pressure and their discipline was buttressed by the ingenious magazine system. There was a deep cleavage between state and society. The nonmilitary classes held militarism in contempt. Public opinion entertained expectations of lasting peace because it believed in reason, progress, and commerce. Attempting to formulate antimilitary attitudes, which were not strictly confined to the nonmilitary classes, literati devaluated courage and honor, the basic elements of the aristocratic code. The methods they developed for this purpose, however, contained philosophical implications which made it difficult to redefine honor and courage in a nonmartial way and to preserve the value which lies beyond the historically limited, relative, forms.

NOTES

1. I use the term militarism not merely to represent a philosophy or a bellicose foreign policy but to signify and interdependent social system. This usage may be roughly compared with the sociological conception of feudalism or industrialism.
2. Henri Carré, *La Noblesse de France et l'Opinion Publique au XVIII Siècle*, Paris, 1920, p. 168. The case occurred in 1746.
3. *Acta Borussica, Getreidehandelspolitik*, vol. 3, p. 183, and vol. 4, p. 51.
4. Ibid., vol. 1, p. 435.
5. Cf. Werner Sombart, *Krieg und Kapitalismus*, Munich and Leipzig, 1913, p. 141.
6. Cf. *Acta Borussica. Getreidehandelspolitik*, vol. 4, pp. 100ff.
7. This famous maxim was much discussed in the eighteenth century. Cf. Christian Garve, "Über die Maxime Rochefoucaulds: Das bürgerliche Air verliert sich zuweilen bei der Armee, niemals am Hofe," in *Versuche über verschiedene Gegenstände aus der Moral, der Literatur und dem gesellschaftlichen Leben*, Breslau, 1801, pt. 1, pp. 263–402; and Addison and Steele, *Spectator*, Everyman's Library, vol. 8, pp. 39–40. Notice the characteristic difference in interpretation.
8. Cited by Louis Ducros, *French Society in the Eighteenth Century*, trans. W. de Geijer, London, 1926, p. 294.
9. Cf. C. W. C. Oman, *Wellington's Army 1809-1814*, New York and London, 1912, pp. 198ff. Nor did the Duke ever adopt the principle of promotion by merit. On the old rankers he passed harsh verdicts: "Their origin would come out, and you could never perfectly trust them." Ibid., p. 206.
10. From the Order of May 1, 1733, cited by Curt Jany, *Geschichte der Königlich-Preussischen Armee*, Berlin, 1928, vol. 1, p. 692.
11. Max Jaehns, *Geschichte der Kriegswissenschaften*, Munich and Leipzig, 1891, vol. 3, pp. 2254–55.
12. As late as 1800 the king refused the resignation of a noble officer because of his obligation to serve as a vassal. Cf. Jany, op. cit., vol. 3, p. 417 note.
13. Oscar Bezzel, *Geschichte des kurpfalzbayerischen Heeres von 1778-1803*, Munich, 1930, p. 176. I do not think that the difference between the Bavarian and the Prussian corps of officers was quite so great in the eighteenth century as Karl Demeter suggests in his book, *Das deutsche Offizierskorps in seinen historisch-soziologischen Grundlagen*, Berlin, 1930.
14. Karl Staudinger, *Geschichte des kurbayerischen Heeres 1726-1777*, Munich, 1908, pp. 430ff.; Oscar Bezzel, *Geschichte des kurpfälzischen Heeres bis 1777*, Munich, 1925, p. 469.
15. Bezzel, *Geschichte des kurpfälzischen Heeres bis 1777*, pp. 477ff.
16. Ibid., p. 368.
17. Justus Möser, *Gesammelte Werke*, ed. by Heinrich Schierbaum, Munich and Leipzig, 1915, vol. 1, pp. 146–68. Similar ideas were expressed by Christian Garve in German; cf. his *Philosophische Anmerkungen und Abhandlungen zu Ciceros Büchern von den Pflichten. Anmerkungen zum ersten Bande*, 4th ed., Breslau, 1794, pp. 49–50.
18. *Observations on the Military Establishment and Discipline of His Majesty the King of Prussia*, translated from the French by J. Johnson, London, 1780, p. 96.
19. Liddell Hart, *The Ghost of Napoleon*, New Haven, 1934, p. 23.
20. Heinrich Dietrich von Bülow, *Geist des neuen Kriegssystems*, 1799, cited by Hans Rothfels, *Carl von Clausewitz*, Berlin, 1920, p. 49.

21. Cf. the highly interesting letter of Clausewitz to Fichte, in which the term "der bürgerliche Krieg" appears; reprinted as appendix to "Machiavell," pp. 59ff., in Fichte's *Staats-philosophische Schriften*, ed. by H. Schulz and R. Strecker, Leipzig, 1919. Guibert's *Essay Général de Tactique* appeared in 1770. Some passages from it are easily accessible in English in Spencer Wilkinson's *The French Army before Napoleon*, Oxford, 1915. For a convenient summary of Napoleonic tendencies in warfare before Napoleon cf. Lidell Hart, op. cit.

22. Figures from Werner Sombart, op. cit., pp. 51–60.

23. For an account of how far the system of European politics was penetrated by the ideas of enlightenment in the last thirty years of peace before the French Revolution cf. Ph. Sagnac, "La rénovation politique de l'Europe au XVIII siècle," in *Mélanges d'histoire offerts à Henry Pirenne*, Brussels, 1926, vol. 2.

24. Louis Ducros, op. cit., p. 294.

25. *Johnson's England*, ed. by A. S. Turberville, Oxford, 1933, vol. 1, p. 81.

26. Fichte, "Beiträge zur Berichtigung der Urteile über die französische Revolution, 1793," op. cit., p. 116.

27. For a comprehensive survey of the writers and the arguments which they used cf. Max Lehmann, *Scharnhorst*, Leipzig, 1886, vol. 1, pp. 54–69 and 204–11. The few nonmilitary writers who did not oppose standing armies included Adam Smith.

28. Isaak Iselin, *Über die Geschichte der Menschheit*, new ed., Zurich, 1768, vol. 2, p. 395. That the theory of progress cannot be understood simply as an ideology of the bourgeois middle classes is an important inference to be drawn from Ronald S. Crane's articles on "Anglican Apologetics and the Idea of Progress, 1699–1745," in *Modern Philology*, February and May 1934.

29. J. B. Bury, *The Idea of Progress*, Amer. ed., New York, 1932, p. 140.

30. Also in art; cf. Edgar Wind, "Humanitätsidee und heroisiertes Porträt in der englischen Kultur des achtzehnten Jahrhunderts," in *Vorträge der Bibliothek Warburg 1930-31*, Leipzig and Berlin, 1932, pp. 156–229.

31. Cf. also Sir William Temple's essay "Of Heroic Virtue" in *Works*, new ed., London, 1814, vol. 3, pp. 313–405.

32. David Hume, *A Treatise on Human Nature*, Everyman's Library, vol. 2, p. 294.

33. Cf. the 64th letter.

34. Thomas Abbt, *Vom Verdienste*, 4th ed., Berlin and Stettin, 1790, p. 224.

35. Jay Barrett Botsford, *English Society in the Eighteenth Century*, New York, 1924, p. 180.

36. Cf. the interesting account of the eighteenth-century discussion on the "question de la noblesse commerçante" in Henri Carré, op. cit., pp. 135–53.

37. For the conception of the philosophe cf. Hans Schommodau, *Der psychologische Wortschatz in Frankreich in der zweiten Hälfte des 18. Jahrhunderts*, Leipzig, 1933.

38. Cf. D'Alembert, "Essay upon the Alliance betwixt Learned Men and the Great," in *Miscellaneous Papers in Literature, History and Philosophy*, English translation, London, 1764, p. 150. This essay is important for an understanding of the aristocratic background of modern pragmatism; cf., for example: "A philosopher should know how to manage and not how to influence the prejudices of a nation," p. 149.

39. Cf. Ira O. Wade, "Middle Class Philosophes. Middle Class Philosophy in the Drama of the Eighteenth Century," in *Modern Philology*, vol. 26, Nov. 1928, pp. 215–29.

40. Christian Thomasius, *Ausübung der Vernunftlehre*, Halle, 1691.

41. Baron d'Holbach, *Système Social*, London, 1773, vol. 1, p. 112.

42. Emeric Crucé, *The New Cyneas of Discourse or the Occasions and Means to Establish a General Peace, and the Liberty of Commerce Throughout the Whole World*, 1623, French and English ed. by Thomas W. Balch, Philadelphia, 1909, p. 78.

43. Ibid., p. 58.

44. The first modern writer who suggested this was, according to my knowledge, Erasmus.

45. Ibid., p. 24.

46. Holbach, op. cit., vol. 2, p. 166; cf. also vol. 1, p. 162.

47. Hume, op. cit., vol. 2, p. 294.

48. Kant, *Critique of Aesthetic Judgment*, ed. by J. M. Meredith, Oxford, 1911, p. 112.

49. Cf. the remark of Erwin Panofsky, in *Idea*, Berlin and Leipzig, 1924, p. 2, that a separation of the aesthetic from the theoretical and the ethical was not made before the eighteenth century.

50. For further references concerning the devaluation of courage and honor see the bibliography under the headings "Contre le Héroïsme Guerrier" and "Contre le Point d'Honneur," in Paul Hazard, *La Crise de la Conscience Européenne*, vol. 3, Paris, 1934, pp. 120–21.

51. "Même sans les lumières de la foi, la raison livée a elle-même suffit à découvrir la vanité de cet ideal," says G. de Bidois in this connection; cf. his *L'Honneur au Miroir de nos Lettres*, Paris, 1921, p. 281.

52. Voltaire, *The Age of Louis XIV*, Everyman's Library, p. 79.

4

Ludendorff: The German Concept of Total War

Erich Ludendorff's contribution to the development of military thought is that of a general who lost a war. He began to write almost immediately after the defeat of the German armies in 1918. Although his books are born of a rich strategical and organizational experience, they are full of conceit and resentment, and are apologetic in character. They attempt to prove that, in a military sense, Germany did not lose the First World War. Considering the vital importance of this opinion, known under the slogan of "the stab in the back" in German domestic politics in the time of the Weimar Republic, one is justified in regarding Ludendorff's literary activity as political pamphleteering. Certainly, his writings are not distinguished by detachment or subtlety. It was Ludendorff's fame as a great general rather than the intrinsic merit of his works which accounted for his amazing literary success in republican Germany.

Ludendorff wrote on three main subjects, of which only one is of immediate interest to this study. He specialized in reminiscing, debunking, and forecasting. In reminiscing about the military events of the First World War, he tried to enhance his historical stature as a general and he polemicized against those who belittled his generalship. Amplifying his prejudices against Freemasons, Jews, Jesuits, and

From Edward Mead Earle, ed., *Makers of Modern Strategy: Military Thought from Machiavelli to Hitler*, Copyright 1943 © 1971 renewed by Princeton University Press. Excerpt reprinted with the permission of Princeton University Press.

Christianity at large, and advocating under the influence of his wife a martial religion of his own, he tried to expose those sinister forces which he held responsible for Germany's defeat in the First World War. He was convinced that both his political enemies and his National Socialist competitors after the war were also under the influence of those forces. Finally, in putting forth his ideas on total war, Ludendorff outlined the conditions which in his opinion would have enabled him to operate more effectively as a general in the First World War.

Ludendorff's theory of total war is not based on a study of military developments between the two world wars. Nor is it derived from a careful consideration of the interrelations between politics, warfare, technology, economics, and popular morale. In fact, there are few military writers to whose historical works Friedrich Schlegel's statement that "history is retrospective prophecy" can be applied with more justice. And in appraising Ludendorff's writings on total war one is sometimes tempted to modify Schlegel's aphorism by saying that the general's prophecies were history projected into the future.

For the historian of military thought Ludendorff's criticism of Clausewitz' ideas on war is particularly arresting. The carelessness of this criticism makes it easy to note Ludendorff's intellectual inferiority to the master of German military thought, but the point of interest is the political motive of the criticism rather than its content. Not as a military scientist and historian, but as a politician, did Ludendorff, the advocate of total war, renounce Clausewitz, the theoretician of "absolute war." After stating his unqualified demand of complete authority of the supreme military leader in all *political* matters as well, Ludendorff adds, "I can hear how politicians will get excited about such an opinion, as they will about the idea in general that politics is to serve the conduct of war, as though Clausewitz had not taught that war is but the continuation of politics with different means. Let the politicians get excited and let them regard my opinions as those of a hopeless 'militarist.' This does not change any of the demands of reality, which require precisely what I demand for the conduct of war and thus for the preservation of the life of the people."[1] In such phrases, which abound in his work, Ludendorff discarded the principles of Prussian statecraft and militarism as they existed in the latter half of the nineteenth century, and suggested a return to the days of his hero, Frederick the Great.[2]

Like Hitler, Ludendorff was not only opposed to the German republic, but also to the political structure of the Reich under Wilhelm II. The resemblance between the two men, however, does not go very far.

Ludendorff was a reactionary who differed from other reactionaries at the time of the republic only in two respects. He was violently anti-Christian, and he was not concerned with years or decades but with more than a century in his desire to turn back the wheel of history. At the same time, he had a keen understanding of the advantages of centralized power in the direction and administration of modern politics but measured these advantages only with the yardstick of bureaucratic efficiency. His understanding of the masses in modern society was limited and so was his experience as a demagogue. By contrast, Hitler is the political leader of a modern, subversive, mass movement. He comes from nowhere, that is, from one of the many interstitial groups which modern industrial society produces. He conquered power as a political upstart and transformed the society which allowed him to ascend. His rise to power and his conduct of the Second World War have been predicated in part upon his ability to sway the German masses as a demagogue. Hitler's regime is a political dictatorship over all social institutions and groups, including the military ones. Ludendorff, on the other hand, drew up the blueprint of a military dictatorship to eliminate politics for purposes of total war; mass movements would have been crushed by this dictatorship. In National Socialist Germany, the corps of officers is altogether relegated to positions where they exert violence in an expert fashion but without political momentum of their own. Certainly Hitler is not the general who Ludendorff thought would control politics in the war of the future, but rather the plebiscitarian mass leader who, after a prolonged struggle, has succeeded in forcing generals to obey his orders.

Thus, while Ludendorff was a reactionary, military bureaucrat, who advocated what may be called a technical dictatorship for purposes of the conduct of mass warfare, Hitler is a political dictator thriving on, rather than disregarding, the social tensions of modern mass society.

I

To understand Ludendorff's ideas on total war one must keep in mind the nature of German militarism before the outbreak of the First World War. It was a widely accepted class militarism on a half feudal basis within the bounds of an otherwise capitalistically stratified society. The conflict between the military traditions of the monarchy and the aspirations of the industrial middle classes was not resolved but institutionalized. Military power and social prestige were so distributed as to favor the aristocracy and the owners of large and medium-sized landed estates while economic power was concentrated in the hands of the politically inexperienced leaders of industry, trade, and finance.

The tradition of German militarism was rooted in the social structure of eighteenth-century Prussia in which the armed forces had been exempt from industry and the productive classes, in turn, exempt from military service. In the second half of the nineteenth century with its widespread literacy and industrialization such conditions no longer prevailed. The monarchy and the preindustrial political institutions were modified by a liberal constitution.

In 1934 Carl Schmitt put it thus: "The liberal movement of the year 1848 had forced the Prussian state to come to terms with a 'constitution' and to expose itself to the danger of losing no less than its character, as its government became parliamentarian and its army a parliamentary army."[3] According to Schmitt, this represented "a victory of the citizen over the soldier." In point of fact, this was hardly true, since the political leaders did not succeed in assuming political leadership, in molding the state according to their interests, and in determining foreign and domestic policies.

Germany had no class that produced political leaders with foresight and with experience in international affairs. Germany's most prominent statesmen succeeded in corrupting the bourgeoisie politically by forcing it to endorse their military successes after they had been accomplished and by exploiting its fear of the working class movement.

Wilhelm II, while admitting representatives of the economic elite to his court, tried to maintain political independence and military control. Until 1914, the military cabinet, through its influence on the selection of the highest military personnel, and the general staff, through its jealously guarded competence in planning future campaigns, were actually in control of military policy. The naval armament, on the other hand, was carried out with the help of tremendous propaganda campaigns conducted by the German Navy League. The younger branch of Germany's armed forces, under the influence of von Tirpitz with his keen sense for patriotic publicity, was socially more aggressive than the conservative army. The Navy League, founded in 1898, constituted the first social organization in Germany whose propaganda activities regarding armaments can be compared with those of the National Socialist Party after 1933. The League was sponsored by heavy industry.[4]

A fair indication of the political power wielded by the various agencies among which military authority was distributed is the access each of them had to the monarch. Wilhelm II preferred to listen to advisers who were not responsible to the Reichstag, that is, to the chiefs of the civil, military, and naval cabinets, and to the chiefs of the general staff and of the admiralty. The heads of the various ministries who were responsible to the Reichstag did not report regularly to the kaiser. They could get the ear of the monarch only through the civil cabinet. Even the chancellor of the Reich did not see the kaiser regularly. An exception to the emperor's preference for irresponsible advisers rather than constitutionally responsible ministers existed only with regard to the minister of war. The war minister's influence, however, was contested by the military cabinet and the general staff. During the reign of Wilhelm II the power of the war department was more and more restricted, paradoxically enough with the help of the secretaries of war. While the opposition in the Reichstag tried to strengthen the position of the war department and to curb that of the military cabinet, the secretaries of war refused to accept this help and regarded themselves as generals who took their orders from the emperor.[5]

The time schedule of Wilhelm II clearly showed the predominance of the military over the civil authorities, and among the military authorities the predominance of the parliamentarily irresponsible agencies. The chief of the military cabinet saw the kaiser three times a week while the secretary of war reported only once. In addition, the representative of the military cabinet was present when the kaiser received the secretary of war, while the latter had no right to attend the audience for the military cabinet. When the kaiser was not in Berlin, the heads of the cabinets took over all the reports.

The power of the military cabinet, a small body of men growing from four persons in 1872 to seventeen after 1900, rested not only on close contact with the kaiser but also on its watertight control of the personnel policy in the army. The Reichstag had no influence whatever on promotions, resignations, and transfers in the corps of officers. By the same token, the inferior authority and restricted competence of the ministry of war was reflected in the composition of its personnel. With very few exceptions the secretaries of war were generals of no military distinction. The most energetic and most intelligent officers had the ambition to get into the general staff. Only second rate staff officers were transferred to the war department and the rest of the personnel came from the Military-Technical Academy (known in the snobbish circles of the officers corps as the "plumbers' academy"), from the Artillery-Inspection Commission, and from officers of the line.

The military elite was primarily interested in retaining its high social status and in defending its political independence against civilian control. Both their status and power were jeopardized by the industrialization of German society, which created an economically powerful counterelite and urban masses which would not fit in with the preindustrial pattern of politics. To illustrate, from 1870 to 1910 the production of hard coal had increased from 34,000,000 to 153,000,000 tons, that of iron ore from 5,300,000 to 28,700,000 tons. In 1870 Germany had 18,560 km of railways and about 4000 telegraph offices as compared with 59,031 km of railways and 45,000 telegraph offices in 1910. In 1871 almost two thirds of the German population were rural, living in places with less than 2000 inhabitants; in 1910 about three fifths of the population were urban, and one fifth lived in large cities with more than 100,000 inhabitants. From 1882 to 1907 the number of independent persons among the gainfully employed had increased only slightly, from 4,995,000 to 5,332,000, while their position in relation to other classes had decreased sharply from 45 percent to 20 percent of all gainfully employed. The number of workers, on the other hand, had increased from 10,705,000 to 17,836,000 in the same period, a gain of 60 percent.

In this context it should be noted that the military elite in the imperial era was not imperialistic. They expended their energy in the struggle to maintain their prestige and power in a process of economic change which endangered their privileged position. The military elite was not responsible for developing schemes of national aggrandizement and conquest. Social organizations like the German Navy League, the Pan-German League and the various societies interested in the acquisition and development of colonies were controlled and sponsored by the economic counterelite and by intellectuals coming from the middle classes.[6]

The peculiar class structure of German militarism in the imperial era stood in the way of wholly efficient preparedness and even of that measure of efficiency in the conduct of war which the progress of technology had rendered possible. These limitations manifested themselves chiefly in four sectors of military life: in the social composition of the army, in war economics, in the attitudes of the military toward technology and in the lack of comprehension of the importance of propaganda in the case of armed conflict.

German militarism extended its social basis by half measures in order not to isolate itself from the economically and ideologically powerful groups. Apart from the frequent occurrence of intermarriages between the aristocracy and the bourgeoisie and from a tight control of positions in the higher bureaucracy through the alumni of socially exclusive student fraternities, the prevailing system of education was utilized in the interest of the military elite. The shorter one-year service in the army was contingent upon a certain amount of high school education and thus upon economic status. Those privileged in the economic hierarchy were given moderate privileges in the army. This was particularly important for the social composition of the corps of reserve officers, an institution which forced upon the sons of the bourgeoisie the standards of the aristocratic military elite. In the years before the war there were about 15,000 officer candidates—the so-called *Einjährige*—in Germany every year, while the total number of reserve officers was only 29,000 in 1914.[7] The actual control of the selection of officers was exercised in the mess of the officers of the line, where the aspirants were inspected as to their social background and political opinions. No liberal was allowed to pass.

The increase in the ratio of commoners to aristocrats in the corps of officers which proceeded apace under Wilhelm II created a special problem. The fear of destroying the conservative character of the officers corps and the apprehension that the political stability of the Reich would be endangered by enlarging the army from the urban areas functioned as brakes to the full utilization of the available man power. The demands of efficiency were overruled by considerations of status and power in the state. For example, in 1904, von Einem, secretary of war, wrote to Count von Schlieffen, chief of the general staff, that the scarcity of officers could be remedied if requirements were lowered. He added, "This can not be recommended because we could then not help accepting in a large measure democratic and other elements unfit for this profession."[8] Similar opinions were expressed with regard to both commissioned and noncommissioned officers by the secretary of war, von Heeringen, in a memorandum to the chief of the general staff, von Moltke, in January 1913.

The limitations of the prewar German military caste is also apparent in the fact that there was little understanding of the economic aspects of war in Germany before 1914. Most military and financial circles held the opinion that a future war would not and could not last long.[9] The inquiries into the food supply of the army in case of war, which were conducted by the ministry of war in 1884, 1906, and 1911, were based on the assumption that a war would not last longer than nine months. This notion was based partly on the experiences of the preceding wars in the nineteenth century which had lasted only weeks or months and partly on considerations of the destructiveness of modern armament. Modern industrialized nations were not expected to be able to conduct a long war.

It is noteworthy that the military elite had a marked professional interest in a short war. The general staff was afraid that preparation for a *long* war would lead to a curtailment of the military monopoly in the control of war, or would at least increase the importance of the economic and social factors in war. Economic mobilization for a long war would have required a new budgetary and a new social policy: the money to be invested in an adequate storage of food and raw materials would not have been available for military purposes in the narrower sense of the term, and the assignment of armies of skilled workers to war industries might have meant the reduction of military man power. Thus, it appeared that the preparation of a long war would reduce the military strength with which the general staff hoped quickly to force a military decision. The plans of the general staff were focused on the necessity and feasibility of shock strategy. Schlieffen rejected the idea of a strategy of attrition because it would endanger the existence of the nation by the disruption of all commercial and industrial activities. Similar opinions were expressed by General von Blume, a pupil of von Moltke, in his book on strategy in 1912.

The technological limitations of German prewar militarism are perhaps best reflected in the early development of air power. The following figures speak for themselves. From 1909 to 1912 France spent 30,610,000 francs for military aircraft, while the German expenditures amounted to only 6,486,000 marks. In 1912 the French army had 390 airplanes and 234 pilots, the German army 100 planes and 90 pilots.[10] Thus the German–French ratio for expenditure for aircraft in the period 1909–12 was approximately 1 : 4; with regard to the number of planes, the ratio in 1912 was 1 : 4; and, in number of pilots, the ratio was 1 : 2.5. Shortly before the outbreak of the war, the German general staff became convinced that airplanes were superior to lighter-than-air craft. The ministry of war, however, and especially the treasury, were opposed to spending more money for airplanes and pointed to the difficulties of proper training.[11] In addition, the lighter-than-air craft command was of the opinion that airplanes could never be usable in war.[12]

There was a similar reluctance to strengthen and modernize the technical branches of the army, particularly in the fields of communication and engineering.[13] In 1900 Lieutenant General von der Goltz made a number of important suggestions regarding the sappers in the

German army. Their number, he held, should be increased to three companies per army corps; the technical training of the officers should be intensified; and a closer tactical connection between infantry and technical troops should be effected by exchanging officers and by the formation of a special engineering staff composed of technically trained officers from all arms. The ministry of war and the general staff declined to accept these recommendations. Financial difficulties served as a most convenient excuse for lack of foresight. The general staff was apprehensive of having its competence restricted by the formation of such a technical staff. The Russo–Japanese war taught a number of lessons on the importance of technical troops in modern warfare which could not be lightheartedly disregarded. But again the general staff declared simply that an increase of sappers was superfluous.

Limited by its social composition, by its ignorance of the economic aspects of modern war and by its prejudice against technological innovation, the military caste was also insufficiently aware of the importance of the propaganda factor. At the outbreak of the war, the military authorities were completely unprepared in this field. Despite their fear that war might cause unemployment and social unrest they did not conceive the possibility of upholding morale at home by a concerted effort of the government. Since they had little contact with, or understanding of, modern business methods, they could not learn anything from commercial advertising. Besides, propaganda, like technology, was stained with the spirit of middle-class civilization toward which the military elite had a condescending attitude. The sword, not the pen, was to decide future wars.

Shortly after the outbreak of the First World War the limitations of German class militarism became all too apparent. Theoretically the kaiser was the German commander in chief, with the chief of the general staff as his strategic adviser and the chancellor as his political adviser. In practice, there existed in Germany during the war a military dictatorship from the moment in which von Falkenhayn was replaced by Hindenburg and Ludendorff. In the conflict between military and political authorities Ludendorff was put into a position where he became the advocate of the supremacy of generals over statesmen. Wherever he found constitutional limitations to his power, he disregarded them. That he did feel such limitations, however, is shown by the fact that all of his later reflections on the relation of military and political authorities were inspired by these wartime experiences.

The influence of the military cabinet waned under the impact of war. The restricting influence which the Reichstag through its right of budgetary control might have exerted was effectively counterbalanced by threats of resignation on the part of Hindenburg and Ludendorff. In all decisive conflicts between the politicians and the generals, Ludendorff determined the outcome; not so much because he wanted power for himself as because, when efficiency was the demand of the hour, there was nobody else who wanted it.

Ludendorff did not belong to the socially leading aristocracy. He came from an obscure family and had advanced to a position which was usually reserved for men of noble blood. Considering his background and the newly created position of *Erster Generalquartiermeister*, which he held from August 1916 on, he was socially an upstart. Perhaps for that very reason he felt the political limitations — however ineffective — to his authority and the lack of central responsibility for the far-flung war effort more keenly than an aristocrat with more firmly rooted traditions might have done. His will power was greater than that of the chancellor or the kaiser, and Ludendorff managed to balance his incompetence as a statesman and economist by his will power.

Conflicts between statesmen and generals arise easily in war. Even mediocre statesmen may be able to hold their own against generals if the political institutions and their entrenched traditions operate against the inevitable wartime trend toward redistribution of power in favor of the military elite. Strong personalities are capable of asserting themselves even against heavy institutional odds. Bismarck succeeded in doing so in 1866 and 1871. In a passage of his memoirs which, incidentally, may be taken as the verdict on Ludendorff's political ideas, he declared that "to set up and to delimit the aims to be reached by means of war, and to advise the sovereign upon this matter, is a political function while the war is in progress no less than in times of peace."

The only political statesman of note in Germany during the First World War was Bethmann-Hollweg, and he had neither the personality nor the will to assert himself against the military. Curiously enough, he did not hesitate to check the independence of the admirals. In the most important naval decision of the First World War Bethmann-Hollweg shifted responsibility to general headquarters; and Ludendorff's judgment, which was influenced by his desire for a peace through military victory, was decisive in the introduction of unrestricted submarine warfare.[14] On all other questions, Bethmann surrendered statesmanship to the generals and made no effective attempt to curb their political power.

As a result, Ludendorff emerged as the military dictator of Germany. His role as such is too well known to need more than a bare listing of the events which he determined or influenced by wielding his unconstitutional power over kaiser, chancellor and Reichstag: the dismissal of Bethmann-Hollweg and the appointment of Michaelis as Reich chancellor; the dismissal of von Kuehlmann as state secretary of the foreign office; the decisive influence upon the peace treaties with Russia and Rumania, and the dismissal of von Valentini as chief of the civil cabinet. In addition, Ludendorff exerted a decisive influence in every phase of German economic and social policy during the war.

II

Ludendorff's idea of total war can be stated in the form of five basic propositions. War is total; first, because the theater of war extends over the whole territory of the belligerent nations. In addition to this diffusion of risks, total war also involves the active participation of the whole population in the war effort. Not armies but nations wage total war. Thus, the effective execution of total war necessitates the adaptation of the economic system to the purposes of war. Third, the participation of large masses in war makes it imperative to devote special efforts, by means of propaganda, to the strengthening of morale at home and to the weakening of the political cohesion of the enemy nation. Fourth, the preparation of total war must begin before the outbreak of overt fighting. Military, economic, and psychological warfare influence the so-called peacetime pursuits in modern societies. Finally, in order to achieve an integrated and efficient war effort, total war must be directed by one supreme authority, that of the commander in chief.

Ludendorff's relatively simple idea of total war is not devoid of a few interesting details. The geographical extension of the theaters of total war is a consequence of the technical progress of the means of destruction and of the increasing functional interdependence of modern nations. Not only are the fighting zones widened by the technical improvement of long-range weapons of all kinds, but the regions behind the actual fighting zones are also affected "by hunger blockade and propaganda." The nation at war can thus be compared to the people in a besieged fortress. As the besiegers try to force a fortress to surrender not only by directing strictly military means against its military defenders, but also by starving its civil inhabitants, so total warfare implements the military assault upon the armed forces of a nation by the use of nonmilitary weapons directed against the noncombatant parts of the enemy population. The distinction between combatants and noncombatants loses its former significance.

In order to secure the necessary military supplies and foodstuffs for the sustenance of the besieged nation, Ludendorff advocated economic self-sufficiency. His ideas on war economics, however, are little else than textbook generalities. He dealt with the organizational aspect of war economics rather than with the strategic possibilities of improving the raw material, food, and labor supplies of the nation at war through conquest.[15]

Surprisingly enough, the most original contribution General Ludendorff made to the theory of total war does not lie in the field of military warfare, but in the realm of what is often inadequately called "psychological warfare." Ludendorff is almost excessively concerned with the problem of the "cohesion" of the people. It is in this regard that he differs most strikingly from National Socialist writers on total war. He despised, and regarded as ineffective, any attempt to achieve social unity by force and drill. Such methods he called "mechanical" or "external." "An external unity of the people, achieved by compulsion — a unity in which the soul of the people has no share by common and conscious racial and religious experience — is not a unity which people and army need in war, but a mechanical phantom dangerous to the government and the state."[16] Similarly, he spoke with unconcealed derision of such measures as the Fascists and National Socialists had taken in the field of the premilitary training of youth. He compared this training with that of dogs and doubted that mass drill, which "deprives youth of personalities," prepared young men satisfactorily for military service.[17]

His model of a closely knit social unity is therefore not the old Prussia, nor is it the new Germany of Hitler. Ludendorff thought of Japan when he spoke of unity and cohesion. "Entirely different [from mechanical unity] is the unity of the Japanese people; it is a spiritual one, essentially resting upon Shinto religion, which compels the Japanese to serve their Emperor in order thus to preserve the road to the life of their ancestors. For the Japanese, service for the Emperor and thus for the state is prescribed by his experience of God. Shintoism, stemming from the racial heritage of the Japanese, corresponds to the needs of the people and the state. . . . In the unity of racial heritage and faith and in the philosophy of life erected upon them resides the strength of the Japanese people."[18]

Ludendorff's own racial religion was to provide the Germans with a faith corresponding to Shintoism in Japan. However fantastic this may sound, Ludendorff must be credited with understanding the fact that something more profound than merely a clever propaganda policy is needed in order to produce a state of popular morale which enables people in modern industrial society to endure the hardships of total war. Like Ernst Jünger, Ludendorff realized dimly that "a mobilization may organize the technical abilities of a man without penetrating to the core of his faith,"[19] and that the spirit of sacrifice cannot be injected into the body politic by a clever doctor. Ludendorff realized that the source of concord in society lies in deep rooted traditions rather than in an efficient organization of the police. In fact, he did not advocate violence against dissenters in his book on *Total War*, and when he spoke in his memoirs of the fact that the government may use force against those who jeopardize the common war effort he did so in an almost apologetic fashion.

On the whole, Ludendorff's ideas on the role of propaganda were sounder than Hitler's. In the realm of propaganda techniques as well, Ludendorff's opinions revealed surprising expertness. He deplored the German government's concealment of the defeat in the battle of the Marne from the German people and advocated a policy of frankness in order not to give "free reign to the 'discontended' and the rumormongers."[20] Similarly, Ludendorff wrote in his memoirs that every German, whether man or woman, should have been told every day what a lost war meant for the fatherland. Pictures and films should have broadcast the same story. The presentation of the dangers would have had a different effect than the thinking about profits, or talking and writing about a peace by negotiation.[21] Goebbels, in the propaganda strategy of gloom upon which he embarked a few months after the invasion of Russia, seems to have taken a few leaves from Ludendorff's book. Whenever possible, Goebbels also follows that advice of Ludendorff which several National Socialist authors on propaganda have repeated: "A good propaganda must anticipate the development of the real events."[22] Finally, Ludendorff regarded the circulation of rumors, in which the National Socialists were to become past masters, "the best means of propaganda" against the enemy.[23]

Ludendorff's theory of total war culminates in the role assigned to the supreme military commander. In addition to conducting the military operations he is to direct the foreign and economic policies of the nation and also its propaganda policy. "The military staff must be adequately composed: it must contain the best brains in the fields of land, air, and sea warfare, propaganda, war technology, economics, politics, and also those who know the people's life. They have to inform the Chief of Staff, and if required, the Commander in Chief, about their respective fields. They have no policy-making function."[24] Thus, in Ludendorff's total war there is no place for the civilian statesman. The general rules supreme. And Ludendorff concludes: "All theories [sic] of Clausewitz have to be thrown overboard. War and politics serve the survival of the people, but war is the highest expression of the racial will to life."[25]

Clausewitz had been of the opinion that the French Revolution had removed many of the limitations which in the ancien régime, when cabinets rather than nations waged war, had prevented war from assuming its "abstract" or "absolute" character. Clausewitz had rejected the erroneous idea that war had "emancipated" itself from politics in consequence of the revolution. Instead, he insisted—in a passage which Ludendorff later quoted—that the political forces of the French Revolution had unleashed energies which subsequently changed the type of war. By thus attributing the change in the type of war to politics, Clausewitz defined the prevailing type of war in terms of the structure of the political community that wages it.

According to Ludendorff, on the other hand, total war is a product of demographic and technological developments. The increased size of populations and the improved efficiency of the means of destruction have inevitably created the totality of war. Total war, which has no political cause, absorbs politics.

There is not the slightest suggestion in Ludendorff's writings that he prefers total to limited war on moral or metaphysical grounds. Nor is there any explicit justification of total war in terms of an imperialistic doctrine,[26] or of a value system in which pugnacity, heroism, and the love of sacrifice are so supreme as to demand war for their realization and glorification. Instead, Ludendorff goes so far as to contend that total war is essentially defensive. The people will not cooperate in waging it unless they know that war is waged to preserve their existence. To be sure, it would be expedient to make such contentions for the mere sake of appearance in a culture which, in E. M. Forster's words, "preaches idealism and practices brutality." Yet Ludendorff did not shrink from shocking the public by unorthodox opinions in the field of religion, and it would do injustice to his character to doubt that he meant what he said when he talked about the defensive character of total war. He insists that "the nature of total war requires that it be waged only if the whole people is really threatened in its existence, and determined to wage it."[27] If this insistence upon the defensive nature of war were a mere attempt on the part of Ludendorff to conceal his true opinion as to its nature, he would have to be credited with a Machiavellian attitude toward the masses. There is no trace of such an attitude in his writings. In fact he rejects explicitly the opinion, characteristically to be found in the circles of National Socialist intellectuals, that the masses can and should be psychologically manipulated in the interest of the power holders. As has been pointed out, Ludendorff regarded attempts to manage the masses in this way as futile.

III

The National Socialists have not only organized German society for total war but have also written profusely about it. Their contributions to the development of the theory of total war are built upon Clausewitz' and Ludendorff's basic contention that in modern war all material and moral resources of the nation must be mobilized. The main difference between National Socialist literature and Ludendorff's writings on total war lies in the fact that the National Socialists have attempted to produce ideological justifications of modern war. Racial superiority and the law of nature, Darwinistically and geopolitically understood, are supposed to provide German war and the new militarism with a moral halo. Moreover, some National Socialist writers have pushed Ludendorff's theory to its logical end by denying the *existence* of peace altogether. They no longer regard war as a *phase* in the interrelations of states, preceded and followed by phases of peace, but as "the expression of a new political and social development in the life of peoples."[28] Similarly, geopoliticians have written books about the forms which warfare assumes in times which according to common usage are designated as times of peace. Instead of speaking about peace between wars, they have found the formula of "the war between wars."[29]

One of the most important changes of warfare, without which blitzkrieg methods and the coordination of different arms would have been impossible, was predicated upon a complete removal of resistance to technological change on the part of the new corps of officers. Karl Justrow, who criticized sharply the scarcity of engineers in the German armies of the First World War and contended that engineers had "not the slightest influence" on the conduct of the war, wrote shortly before the outbreak of the Second World War, that "technology — once a stepchild in all organizations — is today treated with more and more understanding in the conduct of war."[30]

This breakdown of resistance to technology has inevitably involved a greater equalization of society. The higher the demands for technological skill and physical fitness on the part of the expert operators of the means of destruction, the less important must be the respect paid to the status qualifications of the soldiers. Status consideration must be sacrificed in favor of high skill requirements, especially when there is a shortage of available personnel. Thus, the technology of total war favors the "egalitarian" militarism of Hitler's Germany. When Hitler reintroduced universal military service, he abolished the privilege of shorter service in the army which boys with a high school education had enjoyed under the kaiser. In this respect and also with respect to promotion from the ranks the military system of this modern despot is more egalitarian than was that of Imperial Germany. Hitler has proceeded in the spirit of what Oswald Spengler has called "Prussian Socialism,"[31] adapting this kind of socialism to the postdemocratic structure of his plebiscitarian dictatorship. With this resolution to liberate destructive techniques from humanitarian fetters and to sacrifice any tradition to military efficiency he has brought to a head the martial equalization of society that began in eighteenth-century Prussia but required the rise of modern political mass movements to become truly effective.

When, in 1733, the so-called canton system of recruitment was introduced in Prussia, the enlargement of the social basis of the army was officially justified by the argument that the inequality among those enrolled should be abolished. Later the introduction of universal military service in Prussia was announced by a cabinet order which stated that "all privileges based on social status cease to exist with the army." This was in 1808, when the liberal Barthold Georg Niebuhr wrote that universal conscription, "this equality which disgusts the true friend of liberty," will lead to "the demoralization and degeneration of the whole nation, universal brutality, the destruction of civilization and of the educated classes."

The two developments which have most incisively changed the social structure of German economy in this war were not discussed at great length before war broke out.[32] The ruthless principle of turning the conquered territories into a reservoir of labor for the conqueror, from which, according to German claims, no less than 12 million foreign workers had been forced to migrate to Germany by 1943, was not fully anticipated in the *Wehrwirtschaft* discussions before 1939. Nor did any German economist dare to reveal the possibility of a virtual destruction of the German middle classes in the war of the future.[33]

The contribution of German intellectuals to the literature of "psychological warfare" has probably been grossly overrated. The contribution of German psychologists to the theories of political mass behavior is smaller than the many volumes written on that subject would have us believe. Nazi literature on political propaganda contains little that has not been known for centuries to less pedantic students of rhetoric and to modern specialists in advertising. The recent overestimation of the German contribution is to a large extent a consequence of the fact that talk about German "fifth columns" and propaganda gave intellectuals in the democratic countries a thrilling opportunity to offer an excuse for the military inferiority of the democracies at the beginning of this war. The prestige of propaganda waxes and wanes with military success and failure. The Nazis as leaders of a modern mass movement have undoubtedly realized more clearly than did the leaders of Imperial Germany in the last war the importance of propaganda. They have invested more money and talent in it and have organized it efficiently. They have not produced any new "theory."

As to their propaganda practice, it is often overlooked that in some respects the National Socialists are in a less favorable position than was Germany under the kaiser. For example, any attempt to create discord in the camp of the enemy coalition must necessarily appear as a move of the German propaganda machine, because the world knows that all German propaganda is centrally planned. The German anti-Bolshevist campaign can at once be recognized as Dr. Goebbels' campaign. It is interesting to compare this predicament with the greater freedom of operation which Ludendorff had in the First World War. In June 1918, Colonel Haeften, the representative of the supreme command at the foreign office, presented the plan of an anti-Bolshevist campaign to Ludendorff for approval. In order to strengthen Lansdowne's peace party in England, influential Germans, acting to all appearances in complete independence from the government, were to advocate in public speeches a united European front against Bolshevism.[34] The less centralized setup of the German propaganda machine at that time permitted maneuvers in political warfare upon which National Socialist propaganda cannot embark without giving itself away.

Ludendorff's ideas on the supreme position of the general in total war, however, were buried with him. German generals are under the domination of the National Socialist Party led by Hitler, a "charismatic" corporal. So complete was that domination that on January 30, 1943 Goering could dare to refer in public to the weak German military leaders who "were whining" before Hitler when he "held" the Eastern front against the onslaught of the Russians.

NOTES

1. General Ludendorff, *Der totale Krieg*, Munich, 1935, p. 115 n.
2. Ludendorff was of the opinion that Frederick the Great was "on his side," even in his attitude toward religion. Ludendorff put out a pamphlet in his own publishing house entitled *Friedrich der Grosse auf Seiten Ludendorffs. Friedrichs des Grossen Gedanken über Religion. Aus seinen Werken*, Munich, 1935.
3. Carl Schmitt, *Staatsgefüge und Zusammenbruch des zweiten Reiches*, Hamburg, 1934, p. 9.
4. In 1910, the League had 300,000 individual members and 740,000 additional members who had joined collectively through no less than 1700 other associations. See Konteradmiral A. D. Weber, "Der deutsche Flottenverein," in *Deutsche Revue*, vol. 35, 1910, p. 177. It had about 100 branches in foreign countries, and spent about 50,000 per year as compared with 3,000 spent by the British Navy League, according to an anonymous article, "The German Navy League," in *National Review*, vol. 46, p. 639. *Die Flotte*, the official organ of the League, distributed 320,000 copies in 1905, at a time when the four principal German newspapers sold 152,000 copies together. On July 1, 1933, Hitler sent a telegram to the general meeting of the reconstituted League declaring "that since his youth the League had been known and familiar to him, that he had always read its literature with the greatest interest and that he welcomed and desired the work of the association continued in its well proved manner." See Admiral A. D. Bauer, "Der deutsche Flottenverein 1898 bis 1934," in *Marine Rundschau*, vol. 40, 1935, p. 64. The article in the *National Review* quoted above says of the League in 1905: "Its political power in Germany is exceedingly great and probably greater than that wielded by any of the German political parties."
5. In 1889 General von Verdy in an attempt to recommend himself as a desirable candidate for the position of secretary of war pointed out that, according to his opinion, the secretary of war should act "as a kind of suicide in relation to his department." R. Schmidt-Bückeburg, *Das Militär-Kabinett der preussischen Könige und deutschen Kaiser*, Berlin, 1933, pp. 174ff.
6. For example, in 1904 no less than 128 of the 276 members of the officials of the Pan-German League were academicians, according to Lothar Werner, *Der Alldeutsche Verband 1890-1918*, Berlin, 1935, p. 64. The proclamation founding the German Colonial Society in 1882 was signed by representatives of the National Liberal Party, university professors, presidents of the chambers of commerce, and industrialists from the Rhineland and from southern Germany. Cf. *Die Deutsche Kolonialgesellschaft 1882-1907*, Berlin, 1908. The German Navy League was founded in 1898 by persons "most of whom belonged to the Central Association of German Industrialists." Cf. Eugen Richter, *Zur Flottenfrage*, Berlin, 1900, p. 31.

7. Herbert Rosinski, *The German Army*, New York, 1940, p. 112.

8. Reichsarchiv, *Der Weltkrieg 1914 bis 1918. Kriegsrüstung und Kriegswirtschaft*, vol. 1, Berlin, 1930, p. 91.

9. There were only few exceptions: von Moltke in 1890 and Max Warburg in 1907 expressed the opinion that future war would last many years.

10. *Kriegsrüstung*, op. cit., vol. 1 (Documents), p. 441, note 1. W. O'D. Pierce, *Air-War*, New York, 1939, p. 92, gives the following figures for certified pilots in 1911: France, 353; England, 57; Germany, 46; Italy, 32; Belgium, 27; U.S.A., 26; Austria, 19.

11. In France, these difficulties were overcome by making army orders of planes conditional upon the training by the airplane factory of one pilot per plane.

12. A. Hildebrandt, "Die Luftfahrertruppe," *Handbuch der Politik*, vol. 3, 2nd ed., Berlin, 1914, p. 305.

13. "Frequently before the war very great artillery ranges were rejected on the ground that no observation was possible over long distances. One forgot that the efficiency of telescopes was constantly increasing and that the telephone permitted an extension of observation." Max Ludwig, "Heerestechnik," *Die deutsche Wehrmacht 1914-1939*, Berlin, n.d., p. 87.

14. For Ludendorff's role as a military dictator during the war cf. Arthur Rosenberg, *Die Entstehung der deutschen Republik*, Berlin, 1928, especially chaps. 4–6, and the literature cited there; Karl Tschuppik, *Ludendorff: The Tragedy of a Military Mind*, translated by W. H. Johnston, Boston, New York, 1932; K. von Oertzen, "Politik und Wehrmacht," *Wissen und Wehr*, vol. 5, 1928.

15. These aspects of war economics were discussed in Germany by the adherents of geopolitics.

16. *Der totale Krieg*, p. 17.

17. Ibid., p. 58.

18. Ibid., p. 17.

19. In this way Ernst Jünger characterized Walter Rathenau's great contribution to the organization of German war economy in the First World War. Cf. his *Die totale Mobilmachung*, Berlin, 1931, p. 16.

20. *Der totale Krieg.*, p. 26.

21. *Meine Kriegserinnerungen*, Berlin, 1919, p. 296.

22. Ibid., p. 300.

23. Ibid., p. 302.

24. *Der totale Krieg*, p. 111f.

25. Ibid., p. 10.

26. It is useless to look in Ludendorff's writings for statements like this: "The genuine International is that of imperialism, of rule over the Faustlike civilization, hence over the whole earth, to be exerted by one singly forming principle, and not through compromise and concessions, but through conquest and destruction." Oswald Spengler, *Preussenthum und Sozialismus*, Berlin, 1919, p. 84.

27. *Der totale Krieg*, p. 6.

28. Guido Fischer, *Wehrwirtschaft*, Leipzig, 1936, p. 23.

29. Cf. Rupert von Schumacher and Hans Hummel, *Vom Kriege zwischen den Kriegen*, Stuttgart, 1937.

30. Karl Justrow, *Der technische Krieg*, vol. 2, Berlin, 1939, p. 13.

31. Oswald Spengler, *Preussentum und Sozialismus*, Berlin, 1919.

32. Henry William Spiegel, in a discussion of *Wehrwirtschaft*, makes the interesting

observation that "there is no academic economist of repute among the godfathers of the new discipline." See his "Wehrwirtschaft. Economics of the Military State," in *The American Economic Review*, vol. 30, 1940, p. 715.

33. On the middle classes in Germany's total war economy cf. *The Fate of Small Business in Nazi Germany*, Washington, 1943, prepared by A. R. L. Gurland, Otto Kirchheimer, and Franz Neumann for the Special Senate Committee to Study Problems of American Small Business.

34. Cf. Arthur Rosenberg, op. cit., pp. 210ff.

5

Risk, Security, and Modern Hero Worship

I

If we are to trust the nonchalance with which the words "hero" and "worship" are used, modern man seems to be singularly predisposed toward hero worship. There are not only heroes proper, but also heroes of nations, science, revolution; we speak of the heroes in novels and motion pictures, which are as far removed from the heroic in the classical sense as Hollywood is from ancient Troy. Any high-school girl may say of her beau, "He is my hero," and boys "worship" their girls. It almost appears that anyone can be a "hero," provided someone admires him, and all kinds of admiration are readily called "worship." Consult the catalog of a large library—the prospectus of the cemeteries where learning and trash are buried side by side—turn to the letter "H," and you will find that Beowulf, the "Hero," rests near the "Heroes of Labor," and that worship blends into mere infatuation.

The most puzzling and the most important case of hero worship in modern times is, of course, that of large, literate masses of the populations in the West hailing the destroyers of their political freedom.

Notes for a paper presented in December 1940 as part of a seminar jointly given by the author with Karen Horney, Kurt Riezler, and Max Wertheimer. First published in Hans Speier, *Social Order and the Risks of War*, New York, 1952. Copyright © 1952 by George W. Stewart, Publisher, Inc. First M.I.T. Press paperback edition March 1969. Reprinted by permission of M.I.T. Press.

Dictators who restrict liberties, demand sacrifices, and may yet ruin the people they rule are revered like demigods. In a German film, Hitler indeed descended upon sleeping, medieval Nuremberg, the city of his party rallies, from wind-swept skies, a divine essence incarnated in an aluminum bird, his airplane. There are men and women in many lands who prostrate themselves before their great tormentors; their dignity has vanished in a bewildering cult of worship which is modern and yet primeval.

Modern social science has little to offer when it is asked to describe and explain modern hero worship. Perhaps the most famous attempt to account for the phenomenon can be found in Max Weber's discussion of charisma, the gift of a leader to be followed beyond reason or tradition. "Charisma," said Max Weber, "is the great revolutionary force in epochs bound by tradition."[1] He defined it as the quality of a "personality" which others under its spell regard as an extraordinary and exclusive source of "supernatural or superhuman or at least specifically non-everyday" forces or properties; this quality causes them to view the great personality "as having been sent by God or as exemplary and for this reason as a 'leader.'"[2]

As the definition indicates, Max Weber discovered charisma in many men throughout history — in prophets, saviors, heroes, magicians, great judges, shamans, "literati like Kurt Eisner"; in kings claiming a divine right to rule as well as in Napoleon whose rule was illegitimate; in certain tribal chieftains no less than in poets like Stefan George.

One suspects that Weber found charisma too often. Indeed, he broadened a category which had served Rudolf Sohm to understand the development of early Christian ecclesiastical authority[3] and subsumed under it the most widely divergent social types of leadership. In this respect Max Weber's usage of "charisma" does not differ much from that of "hero worship" in popular speech. Max Weber's interest in establishing a "value-free" sociology misled him to treat saint and criminal, hero and journalist, as "thoroughly equivalent"[4] (to use his own words), if only their followers treated them as "charismatic" leaders. According to Max Weber, charismatic leadership is constituted like all types of domination through the response of those who admire, worship, and obey rather than by the qualities of the one who leads. The social recognition of the qualities of leadership appeared more important to him than these qualities themselves. For this reason one may expect Weber's theory to be helpful in an attempt to understand hero worship, more helpful, in fact, than it could possibly be to the understanding of heroism, ancient or modern. Weber said about the social recognition of charismatic qualities by those who are under its spell, "This 'recognition' is a devout, wholly personal surrender psychologically born out of misery and hope."[5]

Max Weber's great system of sociology is deficient in psychological insight. His notion of charisma, which has been applied to modern totalitarian leaders like Mussolini and Hitler (though less often to Bolshevik chieftains), does not help us to understand why "misery and hope" may lead to frenzied political mass support of tyrants in modern civilized society, that is, a society we like to regard as moderately "rational" since it has been exposed to enlightenment and industrialization. Nor does Weber's discussion of charisma offer us any precise description of the specific properties of the modern political "hero" which evoke so much admiration.

In one respect Max Weber's theory is more helpful, however, than the reasons other social scientists give for the modern mass admiration of tyrants. In particular, the explanations derived from the Marxian theory of the class struggle offer no insight whatever into motives other than economic interest rightly or wrongly understood. They may lead us to identify the social positions of those who hail the Duce, the Führer, and Stalin (not to mention the lesser gods in the Olympus of modern depravity), but they are no guide to feelings and aspirations. They give no access to understanding the *need* for "recognizing" charisma.

Max Weber does at least suggest that modern hero worship may transcend the realm of economic calculations, although it is related to "misery and hope" at large, and his approach has at least the merit of suggesting to us that we must look for something "extraordinary," not to be found in the routine of life. If the readiness to worship heroes which modern usage seems to indicate is related to the startling and undying fame enjoyed by the great killers and conquerors in history, Max Weber's clue is therefore not without value.

II

Social science has shown little interest in human *violence* and the primary natural threats to physical *safety*. As a rule economic insecurity and economic exploitation are regarded as the worst social evils, whereas the elementary social evil, physical violence, is usually understood as deviant behavior (crime) or as a barbarism of the past (war).

When social scientists in the nineteenth century discussed problems of social structure, they turned their attention to the division of labor, the distribution of economic opportunities and gains, or the recognition of rights. Today it startles us that the elementary experiences of physical risk and physical safety were treated with a silence that was nearly complete. If it is true that "risk" and "safety" have meanings that are not exclusively economic in character, the risk structure of society has not been studied much. I shall suggest that modern hero worship is related to that aspect of social life.

There has been a tendency in capitalistic civilization to regard noneconomic risks as something undesirable and to treat them as irrelevant for the understanding of social structure. Subordinate, economic risks, like unemployment, have been taken as the prototypes of risk. The elementary noneconomic risks, particularly the risks of violent death, were regarded during the nineteenth century as a feature of the "irrational," ignorant, unenlightened prebourgeois world, just as they are sometimes considered now to be barbarous traits of an antibourgeois world.

According to the theory of progress, history was a process of gradual liberation from the "irrational" in all its forms. The essential feature of advance in civilization appeared to be increased efficiency in controlling nature. Control of nature meant, primarily, the control of threats to safety which prior to the advance of science and scientific engineering were uncontrollable or only imperfectly controlled; this was true of floods, famines, epidemics. In this sense civilization appeared as a successful fight against death. Nor was the pride with which modern man viewed his progress entirely unjustified. The mean life expectation of life at birth was very low indeed as late as the second half of the eighteenth century; according to the first life table computed in Sweden for the period 1755 to 1775, 35 years. It now exceeds 60 years in many countries of the West. An infant mortality of 300 per thousand was formerly not unusual; in New Zealand it had dropped to 31 in 1932, which seems to be the lowest rate ever reached.

Similar advances in the fight against death were observed in times of war. Until quite recently the main horror of wars was epidemics. Even in the armies themselves the cases of death from disease far outnumbered combat casualties. In the Crimean War, the ratio of the two kinds of death was still 3.8 to 1 among the English and 3.3 to 1 among the French. The first modern war in which combat casualties were higher than the casualties soldiers suffered in consequence of disease was the Franco-Prussian War of 1870–71, when the ratio in question reached 0.5 to 1 among the Germans. There still were later wars in which the precivilized risks of soldiers dying from disease remained extraordinarily high. For example, in the Japanese–Chinese war of 1894–95, the ratio of noncombat to combat casualties was 3.3 to 1, and in the Spanish-American War, a few years later, it was as high as 5.6 to 1, chiefly on account of typhus and malaria. Only as the technology of destruction in war improved was there a parallel advance in the control of diseases. During the First World War soldiers had indeed a far better chance of being killed by steel than by germs. In the armies of all the belligerents the ratio of the two types of casualties dropped to 0.1 or 0.2 to 1.[6]

The great event reminding civilization that its struggle against death was not entirely successful, however, was war itself. Despite the belief in its barbarous character, it recurred; and as science and technology increased man's comfort, war, too, became more scientific and technologically more efficient. Like conquest, it remained with waxing murderousness and waning limitations one of man's scourges, defying civilization and the believers in progress. The development of long-range weapons led to a diffusion of the risks of violent death to noncombatant civilians who as producers of materiel became integral and vulnerable parts of society at war.[7]

III

For an understanding of risk it is important to note that many risks are *imposed* upon man. They are suffered passively. This holds true of the derived economic risk of unemployment as well as of the risk civilians and soldiers incur of being killed or maimed in war. Yet it is equally important to note that there are other risks, which I shall call *free or active* risks, because they are freely chosen and gladly faced.

Risk as such is not something which the organism avoids. According to the available biological evidence only impaired organisms shun all risks. Sociological evidence corroborates this observation. History abounds with cases in which certain social classes desired to face risks and regarded it as a sign of low social status not to do so.

In our civilization enterprising businessmen do not seem to be penalized by the fact that society permits them to run economic risks. While these risks are derivatives, that is, less taxing than the basic physical risks man is capable of choosing, they are assertions of freedom and activity rather than impositions. In preindustrial civilization free and active risks were more frequently of the elementary physical type. A spectacular form of the free risk is that sought by the hero who challenges death.

Imposed risks can lurk in nature in the form of illness, the danger of drowning, and most of the other chances of death which saddened Aeneas in the netherworld. In the face of such hazards only the strong have a chance to be masters. As Polybius observed, "When, owing to floods, famine, failures of crops or other such causes, there occurs such a destruction of the human race as tradition tells us has more than once happened, and as we must believe will often happen again, all arts and crafts perishing at the same time . . . it is the necessary consequence that the man who excels in bodily strength and courage will lead and rule over the rest."[8]

Imposed risks may reside also in the human organization of society. It is with the derived economic risks of this kind that social science in the nineteenth century found it important to concern itself. The early critics of the industrial system spoke much of the monotonous character of factory work, and in Marxist literature exploitation and unemployment received more attention than starvation and tuberculosis.

Since the rise of modern dictatorial regimes after the First World War we have had occasion to learn again that not all imposed risks are economic in nature. Confinement, torture and violent death imposed upon contestants for power, upon enemies of the government, political heretics, and scapegoats — all these risks are evidently so much more elementary that one can only marvel at the pleasantness of nineteenth-century life in which they were disregarded. Security meant, and for some strange reason still means to many observers, economic security, while its primary meaning is physical safety.

It would be erroneous to assume that "upper classes" have always been privileged with regard to safety. Rather than having been protected against free and active risks, their life has been safer than that of the lowly merely in respect to imposed risks. Up to the end of the eighteenth century the higher middle classes in Europe were not entirely exempt from the risk lurking in famines, not to speak of epidemics, although it is true that they suffered somewhat less than persons of low status. Similarly, there are today certain passive risks from which the higher classes are characteristically exempt, for example, the hazards encountered in mining. As to free and active risks, however, it is members of the upper class in pre- and postbourgeois societies who take them and jealously guard their privilege to do so.

A case in point is the losses suffered by officers in prebourgeois wars. During the seventeenth and eighteenth centuries, when officers were recruited largely from the aristocracy, their losses in war were enormous. It is possible to explain this fact in terms of prevalent military tactics and the requirements of discipline, but the fact remains that the chance of these officers to be killed in war was much higher than that of their men. Losses among officers frequently amounted to 10 percent of the total. Only after the wars of Frederick the Great did these losses decrease to remain fairly constant around 5 percent up to the time of the First World War. Similarly, during the Thirty Years' War, the wars of Louis XIV, and in the war against the Turks, it was not unusual that one general was put to death for every 200 to 300 dead or wounded soldiers. In the eighteenth century, the ratio was 1 to 1400, in the Napoleonic wars 1 to 1000, and thereafter 1 to 2,500.[9]

These figures are a reflection of the fact that in middle-class civilization the elementary active risks of the upper classes have diminished. At the same time the derived economic risks, both active and passive, have become increasingly relevant. Also the free risk of other, socially interstitial and marginal groups have shrunk within the civilized area of modern society; piracy and highway robbery have been reduced and relegated to outlying (colonial) and border areas (e.g., Balkan countries).

Finally, technological progress paradoxically has led to the emergence of experts in high-skill violence who are specially selected and trained for their hazardous tasks. A striking instance of these streamlined buccaneers are the "shock troops" that were formed toward the end of the First World War to break the stalemate at the stationary fronts. The upper age limit for regular fighting at the front at that time lay between thirty and thirty-five years of age; in these shock troops, however, no one was more than twenty-five years of age. It was required that they be unmarried and only volunteers were accepted. The shock trooper was an athlete whose special military training did not culminate in parades or maneuvers but in attacks on realistically duplicated "enemy" positions. In this training live hand grenades were used; the accident rate was high. A special esprit de corps of an archaic type, resembling that which is known from sworn brotherhoods, was cultivated partly with the aim of disengaging this elite from ordinary military and social relations. Privileges in food, honor and pay were granted them. Immediately after the high-skill attack and before the retaliatory bombardment began they were withdrawn from the front. Thus, the regular troops often had to assume a passive, defensive risk in consequence of the aggressive action of the shock troops.

In the postwar literature celebrating the spirit developed in this elite group, they were proudly called "warriors" rather than "soldiers," and one of these warriors who turned to writing, Ernst Jünger, said "that one looked forward to the battle with a certain lust."

IV

In order to gain insight into the nature of modern hero worship, it is useful to glance at classical heroism as it is known to us from the premodern age. This is not to suggest that in modern hero worship an ancient ideal is being embraced. As a matter of fact, I shall try to show how misleading such a suggestion would be. There are, nonetheless, in classical heroism elements of a form of life which may help us to appreciate better the emotional needs as well as the perversions which modern hero worship contains.

In an attempt to describe the heroic, one must not refer too soon to the moral principles which serve to justify or denounce it. Otherwise one may come to praise heroism without understanding it fully or to point out its faults yet be compelled to admit with Hume that there remains "something dazzling" which baffles all moral criticism.

The prototype of the heroic is related more closely to madness of the berserk[10] than to the code of the medieval knight. One is inclined to say that the classical hero invites physiological study rather than moral appraisal. He is strong and proud rather than noble and not necessarily fair; exuberant to the point of a reckless waste of his strength; powerful but not generous and striving for glory rather than justice.

In the early heroic poetry of all cultures, the hero's invincibility is grounded upon physical excellence and often also upon cunning. The delight the poets take in depicting the hero's physique resembles the admiration one feels for the beauty of a strong animal, a stallion or a lion. Indeed, the hero is often compared with animals of superhuman strength. He is not an image of human perfection but a stroke of nature's luck, a man into whom life has thrown more than one of its torches.

The similes used in heroic poetry always point to athletic perfection. Agamemnon's chest resembles that of a bull. When Hector fights it is as though a lion falls upon a herd of cattle. Idomeneus is likened to a boar. When Ajax, Diomedes, Aeneas, or any other great hero throws a stone, Homer never forgets to remind us that among mortals now nobody could lift a rock of such weight, and so heavy was even the spear of Achilles that no other man on earth would have been able to handle it. Beowulf's fantastic exploits as a swimmer are well known. In German heroic legends of the Middle Ages the hero is often represented as a giant. In the *Chanson de Roland* Charlemagne is fifteen feet high, and Turpin's prowess in dealing more than a thousand blows after he is wounded to death inspires our awe.

None of this is moral in nature, indeed all of it is premoral. The Greek term *arete*, which we translate as virtue, was originally applied not only to men but to animals as well. Its meaning centered around a notion of extraordinary fitness comprising those qualities which are necessary to cope with life and its violent dangers. In old Latin *animus* denoted a natural disposition or quality of impetuosity and perseverance which was not acquired and, again, it was possible to speak of the *animus* of animals. Similarly, in German the word *Held* meant originally only a man who bears arms and can fight; it lacked any connotation pertinent to the way we sometimes like to think heroes fight. In Islandic, *agr* was the word for both "coward" and "woman" which illustrates once more the heroic identification of natural and moral qualities.

The hero is not only strong, he is also violent. Yet his is an assertive rather than a resentful brutality. He is brutal because he is strong, so strong, indeed, that he is able to slay monsters and, when enraged, to defy fate. Achilles drags Hector's corpse through the dust to revenge the loss of Patroclos. In Layamon's *Brut* even women are maimed. Hagen swings his sword like a deadly scythe and the heads of his enemies fall as though Hagen was mowing grass. Vainly do the sons of Antimachos implore Agamemnon that he may spare their lives; the hero slays them in his frenzy. It happens not seldom that the classical hero approaches the type of the berserk, the mad fighter who roars and bites the rim of his shield in battle. All this is ferocious enough. Yet while this ferocity is appalling, it is never sickly.

Despite their strength, heroes do not shun treachery. The celebrated hero Yamato-Take in the Japanese legend deceives his enemy by feigning friendship for him; secretly he replaces the good sword of his foe by a wooden one in order to slay him with ease. Another time he lulls his opponent into safety by wearing a woman's garment. Foes may be murdered in their sleep or while they are drunk. All this seems perfectly compatible with the heroism of Japanese epics.[11] Nor is this trait confined to Asia. In the Iliad, Diomedes kills Rhesos, the king of the Thracians and twelve of his retainers at night in their sleep. While in Islandic society honor demanded that an enemy should not be killed in his sleep, a saga tells us that the heroes would observe this rule by awakening the enemy before they struck but never give him a chance to get up and fight.

Likewise, heroism is compatible with treacherous attacks from an ambush. Trickery is not infamous. Dishonorable revenge is better than taking no revenge at all, and the frequency with which the sources relate occasions of such dishonorable revenge is only excelled by the number of words for honor and shame. The Islandic heroes had an institution called *holmgang*, a kind of duel in which two opponents measured their strength under conditions of complete equality of arms. This, then, appears to be an instance of fairness. A competent student, however, whose admiration for ancient Nordic culture cannot be doubted, informs us that in the great majority of cases, "the *holmgang* was resorted to in order to press an unjustified demand."[12] In one of the heroic stories related by Saxo Grammaticus, a hero is so intent upon victory that he treacherously murders one of his own men, dressing him in his own royal garment in order to infuriate his hesitant followers by the supposed death of their chieftain.[13]

We may add that the hero knows no fear. He is capable of braving the terrors dreaded by ordinary men; this means, above all, the terrors of nature — dark forests, deserts, quagmires, caverns, wolfcliffs — which in the language of imagination take the shape of beliefs in monsters, serpents, werewolfs, trolls, and giants. "Others fear the terror, but *his* serenity is the token of his heroism."[14]*

The hero's vital strength prevents his lapsing into indolence and gloom, or, to put it simply in the affirmative, *the hero enjoys life.*

---

*We notice, however, that the Homeric heroes do know fear. Mr. Routh remarks: "The great German, Frankish and Irish warriors are not so ready to confess to their inferiority; in fact a perfect warrior would be immune to such weakness." (H. V. Routh, *God, Man and Epic Poetry*, Cambridge, 1927, vol. 2, p. 17). Hector and Menelaus show unmistakable signs of timidity and are subject to terror. In fact, even the Gods, at times, give counsel to shun a fight with certain powerful enemies. According to all traditional concepts of heroism this is indicative of *cowardice*: Mr. Routh says, "Such attacks of moral exhaustion are perfectly true to life" and, again, "It needs the Homeric sense of sureness and perfection to confess, even in moments of poetic exaltation, that we sometimes fall short of what is required of us." (I, 38). But, if the attacks of "moral exhaustion" which Homer describes are "perfectly true to life," we are led to assume that Homer wants to show that the perfect hero is not true to life. The Homeric "sense of perfection" refutes the idea of a "perfect hero." By admitting that the warrior with the stoutest heart has moments of fear, which are inglorious, also the notion of glory is tainted. Says Mr. Routh: "medieval and modern war poetry shrinks from showing sympathy with human weakness. Our admiration is fixed on too high a dream of self-abnegation and moral heroism . . . " (I, 38). This is a good choice of words: Homer was no dreamer. Is it presumptuous to suggest that instead he was an *interpreter of dreams*, a *critic* of heroism? I believe it can indeed be shown that Homer did *not* want to have Achilles regarded as the greatest man in the Iliad.

Unlike violence and cunning, joy as an attribute of the heroic does not overtly conflict with our moral notions concerning the good life, although Christian ethics has discovered a sting in joy as well. Joy is the radiance of the heroic temper. The hero is proud. He seems pervaded by a feeling of self-reliance and demands praise. As Goethe said in one of his terse, anti-Christian adages, "Only scoundrels are modest."

Heroic accomplishments are decidedly not the outcome of methodical effort, diligence, and sweat. They are not continuous conquests of fatigue or solutions of tasks. They are products of adventure, freely chosen encounters with risk, rather than work. Unlike the saints, heroes never go to the desert. While they live victoriously they seek no victory over themselves, for it is not themselves but the world they face. They accept the challenge of life and rejoice over their deeds.

The heroes of all cultures fear death away from battle. Nothing is more ignominious to them than natural death. Such death denies freedom. Natural death, "*Strohtod*" among the ancient Germans, is insidious death. Drowning, the fate suffered by Achilles (due to Homer's wisdom), death of old age, death even by murder are forms of passivity in which the heroic is eluded. Through such a death, the hero is denied to die acting *securely* in the face of risks.

V

For many centuries prior to the rise of middle class culture, joy was regarded as a state of the soul, which is closely connected with certain virtuous qualities of a man, such as *magnanimitas* and *securitas*. These virtues were thought to be implied in the cardinal virtue of *fortitude*, and fortitude was held to be the source of joy. As to *securitas*, it must not be confused with our notion of security. *Securitas* has no economic connotations. While it is true that "heroes" do not suffer from poverty, their security is not inherent in their wealth. Like power, glory, beauty, and dexterity, wealth was held to belong to the *bona fortunae et corporis*, something by no means without worth, but being in the realm of the *useful* things. *Securitas* was not included in the values which were regarded as *utile*, but was held to belong to the *honestum*: a beautiful quality of the soul, not a consequence of fortune.

The German philosopher Heidegger, under the influence of Kierkegaard's Christian psychology, has pointed out that *Sorge*, anxiety, is a fundamental human experience to which man is exposed in this world; and many modern psychologists talk about "basic anxiety." This is a poignant description of man insofar as he is *not* heroic. Heroes are *secure*, and the most accurate German translation of *securitas* is *Sorglosigkeit*, the opposite of *Sorge*. Again, *securitas* is not carelessness or indifference, but a healthy absence of anxiety.

While anxiety paralyzes action, the "inner" security of the hero enables him to act. In the Latin poetry of the German nun Hrotsvita, which is an important source for the Christianization of the heroic ideal in Western civilization, Gongolf, the hero is depicted in the most decisive and dangerous moments of this life as *secure*. Security in this sense, then, implies profound self-confidence. If the modern notion of security connotes protection against risks, heroic security is of another kind: it asserts itself precisely when man encounters risks. Heroic security makes it unnecessary for a man to be secure in the modern sense.

Closely related to joy and security of the hero is what in middle high German was called *Hoher Muot*. It came close to what the Romans called *magnanimitas* and the Greeks *megalopsychia*. *Hoher Muot* designates a state of feeling (*Hochstimmung*) rather than a state of mind (*Hochsinn*). The opposite of *Hoher Muot* is pusillanimity (*Angst*, anxiety).

For a time, historians assumed that the German *Hoher Muot* is derived from the ancient *megalopsychia* and *magnanimitas*, the connecting link being William of Conches (died 1154), who defined *magnanimitas* in his moral philosophy as "the spontaneous and rational (sic) aggression of that which is difficult." More recently, it has been shown that no historical connection exists between *magnanimitas* and *Hoher Muot*. The similarity, it seems, arises from the affinities of aristocratic cultures; and the differences are perhaps due to the fact that the ancient terms were philosophical terms, while the German one is found in court poetry. *Hoher Muot* is often (e.g., in the *Nibelungenlied*) understood as consequence of love (*Minne*), which in all knightly codes of conduct is both passion and virtue.

The original meaning of the term *Hoher Muot* deteriorated in consequence of Christian and middle class criticism, the degeneration taking place between 1220 and 1500. *Hoher Muot* was identified with robust enjoyment, ridiculous excitement, *merely* physical energy and presumptuous exertion. Horses were said to have this quality, and finally *Hoher Muot* became "pride," arrogance, a "*vice*." This process of devaluation was accompanied by a transformation of the meaning of symbols. The stately stride of the crane, once used to symbolize *Hoher Muot*, became a symbol of *superbia*, i.e., haughtiness and arrogance; correspondingly, in German, *Hoher Muot* assumed the meaning of *Hochmut*.

According to Christian ethics, pride is one of the seven deadly sins. The old hero is incompatible with Christian morals. He gives way to the martyr, or becomes acceptable by fighting the infidels with fortitude in the name of God.

VI

One sin, which was deadly according to Christian teaching, should be briefly considered in relation to the heroic temper. No hero fell into inactivity, or to use the older, more precise term, into *acedia*.[15] According to Chaucer "accidie is the anguish of a trouble (dark) herte"; "Bitterness is the mother of accidie"; "it abates the soul and makes it feeble."

The term is by no means confined to Chaucer. It is traditional in Christian ethics. Cassian in the fourth century devoted a whole book of his *De Coenobiorum Institutis* to the discussion of *acedia*. He said that those who live in the desert are especially assailed by this temper and monks find it most troublesome around noon. The Christian remedies for the affliction of gloom or *acedia* are work and fortitude. Much of what other writers regarded as traits of *acedia* Cassian attributed to sadness. Thomas Aquinas censored this interpretation and restored the connection between sadness and *acedia* by defining the latter as *tristitia de bono divino* (sadness about the divine good). This definition is of great interest because it points to the relation between *acedia* and envy which Thomas defined as *tristitia de bono proximi* (sadness about the neighbor's good).

Envy, I suggest, is one of the roots of modern hero worship, just as "inactivity" is another. These traits will presently be discussed further, but let us note here that we may have to search in modern hero worship for the admiration of qualities which the admirers lack and miss rather than share.

VII

The procedure I have so far followed needs a word of explanation. Technically speaking, hero worship is the worship of dead warrior and modern hero worship has of course little to do with it, although the staged solemnity of contemporary state funerals or the exhibition for purposes of veneration of an embalmed corpse at the Red Square in Moscow invites a more careful delimitation of the dissimilarities than I shall attempt. The fact, however, that the traits of the classical hero are taken from imaginative material need not disturb us unduly, regardless of whether this material can be traced to ritual, as some writers suggest,[16] or to actual early social conditions. What matters in the context of this discussion is the fact that human imagination created the picture of the heroic which we find in old epics and that Christian moral doctrine as well as later middle class ethics transformed and eventually devalued that image. The forms of life in which heroic poetry expressed the prevalent feelings of man differs from modern civilized life. The point need not be labored. James Joyce's *Ulysses*, science fiction and "true" romances are more popular today than Homer, the literature on foreign travel in the age of discovery or songs of the troubadours. By the same token modern hero worship must be expected to reflect traits of modern man in modern society, no matter how much it may also betray something unchanged and unchangeable in man's nature.

It has been suggested that in the West today the social conditions most closely approaching those of ancient "heroic society" can be found in backward countries, particularly the Balkans. Indeed, the description of fairly recent Serbian society given by Gesemann and others[17] corresponds closely to that emerging from ancient sources; many of its salient features virtually coincide, for example, with those of the Norsemen as they appear in Icelandic sources.[18] The country is mountainous, divided into numerous regional units with difficult communication among them. The absence of a centralized political power and the poverty of the country put a premium on self-reliance and lend economic importance to "heroic" raids and robbery. Society is organized in clans (*zadruga* in Serbia); sworn brotherhoods are sanctioned in churchlike marriages. In Serbia there was continual border warfare with the "Turks," that is, mostly "Serbo-Croats" of Mohammedan caste but of the same language. It was therefore possible to exchange heroic songs with the enemy and to engage in the poetic challenges prior to fighting well known from Homer and to be found in many other early cultures as well (e.g., "*Reizrede*" among ancient Germans). The "hero" in such societies must take active risks in order to survive, and heroism is self-centered, entirely devoid of the notion of sacrifice. Heroic society should not be understood, however, as a continuous war of all against all, since within the clans and the (sworn) brotherhoods, within certain contractual arrangements and wherever hospitality was extended to guests, certain cells of precarious peace always existed (*frith* in Icelandic Society).

Finally, in heroic society the technology of weapons has not yet made death "invisible," to use Adam Smith's felicitous phrase. Man meets man in combat. King Archimados III has not yet had an occasion to exclaim, as he did when the catapults were introduced from Sicily, "O Heracles, gone is the valour of man" nor Martin Luther to deplore guns and cannons which "throw men up in the air" as "the devil's work and of hell," and "invented by such a one as could not otherwise fight with his corporal weapons and fists."

VIII

There is sharp contrast between heroic society and modern social organization. Power now is centralized and largely anonymous; law has restrained self-reliance and not only the great, as in Homeric society, eat meat. We are scientific and can prolong the life span of man if it is not shortened by crime and the accidents of the machine age or by its wars.

A truly bewildering specialization of work — inventive, productive, administrative, and otherwise — has created a web of interdependence which all of us help to spin and in which each of us seems caught as a methodically crippled part of his self. As Schiller put it more than a hundred years ago, we must go around from specialist to specialist to piece together a composite picture of man. We are divorced from the naive and full assertion of life, of which we catch veiled glances in our dreams when we are less well shielded from the terrors of nature and when the Christian traditions of humility and work loosen the grip they have on our impulses.

To large insecure masses of the population the ubiquitous risks of modern civilization are ever impending like natural disasters, and the masses demand social security. It should be noted that in the midst of a civilization dedicated to making life less dangerous this demand is born of the same "misery and hope" which has led adventurers, adolescents, and declassés of all kinds to embrace the antibourgeois creed of the "dangerous life."

All modern so-called charismatic leaders claim to offer to their mass following increased security from hazards to be suffered passively and to a select youthful "elite" encounters with elementary, active risk. The former are presented as concessions to envy and reductions of social inequality and the latter appear as a postbourgeois and anti-Christian enrichment of life.

Modern hero worship is a devastating inarticulate criticism of the shortcomings of a civilization in which the goals of socially approved aspirations are difficult to attain, in which the rewards of conformity bring only scant and clandestine release from the self-restraint expected of conformists and in which the nature and distribution of risks leaves even those who are "secure" in a state of bewildering indifference. Modern man, brought up with the expectation that happiness is a right, finds at best that life offers diversions — "fun," but not "joy." While he may not be fully aware of the difference, it is in hero worship that he betrays a deep need for release from the yoke of civilization.

Modern hero worship is a safe and underhanded way of obtaining vicariously what life refuses to give freely. Hero worship is a worship of active unbridled life. Ferrero observed that "The Napoleon-worship is to the higher classes what brigand-worship is to the lower."[19] One wonders whether this remark still is quite true. Many great brigands become popular not only because of their daring and recklessness, but also because they right social wrongs. They pursue justice in the raw. Often, the tales of their sparing or helping the poor while they rob the rich linger on long after the guardians of the law put an end to their exploits. By contrast, the Napoleon-worship, like that of the more recent worship of national tyrants, which is by no means confined to the upper classes, appears to be a worship of great energy and dazzling success as well as a mistaken acclaim of social justice.

Low social origin, moreover, is a prerequisite of tyrannical leadership in modern society; both Napoleon and Hitler were "corporals"; Stalin was one among many conspirators of undistinguished social origin. The new dictatorships have a strongly plebeian tinge. Low social origin of the modern caesars not only facilitates identifications of the admirers with their leaders but also serves as a reminder that social obscurity need not always be a bar to great power. The modern caesar is an upstart whose lowly beginnings throw his high station into relief. In modern hero worship there is probably admiration of meteoric *careers* in which the ordinary obstacles to success have been overcome by luck, ruthlessness, and hazardous disregard of the law. Unlike the saints, whose history comprises struggles with temptations and life in the desert, modern heroes early in their careers often spend time in jail. Their background resembles that of outlaws, but different from criminals they have successfully proved the fickleness of norms which restrain the conduct of their worshipers. It seems plausible to assume that the caesar's extraordinary nonconformism answers a deep emotional need of ordinary men. The followers of the modern "charismatic leader" are not only those who receive tokens of his spoils and revolutionary power and function as a brutal substitute for the law; they include also the mass of the feeble who enlarge the domain of their apathetic lives by vicarious participation in what they conceive to be greatness.

If an effort will ever be made to verify Max Weber's contention that the recognition of charisma springs from "misery and hope," it will be worthwhile studying the resemblance of hero worship with the belief in great charlatans and with the character of notorious gossips.

In a study of *The Power of the Charlatan*[20] it has been shown that the disposition to be duped by a charlatan has its roots in desires for "transformation." The poor want to become rich and try to avail themselves of the secret which turns copper into gold. The sick want to be healthy and trust a quack. The aged yearn for rejuvenation and squander their wealth in a futile chase. The power of the charlatan is dependent upon the fact that his clients consist, as it were, of passive charlatans. Correspondingly, the grip which the modern caesar has on popular imagination may result from the fact that his public leads a feeble, thoroughly unheroic and dissatisfied life, in which few risks are freely chosen. Their worship of the heroic may be a substitute for action from which they are barred by circumstance, fear, and convention.

Similarly, gossip is a form of vicarious enrichment of one's stifled experience. It typically occurs in narrow conditions of personal and social life. Gossip, like modern hero worship, is indicative of sterility, a flower blossoming on the stagnant waters of an arrested life. It is parasitic participation in the envied romance of others, the vicarious experience of crime one does not dare to commit or a clandestine taste of the thrilling risk which is feared and admired. A person fond of gossip is indeed never more alive than when he indulges in talk, just as many people parading before their "leader" awaken from passivity to a counterfeit of active life.

Gossip is a form of envy, the envy of liberties which others take, of passions one cannot satisfy and of scandals one's own life refuses to provide. It is impotent love of the extraordinary. Those whose life is active and happy do not gossip; nor are they likely to join the ranks of the anxious who find charisma in the caesars of our time.

In summary, I suggest that modern hero worship comprises three main components; first, the primeval veneration of strength and freely chosen risks in defiance of Christian and middle-class ethics; second, the specific misery created by the clash of the socially approved values of work, humility, and self-sought happiness as a right with a life experience in which aspirations are curbed, desires censored and in which risks are ubiquitous but imposed; third, the passivity which modern civilization promotes as it catches man in its incomprehensible web of depersonalized "forces" and "relationships."

NOTES

1. Max Weber, *Wirtschaft und Gesellschaft*, Tübingen, 1922, p. 142.
2. Ibid., p. 140.
3. Ibid., p. 753.
4. Ibid., p. 140.
5. Ibid.
6. Oberstarzt Dr. Jungblut, "Kriegsverluste," in *Militärwissenschaftliche Rundschau*, 1938, p. 250.
7. Harold D. Lasswell has aptly spoken of "the socialization of threat in modern war" and of the importance this socialization may have in the "garrison state." See his "The Garrison State," in *American Journal of Sociology*, vol. xlvi, 1941.
8. Polybius, VI, 5.
9. Gaston Bodart, *Militär-historisches Kriegs-lexicon 1618–1905*, Vienna and Leipzig, 1908, pp. 853ff., 869.
10. On the *Berserker*, see Gunnar Rudberg, *Zum antiken Bild der Germanen*, Oslo, 1933, p. 10, and Ernst Herwig Ahrendt, *Der Riese in der mittelhochdeutschen Epik*, Güstrow, 1923, pp. 114ff.
11. Walter Donat, *Der Heldenbegriff im Schrifttum der älteren japanischen Geschichte*, Tokyo, 1938, pp. 26–27.
12. Walther Gehl, *Ruhm und Ehre bei den Nordgermanen*, 1937, p. 53.
13. H. V. Routh, *God, Man and Epic Poetry*, Cambridge, 1927, vol. II, pp. 49–50.
14. Routh, op. cit., vol. II, p. 22.
15. See the introductory essay on *acedia* by Francis Paget in his *The Spirit of Discipline*, 12th impression, London, 1911, pp. 1–50.
16. E.g., Lord Ragan, *The Hero* (various editions), and the anthropological literature on the culture hero.
17. Gerhard Gesemann, *Der montenegrinische Mensch*, Prag, 1934; Maxim Braun, "Zur Frage des Heldenliedes bei den Serbokroaten," in *Beiträge zur Geschichte der deutschen Sprache und Literatur*, vol. 59, 1935; Jovan Cvijic, *La peninsule balcanique Géographie humaine*, Paris, 1918.
18. Gustav Neckel, *Altgermanische Kultur*, 2nd ed., 1935; Walther Gehl, op. cit.; Andreas Heusler, "Altgermanische Sittenlehre und Lebensweisheit," in *Germanentum*, 1935, pp. 7–62.
19. Guglielmo Ferrero, *Militarism*, Boston, 1903, p. 196.
20. Grete de Francesco, *Die Macht des Charlatans*, Basel, 1937.

PART TWO

Communication and Propaganda

6

The Changing Function
of Communication

In one of Pieter Bruegel's paintings, dated 1560, more than eighty different children's games are depicted. Almost all of them are still familiar to us. We used to play them ourselves when we were young. We learned the games from other children who transmitted them to us, as they had been transmitted to them and as we in turn handed them on, along with rhymes and riddles and nonsense verse, in face-to-face contact with younger children. Thus a long chain of communication extends backward for many centuries and, let us hope, forward into the distant future. The games live on without the aid of writing and reading.

From the dawn of history to this day, most communication has been by word of mouth. Oral communication without the help of technical devices, such as loudspeakers, wireless transmitters, and telephones, occurs not only among children but in many other relationships: in the household among family members, among neighbors and friends; in schools, courthouses, barracks, jails, and churches; in the market-place, barbershops, coffeehouses, and the theater; in factories and offices; on pilgrimages, stage coaches, riverboats, trains, and air-planes; in taverns and at court; in parliament and other meeting plac-es. Much of language itself, a great deal of the information needed for

From *Propaganda and Communication in World History*, vol. 1, edited by H. D. Lasswell, D. Lerner, and H. Speier. © 1979, University of Hawaii. An East-West Center Book. Reprinted by permission.

meeting the demands of everyday life, our manners and morals – all these depend largely on oral communication. So do religious beliefs and rites, and the lore about nature, folksongs, folktales, proverbs, and many other parts of practical wisdom.

Although oral communication with each new generation can keep pace with time, *continuous* relays of both message and memory are required to bring the past up to the present ever anew. Once the chain of communication is broken, tradition fades with the passage of time unless memory is stored and can be retrieved at will. There must be writing and reading for such *discontinuous* communication to occur. Thus today, we can return to the immediate and distant past by reading what was recorded for future use a short or a long time ago.

Similarly, the realm of oral communication in space is bounded by the range of the human voice. This limits the transmission of information over long distances to the speed with which messengers can travel. We tend, perhaps, to underestimate the speed of disseminating news in times when its transmission altogether depended on a spontaneously operating human relay system. A famous instance in this regard is the fact that the news of the victory of Macedonicus over Perseus at Pydna in Macedonia in 168 B.C. took only four days to arrive in Rome. Certain ancient regimes employed a technique, known also from primitive societies, of posting men as links in a chain of oral communication capable of outpacing fast riders. The ancient Persians are credited with the ability to transmit important news at the speed of fifty miles a day. To be sure, only news relevant to the exercise of government was handled in this manner, and it could not travel across the sea. Even in modern times, until fairly recently, diplomats overseas were dependent on the packet boat for receiving instructions from the home center and sending intelligence back. As late as the beginning of the nineteenth century, a diplomatic despatch posted in London took sixty days to reach Washington, D.C. The situation changed drastically only with the invention of telegraphy. By the momentous increase in the speed of transmission it became possible for the diplomat abroad to inform the home center promptly of changes occurring in the host country and for the center to control more tightly the activities of its diplomatic representatives in foreign countries.

In modern times, messages characteristically travel faster than messengers, but this is only secondarily the result of advances in the technology of transmission; it is primarily the consequence of the dissociation of the message from the messenger, that is, the ability to encode messages in such a way that they can be seen rather than heard.

Beginning with the invention of writing and ending with the modern revolution in communication that owes so much to the transistor and to the computer technological advances have enabled man to surmount the natural barriers to oral communication in four principal ways: by storing messages for retrieval, by speeding up the transmission of messages far beyond the performance of messengers, by bridging virtually any spatial gap, and by ensuring simultaneous reception at widely separated locations.

Technological progress in the field of communication must not be envisioned as linear advance, in which each later phase, marked by increased speed or range or by lower cost, renders earlier technologies altogether obsolete. At any point in time, there is room for some overlapping use of simple and advanced techniques. Such overlapping may obtain for different reasons. First, although an advanced technology may be available, simpler forms may persist for purely social reasons. For example, in Cicero's age Roman literature was produced to be read out loud to friends, but much of it was preserved by the *bibliopola* to whom the author gave his work for copying and distribution to buyers who were unknown to the author. The same situation had prevailed in Athens since the fifth, and in Alexandria since the third, century. Written copies of ancient literature thus survived the long period from the fifth to the tenth century when no literary public existed in the West. Similarly, the poetry of the troubadours, largely produced for oral delivery to illiterate listeners, flourished at a time when clerics were capable of writing and reading.

Second, different technologies of communication may overlap because of a lack of centralization in society. Parochial modes of communication, for example, village gossip, may coexist with fairly sophisticated networks controlled by the government reaching distant areas by printed documents issued to subordinate local authorities.

Third, different technologies of communication may overlap in a given society for political reasons. Just as nonmilitary counterelites in the modern state lack means of violence as efficient as those controlled by the legitimate government, so the means of communication employed by counterelites often are woefully inferior to the dominant ones. This is particularly, but by no means exclusively, true of illiberal regimes. Prior to Hitler's seizure of power, Nazi propaganda operated without the help of press and radio. It scored its successes despite the fact that control over these media was exercised by political and economic groups whose power Hitler wanted to usurp. He succeeded in his propaganda by means of the spoken word, mass meetings, and terror in the street. Similarly, opposition to repressive regimes is regularly forced to use a backward technology of communication for conveying intelligence information and all other messages and for its propaganda. In fact, usually this is one of the major handicaps the opposition must overcome when bidding for power. More generally speaking, the control by totalitarian governments of news appearing in the mass media and the suppression of public dissent typically entails the resurrection of earlier, more primitive, modes of communication: dissenters resort to graffiti, rumors, inefficient ways of duplicating and disseminating news, and so on.

Finally, the introduction of an advanced technology of communication may reinforce the use of earlier technological means instead of rendering them obsolete in practice. It has been claimed that the Hussite revolt might have spread in Europe like the Lutheran Reformation, had its religious propaganda been able to benefit, as did Luther and Calvin, from the invention of the printing press. But the astonishing increase in religious pamphleteering in the Reformation era triggered an equally notable growth of reformist preaching. In analytical perspective the case is similar to the increase in newspaper reading as a result of the introduction of the wireless distribution of news in this century.

At all stages of development, communication is embedded in the form society has assumed, its religious, political, military, and economic life, its given social differentiation, and its territorial organization. What are the requirements in the field of communication for the population to participate in the political life of the community? Above all, there must be no monopoly on learning held by a privileged and socially closed minority, be they a class of priests in command of esoteric knowledge or a political class in possession of politically relevant information withheld from the population at large. Such minorities may even serve supreme political power holders who are themselves illiterate. Charlemagne vainly tried to learn how to write while attracting from afar monks who were responsible for the cultural renaissance under his reign.

Generally speaking, for politics actively to involve large parts of the population, the political language must be a common tongue and public records must be widely accessible. Those who speak the common tongue must be able to read and write. They must also be interested and educated enough to reflect upon political life and powerful enough to act. In a word, they must be literate citizens. It is not necessary, however, for the citizenry to be unilingual. In ancient Rome, both Greek and Latin were spoken, just as modern Switzerland has four official languages and many other countries have polyglot populations without loss to political integration. Although multilingualism contains the potential of divisiveness if nationalist feelings are associated with each tongue, it is more important to note that a monopoly on any language for magical, religious, or political use necessarily precludes the idea of common citizenry and institutionalizes instead through the medium of language the rule of an active minority over an illiterate or ignorant mass of subjects condemned to passivity.

From the vantage point of communication and its social functions, the main requirements of political participation in Western society were the ascendency of the vernaculars over Latin, widespread literacy and the rise of free markets for printed information on politics, a market, that is, to satisfy the needs of the impecunious as well as the rich.

Humanists in the period of the Renaissance initiated in the West the replacement of Latin as an exclusive language by the vernacular as a dignified medium of learning and literature. This momentous shift away from Latin as the language that unified a small educated stratum across geographical and linguistic boundaries contributed to the later rise of national consciousness and pride. It might even be argued that a high price was ultimately exacted for this progress: the division of the formerly unified culture of the West. But this happened only in the era of nationalism, ushered in by the French Revolution, when large masses in peacetime and in war passionately embraced, or recoiled from, the political causes their governments espoused.

Another impetus toward the replacement of Latin by the vernacular and, ultimately, toward the formation of a literate public came from the religious reformers. They insisted on the study of God's word without the help of priestly intermediaries and preached in the mother tongues of the faithful who did not know Latin. John Wyclif (1328–1384) preached at Oxford and London in the vernacular. So did John Milíč (circa 1325–1374), the father of Czech Reform, a forerunner of John Hus, and Matthew of Janov (circa 1355–1393), his immediate successor, at Prague. Toward the end of his life, Milíč preached every day in three different churches in Latin, Czech, and German. And Matthew, like Wyclif, translated the Bible into his mother tongue. In the fifteenth century the Lollards extended the use of the Wyclifite translation, and in 1500 — seventeen years before Luther published his ninety-five theses — no less than thirty Bible translations had been printed in vernacular versions. After 1522, the Scriptures were available to every European nation in its mother tongue.

The literature inspired by the religious reformers was devotional and edifying in the first place. For the modern political public to arise, additional forces had to change the fabric of society. The secularization begun in the Renaissance was brought to fruition in the period of the Enlightenment. Now education was expected to ensure freedom from superstition and prejudice, and the dignity of man's reason to replace the dignity of tradition. Among the middle classes moral and political concerns began to attract more attention, while purely edifying literature lost ground. But the philosophers of the Enlightenment were "elitists," to use a modern term. Their interest was not the liberation of the masses but the liberation of the mind, and modern public opinion as a force in political life would not have asserted itself had it not been for the vital concern on the part of economic innovators, usually referred to as the modern bourgeoisie, with fiscal and budgetary matters. Once the government yielded to demands that these matters no longer be kept secret, the solid foundation for public opinion and public information on politics was laid.

On the moral and philosophical plane in the same era, the ardent faith in the rights of men to govern themselves as free and equal brothers became the great modern utopia. It spawned momentous institutional changes in society as well as liberal, radical, and communist ideologies and the associated propaganda efforts that still are an integral part of modern civilization.

7

The Rise of Public Opinion

I

Public opinion is often regarded as opinion disclosed to others or at least noted by others, so that opinions that are hidden or concealed from other persons may be called either private or clandestine opinions. The criterion for distinguishing between private and public opinion thus appears to lie in the realm of communication. In expressions like "public good," "public ownership," "public law," however, our point of reference is not communication but rather a matter of general concern, more precisely, *res publica*. This political meaning of the word is older than the meaning we customarily associate with the term "public opinion."

Thomas Hobbes, for example, distinguishing public worship from private worship, observed that public is the worship that a commonwealth performs "as one person."[1] According to this usage, the distinctive mark of private worship need not be secrecy; it might rather be heresy. Hobbes mentions indeed that private worship may be performed in "the sight of the multitude," which is an old-fashioned, if more concrete, way of saying "in public." Private worship performed in public he regarded as constrained either by the laws or by the

From *Propaganda and Communication in World History*, vol. 2, edited by H. D. Lasswell, D. Lerner, and H. Speier. © 1980, University Press of Hawaii. An East-West Center Book. Reprinted by permission.

"opinion of men." Correspondingly, in considering the nature of here-sy, Hobbes remarked that it "signifies no more than private opinion."[2] If we follow the lead Hobbes gives us, we may arrive at an understand-ing of public opinion that makes political sense and is useful for the purposes of this historical review.

Let us understand by public opinion, opinions on matters of con-cern to the nation freely and publicly expressed by men outside the government who claim as a right that their opinions should influence or determine the actions, personnel, or structure of their government. In its most attenuated form this right asserts itself as the expectation that the government will publicly reveal and explain its decisions in order to enable people outside the government to think and talk about these decisions or, to put it in terms of democratic amenities, in order to assure "the success" of the government's policy.

Public opinion, so understood, is primarily a communication from the citizens to their government and only secondarily a communica-tion among the citizens. Further, if a government effectively denies the claim that the opinion of the citizens on public matters be relevant, in one form or another, for policy making or if it prevents the free and public expression of such opinions, public opinion does not exist. There is no public opinion in autocratic regimes; there can only be suppressed, clandestine opinion, no matter how ingenious or careful the government may be in permitting an organized semblance of truly public opinion for the sake of democratic appearances. By way of illustration, no German public opinion existed in occupied Germany after the Second World War under the rule of military governments, despite the speedy liberalization of press and radio in the Western zones, and despite the expression of many opinions in public. This was because the Germans were neither free to act politically according to their own decision, having been deprived of sovereignty, nor free to criticize the actions of the military governments or of the Allied Con-trol Council.

Finally, for public opinion to function, there must be access to information on the issues with which public opinion is concerned. This means, above all, that the actions of the government must not be kept secret. Thus, Jeremy Bentham demanded full publicity for all official acts so that what he called "the tribunal of public opinion" could prevent misrule and suggest legislative reforms. Public commu-nication of governmental acts (*Oeffentlichkeit*) was demanded by the political philosophers of enlightenment. The practice of submitting a budget to popular representatives, if not to the public at large, was established in England by the time of the revolution in 1688 and in France at the time of the French Revolution of 1789. The more democracy progresses and the more intensely public opinion is cherished as a safeguard of morality in politics, the louder become the demands for the abolition of secrecy in foreign policy as well. After the First World War such demands led to the so-called new diplomacy. Under the system of the League, international treaties had to be registered so as to prevent the inclusion of secret clauses.[3]

If public opinion be regarded primarily as a public communication from citizens *to their government*, it may be distinguished from policy counseling by policy advisers or governmental staff members, which is one of the processes of communication bearing on decision making *within the government* (whether it is democratic or not). Public opinion is also distinguished from diplomacy, which may be regarded as communication *among governments*. Finally, one may speak of governmental information and propaganda activities as communications *from a government* to its own citizens, other governmental personnel, or foreign audiences in general.

Public opinion can of course be studied also with a view to what I have called its secondary communications process, that is, with respect to the communications it involves *among the citizens*. In this context questions of the relations between opinion leaders and followers arise, as do problems of the size and anonymity of the public, the competence and representativeness of its organs, the direction and intensity of the interest taken in matters of public concern, the level and organization of public discussions, and so on. On many of these aspects of public opinion our historical knowledge is limited. In the history of public opinion the most conspicuous landmarks are the dates when governments ceased to censor the public expression of political dissent. In France, free communication of thought and opinion was proclaimed as "one of the most valuable of the rights of men" during the Revolution of 1789. In England, censorship in the form of licensing was abolished with less fanfare about a century earlier (1695).

II

Older discussions of our subject do not differ much from modern writings in estimating the influence popular opinions exert upon the actions of men; they differ in assessing the influence popular opinions have or should have upon the actions of statesmen and philosophers. It was common knowledge among older writers that opinions hold sway over the success, conduct, and morals of men. Shakespeare called opinion a mistress of success, and Pascal regarded it as the queen of the world. John Locke pointed out that men judge the rectitude of their actions according to three laws, namely, the divine law, the civil law, and the law of opinion or reputation, which he also called the law of passion or private censure. He attributed overwhelming power to the third law, the law of opinion, because man fears the inexorable operation of its sanctions. Dislike, "ill opinion," contempt, and disgrace, which violators of the law of censure must suffer, force men to conform. When Locke was attacked for his allegedly cynical view of morality, he defended himself by saying that he was not laying down any moral rules but was "enumerating the rules men make use of in moral relations, whether these rules are true or false. . . . I only report as a matter of fact what *others* call virtue and vice."[4]

Locke did not advance the view, however, that popular opinion should govern the actions of government. Characteristically, he used the phrase "the law of *private* censure" as a synonym for "the law of opinion." Moreover, he described the law of opinion "to be nothing else but the consent of private men, *who have not authority enough to make a law*."[5]

Locke did not say that he shared popular opinions about morality. He knew that independent minds examine such opinions, although they cannot lightheartedly provoke the censure of others in whose company they live by showing disregard for what others consider to be right and wrong; the philosophers would otherwise "commit the fault of stubbornness," as Montaigne charmingly put it.[6]

Sir William Temple's essay *On the Original and Nature of Government*, written in 1672, has often been cited as an early discussion of public opinion. Temple observed that it cannot be that "when vast numbers of men submit their lives and fortunes absolutely to the will of one, it should be want of heart, but must be force of custom, or opinion, the true ground and foundation of all government, and that which subjects power to authority. . . . Authority rises from the opinion of wisdom, goodness, and valour in the persons who possess it."[7]

But Temple did not speak of public opinion. He spoke of opinion or "general opinion." In fact, he used the old term "vulgar opinion" when he wished to designate opinions critical of authority. "Nothing is so easily cheated," he said in his essay *Of Popular Discontents*, "nor so commonly mistaken, as vulgar opinion."[8] Temple's concern was with the nature and stability of government. He opposed the contractual theories of government, no matter whether they advanced a sociable or a bellicose view of man in the state of nature. If men were like sheep, he once wrote, he did not know why they needed any government; if they were like wolves, how they could suffer it. Contending that political authority developed out of habits and feelings formed in relation to the father of the family, he regarded opinion as a conserving force that helped the few to govern the many. The word "public," however, he reserved for the common good or the common interest of the nation: the "heats of humours of vulgar minds" would do little harm if governments observed the public good and if they avoided "all councils or designs of innovation."[9] It was precisely such innovation with which public opinion was concerned when it came to be called "public opinion" in the eighteenth century.

Even Rousseau, who put public opinion in its modern political place, demanding that law should spring from the general will, still spoke of opinions also in the traditional, predemocratic way. In his *Nouvelle Héloïse* he equated "public opinion" with vain prejudices and contrasted them with the eternal truths of morality; and in his *Considerations about the Government of Poland* he said: "Whoever makes it his business to give laws to a people must know how to sway opinions and through them govern the passions of men."[10]

The discussions of popular opinions up to the eve of the French Revolution lay much stress upon the power of opinions as means of restricting freedom, upon their prejudicial character, their changeability as to both time and place; they also indicate that men of judgment, whether philosophers or statesmen, deal prudently with popular opinion. Especially during the eighteenth century there are discussions to the effect that governments should take account of popular opinion instead of merely imposing their laws on the people. Finally, in the traditional views popular opinion was seen in close relation to imagination and passions rather than to intelligence and knowledge. Jacques Necker, who was the first writer to popularize the notion and the term "public opinion" throughout Europe at the eve of the French Revolution, still spoke of "imagination and hope" as "the precious precursors of the opinion of men."[11]

It did not occur to older writers that the "multitude" should know more about government than a good ruler, an experienced counselor, or a political philosopher. Only when economic and social inequalities were reduced and the rising elements in the population became unwilling to put up with political inequality could the claim be advanced that the government should make concessions to public opinion. Public opinion is a phenomenon of middle-class civilization. At the end of the ancien régime in France, Count Vergennes, one of M. Necker's colleagues, wrote in a confidential report to the king: "If M. Necker's public opinion were to gain ascendancy, Your Majesty would have to be prepared to see those command who otherwise obey and to see those obey who otherwise command."[12] With reference to Locke's remark about "the law of opinion" one might say that Count Vergennes warned the king of public opinion, because the people who formed it had gained enough authority to make a law.

III

In his fierce criticism of Edmund Burke's ideas on the French Revolution, Thomas Paine remarked that "the mind of the nation had changed beforehand, and the new order of things has naturally followed the new order of thoughts." [13] The observation that the habits of Frenchmen had become republican while their institutions were still monarchical is well sustained by modern research, although it should be borne in mind that it was a numerically small class that had slowly changed its habits.

Lord Acton attributed the growing influence of public opinion in eighteenth-century France to the rise of national debts and the increasing importance of the public creditor.[14] It is curious that this important insight into the origin of public opinion has not led to more detailed research by the historians of public opinion. The history of public opinion has been written primarily with reference to channels of communication, for example, the marketplace in ancient Greece; the theater in Imperial Rome; the sermons, letters, ballads, and travels in the Middle Ages; pamphlets, newspapers, books and lectures, telegraph, radio, film, and television in modern times. We know more about the history of literacy, the press, the law of sedition, and censorship than about the relationship between the struggle for budgetary control and the history of public opinion or about the emergence of social institutions, other than the press, which were instrumental in the political rise of public opinion.

In some older sources the close interconnection between public finance and public opinion is fully recognized. In the French ancien régime publicists and financiers no less than the middle classes at large condemned public loans. Bankruptcy was demanded by courts of justice and by political philosophers like Montesquieu. "It was a reaction against these proposals of bankruptcy that the French constitutions at the end of the eighteenth century proclaimed that the public debt was sacred."[15]

Jacques Necker had occasion to observe as minister of finance that his contemporaries were much concerned with his fiscal policies. He, in turn, regarded it as the "dear object" of his ambition to acquire the good opinion of the public. He contrasted the "extensive horizon" of the public with the court at Versailles, the place of ambition and intrigue, and made the interesting observation that the minister of finance could not consider the court as a "suitable theater" for himself; Versailles, he said, was a place appropriate perhaps for ministers of war, the navy, and foreign affairs, "because all the ideas of military and political glory are more connected with the pageantry of magnificence and power."[16] By contrast, the minister of finance "stands most in need of the good opinion of the people." Necker recommended that fiscal policies should be pursued in "frankness and publicity" and that the finance minister "associate the nation, as it were, in his plans, in his operations, and even in the obstacles that he must surmount."[17] Necker's great contribution to the history of public opinion was not so much what he wrote about its power but rather his important innovation of publishing fiscal statements (*compte rendu*) so that the merits and faults of governmental policy in this field could be appraised in public. He did so "to calm the public which began to distrust the administration of finances and feared that the income of the treasury would not offer any security to the capital and interests of its creditors."[18] Mme de Staël, Necker's daughter, regarded this innovation as an important means for pacifying public opinion. The government, she observed, was forced by its need for public credit not to neglect public opinion; but Necker did not yet hold the view that the general will of the public should take the place of the government. He represents a transitional phase between the predemocratic and the revolutionary–democratic views of public opinion.

The institutional changes that preceded the restriction of absolutist rule and contributed to the rise of public opinion can be stated in this historical sketch only in bare outline. Gains in economic power of the middle class and the gradual spread of literacy are merely two aspects of this process.

The first impetus toward increasing literacy was given by the Reformation, which created a broad reading public seeking edification without the mediation of priests in religious literature written in the vernacular. As Sören Kierkegaard noted with extraordinary perspicacity about Luther, he "unseated the Pope — and put 'the public' on the throne."[19] During the eighteenth century, popular religious literature gradually was replaced by secular reading materials. Content and style of fiction changed in the process. The novel of manners and the episto-lary novel, both primarily addressed to women, made their appear-ance, and the moral concern of the readers was shared by their au-thors. It became possible for them to earn a livelihood by writing. The professionalization of writing was furthered by the breakdown of the patronage system and its replacement by the collective patronage of the anonymous public.[20]

Parallel with the formation of a broader literary public, the middle classes transformed musical life. Public concerts to which an anony-mous audience paid admission fees took the place of concerts given by the personal orchestras at the courts of European rulers and in the luxurious residences of distinguished aristocrats.

The expansion of the reading public was accompanied by the devel-opment of related social institutions such as reading societies, reading clubs, circulating libraries, and secondhand bookstores. The establish-ment of the first circulating library in London coincided with the publication of Richardson's *Pamela*. Secondhand bookstores ap-peared in London during the last third of the eighteenth century. Euro-pean reading societies were influenced by the model of the American subscription libraries, the earliest of which was founded by Franklin in Philadelphia in 1732. Thirty years later there were several *cabinets de lecture* in France, and the first German reading circle seems to have been established in 1772.[21] In addition to fiction—the favorite litera-ture of the ladies—books on history, belles lettres, natural history (that is, science), and statistics were read in these circles. But the favorite reading matter was political journals and scholarly magazines. In fact, the reading societies of the eighteenth century must be considered as the collective patrons of the moral weeklies that contributed so much to the articulation of middle-class opinion on matters of moral con-cern.

In German social history one looks in vain for the social institutions that contributed powerfully to the formation of public opinion in England and France, the coffeehouse and the salon, respectively. Ger-many's middle classes lacked the commercial strength that made the coffeehouse so important in England. In Europe, coffeehouses date back to the middle of the seventeenth century; they became popular as centers of news gathering and news dissemination, political debate, and literary criticism. In the early part of the eighteenth century, Lon-don is said to have had no fewer than two thousand coffeehouses. Addison wanted to have it said of him that he had brought philosophy out of closets and libraries "to dwell in clubs and assemblies, at tea tables and in coffee houses."[22] The English middle classes began to accomplish their own education in the coffeehouses.

Like the history of the coffeehouse in England, that of the French salon goes back to the seventeenth century and even farther to the Italian courts of the Renaissance. In the history of public opinion the French eighteenth-century salons were important because they were the gathering places of intellectually distinguished men and women who cherished conversation, applauded critical sense, and did not regard free thought or irreverent ideas as shocking unless they were advanced pedantically. During the second half of the eighteenth century the salons governed opinion in Paris more effectively than the court. Men of letters were received regardless of their social origin and met on terms of equality with the most enlightened members of society. The salon, a place where talent could expect to outshine ancient titles, was an experiment in equality that assumed paradigmatic importance within a hierarchically organized society.[23] As d'Alembert said in his *Essay upon the Alliance betwixt Learned Men and the Great*, "the man of quality, whose ancestors are his only merit, is of no more consequence in the eye of reason, than an old man returned to infancy, who once performed great things."[24]

In Germany the salon never exercised the influence on the dignity and the literary style of authors or on the manners and opinions of their public that it did in France. Germany was a poor, divided, and in part overmilitarized country; it had neither a Versailles nor a Paris. The social institutions that helped to pave the way toward the social recognition of the ideas of enlightenment in Germany were the predominantly aristocratic language orders of the seventeenth century and the stolid moral and patriotic societies of the eighteenth century in which civil servants played an important role. Both of them may be regarded as forerunners of the Masonic lodges in Germany. They practiced egalitarian rituals, opposed the conventional customs of the courtier, extolled merit and virtue as the new principles of prestige, read and discussed John Locke, and cultivated mutual confidence as a bulwark against the dangerous intrigues in politics.

These institutional changes in European society that led to the emergence of public opinion as a prominent factor in politics may be summed up without regard to national differences as follows. A closed, restricted public gradually developed into an open one, enlarging both its size and its social scope as illiteracy receded. This movement ran its full course only during the nineteenth century. It extended to the lower classes much later than the late eighteenth-century attempts to parade the Third Estate as the nation would make us believe. From the end of the eighteenth century we have glowing accounts of the widespread eagerness of people to read and to learn, but illiteracy was still widespread. It has been estimated that about 57 percent of the men and 27 percent of the women could read and write in France at the time.[25]

Geographically, the process of diffusion spread out from urban centers, with the United States, England, and Germany taking the lead over France, where printing presses as well as the socially influential circles were concentrated in Paris.

The economic and technical landmarks of this process of diffusion are reflected in the cost of mass communication to the poorer classes of society. Here again progress was made more rapidly during the nineteenth century than the eighteenth century. Taxes on newspapers and advertisements were fairly high until 1836 and partly until 1845; the poor could not afford to buy them. Even postal service was not readily available to them until 1839, when penny postage was introduced. Harriet Martineau said at the time that the poor now can "at last write to one another as if they were all M.P.'s."[26]

As regards the men of letters and the publicist, the prerequisite of their wider influence was the recognition of merit as a criterion of social status, so that authors could climb the social ladder regardless of origin merely on the strength of performance. It might be added that the rise of public opinion presupposed a redefinition of scholarship and a program of its missionary diffusion to laymen, a process in which "the world" took the place of "the school' and education became a technique for the establishment of a classless society.

One of the earliest and most radical instances illustrating this missionary zeal can be found in Christian Thomasius' *Einleitung zur Vernunftlehre*, published in 1691. Thomasius believed that it was the result only of differences in social status that not everybody arrived at wisdom; science ought to be the common property of all mankind. Everybody was capable of becoming learned, and the scholar should disseminate rather than attain knowledge.[27] It has been said that Thomasius repeated "the Lutheran teaching of general priesthood in the secularized form of general scholarship."[28]

Thomasius' notion of scholarship is close to Condorcet's doctrine of education or Sieyès' views of public opinion. Condorcet's aim was to render it impossible through education to use the masses as "docile instruments in adroit hands" and to enable them to avoid the "philosophic errors" on which he believed "all errors in government and in society are based,"[29] And Sieyès wrote: "Reason does not like secrets; it is effective only through expansion. Only if it hits everywhere, does it hit right, because only then will be formed that power of public opinion, to which one may perhaps ascribe most of the changes which are truly advantageous to mankind."[30]

IV

The elimination of prejudice, ignorance, and arbitrary government that the advocates of enlightenment wrote upon their banner in order to base the commonwealth upon reason and civic virtue is frequently regarded as a rationalistic program in which no cognizance was taken of the so-called irrational factors of human nature. For this reason, propaganda has often been presented as a counterpart to the process of public opinion. It is erroneous, however, to believe that the advocates of enlightenment neglected or overlooked the emotional facets of life.

The advocates of enlightenment themselves proposed the equation of government with adult education. They suggested, for example, that the government should engage orators for political instruction as it paid priests for religious service (Weckherlin); that attendance of courses on the nature of society should be made obligatory for the acquisition of citizenship (Mercier de la Rivière); that the government should control and publish newspapers to increase loyalty to the sovereign (Quesnay); and that historical works should be written to increase patriotism and national pride (Voss).

Perhaps even more important than these suggestions of political indoctrination were the proposals for the organization of public spectacles and celebrations in order to evoke enthusiasm for common causes and enlist the sentiments of those who did not think. Dupont de Nemours in *Des Spectacles nationaux* developed a theory of national celebrations based on the idea that the desire for pleasure is the driving force of mankind. The people should be brought to develop their patriotic virtues by way of exaltation over public celebrations in which they were to participate—an idea, one might say, that was realized in both the institutionalized public celebrations of the French Revolution and in the Nuremberg festivals of the Nazis or in May Day celebrations. Other writers who pointed to the educational function of national festivals and public plays were Diderot, Condorcet, and Rousseau, and, in Germany, among others, Stephani, Voss, and Zachariä.

In view of these facts it cannot be maintained without qualification that the modern advocates and practitioners of totalitarian government propaganda have superseded the theory and practices of the reformers who helped public opinion on its way to political prominence. It would be more correct to say that the participation of large masses of the population in public affairs, characteristic of both government by public opinion and modern tyranny, is spurious in character under totalitarian regimes in that it is demonstrative rather than determinative of governmental action. It may also be said that in totalitarian regimes mass participation in politics is regarded by the intellectuals as a design to conceal the truth about power processes, whereas in the eighteenth century such participation was considered as a measure toward the ultimate elimination of the irksomeness of power, if not of power itself.

It was believed that man guided by reason and inspired by rectitude would reduce politics to a calculation in happiness and do away with war. Nevertheless, the French Revolution gave rise to war and to war propaganda, and it lifted many restrictions on warfare. It created what William Pitt called "armed opinions" and Jomini "wars of opinion." Liberty, equality, and fraternity were not merely the aims of Frenchmen; they were held to be rights of man regardless of political and national affiliation. The French revolutionary armies did not wage war against other countries but for the liberation of man from old, oppressive governments.[31] Foreign exiles in sympathy with the new regime were admitted to the French clubs, the national guard, and the public departments. They could be found even in the Ministry of Foreign Affairs.[32] They were organized in foreign legions fighting the battle for France. Indeed, the foreigners fighting on the side of the French for the ideas of the French Revolution may be regarded as the prototype of the armed contingents that, hailed by their respective "governments-in-exile," joined the British, American, and Soviet Russian forces of World War II in "the crusade" to end Hitler's tyrannical rule. Similarly, the Girondists imagined that foreign nations in their desire to be delivered from the tyranny of their rulers and priests would rally in support of revolutionary principles. Robespierre's program of April 24, 1793 envisaged a universal republic in which all citizens in all countries would unite against the aristocrats and the tyrants.[33] As Burke pointed out, before the time of the French Revolution there had been no instance "of this spirit of general political factions, separated from religion, pervading several countries, and forming a principle of union between the partisans in each."[34]

It was not only the conquest of foreign territory and the subsequent provisioning of the French armies by plunder, but also revolutionary, cosmopolitan enthusiasm and the leveling of social inequalities that enabled 25 million Frenchmen to defeat a coalition of 75 million enemies. The royalist adversaries put twice the number of soldiers in the field as did the young republic. But although the French armies lost two thirds of their nine thousand royalist officers through defection, the *levée en masse* mobilized hitherto untapped human resources for war. As the Committee of Public Safety decreed in 1793:

> The young men will go to battle; the married men will forego arms and transport food; the women will make the tents, garments, and help in the hospitals; the children will cut old rags into strips; the old men will place themselves in the public squares to influence the courage of the warriors, incite hatred against the kings, and recommend the unity of the Republic.[35]

The most important change in military tactics brought on by revolutionary enthusiasm was the emergence of the *tirailleurs*, marksmen, who aimed their shots at a target instead of relying on volleys, as the disciplined armies of the ancien régime had done. The new tactic was known only from the American War of Independence and, in Europe, from the fighting of the notoriously cruel Pandours of Croatia. Advocates of the old Frederician tactics regarded the behavior of the *tirailleurs* as "militarily superfluous," "politically odious,"[36] and indicative of "the scoundrel hidden in every man."[37] Indeed the new tactic was adopted by the conservative enemies only after their defeat, in Austria (1806) and in Prussia (1809 and 1812).

The leveling of social distinctions in the French nation also affected the status of officers and had repercussions in the logistics of war. In Prussia every lieutenant had two horses, one for riding and one for his baggage, captains could not do without three to five baggage horses each. In the French revolutionary armies no such luxury existed. Privates had to shift without tents, whereas no less than sixty pack horses carrying tents followed each Prussian regiment.[38] In 1806, the French baggage train was one eighth to one tenth that of the Prussians.[39]

In the international turmoil following the French Revolution, the enemies of France were incapable of restricting the war to its former, military dimensions. They responded to the ideological challenge. In

October 1793, His Majesty's Government sent a declaration to the commanders of the British forces in which France was accused of attacks on "the fundamental principles by which mankind is united in the bond of civil society."[40] And William Pitt found the most eloquent expression for the ideological issue raised by the French Revolution. On June 7, 1799 he spoke in the House of Commons, moving that the sum of £825,000 be granted to His Majesty to enable him to fulfill his engagements with Russia. Pitt pointed out that this subsidy would be used for the deliverance of Europe. In reply Mr. Tierney contended that the funds were to be used against the power of France "not merely to repel her within her ancient limits, but to drive her back from her present to her ancient opinion." Mr. Pitt rose once more and said, among other things:

> It is not so. We are not in arms against the opinions of the closet, nor the speculations of the school. We are at war with armed opinion; we are at war with those opinions which the thought of audacious, unprincipled and impious innovations seeks to propagate amidst the ruins of empires, the demolition of the altars of all religion, the destruction of every venerable, and good, and liberal institution, under whatever forms of policy they have been raised; and this, in spite of the dissenting reason of men, in contempt of that lawful authority which, in the settled order, superior talent and superior virtue attain, crying out to them not to enter on holy ground nor to pollute the stream of eternal justice; admonishing them of their danger, whilst, like the genius of evil, they mimic their voice, and, having succeeded in drawing upon them the ridicule of the vulgar, close their day of wickedness and savage triumph with the massacre and waste of whatever is amiable, learned, and pious, in the districts they have overrun.[41]

V

After the Congress of Vienna the utilization of public opinion in international affairs became, as it were, respectable also among statesmen who did not pursue any revolutionary cause. Once the importance of public opinion was discovered as a new factor in international relations, it became tempting on moral as well as on expediential grounds to utilize it. Neither Canning, who believed that public opinion should be invoked in the pursuit of British foreign policy, nor Palmerston, who held that public opinion founded on truth and justice would prevail against the force of armies, realized that they were continuing to revolutionize European diplomacy by their actions. A diplomat of the old school like Metternich was appalled by Canning's enthusiasm and could see only preposterous folly in the Englishman's notion of public opinion as "a power more tremendous than was perhaps ever yet brought into action in the history of mankind."[42]

The art of arousing public opinion nevertheless became a valued skill during the nineteenth century even of statesmen like Bismarck, who failed to respect public opinion, remained indifferent to its moral claims, and made no attempt to raise its level of competence. Bismarck condemned policies inspired by sentiments or moods. He regarded public opinion as dependent, to a large extent, on mood and sentiment, incapable of the calm calculations that had to precede political decisions. Nor did he believe in the political insight of public opinion. "As a rule," he said, "public opinion realizes the mistakes that have been committed in foreign policy only when it is able to review in retrospect the history of a generation."[43] Given the political constitution of Prussia and the Reich, Bismarck could afford to make foreign policy against public opinion, if he regarded such action as necessary and if he had the confidence of his monarch. Thus, in 1866 he waged war against the will of almost all Prussians, but he also refused to risk war against Russia by interfering in Bulgaria, a course rashly sponsored by the liberal press. Similarly, in the Boer War, Chancellor von Bülow disregarded German public opinion, which strongly favored interference, in the well-considered interest of the country.

The scope of governmental influence upon public opinion was limited throughout the nineteenth century and, if compared with recent activities in this regard, had an almost patrimonial character. In nineteenth-century Europe public opinion was a synonym of opinions expressed by the political representatives of the electorate, by newspapers, and by prominent members or organizations of the middle class. In England their faith in the beneficial effects of discussion and the persuasiveness of liberal opinion upon conduct of domestic affairs grew particularly under the influence of Bentham and his followers.[44] Toward the end of the nineteenth century, Lord Bryce pointed out that in England the landowners and "the higher walks of commerce" not only form the class which furnish the majority of members of both houses but also express what is called public opinion. He held that in Germany, Italy, and France as well public opinion was "substantially the opinion of the class which wears black coats and lives in good houses."[45] He contrasted these conditions with those prevailing in the United States, where he believed government by public opinion to exist, because "the wishes and views of the people prevail even before they have been conveyed through the regular law-appointed organs."[46]

Like de Tocqueville and other nineteenth-century writers,[47] Lord Bryce recognized the decisive importance of class distinctions in limiting participation in public opinion, although he failed to appreciate the limiting influence upon public opinion exercised by pressure groups in the United States. He also lacked the perspicacity of de Tocqueville, who detected the threats to freedom of thought that public opinion in conditions of social equality presents. Reactionaries, romantics, Saint-Simonians, and Marxists attacked liberal convictions and threw doubt upon the morality, disinterestedness, and representativeness of middle-class opinions in the nineteenth century. They were not concerned, however, with freedom of thought; they contributed, in fact, to its modern decline. De Tocqueville, however, clearly saw that in "ages of equality" the liberation of the people from ignorance and prejudice by enlightenment may be purchased at the price of equalizing thought.

> There is, and I cannot repeat it too often, there is here matter for profound reflection to those who look upon freedom of thought as a holy thing and who hate not only the despot, but despotism. For myself, when I feel the hand of power lie heavy on my brow, I care but little to know who oppresses me; and I am not the more disposed to pass beneath the yoke because it is held out to me by the arms of millions of men.[48]

Perhaps the most wrathful condemnation of public opinion and its architects, the journalists, was advanced by Sören Kierkegaard. It shocked him deeply that a single person should be able every week or every day to get forty thousand or fifty thousand readers to speak or think like him.[49] His shock might have been cushioned, had he known that the ways men act — to judge by political elections in nineteenth-century Europe as well as twentieth-century America — do not necessarily reflect the preferences of the press they read.

NOTES

1. Thomas Hobbes, *Leviathan*, vol. 2, p. 31.
2. Ibid, vol. 2, p. 11.
3. For a discussion of secrecy in international negotiations versus secrecy of international agreements see, Harold Nicolson, *Diplomacy* (London, 1939), and *Peacemaking 1919*, New York, 1939, pp. 123ff.
4. John Locke, "The Epistle to the Reader," in *An Essay Concerning Human Understanding*, ed. by A. C. Fraser, Oxford, 1894, vol. 1, p. 18. The italics are Locke's.
5. Ibid., book 2, chap. 28, section 12. My italics.
6. Montaigne, *Essays*, book 3, chap. 8.

7. *The Works of Sir William Temple: A New Edition*, London, 1814, vol. 1, pp. 6–7.

8. Ibid., vol. 3, p. 39.

9. Ibid., p. 44.

10. Rousseau regarded public opinion as "the standard of free society," but as questionable from a "transpolitical point of view." See Leo Strauss, "On the Intention of Rousseau," *Social Research* 14 (December 1947):473.

11. J. Necker, *A Treatise on the Administration of the Finances of France*, 3rd ed., London, 1787, vol. 1, p. 17. The two best expositions of the treatment of "opinion" and "public opinion" by political theorists are Paul A. Palmer, "The Concept of Public Opinion in Political Theory," in *Essays in History and Political Theory in Honor of Charles H. McIlwain*, Cambridge, Mass., 1936, and Hermann Oncken, "Politik, Geschichtsschreibung und öffentliche Meinung," in *Historisch-politische Aufsätze und Reden*, Berlin and Munich, 1914, vol. 1, pp. 203–44. See also Wilhelm Hennis, "Zum Begriff der öffentlichen Meinung," in *Politik als praktische Wissenschaft*, Munich, 1968, pp. 36–48.

12. Cited from Soulavie's *Mémoires historiques*, in Ferdinand Tönnies, *Kritik der öffentlichen Meinung*, Berlin, 1922, p. 385.

13. Thomas Paine, *Rights of Men*, Modern Library edition, p. 141.

14. Lord Acton, "The Background of the French Revolution," reprinted in *Essays on Freedom and Power*, ed. by Gertrude Himmelfarb, Boston, 1948, p. 267.

15. Gaston Jèze, "Public Debt," in *Encyclopaedia of the Social Sciences*, vol. 12, p. 602. Cf. Thomas Paine's remark: "The French nation, in effect, endeavored to render the late government insolvent for the purpose of taking government into its own hands: and it reversed its means for the support of the new government." Paine, p. 175.

16. Necker, p. 54.

17. Ibid., p. 73.

18. August Wilhelm Rehberg, *Über die Staatsverwaltung deutscher Länder*, Hanover, 1809, p. 58.

19. Sören Kierkegaard, *Die Tagebücher*, selected and translated by Theodor Haecker, Innsbruck, 1923, vol. 2, p. 340.

20. See Charlotte E. Morgan, *The Rise of the English Novel of Manners*, New York, 1911; Leo Lowenthal, *Literature, Popular Culture and Society*, Englewood Cliffs, N.J., 1961; Martin Greiner, *Die Entstehung der modernen Unterhaltungsliteratur; Studien zum Trivialroman des 18. Jahrhunderts*, Hamburg, 1964.

21. Walter Götze, *Die Begründung der Volksbildung in der Aufklärungsbewegung*, Berlin and Leipzig, 1932, p. 64.

22. On the history of coffeehouses in England, see E. F. Robinson, *The Early History of Coffee Houses in England*, London, 1893; Ralph Nevill, *London Clubs: Their History and Treasures*, London, 1911; Hermann Westerfrölke, *Englische Kaffeehäuser als Sammelpunkte der literarischen Welt im Zeitalter von Dryden und Addison*, Jena, 1924.

23. See Helen Clergue, *The Salon: A Story of French Society and Personalities in the Eighteenth Century*, New York and London, 1907; Erich Auerbach, *Das französische Publikum des XVII. Jahrhunderts*, Munich, 1933; Chauncey B. Tinker, *The Salon and English Letters*, New York, 1915; Conférences du Musée Carnavalet, *Les grands salons littéraires*, Paris, 1928.

24. Jean d'Alembert, *Miscellaneous Pieces in Literature, History and Philosophy*, London, 1764, p. 149.

25. As Aulard has pointed out, "It was by the political song, sung in the theatre, in the cafés and in the street, that the Royalists and Republicans succeeded, principally at Paris, in influencing the people," during the French Revolution. Quoted by Cornwall B. Rogers, *The Spirit of Revolution in 1789*, Princeton, N.J., 1949, p. 26. This book is a monographic study of the propagandistic importance of oral communication, especially lyrics, during the French Revolution.

26. Quoted by Howard Robinson, *The British Post Office*, Princeton, N.J., 1948, p. 302.

27. In chapter 13, Thomasius discussed the origin of error, distinguishing between the "prejudice of human authority" and "the prejudice of precipitation." See the reprint of this chapter as well as the equally relevant chap. 1 of Thomasius' *Ausübung der Sittenlehre* (1696), in F. Brüggemann, ed., *Aus der Frühzeit der deutschen Aufklärung*, Deutsche Literatur, Sammlung literarischer Kunst-und Kulturdenkmäler, Reihe Aufklärung, vol. 1, Berlin and Leipzig, 1928. For the relation between prejudice and the demand for enlightening education, cf. especially Thomas Hobbes, *Elements of Law*, ed. by Ferdinand Tönnies, London, 1889: "The immediate cause . . . of indocibility is prejudice; and of prejudice, false opinion of our own knowledge" (I, 10, section 8), and *Leviathan*, chaps. 13 and 15.

28. Götze, p. 20.

29. For a convenient summary of Condorcet's views on education contained in his "Report on Education," presented to the Legislative Assembly on April 20–21, 1792, see Salwyn Schapiro, *Condorcet*, New York, 1934, chap. 11, pp. 196–214. On the educational views of leading writers in the eighteenth century, see F. de la Fontainerie, ed., *French Liberalism and Education in the Eighteenth Century*, New York, 1932.

30. Sieyès, *The Third Estate*, chap. 6.

31. According to Alexis de Tocqueville, the Revolution "a considéré le citoyen d'une façon abstraite, en dehors de toutes les sociétés particulières, de même que les religions considérent l'homme en général indépendamment du pays et du temps." *L'Ancien Régime et la Révolution*, 8th ed., Paris, 1877, p. 18.

32. Albert Mathiez, *The French Revolution,* New York, 1928, p. 217.

33. Corneliu S. Blaga, *L'Évolution de la technique diplomatique au dixbuitième siècle*, Paris, 1937, p. 421.

34. Edmund Burke, "Thoughts on French Affairs," in *Reflections on the French Revolution and Other Essays*, Everyman's Library edition, p. 289.

35. Quoted in Shelby C. Davis, *The French War Machine*, p. 100.

36. Max Lehmann, *Scharnhorst*, Leipzig, 1886, vol. 1, p. 323.

37. Hans Delbrück, *Geschichte der Kriegskunst*, Berlin, 1920, vol. 4, p. 469.

38. Ibid., p. 461.

39. Ibid., p. 479.

40. Quoted in W. Allison Hillet and Arthur H. Reede, *Neutrality*, vol. 2: *The Napoleonic Period*, New York, 1936, p. 8.

41. *British Historical and Political Orations from the 12th to the 20th Century*, Everyman's Library edition, pp. 146 48.

42. Nicolson, p. 73.

43. Bismarck, *Memoirs*, vol. 3, p. 157.

44. The Benthamites did not share the belief in natural rights. Bentham had deplored the Declaration of Rights in France because he regarded them as metaphysical and

did not believe that political science was far enough advanced for such declarations. Cf. A. V. Dicey, *Law and Opinion in England*, New York, 1930, p. 145, n. 1.

45. Lord Bryce, *The American Commonwealth*, New York, 1919, vol. 2, p. 260.

46. Ibid., p. 257.

47. Thus Bluntschli in his *Staatswörterbuch* (1862), said of public opinion that "it is predominantly the opinion of the large middle class." This notion was predicated upon the conviction that public opinion was a matter of free judgment. "Without training of the reasoning power and the capacity to judge there is, therefore, no public opinion." For the same reason, Bluntschli observed that public opinion is possible in political matters but alien to religious piety (*Ergriffenheit*). Cf. Oncken, pp. 229ff.

48. Alexis de Tocqueville, *Democracy in America*, New York, 1948, vol. 2, pp. 11–12.

49. *Kierkegaard in 1849*; cf. *Kierkegaard*, vol. 2, p. 37.

8

Psychological Warfare

Inadequacies of the Term "Psychological Warfare"

The term psychological warfare has gained wide currency in popular and scientific discussions, but its meaning is not clear. For three reasons the term is debated among those who use it freely.

First, warfare cannot readily be expected to be waged in times of peace or, for that matter, against the populations of neutral and allied countries in wartime, unless it is felt that by virtue of being "psychological" this kind of warfare is not "real" warfare. During the Second World War, psychological warfare was indeed regarded primarily as a responsibility of the military who fought the enemy, whereas the civilian Office of War Information never officially professed before the Congress and the public its concern with it. Soon after the end of the war the relationship between the Soviet Union and the Western powers began to be characterized as a state of cold war — incidentally no less ambiguous a term than "psychological warfare" — but while, according to many observers of the international scene, the traditional distinction between war and peace cannot be applied in the postwar period, no government involved in the cold war has as yet stated that it is

First published in Hans Speier, *Social Order and the Risks of War*, New York, 1952. Copyright © 1952 by George W. Stewart, Publisher, Inc. First M.I.T. Press paperback edition March 1969. Reprinted by permission of M.I.T. Press.

engaged in psychological warfare against other nations. Rather, there is talk of "international information" and, reluctantly, of propaganda.

Second, the terms "psychological warfare" and "political warfare" (as the British prefer to call their activities in this field) are misleading if they designate exclusively propaganda to enemy countries in times of war. Wars are waged against enemies in order to defeat them; yet during a war, psychological warfare comprises not only ancillary activities to the same end by certain nonlethal means but also actions which attempt to reach and make friends in the enemy camp.

For yet a third reason, the term psychological warfare is easily misunderstood. When it is used as a synonym for combat propaganda and related activities in wartime, it seems to be implied that other forms of warfare have no psychological effects, but only physical consequences, and are conducted without regard for the mind of the enemy and the moral forces at his command. In this context, then, psychological warfare emerges as a specialized activity which injects into the "unpsychological" wars of the machine age the recollection and rediscovery of man as the agent of aggression, the object of suffering, the human element in bureaucratized strategy and industrialized battles.[1]

The ambiguities of meaning from which the term psychological warfare suffers stem from the lack of a more basic agreement on the nature of war. It is inadvisable as well as tedious to begin this reconsideration of psychological warfare with a proposal of new definitions. The following discussion will cover activities which the reader should feel free to include or exclude from the field of psychological warfare as he delimits it. Fortunately, it will be possible to engage in this inquiry without using the word "psychological" at all.

The Ability and the Will to Fight

Military writers are in the habit of distinguishing between the ability and the will to fight. An enemy can be defeated by destroying his capability of resistance, but failing this he will also succumb when his will to fight is broken. These two elements of war are not independent of one another. The will to fight is likely to be stronger if the ability to fight, compared with that of the enemy, promises a chance of success. Capability counts for nothing, however, if resolution to use it is wanting, and within certain limits strong will can offset the disadvantage of inferior capability, particularly when the opponent's resolution and perseverance do not match his superiority of force.

Incapacitation of the enemy by destruction, conquest of territory, capture or denial of men and material, blockade, etc., and incapacitation by demoralizing the enemy are two roads to victory. To assume that only destruction wins wars is tantamount to denying the intellectual and moral elements in war. It is obvious that demoralization, that is, breaking the will to resist, may in turn be achieved by physical destruction, but statesmen and generals throughout the ages have also used less crude and more ingenious means to win wars. The amount and kind of destruction necessary for victory varies not only with the state of technology but also with the political conduct of the war.

The distinction between capability and will can be profitably applied to the analysis of international relations in times of peace, since in peace as well as in war the status of nations depends upon their ability and their will to change or maintain the prevailing distribution of power. Organized violence by means of military power is not brought to bear upon other nations in times of peace. For the citizen life is safer and more comfortable than it is in wartime. His risk of suffering violent death is low and so are, relatively speaking, his deprivations. The potential use of organized violence, however, bears on the policies which are pursued in peacetime. The same holds true of scientific and technological developments which affect the protective and striking power of arms; of threats, warnings, denunciations of their possible use; of demonstrations that they exist and are efficient; of reorganizations and redispositions of the available forces; and of partial mobilizations. Nor are the other instruments of international policy invariably and exclusively reserved for either wartime or peacetime use: diplomacy, espionage, counterintelligence, economic measures, organizational activities ("fifth columns"), propaganda—all these means are used in the pursuit of international policy in peace as well as in war. The erroneous opinion that the employment of any of these instruments is confined to wartime breeds illusions about the nature of peace, impairs the pursuit of foreign policy goals in peacetime and may render wars, when they come, more ferocious. It is quite possible that the recent popularity of the term "cold war" indicates not only the precarious nature of the postwar relations among the great powers allied during part of World War II but also the unjustified demand that peacetime relations ought not to reflect a struggle for power.

There are, of course, secular trends in the use and function of the instruments of policy. Military force has been applied with fewer political and moral restrictions in the wars of the twentieth century than in the conflicts of the two preceding centuries. Correspondingly, the function of diplomacy in eighteenth-century international affairs was more continuous, that is, less subject to modification and disruption by war, than has been true in the twentieth century. The effort of all great nations during the last four decades in using propaganda as an instrument of foreign policy in peace as well as in wartime has been more formidable than the effort these nations made in this field during the preceding four decades.

Regardless of secular trends in the use of foreign policy instruments and regardless of the different modes of their employment in war and peace, war is not a state of affairs in which military force replaces all other means of policy. Nor is the state of international affairs in periods of peace independent of the balance of national war potentials. The national ability to attain or defend positions of international power, which is put to a test in war, influences the state of peace. So does the will to resist or commit aggression. But it now is necessary to determine more closely what "will" means in this context.

The Will to Fight Reconsidered

Unless we ascertain *whose will* we have in mind when speaking of "the will to fight" we are in danger of committing an anthropomorphic fallacy: clearly, not everybody in a nation at war is really fighting. Unless we ascertain further what is being done and "willed" by those who are not fighting as the nation pursues a given course of action, we miss the various *aims* of "the will" that matter: evidently, not only "the will to *fight*" is necessary for victory. Finally, if we are satisfied with the simple juxtaposition of "capability" and "will," we neglect the intellectual functions in warfare and peacetime foreign affairs: there must be knowledge and thought if a will is to use means for a purpose. The following discussion will attempt to clarify these three issues.

If wars were still waged by armed forces alone and if their leaders could count on blind obedience to command, the only will to fight that would count would be that of the officers—a situation which was approximated in the European wars of the eighteenth century prior to the French Revolution. Soldiers then were disciplined, unhappy, and more afraid of their own superiors than of the enemy. Nor did they depend at that time on a continuous flow of freshly-produced supplies to replenish and improve their arms and ammunitions while the war lasted.

Today, war efforts can no longer be sustained from arsenals or loans with which to buy foreign manpower and available weapons. The physical resources of the country must be exploited and the human resources of the whole nation be mobilized in order to insure survival in large-scale war. A large part of the noncombatant population must be put to work in order to equip and reequip, arm and rearm the fighting forces of the nation. The industrialization of the economy has changed both the standard of living and the standard of dying. The functional role of the noncombatants in the war effort is buttressed by widespread emotional participation and intellectual interest in the war, which rarely existed prior to the modern nationalistic, literate, age. Finally, civilians as well as the armed forces are exposed to the danger of violent death, since the modern means of destruction permit attacks on the enemy's sources of armament, the urban centers of his industrial war production.

The will to fight is essentially a *will to work* on the part of the civilians in a nation at war. Moreover, while both combatants and noncombatants must be ready to die and suffer deprivation (regardless of any attractions and profits war may offer to some of them), the latter do not need to have a will to kill; the former do. They are victims rather than executioners of violent death. These differences have an important bearing on any intelligent enemy effort to break the national will to resist, and require differentiated warfare.

The large noncombatant part of the population comprises at least four general classes of persons, which are of importance to this analysis.

There are, first, those who hold political power—the political elite. Assuming that they, rather than the rulers of the military hierarchy, determine the policy of the nation as a whole, their "will to fight" is of supreme importance indeed at the outbreak of war, for the conduct of the war, and for its conclusion. Similarly, they are responsible in times of peace for the international policy which the nation "as a whole" pursues. But this elite cannot be said to have a will to fight (or not to fight) in the same sense in which such will is asserted in combat. It is more appropriate to speak of the elite's function to decide what is to be done by the nation. Here we are primarily concerned with elite decisions in the field of foreign policy; but the relative stability of the domestic regime bears upon the process in which these decisions are made, and its outcome. The conduct of foreign affairs requires, of course, elite decisions which affect the domestic conditions of life, so that the stability of the regime necessarily narrows or widens the scope of choices which confronts the decision-making elite. Instead of ascribing to the political elite a will to fight (or not to fight) we shall therefore speak of its *ability to govern* (at home)—taking it for granted that they have a will to do so if they can — and its *deciding of foreign policy*.

Those who hold power govern by means of staffs and control personnel; this personnel will be considered here as part of the elite. The function of this auxiliary personnel is to render it possible for the elite to avoid foolish decisions[2] and to see to it that decisions, whether foolish or not, are acted upon, once they are made. Among other things, the elite relies on foreign intelligence about capabilities and intentions of other powers, domestic intelligence on the stability of the regime and the capabilities of the country, advice in estimating the consequences of alternative foreign and domestic policies, control and suppression of domestic opposition (however defined), and communication with other groups holding less power. Note that the disruption of any of these functions impairs the elite's ability to govern and to make sound decisions, possibly with repercussions on the political elite itself, and particularly in times of war, on the nation as a whole.

The second and largest group of the noncombatants will be considered here as a unit and be called the working populations. Its function in modern war has been mentioned. It must have "the will to work." In addition, the working population is required to obey the laws of the country. To the extent that the political elite has authority, instead of merely exercising its rule by means of sanctions, the working population may, therefore, be said to have also a *will to obey* (or not to obey) the law of the elite.

The will to obey meets the minimum requirements of efficiency and authority, but in a well functioning society the working population does in fact always perform "above and beyond the call of duty." If the performance is reduced to mere obedience to orders the control functions of the auxiliary elite personnel are inevitably overloaded.

The relation between the political elite and the working population varies, of course, with the formal and informal political structure of the state. The bearing which this fact has on attempts to break the will to work and the will to obey will be discussed in due course.

The working population comprises people of different skills. Persons of high skill are scarcer than persons of low skill. The loss of experts to the community through death, abduction, desertion, or disloyalty, therefore, has grave consequences since they cannot be replaced easily. The top group of such "irreplaceable" skilled specialists within the working population, including selected scientists, administrators, businessmen, inventors, intelligence experts, engineers, and so on, form the civilian key personnel. Like the working population to which they belong, the civilian key personnel must be willing to *work and obey*. Any successful enemy effort to weaken their will to work and obey, which is especially directed at this part of the community, is likely to have particularly high returns not only because substitutes for key personnel are difficult to find but also because malfunctioning members in this group affect the operations of many others. Inefficiency of a charwoman is a nuisance, that of a top administrator a calamity. Moreover, many persons in key positions possess knowledge of high intelligence value. If they become talkative or disloyal, their value to the enemy as a source of information may exceed the value of their elimination.[3]

The noncombatants include a number of dependents, whose age or state of health makes them worthless to the war effort. Their will does not matter. The graphic military term for describing such dependents under conditions of siege warfare will here be used: these noncombatants are useless mouths (*bouches inutiles*).[4] While useless, such mouths may cry or sing and thus affect the feelings and actions of those who care for them.

Corresponding to the distinction between political elite and working population, we shall speak of military elite and fighting population in the combatant sector of the nation. (There are no military useless mouths, unless one were to regard nonfatal casualties as such.)

It will be assumed that the military elite determines military strategy and tactics in accordance with foreign policy decided by the political elite.[5] Under this assumption, the military elite has a *will to obey* the political elite or must expect sanctions in case of disobedience. In this respect the military elite does not differ in principle from the working and fighting populations. As the military elite holds power over the latter, however, it must have *ability to command* (corresponding to the ability to govern of the political elite). Furthermore, since the military elite and its staffs plan and execute military operations, we shall speak of its *determination of military missions* to attain policy goals. Finally, it shares with the fighting population the *will to fight* (or not to fight), although it should be observed that a large part of this elite holds planning, administrative, and other posts which in some ways resemble top positions in civilian life.

Strictly speaking, the *will to obey* military superiors (and to act "above and beyond the call of duty") is of greater importance than the will to fight even in the fighting population, inasmuch as under modern conditions of warfare the majority of those "under arms" does not fight the enemy but supports combat troops which do.[6] This division of labor, or rather of the broad combatant function, is reflected in the differential casualty rates of various services and branches in the armed forces. Thus, the Infantry in the U.S. Army, while constituting about 10 percent of the strength of the Army, accounted for 70 percent of all the battle casualties in World War II.[7] In planning combat propaganda this stratified distribution of risks, which is associated to a significant extent with differences in social recruitment and civilian background, merits close study, but for present purposes the whole combatant part of the population will be held to possess a will to fight (or not to fight).[8]

There are of course rare and common skills in the fighting population as well as among noncombatants, and the existence of key military personnel, distinguished by high skill and highly specialized training, needs special attention. Tribute has often been paid to these experts, because their contributions to war efforts are great. The function of key combatant personnel in war seems to have increased with increasing industrialization of warfare. Illustrations abound: the German shock troops introduced at the end of the First World War after the collapse of linear infantry tactics, the fighter pilots who defended the British Isles in the battle of Britain in 1940, commandos, airborne contingents, etc. An extreme case has been related in Churchill's account of the Second World War. In March 1941 the British succeeded in sinking the German submarine U-47 commanded by "the redoubtable Prien" as well as U-99 and U-100 commanded by two other "tiptop" officers. "The elimination of these three able men," Churchill comments, "had a marked effect on the progress of the struggle."[9]

In summary, a glance at the broadest outline of the functional and political structure of the nation at war has led to a considerable refinement of the notion with which we started and which plays so important a role in psychological warfare. The general notion of "the will to fight" has been replaced by six factors. Consequently, there are six ways of weakening "the will to resist," namely, interference with:

1. the deciding of foreign policy (by the political elite),
2. the determination of military missions (by the military elite),
3. the ability to govern (of the political elite),
4. the ability to command (of the military elite),
5. the will to obey (of the military elite, the working population and the fighting population),
6. the will to fight (of the military elite and the fighting population).

If the indispensable functions of the auxiliary personnel attached to the elites are borne in mind, it appears that hostile action against foreign political and military elites can be taken especially by interfering with:

a. intelligence on foreign capabilities and intentions,
b. intelligence on domestic capabilities and obedience,
c. estimates of the consequences of alternative policies,
d. control of the working and fighting populations and of the military elite by the political elite,
e. communication with these groups.

Finally, we have found that combatant and noncombatant key personnel is crucial for the functioning of society in peace and war and thus a rewarding target in the international struggle for power. This is due to the fact that key personnel is difficult to replace and often possesses information of high intelligence value.

The Democratic Fallacy in Mass Propaganda

The political influence which the mass of the population is constitutionally able to exert upon the elite, that is, their recruitment and their decisions, determines in large part the structure of the political community. Account must be taken of this structure in the international struggle for power. When the political regime is despotic, the mass of the population has no chance of affecting the recruitment of the elite, filling vacant elite positions, and passing public judgment on elite decisions. In modern despotism, that is, in totalitarian regimes, the political elite disseminates its *exoteric* opinions to the masses of the population. Moreover, the population is tightly organized and thus controlled. All deviant political opinions are either *esoteric*, or are in any case kept secret, because of terroristic measures against those who are alleged to lean toward heresy.

An understanding, however false, of domestic and international events of the past and the future is offered through an official "ideology" — a phenomenon absent in older tyrannies. These ideologies also contain the political definitions of friend and foe, law and moral standards. The ideology invests reality with meaning, however simplified, and provides the masses of the population with permitted language. Ideologies are therefore a comfort in a world which appears incomprehensible and menacing without them. As the political elite blankets the area it controls with approved opinions fitting into the official ideology,[10] it offers security, however costly, to the minds of all as it stabilizes the regime.

In view of these considerations it is folly to expect that the dissemination of another ideology by foreign propagandists can convert the masses of a population living under despotic rule to become adherents to a new ideology or to shake off the shackles of ideology altogether.

The political elite is on guard against the emergence of counterelites, that is, those aspirants to power who attempt to reach their goals against the will of the ruling elite. In despotic regimes counterelites, like less consequential opposition, can operate only underground or abroad.

The subordinate military elite is regarded as a potential counterelite by those who hold supreme power. It is, therefore, distrusted, infiltrated, controlled, and purged from time to time. In the Soviet Union so large a proportion of senior officers were liquidated before the outbreak of the Second World War that the efficiency of Soviet military power was considered in the West to be seriously impaired.[11] Similarly, the national socialist leaders fought more relentlessly against the German military elite than the resistance of its members to Hitler's regime seemed to warrant.[12]

Since in modern societies the mass of the population cannot overthrow, or actively influence the policies of, despotic regimes without armed domestic or foreign support and without organized leadership, the population at large is no rewarding target of conversion propaganda from abroad. Any notion to the contrary may be called the democratic fallacy of democratic propagandists who disregard the differences in political structure between the regimes under which they and their audiences live.

The will to obey and work, or at least the inclinations to progress "above and beyond the call of duty," will be weakened as satisfaction with the regime is lessened; but such demoralization is not likely to be furthered by conversion propaganda and may in fact be hindered by it. Dissatisfaction with the regime may result from experiencing deprivations which are unexpected and regarded as unnecessary, futile, or unjust. Such experience is not likely to be sharpened by the promotion of strange beliefs, that is, by ideological propaganda.

Ideological propaganda to the mass of the population living in despotic regimes is sometimes advocated because of the cumulative effect it is alleged to have. As its effect increases over a period of time, it is presumed to lead to explosive action. Evidence for this proposition is lacking.[13] Politically relevant mass action presupposes the destruction or disorganization of controls by means other than propaganda, especially military force or subversion. It also requires leadership by a counterelite. The control apparatus at the disposal of the elite may crumble in consequence of disruption from without and within but hardly on account of attempts at converting those who are controlled.

Similar considerations apply to combat propaganda directed at the fighting population. Without prejudice to the need for propaganda directed at the combatant population in time of peace and during a war in stalemate and defeat situations, there can be little doubt that the wartime conditions favoring success of such propaganda are military superiority, victory, pursuit, and stalemate. A propagandist speaking for the side that retreats, has lost a battle, or is militarily weak, must fight uphill. Propaganda in war is an auxiliary weapon. Auxiliary weapons cannot turn the wheel of fortune if the main weapons are blunt, scarce, or lost.

Deviant Political Behavior and Its Inducement

In the conduct of psychological warfare sight must never be lost of the fact that a change in attitudes and private opinions amounts to little if it fails to result in deviant, politically relevant behavior.[14]

Generally speaking, deviant, politically relevant behavior comprises all action which weakens the ability of the elites to govern and command. In war, those who fight may cease fighting, fight their own authorities and resist the enemy inefficiently. Those who work or fight may give information to the enemy, cooperate with him by fighting on his side once they are taken prisoner or have deserted. Members of the working population may slow down in their work or commit sabotage, spread rumors, organize those who are disaffected, engage in illegal activities, etc.

Like mutiny in the armed forces, revolution at home or secession under the leadership of a counterelite are the most dramatic instances of disorder, weakening the regime or incapacitating it to pursue its foreign policy.

The conditions of politically relevant actions taken by the working population and by those who fight differ significantly in one respect. The latter have, in favorable military circumstances, a chance, however small, to desert or surrender to the enemy if their will to fight is broken. By contrast, the working population has no such opportunities. There is no line its members can cross in order to get out of the war. Once an enemy soldier deserts or surrenders, he increases his chance of survival. If an enemy worker wants to disobey his authorities, he cannot avail himself of the protection of foreign powers; as a rule, not doing what his authorities expect and want him to do considerably decreases the margin of his safety and adds to his chance of violent death by enemy action the risk of losing his life through sanctions by the domestic police.

It is not certain that military personnel can desert more easily in times of peace than in wartime: its moves can be supervised and controlled more closely in garrisons. For example, while the defections of Soviet soldiers during World War II surpassed in magnitude those of any other belligerent nation, the Soviet armed forces stationed in occupied countries after the war live in so strictly enforced isolation from their foreign environment that desertions are rare.

Civilians can leave their country more easily in peace time, despite emigration and immigration laws which restrict such movements particularly from and to countries with despotic regimes. The only groups with ample opportunities to defect are diplomatic and other personnel, including individuals belonging to the civilian key personnel, whose business takes them abroad.

Some of the deviant, politically relevant actions do not require joint efforts but can be taken individually, others cannot possibly succeed without organization. The power interested in breaking or weakening the will to obey must give thought to the *organizational requirements* of the deviant behavior it tries to induce, and to the magnitude of the *risks* incurred by such behavior.

Finally, intelligence estimates must be made of the *self-interests* of enemy noncombatants and combatants in deviant behavior, since these interests may be compatible with the interests pursued by the rival foreign power itself. Such compatibility signifies what may be called the chance of alliance in noncombat warfare, and it is a matter of elementary statesmanship to assess the political worth of its exploitation.

Not much need be said here about the measures the rival power can take to help meet the *organizational requirements* of deviant behavior in an enemy regime. These measures range from the formation of counterelites abroad (governments-in-exile) to their clandestine or overt support if they operate in the enemy country; from giving material aid and organizational assistance to the opposition in the enemy camp (such as arms and communications facilities) to assigning liaison personnel[15] or leadership to them[16]; from advice to bide time to strategic coordination of joint, foreign and domestic, moves against the regime.

Intelligent noncombat warfare attempting to induce deviant actions in the enemy camp must try to reduce the *risks* of such actions and show awareness of the irreducible risks even in its propaganda. Since in war some of these risks can be curtailed by foreign military action, coordination of the use to which the various instruments of policy are put is of great importance if good will, that is, the will to disobey, in the enemy camp is not to be lost. Apart from military damage to the control apparatus, there are three principal ways of reducing the risks of deviant behavior.

1. Psychological warfare can be careful to encourage only such actions which in view of the prevailing conditions are feasible without decimating the "resistance" in the enemy camp. If this care is not taken, the directors of the psychological warfare effort will appear either stupid or callous and lose whatever influence they are able to wield abroad.

2. By the same token, psychological warfare can warn "allies" in the enemy camp of perils which threaten them. For example, RIAS (Radio in the American Sector of Berlin) broadcasts to the Soviet zone of Germany the names of informers so that anticommunists can be on guard against them. Moreover, specific advice can be given on how to minimize or avoid the hazards of deviant behavior. To cite a case of dubious value, during the last war soldiers were occasionally informed by the enemy how to produce undetectable symptoms of disease which would put them on the sick roll.

3. Instead of attempting to induce deviant behavior in the enemy population at large—a practice predicated on the absurd assumption that whole populations are imbued with the spirit of heroism and self-sacrifice—psychological warfare can concentrate on selected groups whose self-interest, predispositions, and organization are conducive to deviation. Work with and through existing cells of resistance and disaffected parts of the population is likely to be more effective and will boomerang less easily than indiscriminate agitation. Correspondingly, in foreign propaganda, attention must be paid to the fact that talking the way one talks to friends, even though their existence in the enemy camp may be unknown or doubtful, is preferable to a verbal combat with the enemy at large, since such combat is bound to reinforce the opinion of hostile foreign intentions which the enemy elite spreads assiduously in the area it controls. Foreign propaganda of this sort may strengthen rather than weaken the will to obey among the large

mass of those who, in situations of stress, derive comfort and security from the support they give to their leaders.

The *self-interests* of groups and individuals in the enemy population which can be exploited for "alliances" through noncombat warfare comprise a wide range of possibilities. Broadly speaking, there may be political interests of ethnic minorities in secession or liberation, a case skillfully utilized by the British against the Austro-Hungarian Empire in the First World War; there may be interests in the removal of controls which are felt to frustrate the aspirations of counterelites and organized support of the will to disobey, as was the case among the European resistance movements in World War II during the period of German occupation; there may be dissatisfaction with social injustice, etc. Important opportunities for political warfare have arisen throughout history in wars of coalition, since combined national self-interests always are a somewhat brittle foundation for the pursuit of a common policy, particularly in successful offense. In World War II, Goebbels exploited adroitly the mass murder at Katyn to intensify discord between Poland and the Soviet Union, and until the very end of the war, Hitler and his lieutenants hoped for a split between the Western powers and the Soviet Union. Similarly, the Japanese astutely exploited political differences among the Filipinos when at the beginning of 1942 Tojo promised that independence of the Philippines be established at an early date.

Apart from these and other kinds of deviant political self-interest, which are of great value to judicious political warfare, there is elementary self-interest in survival which noncombat warfare can utilize. This is especially true when the employment or the threat of physical weapons intensifies the fear of violent death among the subjects of attack. As has been pointed out, civilians cannot surrender when their courage wanes or their will to obey is broken. They exhibit panic, become apathetic or die. Yet impelled by the need for self-preservation they may also take to flight. Flight in response to propaganda is obviously confined to wartime operations when the subjects of attack are warned that they may be killed unless they take precautionary action in order to survive. Since noncombatants are not expected to have a will to fight and still are in some measures less reconciled than are combatants to the prospects of death through enemy action, they are perhaps more susceptible to warning than soldiers.

Warnings of impending attack differ from ultimata. An ultimatum tries to force one course of action upon the enemy by threatening severe reprisals if another course of action is followed. By contrast, warnings to noncombatants of attacks to come, which were often delivered during World War II, offer escape from the horrors of action which the warning power has resolved to take. Those who are thus warned are again treated as "allies" rather than as enemies. The political interest of the foreign propagandist in disabling the enemy elite to govern a well organized population is reconciled with the interest of the warned population in its own self-preservation. Instruction or advice to the target population as to what it should do in view of the warning is a more powerful noncombat warfare measure than mere warning which leaves to the resourcefulness of the target population and its government the kind of evasive action to take.

The latter type of pure warning may be illustrated from Admiral Halsey's memoirs. In January, 1943, at Bougainville, the following type of message was dropped in pidgin English on native villages.

> "A serious warning from the big white chief to all native of Puka Passage, Buin, and Kieta:
> This is straight talk. You must listen.
> The village of Sorum has been disloyal, has taken orders from the Japs, and has helped the Japs.
> We have now bombed them.
> We have also bombed Pidia, Pok Pok, Toberoi, and Sadi when they helped the Japs.
> If any villages help the Japs, we will bomb them and destroy them altogether.
> We have many planes, many bombs, and many soldiers.
> We will not hesitate to carry out this work.
> Before long we will come with all the American Soldiers to dislodge the Japs and kill them all and punish all natives who helped them.
> > That is all.
> > You have been warned."[17]

It will have been noted that by having regard for organizational requirements, risk and self-interest, those engaged in noncombat warfare play a role quite different from that which the conversion propagandist assumes. The latter is like a missionary, possessed of a faith which he deems superior to that of the heathen, but unlike the missionary he talks from a safe distance. The former identify themselves with the persons whose hazardous political conduct they try to guide; they talk, or at least appear to talk, to allies and friends. To the extent that their careful consideration of what is expedient from case to case is governed by a sense of responsibility, they are less likely to be tempted by the ruinous gratifications which all tasks of human manipulation offer. Political warfare requires many skills, but also certain moral qualities. Its directors must be able to move against the currents of popular passion and to forego adventurous showmanship. In addition, they must know the foreign policy objectives of their country.

The Range of the Planning and Shaping of Expectation

Decisions reflect varying degrees of foresight. Foreign policy decisions are reactive, when they are taken in response to *faits accomplis*; in this case other powers move according to *their* plans, and the reactive elite "muddles through." Decisions taken according to a plan are not strictly speaking predetermined by that plan but issue rather from a reexamination of a given plan in view of a new situation. In other words, all plans of action embody estimates of future countermoves, and each new decision to respond to a countermove enables the planners to reexamine the adequacy of their foresight as well as to bring their plan up to date. Since the pursuit of a foreign policy is affected not only by the ability to carry out intentions, but also by the execution of the opponent's policy, the foresight becomes dimmer the farther it penetrates the future. It would be irrational to predetermine in a political plan the exact decisions to be taken in the more distant future, because the intervening countermoves are matters of probability rather than fact and unforeseeable events are matters of chance. Good plans of action are therefore based on the determination of attainable objectives, but since the estimates of what is feasible change with time, they allow for flexibility through a change of moves to reach these objectives. Good plans of action also reflect a preference for initial moves which do not irrevocably commit the decision maker to subsequent moves nor restrict his freedom to revise subsequent moves in view of unforeseen events. If planning ahead frees the political elite from the pressure of unconsidered countermoves, rational, (i.e., flexible) planning may be paradoxically said to free it from the pressure of irrational (i.e., rigid) plans. This rationality of planning is well illustrated by a phrase which Churchill repeatedly used in setting forth possible courses of action to be taken against the Axis during World War II: after determining feasible objectives and certain suitable moves to obtain them, he pointed out that the moves might have to be modified "as events serve us."

Military elites engage in planning as a matter of course, and in modern wars, at least, are able to state exactly how many days ahead of, or behind, schedule a campaign has progressed. The dependence of modern warfare on the time consuming processes of mobilization, training, the development and production of new weapons as older models become obsolete, and on logistical requirements, renders such planning imperative and constitutes, in fact, a powerful stimulus toward planning the economy of the nation as a whole. Planning in the field of foreign policy is more difficult, chiefly because the control of the future embraced by the plan is shared with opposing elites. The time through which the considerations of political planners extend, moreover, is longer than the time range of military plans. Broadly speaking, it is a military short-range objective in war to complete successfully a phrase in a battle; winning a battle means reaching a medium-range objective; and victory in a campaign attains a military long-range objective. For the political elite in war, the victorious end of a military campaign is, as it were, tantamount to attaining a political short-range objective; the winning of the war is a matter of medium-range considerations, and the best utilization of the international distribution of power at the conclusion of hostilities is a long-range matter. Any consideration to establish *peace forever*, that is, *to abolish foreign policy*, may be said to be politically out of range or utopian.

There are probably historical and national differences in the extent of foresight which various political elites incorporate into their foreign policy plans and decisions. Given the lack of research on this intriguing subject all propositions concerning it must be hypothetical in nature:

1. Utopianism, including the belief that the international struggle for power can be replaced by a harmony of interests, is associated with a lack of articulateness in defining political objectives of any range.
2. Relative military weakness is associated either with attempts to extend the time range of planning or with "reactive" moves.
3. Political elites that have risen to power from a state of persecution (when they were counterelites) are more likely to plan far ahead than elites without such history.
4. Unless the staff of democratically constituted elites is powerful and has a slower replacement rate than the top elite itself, decisions are "reactive," short-range or utopian; by contrast decisions by elites recruited from a political class (e.g., an aristocracy) are governed by considerations of medium- and long-range objectives.

5. Preoccupation of the political top elite with administrative staff functions is indicative of "reactive" decisions in foreign policy; with domestic intelligence: of short-range aims; with foreign intelligence: of medium-range objectives; with history: of long-range goals.

Propaganda reflects in any case the time range prevalent in the decisions of the political elite. If the policy is reactive, propaganda is likely to be an uninspired news service, because it lacks any relation to policy objectives. In that case news has no political focus and the propagandist cannot establish the "meaning" of the events, although facts often do not speak for themselves and if they do, not the same way to all people.

If the political thinking of the elite is utopian, the propaganda effort will be missionary; against recalcitrant opponents who refuse to become converted it will turn fanatical. Only when the foreign policy objectives of the political elite are both articulate and "within range" can foreign propaganda perform a useful function. It does so, broadly speaking, by deriving the political meaning of events from policy objectives in order to influence the expectations of future events.

For it is the *expectations* of the enemy population on which psychological warfare can exert its most profound influence by disseminating "news." What has happened or what has been done, especially by another power, heightens or lowers expectations and changes their content.

In an intelligent psychological warfare program propaganda does not attempt to convert the foreign population to another ideology by claiming its superiority. Rather, the propagandist tries to *shape expectations* by interpreting events as tokens of the future. In doing so he creates an image of intentions. Moving from ideology to the concrete and specific concerns of the people he talks to, he descends, to use a phrase of Karl Marx, from language to life.

The propagandist can sometimes predict what the enemy elite will do in its domestic policy and what the masses he addresses will have to suffer in consequence. Such propaganda presupposes not only good intelligence about the prospective moves of the enemy elite (e.g., curtailment of food rations), but also reliable estimates that increased deprivations will be resented rather than accepted with patience or austere fervor.

More important, however, are the expectations of the population concerning the plans of the power for whom the propagandist speaks.

Theoretically, the propagandist gains access more easily to his own elite than to the secrets of the enemy elite. In practice, however, the effort of the propagandist in influencing expectations depends on the extent to which his own elite permits him to share some of its secrets.

The members of the political elite and its staff concerned with decisions on what is to be done rather than on what is to be said have a natural desire for secrecy because premature disclosures may enable the enemy to parry prospective moves. Even in Nazi Germany, ruled by an elite that attached great importance to international propaganda, the coordination of propaganda and policy was far from perfect. The propagandist is a professional talker. Who likes to confide secrets to professional talkers? The fallacy hidden in this question lies in the implication that the progandist will divulge the secrets he learns. As every diplomat knows, it is possible to hide and betray secrets by both silence and talk. By the same token, the propagandist may conceal by talking or reveal by silence[18] what he is supposed not to disclose, but he cannot do either unless he is informed about the secret. It should be noted, however, that the usual differences in social background and career of policy makers and propagandists increase the secretiveness of the former.

The propagandist does of course not need to know all secrets of his political elite. Yet in order to influence expectations abroad and to be effective in the timing and direction of this effort, he must be able to derive propaganda policy from the foreign policy decisions of the elite. Otherwise he is thrown back to get his inspirations from news or ideology. More generally speaking, the *existence* of policy objectives — short-, medium- and long-range — is a prerequisite of political warfare. The *communication* of these objectives to the directors of propaganda merely insures coordination in the use of policy instruments.

Who, precisely, in the opposing nation is the enemy? Is it the military elite as much as the political elite? Who, in the enemy camp, are potential or actual allies? Which groups should have more power, which less? Is it the foreign policy of the other nation that is to be modified, or also its social institutions? Precisely which, if any, of the latter and in what way? Are revolution and secession permissible, required, or not permissible (since they cannot possibly be a matter of indifference)? If required, precisely what means are to be applied to produce the desired state of affairs: incitement, infiltration, support? If support, what kind? What is the time scale of operations, that is, the relation of short-term to medium-term objectives? In war, what are the political long-range objectives, if victory is a medium-range aim?

In peacetime, what are the elements of a desirable relationship between the powers concerned? It is answers to questions of this kind which furnish the basis of political warfare, as distinguished from the gossip of news, the preaching of ideology, the performance of tricks, and the projection of the self.

Political Warfare Against Elites

In this section we shall turn to political warfare against elites. According to the assumption made throughout this essay, these elites are hostile or at least have designs to maintain defensively, or attain offensively, positions of international power at the expense of other nations. Elite decisions to surrender, to disarm, to form an alliance, to yield or to compromise are goals of political warfare in the same sense in which mutiny in the fighting population, sabotage among the workers, the rise of strong counterelites or the defection of key personnel may be such goals. Maintaining the assumption of "warfare" as the specific state of international affairs with which we are here concerned, the decisions of other elites, if taken *without interference*, are not only in the interest of the nations they govern but also disadvantageous to the power engaged in political warfare against them. Hence the special task of political warfare to influence enemy decisions in order to reduce the power gain which they are intended to bring about and to turn it possibly into a loss.

Decisions by the political elite concerning foreign policy and the determination of military missions by the subordinate military elite require cooperation among the elite members. It is also necessary that certain staff functions be performed and coordinated. Political warfare can therefore attack the cooperation among elite members or the performance of their staff functions.

Cooperation is dependent upon a modicum of mutual trust. In this respect despotic elites are more vulnerable than democratic elites. It has already been mentioned that the subordinate elite in totalitarian regimes is easily suspected of treason and easily regarded as a potential counterelite. A study of relations between the political and military leaders in Germany during the Hitler period is especially revealing in this respect.[19] During World War II it was not fully appreciated how easily distrust can be created.[20] A systematic exploitation of these predispositions of a despotic political elite requires reliable intelligence on frictions within the enemy elite and need not be confined to the use of propaganda. It appears that subtler, less public means, such as studied diplomatic indiscretions in neutral countries or the sacrifice of intelligence for the purpose of compromising certain elite members in the eyes of others are more suitable means.

Desertions of elite members are rare and difficult to induce. If they occur, however, they provide great opportunities to political warfare. The sensational defection of Rudolf Hess, Hitler's deputy, was not exploited by the British, which characteristically aroused rather than allayed suspicion of the British on Stalin's part.

There is also evidence from the last war, particularly in *The Goebbels Diaries*, that propaganda directed at the masses may directly or indirectly through the monitoring services reach the political elite, which is subject to less censorship than the population at large, and thus have an unintended effect. It would therefore appear possible to use this channel for communication with the elite intentionally for specified purposes rather than by default. The same holds true of using mass communications for contacts with members of the military elite. Virtually all memoirs of military leaders in the last war cite enemy propaganda statements, and there are a few instances in which action was influenced by them.[21]

More important, however, than these relatively minor weapons in the arsenal of noncombat warfare against enemy elites are the measures that can be taken to interfere with the performance of staff functions. The following remarks are confined to the subject of interference with foreign intelligence and with advice on the consequences of alternative decisions by means of deception.[22]

According to the saying which Plutarch ascribed to Lysander, "Where the lion's skin will not reach, you must patch it out with the fox's," deception has been used throughout history in order to confuse the enemy. All deception is aimed at creating erroneous estimates of enemy capabilities or intentions and thus at inducing countermoves which are wrong but appear to be right to the enemy.

Like successful secrecy, successful deception produces surprise and helps put the opponent off guard. Secrecy attempts to keep intelligence from the enemy, whereas deception provides him with misinformation. If secrecy about the next planned move were complete the enemy elite would still make the best possible estimate of this move and act in accordance with this estimate. Deception is superior to secrecy in that it attempts to *influence* the estimate; at the same time it aids in obscuring real intent by disclosing a fake intent. Since deception is a form of communication with the enemy elite which it expects to be withheld, the disclosures instrumental to deception must appear either unavoidable or as mishaps: in either case the disclosure may be mistaken by the enemy as the result of its own reconnaissance or intelligence activities. Seemingly *unintentional disclosures* are studied indiscretions, planted misinformation, etc. Seemingly *unavoidable disclosures* result from staging a dummy reality in the hope that enemy reconnaissance will spot and mistake it for an indication of genuine capability or intent.

Many paradigmatic forms of deception occur in the animal world. Friedrich Alverdes distinguished between the following forms of animal deception.[23]

1. *"Sympathese,"* that is, sympathetic coloration and behavior in relation to the environment in order to deceive for aggressive or protective purposes the sense of sight. Since *"Sympathese"* covers behavior as well as coloration, "playing possum" (*"Thatanose"*) is included under this heading. So are forms of protective "dissolves" into the environment, for example, the stripes of the zebra (called by Alverdes *"Somatolyse"*). Finally, there are forms of deception which create the impression that the persecuted, fast-moving, and vividly colored animal suddenly appears to change into one that is not moving and is protectively colored. Such *"Heteropsie"* may also be directed at the sense of hearing, as in the case of locusts whose whirring stops when they settle down.

2. *Mimesis* consists in protective similarity with indifferent elements in the environment. Alverdes distinguished between *"Allomimesis,"* that is, imitation of inanimate things, *"Phytomimesis,"* that is, imitation of plants or parts of plants, and *"Zoomimesis,"* that is, imitation of another species.

3. *Mimicry*. Alverdes used *"Zoomimesis"* to denote cases of deception producing failure to detect whereas *mimicry* is deception producing avoidance by adaption of unprotected animals to the appearance of others which are protected by poison, smells, etc.

4. *"Phobese,"* that is, means which defenseless animals use to ward off their enemies by terrifying colors or behavior.

5. *"Allektation,"* that is, coloration or behavior which lures other animals into the vicinity of those which prey upon them.

It may be added that animals (especially birds) may simulate being wounded in their flight in order to divert the attention of the aggressor from their young. There are also cases in which animals actively use parts of their environment in order to mask themselves.

The obvious similarity between deception "techniques" in the animal world and those used in human warfare is evident, but should not be overemphasized inasmuch as man can add to the deception of the senses the deception of the mind. There is, then, a premium on inventiveness in the field of human deception.

Military history abounds with attempts to mislead the enemy by deceiving his intelligence service through ruses.[24] Military deception is used to mislead enemy intelligence concerning place and time, strength and objectives of offensive or defensive operations in order to induce the enemy either to overlook the imperative need for making a decision or to reach faulty decisions which increase his vulnerability. Major deception schemes to mask operations that involve a large number of combatants are often accompanied by self-deception, that is, cover schemes which conceal the purpose of preparing the real operation from those who are supposed to execute it.

It is doubtful that propaganda can effectively contribute to military deception, although some major efforts to that effect were made in World War II. U.S. propaganda after the invasion of Normandy kept calling attention to the possibility of additional landings elsewhere in France in order to tie down German reserves. These verbal efforts would probably have been of little avail, had it not been for the deception measures taken in Great Britain which strengthened German expectations of further landings. As has been pointed out, the effectiveness of communications with the intent to deceive is altogether dependent on the credible appearance of a mishap and on supporting evidence provided by "dummy reality." It is not sufficient to claim that a move is afoot if observable deceiving preparations of this move are not actually made or if the preparations that are observed clearly deny the claim.

This simple principle of military deception was disregarded by Goebbels who thereby testified to both his ignorance of military matters and his ludicrous overestimation of the power of cunning. Twice he attempted to deceive enemy intelligence about imminent German offensives. The first effort was directed in June 1941 at creating the impression that England rather than the Soviet Union was about to be invaded by German forces. The scheme involved self-deception at a confidential conference when the department heads of the propaganda ministry were told that operations planned in the East had been called off. Then Goebbels himself described in an article published in the *Völkischer Beobachter* the invasion of Crete as a rehearsal for a great airborne operation and implied that an invasion of the British isles was imminent. On secret orders from Goebbels the article was immediately withdrawn, but not until foreign correspondents had cabled the contents of the article out of the country. As soon as it was known through tapping telephone wires that the order for confiscation had also been telephoned abroad, all foreign lines were closed.[25] It is not known what happened to British and Soviet Russian intelligence estimates in consequence of this ruse, but it is safe to assume that the massing of more than 100 divisions on the German-Russian border spoke louder than Goebbels' propaganda and censorship measures.[26]

A similar ruse was tried by Goebbels in the spring of 1942 in order to divert attention from the impending German summer offensive on the Southern front in the U.S.S.R.[27] It again involved an article by Goebbels and the dispatch of a German journalist first on a trip to the Eastern front, which was much publicized, and then to Lisbon where he was instructed to let it be known in a state of feigned drunkenness that the Germans would attack on the *central* front.

These cases illustrate the wasteful histrionics of zealous propagandists. They do not prove the futility of efforts to mislead enemy intelligence by appropriate means.

It is likely that deception of political elites is more easily accomplished than that of military elites, because in efforts directed at political intelligence relatively less attention need be paid to producing "dummy *capabilities*" or to camouflaging them and more reliance can be placed on the effectiveness of producing false notions of *intent*. A given capability can be used for various purposes and the intent to use it in any definite way cannot be safely derived from it, but the margin of error in deriving intent from capability grows in proportion to the scope of the enterprise under review. Whether or not a field commander is preparing for attack in times of war may be safely derived from the observation of certain unmistakable preparations for battle. Evidence of preparations for war itself may be less conclusive, simply because the political elite may decide to confine the "use" of national capabilities to rendering threats of war more effective. Deception in this case would be successful if the intent of war were conveyed in order to heighten the impact of the threat.

Furthermore, there are many political actions, for example, the conclusion of treaties, which do not require observable physical capabilities. In these cases, again, induced mistakes in assessing the intent of foreign political elites suffice for deception.

Finally, to the extent that political elites are concerned with longer range objectives, deception bearing on these objectives may succeed without arranging elaborate "dummy capabilities." An illustration may be taken from Hitler's military conferences. On January 27, 1945, Hitler said to General Jodl,[28]

"I have ordered that a report be played into their hands to the effect that the Russians are organizing 200,000 of our men, led by German officers and completely infected with Communism, who will then be marched into Germany. I have demanded that this report be played into English hands. I told the Foreign Minister to do that. That will make them feel as if someone had stuck a needle into them."

In conclusion, it should be stressed, however, that the use of deception in attempting to influence the expectations and intelligence of opposing political elites is not confined to actions perpetrated by ingenious specialists in trickery. The highest form of political deception consists rather in major political *actions* which lead the opposing elite to misjudge the political strategy it attempts to fathom. Like political warfare in general this kind of deception is no substitute for policy planning: it presupposes the determination of the objectives which deception can help attain, particularly by actions which mislead the opposing elite in assessing the nature of these objectives and their interrelation in time and space.

NOTES

1. I once was asked by an officer, "Does psychological warfare include warfare psychology waged?"
2. Cf. Harold D. Lasswell's and Abraham Kaplan's proposition, "Upper elites tend to be skilled in the practices of inter-personal relations rather than of the area in which decisions are to be made." *Power and Society*, New Haven, 1950, p. 203.
3. On the importance of secrecy among key scientific personnel *in peacetime*, see H. D. Smyth's *General Account of the Development of Methods of Using Atomic Energy for Military Purposes*, 1945, chap. 3. The hypothesis of fission was announced and its experimental confirmation took place in January 1939. "At that time," reports Smyth, "American-born nuclear physicists were so unaccustomed to the idea of using their science for military purposes that they hardly realized what needed to be done. Consequently the early efforts at restricting publication . . . were stimulated largely by a small group of foreign-born physicists. . . . "
4. For an early recognition of this social stratum, see Des Byzantiner Anonymous, "Staatswissenschaft der That oder Kriegswissenschaft," in H. Köchly and W. Rüstow eds., *Griechische Kriegsschriftsteller*, Leipzig, 1855, sec. 1, par. 4. ("The useless people wo cannot do anything for the common good . . . "), sec. 2, par. 9 ("neglected by nature and fate . . . "), and sec. 3, par. 13.
5. In practice, the functions of determining political and military strategies are neither easily distinguished nor always clearly separated. During the Second World War the supreme authority in both spheres of power was in fact held by the same person in the United States, the United Kingdom, China, the Soviet Union, and Germany. (The situation differed during the First World War notably in the United Kingdom and Germany.) Concerning the place occupied by "psychological warfare" in the decisions of the political and military elites in World War II, see for the United States: Wallace Carroll, *Persuade or Perish*, Boston, 1948; Ellis Zacharias, *Secret Missions*, New York, 1946; Charles A. H. Thomson, *Overseas Information Service of the United States Government*, Washington, D.C., 1948, part I; Daniel Lerner,

Sykewar, New York, 1949; for Great Britain: Bruce Lockhart, *Comes the Reckoning*, London, 1947; for Germany: Derrick Sington and Arthur Weidenfeld, *The Goebbels Experiment*, London, 1942, American edition: New Haven, 1943; Rudolf Semmler, *Goebbels — The Man Next to Hitler*, London, 1947; *The Goebbels Diaries, 1942-1943*, ed. by Louis P. Lochner, New York, 1948. — For the First World War, see Harold D. Lasswell, *Propaganda Technique in the World War*, New York, 1927, and Hans Thimme, *Weltkrieg ohne Waffen*, Stuttgart, 1932.

6. On January 5, 1951, Senator Taft asked in the Senate, "Is it necessary for this country to provide from sixty to seventy thousand men in uniform and half as many more civilians in order to put a division of 18,000 men in the field?" *Congressional Record*, vol. 97, p. 64.

7. Samuel A. Stouffer, et al., *The American Soldier*, vol. I, Princeton, 1949, p. 330.

8. In times of peace, the will to fight should not be taken as a desire to break the peace.

9. Winston Churchill, *The Grand Alliance*, Boston, 1950, p. 127.

10. Alexander Inkeles, *Public Opinion in the Soviet Union*, Cambridge, 1950.

11. Erich Wollenberg, *The Red Army*, London, 1938.

12. During World War II of 36 Lt. Generals twenty-one were dismissed by Hitler, two were expelled from the Army, and three were executed after July 20, 1944. Of 800 officers of the General Staff, 150 are said to have lost their lives as opponents to the regime. See Walter Görlitz, *Der Deutsche Generalstab*, Frankfurt, 1950.

13. But there is evidence for cumulative effects of propaganda on opinions and attitudes, particularly when propaganda is monopolistic. Cf. Joseph T. Flapper, *The Effects of Mass Media*, New York, 1949 (mimeographed by the Bureau of Applied Social Research of Columbia University). Cf. also the review article by Wilbur Schramm, "The Effects of Mass Communications," in *Journalism Quarterly*, December 1949.

14. Goebbels distinguished between "*Stimmung*" and "*Haltung*," the former being politically irrelevant internalized responses (attitudes), the latter representing externalized responses (behavior) which matter. As long as the authorities could prevent the transition from "*Stimmung*" to "*Haltung*."Goebbels was entirely right in deprecating concern about depressed "*Stimmung*."

15. E.g., Fitzroy MacLean's airdrop in wartime Yugoslavia to work for the British with Tito.

16. E.g., Lenin's famous journey in a sealed German train to Russia in 1917.

17. William F. Halsey and Joseph Bryan III, *Admiral Halsey's Story*, New York, 1947, pp. 150–51.

18. For example, National Socialist propaganda directives (so-called *Sprachregelungen*) prohibited at a certain date during the last war any mention of heavy water in magazines. If *previous* references to heavy water had been noted from time to time, the abrupt silence about the matter would have been a disclosure.

19. Similarly rewarding is a study of military failures and misfortunes of German and Italian commanders during World War II compared with those of British and American generals.

20. Liddell Hart quotes General Blumentritt, "Hitler knew that Field Marshal von Rundstedt was much respected by the army and by the enemy. Allied propaganda broadcasts often suggested that the views of the Field Marshal and his staff differed from those of Hitler. It was notable, too, our headquarters was never subjected to air attacks. Nor was the Field Marshal ever threatened by the French resistance movement — presumably, because it was known that he had always been in favor of good treatment for the French. All these things were brought to Hitler's notice, of

course, in reports from his own agents. While he treated the Field Marshal with respect — more respect than he showed other soldiers — he kept him under careful watch." See *The German Generals Talk*, New York, 1948, pp. 260–61.

21. See, for example, the entry under June 20, 1944 in Lt. Gen. Lewis H. Brereton, *The Brereton Diaries*, New York, 1946, p. 289, "Owing to the enormous enemy propaganda on damage done by V–I's, it was decided at commanders' meeting to stage a strong air attack on Berlin tomorrow to counteract it."

22. Interference with the control and communication functions of the auxiliary elite personnel have been touched upon when measures to reduce the ability to govern and command were discussed.

23. Friedrich Alverdes, "Täuschung und 'Lüge' in Tierreich," in *Die Lüge*, ed. by Otto Lippmann and Paul Plaut, Leipzig, 1927, pp. 332–50.

24. See General Waldemar Erfurth, *Surprise*, and the introduction to this book by Stefan T. Possony, Harrisburg, 1943, from which the following illustration is taken. During the First World War the British misled the Turks at Gaza to believe that the main blow of Gen. Allenby's forces would fall at the left flank.

    "A whole month was spent in sending 'misleading messages by wireless telegraphy in a code which the Turks, by various ruses, had been taught how to solve, without realizing the situation.' In addition, a British staff officer on patrol ride let himself be surprised by a Turkish guard. He feigned to be wounded and ostensibly lost his haversack with an especially prepared notebook, including money, love-letters and several purported orders and military documents. The haversack was picked up by the Turks. The next morning, a notice appeared in the paper that was issued to the Desert Mounted Corps, stating that a notebook had been lost by a staff officer on patrol and that the finder should return it at once to Allenby's headquarters. 'A small party was sent out to search the country for the pocketbook . . . An officer was stupid enough to wrap his luncheon in a copy of these orders, and to drop it near the enemy.' These ruses were successful," p. 10.

    For a few illustrations from World War II, cf. Field Marshal the Viscount Montgomery of Alamein, *El Alamein to the River Sangra*, New York, 1949, p. 31ff., 57, 78–80; Desmond Young, *Rommel*, London, 1950, pp. 173–74; Sir Giffard Martel, *An Outspoken Soldier*, London, 1949, p. 206; Brereton, op. cit., pp. 273–74; Anthony B. Martienssen, *Hitler and His Admirals*, New York, 1949, p. 79, 101; George C. Kenney, *General Kenney Reports*, New York, 1949, pp. 268, 281–82, 330, 374, 384, 501; Admiral Halsey, op. cit., pp. 197, 207–08; Field-Marshal Lord Wilson of Libya, *Eight Years Overseas*, London, 1948, p. 40; Sir Frederick Morgan, *Overture to Overlord*, New York, 1950; Sir Francis de Guingand, *Operation Victory*, New York, 1947, pp. 108, 155–56. See also Jasper Maskelyne, *Magic-Top Secret*, London, no date.

25. Rudolf Semmler, op. cit., pp. 39–42.

26. I am indebted to Miss Jean Hungerford for an examination of the *New York Times*, the *London Times*, the *Daily Mail*, and the *News Chronicle* from June 9 to June 22, 1941, for possible public effects of Goebbels's article. The incident was duly reported but was completely overshadowed by reports of the massing of troops on the Russian frontier, the possibility of war between Germany and the U.S.S.R., etc.

27. See the *Goebbels Diaries*, op. cit., pp. 162–227.

28. *Hitler Directs His War*. The Secret Records of his Daily Military Conferences, selected and annotated by Felix Gilbert, New York, 1950, p. 118.

9

The Communication
of Hidden Meaning

Disclosing and Withholding

Informative and propagandistic statements have an overt meaning
(M_o) that is clearly apparent to the recipient (R). If the communicator
(C) tries to enlighten R by presenting information or a logical conclusion to him, or even if he speaks of certain beliefs or of a design to
shape the future, the meaning always lies, as it were, on the surface of
his statements. This is true whether he ways "$2+2=4$," "God created
the world," "Paris is the capital of France," "Black is beautiful," or "To
preserve peace we must arm."

But the object of communication is not necessarily to inform and
obtain understanding. It may be not to spread knowledge to a given
ignoramus but to maintain his ignorance; not to profess feelings but to
hide or feign them; to lead astray rather than to guide the perplexed;
not to give the best advice but the next best; not to enlighten but to
obscure, to explain inadequately, to oversimplify, to slant, to popularize, to tell only part of the truth, to mask it, or simply to lie.

Aside from that, a person often renders the same subject in different
terms when talking to different persons: discourse is role-differentiated. Observe a physician speaking about an illness to his colleague
and to his suffering patient, or a father conversing about God with his

First published in *Social Research*, vol. 44, 1977. Reprinted by permission of *Social
Research*.

child in the morning and his priest at noon. Matters kept secret from laymen can be expressed precisely in technical language to experts. If this communication is "translated" into popular terms for purposes of communicating with a larger audience, precision is inevitably lost. In his hearing before the Personnel Security Board, J. Robert Oppenheimer testified:

> I know of no case where I misrepresented or distorted the technical situation in reporting it to my superiors or those to whom I was bound to give advice and counsel. The nearest thing to it that I know is that in the public version of the Acheson-Lilienthal report, we somewhat overstated what would be accomplished by denaturing. I believe this was not anything else than in translating from a technical and therefore secret statement into a public and therefore codified statement, we lost some of the precision which should have gone into it, and some of the caution which should have gone into it.[1]

Role-differentiated discourse about the same subject will appear elusive to those observers who expect every communication to be a full disclosure of that which is on the speaker's mind. Similarly, such observers may easily overlook the fact that a person may not only deliberately delete from his speech some information concerning the subject he dwells on but also deliberately say something to indicate that he is withholding something else.

While often everything is disclosed and nothing withheld, there are many other communications in which something remains unsaid. From the vantage point of the recipient, the communication may then be said to resemble a view that is partially veiled or a tune reaching him only in fragments from afar. Finally, there are communications in which withholding is indeed total: evasive answers, lies, deliberate obscurities, loquacious flooding of the channels with socially acceptable nonsense, etc.

In the following discussion we shall not view communication as efforts at enlightenment or propaganda. Instead, we shall regard the whole realm of communication as a continuum bounded by the two extremes of full disclosure and total withholding of that which is on the communicator's mind. In every communication the communicator discloses and withholds. The specific mixture of the two efforts, that is, the location of any given communication on the continuum, varies among other things with the relationship between C and R and with the political context.

It might be objected that this view of communication is a misanthropic one, since it seems to assume that man is secretive if not deceitful or at least uninterested in enlightening his fellow men. No such opinion of man's nature is meant to be implied.

Let us recall, first of all, Hugo Grotius's distinction between negative and positive stratagems. In negative stratagems we conceal all or part of what we know, as in diplomatic silence or in the withholding of some information available to us when we otherwise speak the truth. This negative stratagem is dissimulation. In positive stratagems, or simulations, we do not speak truthfully. The physician who does not tell his patient that he is going to die, although the physician expects his death, dissimulates; if the physician tells the patient that he is going to live, he uses a positive stratagem.

As this illustration suggests, the use of stratagems is not necessarily reprehensible from a moral point of view and cannot be readily equated with lying. Which stratagems are permissible or indeed mandatory from a moral point of view depends upon the intention with which the stratagem is used and upon circumstances. Grotius cites the instance of King Solomon, who proposed that the contested child be divided and thereby induced the true mother to reveal herself — evidently a morally permissible stratagem used in the pursuit of justice. Similarly, he agrees with Quintilian that children can be taught many useful truths in the dress of fiction. And there are other situations, such as self-defense against an enemy or occasions in which conventional rather than "sincere" conduct is generally expected, where concealment of sentiment, simulation of knowledge or intent, and even feigned respect for values constitute deviations from the truth that leave no moral blemish.

Man communicates for good and evil purposes. Unless he is ill, he knows that not everyone is his enemy to be met with tight lips or lies, and yet only a blabbing fool treats everyone like a trusted friend. Furthermore, just as concealment no less than disclosure may serve a good purpose, so disclosure like concealment may do harm in certain circumstances. Even in talking to a friend, concern or curiosity may be curbed out of respect for his privacy, just as sad tidings may be withheld from him so as to spare his feelings. Conversely, in certain circumstances we conceal nothing from our enemy and give him a full account of our strength — especially if we judge it to be overpowering — and of our good or ill will toward him. In short, while the general view of communication that is being suggested here enables the observer to take account of the fact that the political nature of the social universe impinges upon communication, it does not postulate man to be either angelically straight or fiendishly crooked. Man walks upright, but he can bend.

Before proceeding, we may try to dispose of another possible initial objection. If it be admitted that communication is an act of disclosing and withholding, the extreme case of full disclosure appears more plausible than the opposite extreme of a communicator withholding everything he knows, believes, wants, or feels. For cannot total withholding rather easily be accomplished by silence instead of communication? The argument is fallacious. Neither silence nor the explicit refusal to say anything is necessarily sufficient to avoid disclosure. Silence itself may be communicative. For example, it may express consent or dissent, as the case may be. An audience may be able not only to understand its meaning but to force it upon the silent person, so that he must speak to escape such dictates. Literally or figuratively speaking, a correspondent may receive the message, "If I do not hear from you, I shall assume that you agree with me." Similarly, in a manipulated mass meeting silence at a prescribed moment of cheer or applause is tantamount to a demonstrative act of defiance, as is the silence of a heretic under pressure to recant. In such cases, the communicator cannot remain passive. He has to use words, gestures, or actions if he wishes to avoid disclosing something he does not want to say by remaining silent.[2]

When the significance of silence is not tightly controlled by others, many different meanings may yet be imputed to it, which is often true of statements, gestures, and actions as well. Only an additional communication may prevent the listener from ascribing that particular meaning to silence which "the silent speaker" wants to withhold. For example, although silence may indicate that a person is shy, defiant, indifferent, or proud, the listener may take it to mean that he feels guilty, a meaning which the silent person may have good reason to deny or be anxious to conceal. In either case he must speak up, though in doing so he must swallow the pride that prompted him to be silent at first. Silence among men is always alive. Paradoxically, it is most alive when there is "a dead silence." In short, like other means of communication, silence is a way of disclosing and withholding, although it sometimes lacks the ruthlessness of the "outspoken." Silence in writing on certain subjects can also be used by an author to express an intended meaning obliquely — for example, that he considers these subjects to be unimportant or commonly held views on them to be mistaken.[3]

Silence and a high incidence of withholding in communication need not be stratagems in efforts to gain advantages over others or safeguards against disadvantages possibly to be incurred by disclosure. Instead, such "reticence" may stem from the conviction that everyday language fails to serve since it is blunted by abuse. Modern literature provides ample comment on such despair in contemporary civilization. Indeed, when listening attentively to what we hear today most of the time, then over the distance of half a century the quiet voice of Hans Karl Buehl, the most modern character in Hofmannsthal's plays, touches us to the quick: "But everything one says is indecent. The simple fact that one says something is indecent."[4]

Perhaps this feeling for the "indecency" of all speech reveals a refined sentiment bordering on decadence, but perhaps there reverberates in it the older, profounder, conceit of the romantic and the mystic that ordinary speech cannot reach the truth. The opposing view was most forcefully stated by Hegel in the preface to his *Phenomenology*. Impatient with Jacobi and the romantics, with Schlegel and Schleiermacher, whose "intensity without content" he equated with "superficiality" and "dreams," he thundered: "Die Kraft des Geistes ist nur so gross als ihre Äusserung . . . " ("The power of the mind is only as great as the power of expression . . . ").[5]

Heterogeneous Audiences

In role-differentiated discourse the communicator changes the specific "mixture" of disclosure and withholding according to his intention toward the recipient and according to the latter's known or presumed predisposition (e.g., child vs. priest, patient vs. colleague, friend vs. foe). We may therefore distinguish between role-adequate and role-inadequate discourse. An exposition of Leibniz's monadology to a butler is role-inadequate; so is the aerodynamic explanation of flight to a babe.

While the effort at role-adequacy presents no difficulties to the communicator who addresses a recipient he knows well—say a partner, a friend, or a homogeneous group of recipients—the matter becomes considerably more difficult—and possibly hazardous—for the communicator who faces a recipient whose predisposition he does not know or the communicator who addresses a *heterogeneous* audience. To illustrate, Henry Kissinger once remarked to an audience of congressmen's wives that since World War I there had been "very rarely fully legitimate governments in any European country." The Secretary of State learned too late that "the press office [of the State Department] had invited some newsmen to cover his remarks from an enclosed booth to the side of the auditorium."[6] To cushion the shock he had caused abroad, Mr. Kissinger subsequently issued an apology ruefully stating that he seemed to get into trouble when ladies and the press were present. Thus he managed to put the blame in part on others without admitting that he had rashly yielded to the temptation to be brilliant rather than prudent in public.

In diplomatic discourse, it happens often — indeed, it is almost normal — that the response to a public message is diversified, since the international "community," like "the public," is a heterogeneous audience.

Strictly speaking, for communication to a heterogeneous audience to be fully role-adequate, the same message would have to have multivarious meanings. This requirement is met, of course, only in exceptional cases. Sometimes it is possible by way of a second, corrective, communication to convey once more the meaning which part of the audience missed in the first instance. Thus a teacher may repeat a lesson for inattentive students or amplify for the slow-witted what his bright students had fully understood in the first, brief, rendition.

The class of cases, however, which is of particular interest is that in which the communicator wishes to be understood only by selected members of his audience — "the intended recipient" (R_i) — while wishing not to be understood by others — "the unwanted recipient" of the same message (R_u). Put differently, he endeavors to disclose what is on his mind to R_i while withholding it from R_u.

Even a dog may play the role of R_u when its master speaking to R_i — for example, his servant — avoids pronouncing a word that the dog "understands." By spelling it — "o-u-t" for "out" — he may succeed in communicating with the servant without cueing the dog (until it has learned the new "o-u-t"). Whispering a message to R_i so that R_u cannot get its meaning follows the same pattern. So do the "asides" on the stage, which establish an understanding with the audience in the theater from which actors on the stage are presumed to be excluded. By the same token, Turgenev wrote some of his letters to Pauline Viardot (R_i) in German, because Louis Viardot, her husband (R_u) did not understand German. Turgenev availed himself of what Gibbon once referred to as "the obscurity of a learned language."[7] Resorting to a foreign language may enable parents to convey to each other a meaning which they want to withhold from their children. These may reciprocate by conversing in a contrived "secret" language, which adults are supposed not to understand.[8]

It is possible that the nonsense the unwanted listeners hear may appear to them as a secret shared by the communicator and his equals, while the latter in turn may indeed use a special language whose secret meanings are intelligible only to them. The special language is an instrument of solidarity, social exclusiveness, religious privilege, or power over those who fail to understand the secret. The communicator discloses to some recipient (R_i) what is on his mind and to others (R_u) the fact that he, the communicator, and R_i are in possession of mysterious secrets; but he withholds the *content* of the secrets from these outsiders.

The most important examples of this class of messages are communications transacted in liturgical languages, like Greek, Old Slavonic, Armenian, and Coptic, and the Latin of scholars in medieval Europe.[9]

Covert Meaning

In a heterogeneous audience, certain recipients may either fail to understand or misunderstand the communicator. In the second, more complicated, case, R_u does not hear noise or nonsense; nor does he know and accept the fact that secrets are being withheld from him. Instead, he understands a meaning, but it differs from that received by the intended recipient. The communicator manages to transmit a message which has *two* meanings, an overt one (M_o) and a covert one (M_c). He discloses M_c to the intended recipient (R_i) but withholds it at the same time from R_u by inducing R_u to think that the only meaning he intends to convey is M_o. The intended recipient, whom the communicator wants to receive M_c, understands both M_o and M_c, is able to discriminate between them, and realizes that the overt meaning is meant to preoccupy the unwanted other recipient (R_u), thereby keeping him from noticing the covert meaning. It should be noted that this rather complicated transaction presupposes a common bond between C and R_i as a result of shared knowledge, feeling, experience, belief, or purpose. Conversely, the fact that the unwanted recipient of the message is a stranger or outsider accounts for his naiveté in assuming that M_o is the sole meaning in C's message.

The communication of covert or esoteric meaning occurs in many different situations and for many different reasons. Perhaps the most harmless use is playful, although the limits of harmlessness are sometimes hard to define. Cicero comments at length on the fact that ambiguity of the meaning of words, allegorical phraseology, metaphorical language, and ironical statements may be sources of jests.[10]

Strictly speaking, the metaphorical aspects of language — in the widest sense of the term "metaphorical"—are bound to impede the pertinence of the observation that informational statements have only overt meanings, simply because relatively few communications are entirely free of metaphors. By way of illustration, it may be noted that the words "bound to" in the preceding sentence (in lieu of, say, "inevitably") are derived from "binding," an image under which life and the working of fate were interpreted in ancient Hebrew, Babylonian, Vedic, Roman, Greek, Celtic, Norse, and Slav thought:[11] one of the original functions of metaphors is making it possible to live with the dreadfully incomprehensible by inventing verisimilitudes to something that is comprehended.

Conveying both an overt and a covert meaning in the same message is by no means necessarily playful; it frequently serves very serious purposes, especially in erotic, religious, and political contexts.

Stendhal's *Lucien Leuwen* contains a fine illustration of such a communication in an erotic context. Young Lucien visits for the first time the Countess de Chasteller, whom he loves, but the unexpected presence of a stranger in the room, Miss Bérard, who happens to be a malicious gossip, bewilders him. Although tongue-tied at first, Lucien at last has "a miserable little inspiration." He would be very happy, he says in the presence of both ladies, if he were to succeed in becoming a good officer in the cavalry, for it seems that heaven had not chosen him ever to be an eloquent political deputy. At this point Miss Bérard pricks up her ears because she thinks that Lucien is talking about politics. He continues that as a deputy he would not be capable of presenting in the Chamber matters of deep concern to him. Away from the rostrum he would be plagued by the vivacity of the feelings that inflamed his heart. But were he to open his mouth in front of that highest and stern judge whose displeasure would make him tremble, he could only say, "Look at my diffidence, you fill my whole heart, which lacks even the strength to reveal itself to you." By this time, Countess de Chasteller's initial pleasure has given way to uneasiness; she fears her female companion. Lucien's words appear "too transparent" to her. Hastily she asks him if he really had any prospects of being elected a deputy.[12]

Let us consider this episode somewhat more closely. Lucien (C) evidently assumed that the Countess (R_i) would not betray the covert meaning of his speech to Miss Bérard (R_u), and the Countess in her turn felt that Lucien was expecting her not to betray it. We may therefore say that C and R_i *trust* each other, whereas both of them *distrust* R_u. The awareness of this mutual trust becomes a delicate token of their love, which incidentally neither of them had ever before openly professed: the bond between them as well as the hidden meaning of Lucien's speech is a secret. Had the Countess told Miss Bérard what Lucien "really" meant, she would have disclosed not only the hidden meaning but also various other things: to Miss Bérard she would have revealed that Lucien loved her, but that she did not love him; and to Lucien her brutal response would have told him in addition that she cared so little for his love as to make it and her rejection of it public. It is questionable whether his feelings of shame would have allowed him to protest dissemblingly that she had evidently misunderstood what he has said: he had meant precisely what he had said (M_o). In any event, the reader is inclined to feel that only an unashamedly public profession of love on Lucien's part (in the presence of Miss Bérard) would have deserved so cold and brutal a rejection by the Countess: vulgarity would then have been answered by disdain. Everything would have been different in the absence of Miss Bérard: the Countess might have rejected Lucien's open declaration of love, but then she might have only dissembled her feelings, and Lucien would have known that she had not necessarily spoken her last word.[13]

The Misses Bérard — that is, the listeners who do not understand covert meanings — are often felt to be ludicrous, since they suffer from a defect: like some dull-witted censors, they fail to comprehend what is going on, and dupes are comical characters par excellence.

The Fear of Death and the Love of Truth

The erotic relationship is only one of many possible contexts in which the need arises, in the presence of listeners, to convey meaning covertly to the intended recipient. For one thing, fear of ridicule is not confined to lovers. It is a ubiquitous emotion.[14] Nor is the unwanted recipient always feared merely because he is a gossip who may bring on ridicule, defamation, social rejection, and the like; instead, he may inspire religious or political awe and dread. While fear of social sanctions is a strong motive for cautious behavior, religious and political fear are even more potent, since they are rooted in the fear of death.

The hunter, fisherman, or sailor in preliterate society who imagines he can be overheard or understood by animals, spirits, demons, and the like uses "guarded speech" (Sir James George Frazer) because he is afraid that open discourse would arouse the envy or wrath of uncontrollable powers and entail evil consequences for him. "In place of the forbidden word it is therefore necessary to use some kind of figurative paraphrase, to dig up an otherwise obsolete term, or to disguise the real word so as to render it more innocent."[15] Taboos are observed also with reference to ominous and mysterious physiological functions, events of nature, and in respect of powers that are held in awe, like God. They must not be named; substitute appellations are used.[16]

Like God, great human power as well can inspire awe and fear. If a heterogeneous audience includes persons of great power or their agents, the urge to abstain from the open expression of critical, skeptical, or aggressive opinions is very strong. The fact that it is dangerous to tell the truth to powerful masters is known from the folklore of many lands and is commonplace in the literature dealing with political counseling. Trusted counselors know they must speak cautiously to their princes.[17] Plautus has one of his characters say quite simply, "It's foolish for you to be disagreeable to a person who has more power."[18] Even the life of satirical entertainers is hazardous in illiberal times. They may be ruthlessly punished for as little as a hint in their work, although their subversive intent may be doubtful.[19]

Disclosing the truth is particularly dangerous if it finds fault with authoritative doctrines and sacred beliefs. This is so because even in the absence of a church and a priesthood with their vested interests in guarding the sacred against heresy or blasphemy, the believers do not tolerate any trifling with their gods and their faith and worship. The mere expression of doubt may be intolerable.[20]

However distant the believers may be from the exercise of political power, the rulers themselves must reckon with the religious predispositions of their subjects. Should they not share the communal faith or the ingrained superstitions of their subjects, they had yet better feign respect for them. It is therefore erroneous to equate "the vulgar" with those who have no power. This, of course, has been known to philosophers through the ages. As a rather modern observer, Pierre Bayle, remarked:

> If what is most falsely said by impious Men were true, viz. That Religion is a mere human invention, set up by the Sovereigns to keep their subjects within the Bounds of Obedience, may we not assert, that Princes are the first who have been taken in their own Snares? For Religion is so far from making them Masters of their Subjects, that, on the contrary, it gives their Subjects a Power over them, since they are obliged to profess the Religion of their People, and not That, which seems to them the best: And if they are resolved to profess a Religion different from that of their Subjects, their Crowns will fit loose upon their Heads.[21]

Under certain conditions, then, the powerful must resort to exoteric — religiously orthodox — speech for fear of their subjects, and withhold from them esoteric views that are religiously heterodox or irreligious.

The rulers share the need for such prudence with those philosophers who put reason above faith, although philosophers are not hungry for power. They want to be able to pursue the truth without having to drink poison. While they do not need to manipulate the superstitions of the vulgar, as statesmen and generals sometimes must do in order to achieve their ends,[22] they have reason to fear being deprived of liberty and life in retaliation for questioning powerful popular beliefs. In our time, Leo Strauss reflected more than any other man on the art of philosophical writing in times when those who speak the truth run the risk of persecution. The danger to which they are exposed lies not only with the authorities but, more generally, with those who are ignorant or, to use the older term, with the vulgar; and the authorities may be among them. Strauss pointed out that "premodern philosophers were more timid . . . than modern philosophers": being convinced that "philosophy as such was suspect to, and hated by, the majority of men," they eschewed popularization and concluded "that public communication of the philosophic or scientific truth was impossible or undesirable."[23] It was undesirable not only in view of possible persecution but also because other ills may be engendered by such communication. The wise avoid speaking rashly of God in a manner that may be misunderstood and abused by the vulgar, be they powerful or not.[24]

Aesopic Language

In repressive situations common words may be used to convey covert meanings according to advance agreements so that "insiders" may protect themselves against censors and other dangerous "outsiders." Needs of closeness and solidarity alone tend to foster the use of insider language. But the incorporation of covert meanings into everyday speech may become a matter of survival. Examples of improvised codes in discourse, correspondence, or telephone conversations to mislead eavesdroppers abound.[25]

A farcical instance of an impromptu code can be found in the transcript of the meeting that John W. Dean III and John Haldemann had with President Nixon on March 21, 1973. Dean reported that he telephoned John Mitchell at his home to inquire whether he had been able to raise money to pay Mr. Hunt, a Watergate defendant. Dean said, "He [Mitchell] was at home, and Martha [Mrs. Mitchell: in this case R_u] picked up the phone, so it was all in code. I said, 'Have you talked to the Greek [Mr. Pappas]?' And he said, 'Yes I have.' I said, 'Is the Greek bearing gifts?' He said, 'Well, I call you tomorrow on that.'"[26]

For veiled political criticism in repressive regimes the term "Aesopic language" has gained some currency. It was perhaps introduced by Saltykov-Shchedrin, the author of *The Golovyov Family* (1876) and *Fables* (1885), works in which the author attacked by way of circumlocution government officials, backward landowners, and greedy capitalists. Lenin as well used the terms "Aesopic language" and "slave language" to characterize the practice of the revolutionaries prior to the October Revolution of employing euphemisms in public print in order to hide their radical ideas from the censor. For example, the word "constitution" was understood by properly predisposed readers to mean "revolution." Even in Russia, however, the use of Aesopic language is older than either the Bolsheviks or Shchedrin. In the 1820s the participation of writers in political conspiracies—Pushkin's sympathy and that of other writers with the Decembrists—led the censors to suspect literature of being the cause of uprisings everywhere. When the journal *The European* was forbidden in 1832, and its editor placed under police surveillance, the censors issued a "notification" in which an objectionable contribution to the journal was characterized as follows: "Although the author says that he does not talk about politics, but about literature, he thinks something entirely different. The word 'enlightenment' he understands as 'liberty.' 'Activity of the mind' means to him 'the revolution'. . . . "[27]

Of course, the ruling groups as well as rebels and critics may resort to euphemisms and other devices of conveying covert meanings in public communications. The word for genocide used among Nazi leaders was "final solution." As long as the masses are illiterate and no right to education and active participation in politics is recognized, the need for communication between the rulers and the ruled is small. Many modern regimes, however, insist on adherence by the masses to official ideologies. If in these circumstances the ruling elite considers it important to keep the masses in a state of ignorance about conflicts and struggles for power among the rulers, it may become desirable for them to use exoteric communications with the masses while conveying at the same time esoteric meanings to the subelites. In the political analysis of the Soviet regime and its policies, the understanding of such communications has engaged the attention of many scholars.[28]

Cautious concealment of one's true opinions is possible without loss of self-respect only for those whose secretiveness or mendacity protects cherished persons or values, but there are certain professions that are especially vulnerable to demoralization in consequence of continual dissimulation in public: the professional talkers and writers on political subjects. For example, the political journalists in totalitarian regimes comprise two groups, the zealots and the secret critics. The former have no moral problems, since their zeal impels them to comply and overcomply with the orders they receive. They believe in the ideology they spread. The critics have the choice of leaving their profession or becoming hypocrites, since in this profession everybody is forced to appear as a zealot whether he is one or not. The critics who do not abandon their work must behave in public like zealots. Different from dissenters in many other walks of life, they are compelled by the nature of their work to advocate rather than merely tolerate beliefs they do not share. Writing between the lines then serves not only the objective purpose of spreading criticism obliquely but also the subjective need to gain a respite from pretended zeal for false causes.

The moral stress to which critical journalists are exposed in totalitarian regimes may find release in cynicism and, in the last resort, in the illusion that their esoteric dissent will be detected in their exoteric production.[29] After prolonged compliance with official regulations of language which conflict with reality, or after entertaining for a long time prohibited secret views, the journalist may attribute to his readers an understanding of meanings hidden in his writings which they either no longer possess or have ceased to be interested in: or else the hidden meaning may be so faint as to pass unnoticed. Such illusions indicate that through habituation to fear the subjective need for moral rehabilitation may be stronger than the weak effort or the small opportunity to attain it.

Bruno E. Werner's *Die Galeere*, a novel with an evidently broad autobiographical base, conveys many insights into such moral problems of journalists in the Nazi era. Toward the end of the war, a journalist in the book says to one of his colleagues, "By the way, some people assert that my editorials contain quite a bit between the lines; I have already twice been warned officially." And the author comments that the speaker "belonged to those journalists who did not notice at all that the readers had lost the habit of finding anything in these articles but the official vocabulary. . . . "[30]

Finally, the communicator may wish to include a meaning in his message which, though hidden from *all* recipients, is to modify the overt meaning in his own mind. This is the case of statements made with a "mental reservation" which the communicator expresses in a secret (and possibly magical) way intelligible only to himself. Thus perjury may be avoided in the mind of the perjurer, if not in the eyes of the law, by a publicly imperceptible gesture to which the perjurer attributes redeeming power, because to him it annuls the validity of the oath.

The Audience Seeking Meaning

There is much evidence to support the contention that whenever freedom of expression is suppressed, the sensitivity to allusions increases. A German writer reported about the Nazi regime that at the time

> not only in reading but also in conversation the slightest allusion was understood. Everywhere one smelled a reference to current politics, even when no such reference was made. A conferencier complained to me that his audience was so superkeen of hearing as to interpret politically any joke he was telling.[31]

In 1953, Helmut Thielicke, the distinguished German theologian, published a book of sermons on the Lord's Prayer.[32] He had given the first eight of the eleven sermons in Stuttgart toward the end of World War II, while the city was subject to severe bombing raids. Professor Thielicke told me in 1953 that he recalled the feeling of political audacity he had had when giving these sermons, although they contained no overt political references. He added that, in reading proof in the early fifties, he could no longer discover which specific passages in his sermons had made him feel that way. By the same token, he said, he had experienced after the war that when speaking in a church in Communist East Berlin one had only to whisper what in West Germany required, as it were, the sound of trumpets to be understood. Several other German authors with whom I talked after the war about their experiences in writing and talking between the lines during the Nazi period spontaneously testified in the same way to the heightened sensitivity of the listeners to critical allusions in times of extreme political stress and to the loss of such sensitivity when the stress relaxed.

Indeed, it appears that people who are deprived of voicing and hearing criticism freely tend to find it wherever they can, in old literature as well as in contemporary communications. We may describe this situation, somewhat boldly, as one in which the audience seeks the meaning that it needs so that possibly R, and not necessarily C, is the originator of M_c.

In the years when Hitler ruled Germany, Ernst Jünger wrote a book, *On the Marble Cliffs*, which was widely read in Germany. The author used fantastic imagery to depict certain aspects of modern tyrannical regimes. The main figure in his book was a "Chief Forester." Later, in May 1945, Jünger noted in his diary that in times of censorship "the imagination of the reader cooperates exegetically — much more powerfully than the author wishes. The 'Chief Forester' was understood to be now Hitler, now Göring, now Stalin. This sort of thing I had foreseen, to be sure, but not intended."[33]

In all epochs of history, repressive regimes have encountered the power of allusive criticism contained in older literature. While censors may be able to suppress the contemporary expression of dissent, they cannot possibly prevent associations of suppressed criticism that classical works of the past may evoke in a contemporary audience. For example, in the time of the Roman Empire, theater audiences applauded certain lines in ancient plays which seemed applicable to current abuses as well as to past practices chided by the author.[34]

To this day, many past events and a great deal of old literature have been sources of intense embarrassment to the guardians of prescribed thought. Hence the policy of illiberal regimes to confiscate or burn objectionable books of authors long dead, to restrict access to such books in libraries, to rewrite history, to eliminate certain plays from the repertoire of the theater, to rename cities, to dismantle public monuments, to prohibit old songs and drive certain musical compositions out of concert halls.[35]

The more widely acknowledged the fame and the more deeply rooted the admiration for an old author, the more difficult it is for censors to punish contemporary readers for attributing to his work a timely, subversive, meaning. Sometimes even old poetry may defy the censors despite the fierce criticism which contemporary readers and listeners suddenly read into stanzas whose political meaning has lain dormant for a long time.[36]

Similarly, Rudolf Pechel, for nine years until his arrest in 1942 the courageous editor of *Deutsche Rundschau*, published not only many essays which were obliquely critical of the regime but also excerpts from the writings of old authors whom the readers could suddenly recognize as famous champions of ideas opposed by the Nazis. The authors, whose writings were excerpted under the heading "The Living Past," included Erasmus, Francis Bacon, Balthasar Gracian, Boetius, Marcus Aurelius, Lao-tzu, Montesquieu, Vauvenargues, Manzoni, Kant, Jacob Burckhardt, and Jonathan Swift.

Truly covert meaning, recalled quite often in dire political circumstances, is contained in Tacitus's works. As a senator under the reign of Domitian (A.D. 81–86), whom he regarded as a worse tyrant than Nero, Tacitus witnessed the expulsions of philosophers, book burnings, and death penalties executed upon command of the emperor. Later, he wrote, "as previous ages saw the utmost of liberty, so we saw the utmost of servitude, since we were robbed by spying of speech and hearing. With our voices we would have lost memory itself, if it were as much in our power to forget as it was to be silent."[37] And again, "How few are we who have survived not only others but, as it were, ourselves. . . . "[38] When the good emperor Nerva was chosen to succeed Domitian, Tacitus began to publish his history of the emperors. Long after his death, the Attic brevity and simplicity of his style was associated with unorthodoxy "and even libertinism" in many ages, whereas Cicero's ornate style became that of the church, the universities, the Jesuits, the foreign offices — in general, of orthodoxy.[39]

Interestingly enough, as late as the eighteenth and the early nineteenth centuries, Tacitus was regarded "as a dangerously subversive writer," particularly "under the dictatorships both of the Jacobins and of Napoleon."[40] Similarly, in this century, three years after Hitler had assumed power, the Phaidon Publishing House issued a German translation of Tacitus's works. In a brief note at the conclusion of the volume, signed by the publisher, the reader learned that Tacitus had awaited the end of the arbitrary rule of tyranny in "embittered silence" and that its long duration had made him cautious:

> He did not always want to be understood, not always easily, not always by everybody; many of his sentences are dark as hiding places and brief like riddles. It is remarkable that precisely in such times of anxiety, rather than in times when the press is free, the strongest statements are made and the most intricate thought becomes expressible: severe constraint produces the greatest stylists.[41]

Evidently the German publisher hoped that some readers of the book would discover and cherish in Tacitus's old work certain timely critical views of tyranny.

Sacred literature which embodies lasting values is relatively safe from political censors. Victor Klemperer, distinguished observer of the deterioration of morality and language in the Nazi era, noted triumphantly that sermons which took the authorities and their policies to task, if only by implication, were "quite unassailably timeless."[42] But even sacred literature is not always exempt from political persecution.

When the Chinese Communists decided in 1974 to label all resistance to revolutionary values as Confucian, it became necessary to instruct Chinese youth on a mass scale what abominable "reactionaries" Confucius and Mencius had been. Now Mencius had generally been credited with advocating the right to slay those despised for having outraged humanity and righteousness. But according to a Chinese broadcast in 1974, a meeting of "poor and lower-middle-class peasants" was held in Tsou-hsien County in the eastern province of Shantung, where Mencius had been born more than 2000 years ago. At this meeting it was recalled that "a certain Meng Fan-chi, said to be a 'Mencius descendant of the 74th generation,' gave a banquet for Japanese Army officers during World War II. 'This,' the broadcast said, 'shows the hypocrisy of Mencius.'"[43]

This instance surpasses in delay of censure other cases, such as that of Hobbes's *De Cive*, published in 1642, put on the Roman Index in 1654, and burned at Oxford in 1683; that of Copernicus's *De Revolutionibus*, quickly denounced by Luther, but kept off the Roman Index for almost a century; or the condemnation of John Scot Erigena's heresy by Honorius III in 1225, nearly four centuries after its publication.

Urbane Dissimulation

Covert meaning occurs in communication with "insiders." It excludes unwanted recipients, no matter whether they are in earshot of the communicator or are part of an outside world that is considered to be vulgar, profane, hostile, dangerous. Often the transmission of hidden meaning is associated with consciousness of superiority over those excluded from the communication. It has been said that cultists and sectaries who teach hidden doctrines have a common failing, "the desire to feel superior to others by virtue of esoteric knowledge."[44] While it may be an open question whether or not they have "a desire" to feel superior, the "feeling" itself is indeed common.

It must still be noted that something similar to covert meaning may appear in the *absence* of unwanted recipients, that is to say, in entirely homogeneous groups. This is the urbane dissimulation employed in toning down a painful evocation among civilized people or in softening bad, saddening, news. "Among civilized peoples and especially in refined circles," as Eric Partridge put it in an essay on euphemism,[45] talk about death, sickness, madness, idiocy, ruin, and similarly disturbing subjects is "toned down," if it cannot be altogether avoided.

The relative who has died is said to have "departed," and the person who is very ill may be characterized as *"bien fatigué"* — very tired.[46] Conversely, unrestrained, direct talk among mourners is heartless, as is chillingly shown in Leo Tolstoy's short story "The Death of Ivan Ilyich." Talk about low physical functions and processes as well is avoided in "polite society," or euphemisms, allusions, and abbreviations are employed instead: she "powders her nose," "he spends the night with her," somebody has "TB," etc. Such unpragmatic patterns of speech are capable of extraordinary elaboration and refinement.

All upper classes tend to develop a vocabulary of refined speech, the mastery of which identifies its members. "Correct" pronunciation as well as the "proper" choice of words and, under certain conditions, calligraphy may be indispensable for a successful claim to upper-class status.[47] The understanding of literary allusions may become a mark of distinction.[48]

Since the beautiful must not show the effort it takes to produce it, negligence and carelessness in communication may be regarded as attributes of high standing if speech or writing otherwise clearly meets the required standards.[49]

Similar to allusive discourse in socially exclusive circles is the use of learned allusions by poets in order to display their erudition (to other poets) rather than to please the multitude. In Camoēns's *The Lusiads* (1572), "the bird whose song the Phaetonian death wailed loud and long" is the swan; "the glowing amourist who won fair faithless Larissaea's love" is Apollo, etc. Renaissance poets were much concerned with showing their familiarity with the world of Vergil and Ovid; they referred to "the gods and heroes of antiquity by allusion or association rather than directly."[50] The contempt for the unlettered to be found in medieval Latin poetry survived as disdain for general popularity among serious writers and composers well into the Baroque and Classicist eras.[51] In English poetry the late seventeenth and early eighteenth centuries were the great age of allusion. Only thereafter do allusions of great poets sometimes take on the air of labored futility.[52]

A social class that places a high value on courtesy and good manners observes many verbal taboos. That which is felt to offend, disturb, or frighten man is hidden behind a veil of politeness. Outsiders may be inclined to scorn the artificiality of such conventions, which can indeed degenerate into fastidious niceties indistinguishable from silliness. It should be noted, however, that urbane dissimulation not only is an attribute of social class but also serves to render life bearable and light in defiance of its dark terrors.

Allegorical Interpretation

In this brief essay we have seen that hidden meaning is conveyed to certain recipients in preliterate and literate societies, and particularly, though not exclusively, in illiberal regimes; among those who wield power as well as those who live under its sway; among victims, critics, and detached observers; in high and low social classes. Nor are the efforts to find a way from the overt sense to a deeper "real" meaning confined to everyday political and nonpolitical discourse; they are rather regularly required in the exegesis of sacred texts, the understanding of myths, allegories, parables, and poetic imagery, in the interpretation of philosophical writings, the critical appreciation of fine art and literature.

Inasmuch as the intention of the author or communicator is not always perfectly obvious, it is possible that some hidden meaning is read into the message by a recipient or interpreter. This possibility was not in Dante's mind when he set forth his well-known doctrine that books "can be understood and ought to be explained in four principal senses," which he termed literal, allegorical, moral, and anagogical (or mystical).[53] The notion that the recipient may possibly read these meanings into the text is rather a modern thought having to do with the discrediting of allegoresis by the Protestant Reformation, if not with the modern inclination to favor living readers over dead authors. To Dante, meaning was given in the texts to which he referred for illustration. The notion that meanings might have been invented by readers—that is, merely read into the Scriptures or Ovid, without being intended by God, the Evangelist, or the poet—would have been alien to him.

As regards allegorical interpretation, Dante was merely a link in a long history that went back to the Church Fathers and further to Philo. In the Jewish tradition, no verse in Scripture, whether narrative or law, had to be taken literally but was subject to free interpretation.[54] Philo was also conversant from Greek philosophical literature with the practice of assimilating certain elements of the Greek myths by understanding them as allegories.[55] In general, allegorizing means interpreting a text "in terms of something else, irrespective of what that something else is"—"book learning . . . practical wisdom . . . speculative meditation . . . urging necessities of changed conditions of life," etc.[56] Sometimes, allegorical interpretations were also used "to defeat the crude literalism of fanatical heresies; or to reconcile the teachings of philosophy with the truths of the Gospel."[57]

In the many centuries in which the allegorical interpretation of sacred texts, whether Jewish, Christian or Mohammedan, dominated exegesis, the legitimacy of the method was not questioned, although there were controversies about the number of meanings to be discovered, the rules and methods that were to govern the interpretation, and the correctness of specific instances of exegesis.

In dealing with hidden meaning critically it is necessary to distinguish works written by authors like Maimonides or Rabelais, who state explicitly that meaning is concealed in their writings, from writings like the Homeric poems or sacred texts, in regard to which the assertions of hidden meaning stem exclusively from the interpreters. The names of gods in Homer and Hesiod are not allegories, but to the Stoics Zeus meant *logos*, Ares war, Hermes reason, etc. Many centuries later, John of Salisbury elaborated earlier allegorical interpretations of Vergil and taught that the truths of philosophy were expressed in the *Aeneid* under the guise of a legend. Origen and St. Augustine, following a kindred Talmudic tradition, held that the Song of Songs signified Christ and the Church, although the text itself allows such interpretation only if certain rules of allegoresis are accepted. Philo had laid down the rule "that no anthropomorphic expression about God is to be taken literally"; he assumed that such expressions were "introduced for the instruction of the many."[58] St. Augustine taught that "whatever in Holy Writ cannot properly be said to be concerned either with morality or with the faith must be recognized as allegorical."[59]

The fact that Dante subscribed to the scholastic teaching of the four meanings allows us then to presume that *The Divine Comedy* can be taken as a work in which indeed four meanings can be discovered, because they were intended by the author. In other instances, however, the author's instruction to search for hidden sense is less obvious than in Dante's case and can be established only by very careful inquiry, if at all. In still others it cannot be proved and, if claimed, must be regarded as an invention of the interpreter. In the latter category belongs, for example, the cabalistic methods of gematria.

NOTES

1. U.S. Atomic Energy Commission, *In the Matter of J. Robert Oppenheimer: Transcript of Hearings Before Personnel Security Board, Washington, D.C., April 12, 1954, through May 6, 1954*, Washington, 1954, p. 87.

2. Silence and the pressure to break it provide much of the drama in the play about Thomas More by Robert Bolt, *A Man for All Seasons*.

3. For two illustrations, see Leo Strauss, *Thoughts on Machiavelli*, Glencoe, 1958, pp. 30-31.

4. Hugo von Hofmannsthal, *Der Schwierige* (1921), in *Gesammelte Werke*, 6 vols., Berlin, 1924, vol. 1, p. 445. See also the quotation from a conversation with the poet in Carl J. Burckhardt, *Erinnerungen an Hofmannsthal*, Munich, 1964, pp. 88-89; and the essays by George Steiner, "Der Rückzug aus dem Wort" and "Der Dichter und das Schweigen," in his *Sprache und Schweigen*, Frankfurt, 1969, pp. 44-97.

5. G. W. F. Hegel, *Phänomenologie des Geistes*, 2nd ed., ed. by Georg Lasson, Leipzig, 1921, p. 8.

6. The New York *Times*, March 13, 1974.

7. Edward Gibbon, *Decline and Fall of the Roman Empire*, chap. 40.

8. Secret languages — as distinguished from codes — are contrived by children in many societies (including that of the Maoris of New Zealand), but there is also at least one instance of a secret language designed by a grammarian. In the fifth century A.D., Virgilius Maro invented *berba na filed* ("the poet's language"), a "slang" containing words from Latin, Greek, and Hebrew, native archaic words and distorted common words, that "was preserved by tradition in the Irish schools as a secret language" (Joseph Vendryes, *Language: A Linguistic Introduction to History*, translated by Paul Radin, New York, 1925, p. 255).

9. Ibid., part 4, chap. 2, "Dialects and Specialized Languages."

10. Cicero, *De Oratore* 2: 64-65.

11. See Richard Broxton Onians, *The Origin of European Thought*, Cambridge, 1954, part 3, chaps. 4-5, pp. 349-77.

12. Stendhal, *Lucien Leuwen*, part I, chap. 24.

13. Another very fine illustration of double meaning in erotic discourse may be found in Molière's *The School for Husbands*, act 2, where Isabella and Valère declare their love for each other in the presence of Sganarel, Isabella's guardian. Due to the use of skillfully ambiguous language, Sganarel misunderstands the discourse and believes that Isabella faithfully loves him, addressing Valère in indignation at his advances to her. For an instance from another culture, see the sixteenth-century Chinese novel *Chin P'ing Mei*, with an introduction by Arthur Waley, New York, 1940, p. 678. Consider also the covert meaning hidden in every roman à clef: see Georg Schneider, *Die Schlüsselliteratur*, 3 vols., Stuttgart, 1951-53.

14. Theodore Agrippa d'Aubigné (1552-1630) concluded the preface to his memoirs, published for the first time only in 1729 as *Histoire Secrète*, by an order to his children that they should not keep "more than two copies of this book," that these should be closely guarded, and that neither copy should leave the house. Otherwise those who were envious of the children would punish them by laughing at the divine miracles by which his life had been saved. See Otto Fischer, ed., *Thomas and Felix Platters und Theodor Agrippa d'Aubignés Lebensbeschreibungen*, Munich, 1911, p. 294.

15. Otto Jespersen, *Language: Its Nature, Development and Origin*, London, 1922, p. 289.

16. Heinz Werner, in his important investigation into the origins of metaphor, advanced the opinion that fear is prior to awe: "Furcht ist früher als Ehrfurcht" (Heinz Werner, *Die Ursprünge der Metapher*, Leipzig, 1919, p. 43).

17. See Thomas More's "Dialogue of Counsel" in his *Utopia*, at the end of Book 1.
18. Plautus, *Casina* 2.4.
19. At the time of the ruthless emperor Domitian, "the young Stoic nobleman Helvidius Priscus produced a farce about Paris — not the dancer, but the mythical Trojan prince — deserting the nymph Oenone. Domitian took this as an allusion to his own divorce, and executed Helvidius. It did not matter whether the allusion was intentional or not. It was sufficient if it was likely to be noticed and enjoyed by the public" (Gilbert Highet, *Juvenal the Satirist*, Oxford, 1954, p. 26).
20. According to Cicero (*De natura deorum* 1.23), Protagoras of Abdera opened a book with the statement, "About the gods I am unable to affirm either how they exist or how they do not exist." The Athenian assembly banished him from the city and had his books burned in the marketplace.
21. Pierre Bayle, *Selections from Bayle's Dictionary*, ed. by E. A. Beller and M. du P. Lee, Jr. (Princeton, 1952), p. 4 (article "Abdas").
22. Machiavelli, *The Discourses*, 1.14–15.
23. Leo Strauss, *Persecution and the Art of Writing*, Glencoe, Ill., 1952, pp. 33–34.
24. As late as 1784, Moses Mendelssohn pointed out in his essay "Ueber die Frage: was heisst aufklären?" that the enlightening philosopher will not spread certain truths if they tear down principles of religion and morality. See Norbert Hiske, ed., *Was ist Aufklärung? Beiträge aus der Berliner Monatsschrift*, 2nd ed., Darmstadt, 1977, pp. 449–50.
25. Lali Horstmann reports about Nazi Germany that in her circle of anti-Nazis "Sybil" was used for England, "Pit" for Russia. "The patient's health is unchanged, worse or hopeless, was the expression we agreed on to describe the state of German defence" (Lali Horstmann, *Nothing for Tears*, London, 1953, pp. 39, 62, 67, 73). Similar references to impromptu codes occur in Margret Boveri, *Tage des Überlebens*, Munich, 1968, p. 199; Rudolf Pechel, *Zwischen den Zeilen*, Wiesentheid, 1948, p. 343. An older illustration from eighteenth-century France: "Nicolas Boindin, a man of letters . . . was usually 'at home' at the Café Procope, and was a recognized freethinker there. He had a jargon all his own, and a plentiful assortment of nicknames. Liberty he called Jeanneton, Religion was Jacotte, and God M. de l'Être. 'May I venture to ask,' said a detective who was listening, 'who this M. de l'Être may be who so often misbehaves himself, and with whom you seem to have so much fault to find?' 'Yes, Monsieur; he's a police spy'" (Paul Hazard, *European Thought in the Eighteenth Century*, New Haven, 1954, p. 95).
26. *The Presidential Transcripts*, New York, 1974, pp. 133–34.
27. *Entsiklopedicheskii Slovar*, 41 vols., Petersburg, 1890–1904, 37: 955ff. For Aesopic language in *Pravda* prior to the October Revolution, see Whitman Bassow, "The Pre-Revolutionary *Pravda* and Tsarist Censorship," *The American Slavic and East European Review* 13 (1954): 47–65. More recently, Nathan Leites and Elsa Bernaut in their examination of the Moscow Trials showed in great detail the grammar and syntax of the "veiled language" in which the Bolshevik defendants expressed themselves in order to communicate with other leaders without speaking overtly to the masses (Nathan Leites and Elsa Bernaut, *Ritual of Liquidation*, Glencoe, 1954). For instances of the current use of Aesopic language, see Dina Spechler, "Permitted Dissent in the Decade after Stalin: Criticism and Protest in *Novy Mir*, 1955–1964," in Paul Cocks and others, eds., *The Dynamics of Soviet Politics*, Cambridge, 1976, pp. 28–50.
28. Myron Rush, *The Rise of Khrushchev*, Washington, D.C., 1958; Myron Rush,

"Esoteric Communication in Soviet Politics," *World Politics* 11 (1959): pp. 614–20; Robert Conquest, *Power and Policy in the U.S.S.R.*, New York, 1961; Donald S. Zagoria, *The Sino-Soviet Conflict, 1956–1961*, Princeton, 1962, pp. 24–35; William E. Griffith, *Communist Esoteric Communications: Explication de Texte*, Cambridge, 1967; Leites and Bernaut, *Ritual of Liquidation*, pp. 277–349.

29. A staunch anti-Nazi in Germany observed in 1939 that "the same journalists who only yesterday were up to their neck in their twaddle, crack cynical jokes at their own Byzantine behavior as soon as one speaks to them in the street" (Friedrich Percyval Reck-Malleczewen, *Tagebuch eines Verzweifelten*, Lorch/Württemberg, 1947, p. 97.

30. Bruno E. Werner, *Die Galeere*, Amsterdam, 1949, p. 494.

31. Werner Bergengruen, "Foreword" to Pechel, *Zwischen den Zeilen*, pp. 8–9.

32. Helmut Thielicke, *Das Gebet, das die Welt umspannt*, Stuttgart, 1973.

33. Ernst Jünger, *Strahlungen*, Munich, 1966, p. 147.

34. Moses Hadas, *Ancilla to Classical Reading*, New York, 1954, p. 76.

35. After the Decembrist Revolution in Russia in 1825, all lectures at Petersburg University were read from carefully censored books, and "the students were expected to take them down and repeat them verbatim because to answer 'in their own words' was considered 'subversive free thinking'" (David Margarshak, *Turgenev: A Life*, New York, 1954, p. 54). Schiller's *Wilhelm Tell* was removed by the Nazis from the list of required reading in schools and banished from the stage because of the antityrannical verses the play contains (Theodor Heuss, *Dank und Bekenntnis: Gedenkrede zum 20. Juli 1944*, Tübingen, 1954, p. 23). The opposition of the Nazis to Schiller's *Don Karlos* has a precedent in the removal of the play from the repertoire of the theater in Graz by the Austrian police in 1830. The incident inspired Johann Nestroy the following day to an extraordinarily effective satirical demonstration on the stage (Hans Speier, *Witz und Politik: Essay über die Macht und das Lachen*, Zurich, 1975, pp. 30–31.

36. An especially pertinent instance is a poem written by Gottfried Keller, which became very popular in the Third Reich; see Reck-Malleczewen, *Tagebuch eines Verzweifelten*, p. 97.

37. Tacitus, *Agricola* 2.

38. Ibid., 3.

39. Gilbert Highet, *The Classical Tradition*, New York, 1949, chap. 18. As a certain parallel, it may be mentioned that Stendhal wrote *Lucien Leuwen* in 1836 for "the happy few" who would understand his meaning and appreciate his style fifty years later. He wrote eschewing the popular romanticism of his day and reading the *Code Napoléon* in order to avoid in his own prose the stylistic frills he detested. His novel, which was devastatingly critical of politics in the Second Empire, was published posthumously.

40. Lionel Trilling, "Tacitus Now" (1942), in his *The Liberal Imagination*, New York, 1953, p. 194. In the United States, his aristocratic values have kept liberals from admiring Tacitus (ibid.). On Tacitus, see also Ronald Syme, *Tacitus*, 2 vols., Oxford, 1958.

41. Cornelius Tacitus, *Sämtliche Werke*, Vienna, 1935, "Nachwort," p. 800.

42. Victor Klemperer, *LTI Notizbuch eines Philologen*, Berlin, 1949, p. 279.

43. The New York *Times*, April 4, 1974.

44. Jeffrey Burton Russell, *Dissent and Reform in the Early Middle Ages*, Berkeley, 1965, p. 212.

45. Eric Partridge, "Euphemism and Euphemisms," republished in his *Here, There and Everywhere*, London, 1950, pp. 39–49.
46. Laurence Wylie, *Village in the Vaucluse*, Cambridge, 1957, p. 188. Cf. *abire ad plures* for *mori* in Latin. On euphemisms in Latin, see Otto Keller, *Zur lateinischen Sprachgeschichte*, 2 vols., Leipzig, 1893–95.
47. *The Pillow-Book of Sei Shonagon*, translated by Arthur Waley, London, 1949, "Introduction." For the high esteem in which calligraphy was held in Islam, see Ernst Robert Curtius, *European Literature and the Latin Middle Ages*, New York, 1953, p. 341.
48. *The Pillow-Book of Sei Shōnagon* (p. 65) contains an allusion to Confucius not understood by the man to whom the tenth-century author speaks in the book; nor does she explain it. It is explained by Mr. Waley, the twentieth-century editor of the book.
49. For example, in Lady Murasaki's *The Tale of Genji* it is said about a poem written on a fan: "It was written with a deliberate negligence which seemed to him to aim at concealing the writer's status and identity. But for all that the hand showed breeding and distinction . . . " (Murasaki shikibu, *The Tale of Genji*, translated by Arthur Waley, 2 vols., Boston, 1935, 1:56). There are many other passages showing the importance of calligraphy.
50. William C. Atkinson, in the introduction to his new translation of Camoëns, *The Lusiads*, London, 1952, p. 34.
51. See Hans Speier, "Court and Tavern in the German Baroque Novel," in his *Force and Folly*, Cambridge, 1969, p. 224.
52. See, for example, E. M. W. Tillyard's comments in *Poetry, Direct and Oblique* London, 1948, p. 35, on Ezra Pound's "Ode pour l'élection de son sépulcre." Tillyard speaks of "bogus obliquity" and "would-be obliquity through allusion."
53. See *A Translation of Dante's Eleven Letters*, with explanatory notes and historical comments by Charles Sterrett Latham, ed. by George Rice Carpenter, Boston and New York, 1892, pp. 194–95.
54. On allegory and the allegorical method, see Joh. Geffcken, "Allegory, Allegorical Interpretation," in James Hastings, ed., *Encyclopedia of Religion and Ethics*, 12 vols., New York, 1913–22, 1:327–31; Frederic W. Farrar, *History of Interpretation*, London, 1886; Harry A. Wolfson, *Philo*, 2 vols., Cambridge, 1947, especially 1:115–63.
55. See J. Tate, "The Beginnings of Greek Allegory," *The Classical Review* 41 (1927).
56. Wolfson, *Philo*, 1:134.
57. Farrar, *History of Interpretation*, p. 249.
58. Wolfson, *Philo*, 1:116. "Therefore speak I to them in parables: because they seeing me not; and hearing me not, neither do they understand" (Matt. 13:13).
59. Farrar, *History of Interpretation*, p. 237.

PART THREE

Literature and the History of Ideas

10

Shakespeare's *The Tempest**

I

The work of a great poet lends itself to many interpretations, but the attributes of greatness can never be derived from the dissent among its admirers. The profound and the mysterious should not be confused, and simplicity is not necessarily shallow. The meaning of Shakespeare's *The Tempest* is both simple and profound. Its theme is the nature of authority.

*The following notes were written in 1942 for a seminar in sociology of literature. The discussions dealt less with literature itself than with the size, composition and tastes of the reading public in various periods of history, subjects which lend themselves well to sociological study. It became apparent, however, that among the students there were a few who had not learned to look in great literature for performances other than the grinding of axes. Caliban was cited as a symbol of the masses. Renan rather than Shakespeare was quoted. It seemed an important issue what Shakespeare's *The Tempest* had contributed to the armory of the class war.

Without the guidance of Shakespeare scholars it is difficult to write about Shakespeare and perhaps inadvisable. But then, we should not always remember how many decades or centuries ago a great author lived if he wrote about matters that are of concern to us. Despite the fact that Shakespeare belonged to the Elizabethan age and we to Marx–Lenin–Stalin's or whomever else ours may be named after, we can communicate with Shakespeare as though he were alive. We know what he said.

First published in Hans Speier, *Social Order and the Risks of War*, New York, 1952. Copyright © 1952 by George W. Stewart, Publisher, Inc., First M.I.T. Press paperback edition March 1969. Reprinted by permission of M.I.T. Press.

When reading the play we get a glimpse of an older world. We believe that we have extended its boundaries, but also we may have squandered some if its philosophic treasures.

The Tempest, Shakespeare's most charming play, is pervaded by a truly philosophical spirit: morals and politics, justice, power, work and love — all these human concerns are related to nature.

II

In order to learn from Shakespeare, we may have to change our attitude toward poetry. We are in the strange habit of regarding the poet as an eloquent dealer in imagery, an expert in feelings who does not think. If once we happen not to frown at his uselessness we concede to him that he may startle or move us for an eccentric moment. Then, he had better hurry on and not waste our time, and we often consider it a waste of time when a poet induces us to think. From a poet we demand light and exotic refreshments which can be easily digested — not solid food.

We are victims of the narrow-mindedness of science. We inquire into nature in a way in which only our cunning exceeds our impatience. Like savages who want to extort a secret from a captive we speak to nature, "Yield under torture, reveal your secret or be crucified."

Of course, we cannot really crucify nature; we have merely arranged a crucifixion in effigy. The poet, whom we do not understand, is seized and poeticide becomes a scientific ritual. We interrupt it only when we are tired.

Who is the poet? We are hardly prepared to learn or inclined to believe that the poet is the forgotten You and I who know of nature before it is tortured. In the poet we crucify that part of ourselves which reminds us of knowledge we have forfeited, that knowledge of nature which does *not* enable us to change the world around us but to understand it and live in it.

A long time ago, we developed modern science as veritable outsiders of nature. In order to become scientific observers we had to denature ourselves. We have succeeded. When we say, now, that we are reasonable we mean that we are engaged in calculations. When we hold something to be irrational we are merely indignant that our predictions have not been borne out, or perhaps, we are amused, for we make rash distinctions between the irrational and the stupid. When we say "naturally," we are hardly ever right.

In the age of poeticide even the old poets have to fight an exhausting struggle if they wish us to see with their eyes and to listen, as they listened, to the voice of nature.

They communicated their message as poetic form – an outgrowth of discipline imposed upon imagination and thought, a defiance of infinity. But have we the subtle organs for understanding form? Also form has been replaced by notions which are more easily assimilated to the method of scientific inquiry. When the poet says "form" the scientist speaks of "relationship."

Besides, it is the close affinity between play and form which arouses the suspicion of the scientist. (And distrust is his most obligatory fault: he thinks he cannot do without it.) The scientist is seriously at work until he expires in his laboratory. He even spoils the games which he does play after all. In the seventeenth century, he was called a pedant for that reason. Similarly, he may be said to be the person who does not behave naturally in the world of nature.

The poet gives us the image of nature as form. He uses old symbols. He conveys his message through words. He names what is real, hoping that he will be understood. Words are his only sword with which he defends nature against her modern observers.

We should learn from the poet. The notion that feeling and thought are hostile to one another is true only of perverted and exaggerated feeling or of barren thought. If uncorrupted, thought and feeling are at one. All great poets were wise. Let us leave the detection of an essential enmity between philosophy and poetry to misanthropes whom the dictionary defines as "haters of mankind." Shakespeare, the poet, expects us to think.

III

The cast in *The Tempest* consists of symbols, human, spiritual and subhuman. The human symbols denote both social and moral characters. Sebastian's vice is that of a king's brother, Stephano's vice is the vice of a butler. Virtues and vices, as they appear in *The Tempest*, are specific qualities of men each of whom occupies a specific place in the political world. The cast is a composite symbol of man while no single person, with the possible exception of Ferdinand, can be said to represent the whole nature of man. Only if we take account of all the virtues and vices displayed in *The Tempest* by different persons do we understand what Shakespeare thought of human nature. This is more than a dramatic device enabling the poet to enact in the medium of time what exists at all times: it is a refutation of all notions of human nature which reduce man to one basic drive or quality, be it fear or vanity, greed or goodness. In particular, man cannot be said to be "good" if we regard *The Tempest* as a symbol of his life. We must bear this in mind in order to understand Shakespeare's verdict on modern utopias, which the play pronounces.

Prospero, too, has his vice. He lost Milano because he neglected his business as a duke. He indulged in reading, and this was his vice. In Shakespeare's words, he neglected "wordly ends."

Shakespeare assumes that human virtues can be distinguished from vices because we are able to distinguish order and disorder in the political world. We understand perhaps what virtue in this sense means when we do not hesitate to call the strength and the well-shaped body of a horse its virtue, or to consider a leopard ferociously jumping at his dompteur a virtuous cat. If it is true that water must flow, stagnant water is vicious.

IV

While man is capable of distinguishing order from disorder he can be said to live always in disorder, which is another way of saying that to him order is an idea to be understood rather than a fact to be discovered. The human world is essentially failing, but man is, at the same time, able to realize this failure. Since this realization bears upon man's conduct and his effort to achieve order, it is vicious not to think. The order of the human universe is inevitably a utopia: this is perhaps the simplest way of expressing man's relation to order.

Utopia is an order in which both ruler and ruled are virtuous: the ruler is just and those who are ruled are obedient. While life is infested with injustice and disobedience, a utopia is the body politic in which obedience and justice are in harmony; but a utopia cannot be realized.

Often, we mean by utopia something else. We think that a utopia is a world in which obedience can be dispensed with and, indeed, must be dispensed with in order to establish full justice. This "modern" utopia represents the paradoxical attempt to imagine a political order without regard for a political principle. In modern utopias politics is extinguished. A modern utopia is an idyl and an atrophy.

While either utopia is unreal, only the modern one is phantastic. The lust for happiness which it displays springs from excessive feelings; the denial of authority which it implies betrays a foggy mind. Since it is nonpolitical it serves as a subtle justification for immorality in politics. Under the influence of modern utopian thinking every ruler can justify acts of immoral expediency with the declaration that he is not a utopian, and any subject who obeys may regard his conduct as a morally indifferent act of accommodation.

V

The modern world does not differ much from the world as it has always existed: man has remained the same, although modern man likes to regard his world as a ladder on which he can climb to utopian institutions. Precisely this we have in mind when we say that we are progressing. Modern utopias are devised with a view to realization. This implies a distortion of the relation between fact and truth: only the factual appears now to be true.

In *The Tempest*, the "modern" utopia is presented as Gonzalo's dream. Gonzalo believes that man is good enough for his dream to come true. The mundane courtiers in *The Tempest* sneer at Gonzalo. Shakespeare, more indulgently, calls him an "honest old councillor." Of all the persons in *The Tempest* Gonzalo is the most compassionate politician, so much so that we almost wonder how he can hold his own against the shrewdness and ambitions of his rivals. Gonzalo has saved Prospero's and Miranda's lives when they were expelled from Milano. Gonzalo is decent and honest, but he is not very intelligent. We can trust him when help is needed for somebody in distress, but he is no fit councillor on the affairs of state: he lacks wisdom. Shakespeare's answer to Gonzalo's dream is *The Tempest* as a whole.

VI

While it is unlikely that the stupendous number of utopias produced in the nineteenth century will be reached again in ours we still like to contemplate the momentous effects new inventions may exert on our life. The desire for change, this modern passion, still entices us to obscure the difference between the good and the new. By continuing to apply the phrase "moral progress" to historical epochs we still discriminate against the past in the overbearing manner which adolescents sometimes display toward their parents. In fact, we distrust people who remind us that the excellent is extraordinary but indeed hardly new. The extraordinary we like only when it is not exclusive. This, certainly, is one reason for the wide appeal of technological accomplishments. Contrary to the legendary miracles of the past, technical wonders can be repeated and eventually be understood by everybody who cares to know. It is comfortable to rest assured that they are products of an intelligence in which everybody partakes. The belief in technical progress is our religion — the religion of the detectives of nature.

We still extol progress, but at times it seems that the cult has grown cumbrous. We begin to view with surprise the devout optimism of our forefathers. Sometimes, we hardly shrink from calling it naive. A few centuries after the quarrel about the respective rank of the ancients and the moderns we have become skeptical as to whether gunpowder, the printing press, and the compass have for ever secured our preeminence over the ancients.

We cannot turn for advice to the old apostles of progress. Their message is not addressed to us. Saint-Simon's notion that the "religion of science" is the adequate creed of industrial society appears banal to us, if not like a verdict. Condorcet's fantastic hope that ever progressing man is going to conquer death perplexes us greatly. We do not quite understand the enthusiasm of these writers whose buoyancy time has rendered grotesque. Saint-Pierre held that in comparison with a road, a bridge, a canal, Notre Dame was of little value. How insipid this sounds to us. We ask ourselves whether the author of this remark was an Abbé devoting much of his time to exploring the relations of commerce, progress and peace or an expert in logistics. If the meaning of civilization were merely technological in character, we should be ready now to define it as a state of organized resourcefulness which enables man to rise to the sky in order to erase himself from the earth.

These considerations were no concern of Shakespeare's, but we should not avoid them when reading *The Tempest* today. Regardless of the truly remarkable increase in safety and comfort we owe to technological progress we shall have to learn again how closely technology and utopianism are connected. Through technology we become masters of nature as it endangers us: we change nature. In utopias we fancy ourselves to be masters of our own nature as it threatens to disrupt and destroy social order: in our imagination we change man. We hope to build societies as we build bridges. In *The Tempest* Shakespeare tells us that our hope is vain and futile.

VII

Prospero's island is uninhabited save for Caliban, a heinous demon, and Ariel, a spirit of the air, who was once a servant of Caliban's mother. By means of white magic Prospero frees Ariel, "dainty, delicate" Ariel—a being that is capable of rational and physical sympathies but has no emotions.

Prospero's science, based upon a thorough knowledge of books, is technically known as theurgy which by means of incantations, secret numbers and signs influences the gods for good purposes. It must not be confused with black magic, as it was practiced by Sycorax, the foul witch who worked evil.

Shakespeare's audience was familiar with both white and black magic. Even Dryden held that Caliban, a creature begotten by an aquitarian spirit and a witch, half human, half fish, might indeed exist.

With Ariel and the meaner spirits of nature at his command, Prospero controls fate: his power extends over the forces of nature. Shakespeare's philosophy of nature in *The Tempest* follows closely neoplatonic speculations about the universe.[1] This has been convincingly established by Mr. Curry, yet it does not offer us any clue as to the meaning of *The Tempest*. The play is certainly not a dramatic treatise on Neoplatonism: it is a critique of modern utopias and a dramatic exposition of the nature of authority.

VIII

The first scene of *The Tempest* leaves no doubt as to what we are to expect. It depicts a disaster and shows one of the principal reasons for social disorder. In the danger of shipwreck, threatened by death, the boatswain and the sailors cease to obey their superiors. They are afraid of death, and their fear of death is the source of rebellion: political authority is limited by nature and political philosophy must take cognizance of this limitation. Only that political authority would be impervious to rebellion which could control nature.

The fear of death is rooted in the desire to enjoy life, or to be more precise, those are afraid of death whose supreme good is the enjoyment of life. While it is true that almost everybody regards the enjoyment of life as the highest good there are men who think differently. In *The Tempest*, Prospero is such a man. It is hardly without significance that death casts its shadow in the last scene as well as in the first scene of the play. At the end of *The Tempest*, Prospero declares that he wants to retire to Milano "where every third thought shall be my grave." Prospero does not seem to be afraid of death.

The boatswain and the sailors are of the multitude. They are ignorant. They have fear. Prospero is a philosopher. He has knowledge, and knowledge is a higher good to him than life.

IX

Prospero is not only a philosopher, he is also a magician. He controls the forces of nature. It is Ariel who causes the tempest at Prospero's command, and by invoking the fear of death among the King's subjects he destroys political authority. Nor is his power confined to the direction of the elements. Prospero is master over all other forces which may disrupt the social order.

Two of these destructive forces reside in human nature. The will to power and the greed for gain, or vanity and covetousness, render all order unstable and all authority precarious. Since vanity and covetousness aim at a greater enjoyment of life they are ultimately related to the fear of death.

Ariel, again at the command of Prospero, thwarts the plot to murder Alonso, the King of Naples: pride is punished by madness. He also crushes the conspiracy of Caliban and his drunken companions; greed is chased by dogs. Incidentally, the plebeian revolt is not a satire of the aristocratic conspiracy, for each plot illustrates a specific danger to which the body politic is exposed.

X

Shakespeare took the description of the utopian commonwealth of which Gonzalo dreams from Montaigne's essay on the Cannibals. It is characterized by negations. "I would by contraries execute all things," Gonzalo says. In this utopia there will be no traffic, no magistrate, no science, no contract, no work. There will be no scarcity and no sweat, and there will be neither treachery nor violence. Nor will there be any sovereignty. In short, this commonwealth will not reach, but "excel the golden age." All the aptitudes of man and the dangers of nature which render sovereignty both necessary and precarious are disregarded in Gonzalo's dream, that is the destructive forces of nature to which man is exposed and his own passions which destroy order. In *The Tempest* Shakespeare shows their power in scenes of superb simplicity.

His answer to Gonzalo's dream, however, does more than destroy an illusion. He takes the quest for the perfect social order seriously, and while his "project" is "to please," the wisdom of his answer lies beyond that which merely pleases. The perfect social order presupposes a perfect ruler who has extraordinary power over nature and man's wickedness. This perfect ruler is Prospero.

XI

The Tempest could also have been called The Education of a Ruler. Prospero learns how to rule. In Milano, he had lost his dukedom since he had been a philosopher rather than a ruler. It is therefore not altogether from his books that he acquires the qualities necessary in a ruler. He learns through experience; his brother's treachery in Milano and on the island (which inspires Gonzalo's utopian wish), Caliban's fiendish character urge upon him the duties of a ruler rather than those of a philosopher.

Yet Prospero *remains* a philosopher since he knows how to rule with justice. He combines in himself the qualities of the ruler, the philosopher and the magician. Prospero rules by evoking fear and astonishment, awe and admiration. He works upon the imagination. Those who are driven by passions and for that reason endanger the social order are not led to realize the sublime nature of authority by instruction: they are led to believe in *miracles*. They do not surrender to Prospero the philosopher, but to Prospero the magician. It is as if Shakespeare wants to show us that the world recognizes the "natural" only when it assumes a miraculous appearance.[2]

XII

The principles of conduct we call justice and obedience are elements of law, and the law is impersonal. Man, administering the law as well as man obeying it, is never wholly "at ease." The law which stands above man also stands between him and others. You fear the law, you abide by it, you respect it; but because of its impersonal character you cannot love it as you may love a person.

Now, while it is true that justice and obedience are necessary for concord to be established and maintained in the body politic, it is equally true that there are forms of human association in which concord does not rest upon the law. Friends and lovers need not be reminded by legal rules of the demands of equity. They live in peace. They need no oath to tie them together. In fact, the oath presupposes that the bond of love may be torn. Also, by evoking the majesty of God, the oath deprives love of its human self-sufficiency and thus implicitly admits that love may fail. Strictly speaking, lovers cannot be said to be loyal: they are *in* love, while loyalty is always a return to love. Thus, loyalty is closer to law, obligation, conscience, and possibly anxiety, than it is to love.

While love, which lacks the pedantry of law, is the bond that unites men most firmly, it is neither durable nor inclusive. It is not durable because it involves passions, and it is an intensive rather than extensive force. Montaigne said, doubling oneself through friendship is no small wonder, and those do not realize its greatness who chatter about trebling oneself.

Its exclusive nature renders love incapable of becoming the basis of concord in the state, or to put it in the briefest possible way, love and friendship are nonpolitical (which is not to deny that friendship among the members of a ruling group is a firm base of government). This is what Aristotle must have meant when he declared that there is no need for justice among friends.

The relation of lovers to the world outside the circle of their love has often been described by poets as a transformation of that world. For this reason the man who lives in love is unfit to live in the world. He is separated from it. He neglects the world as does the prince who reads too many books. Goethe once remarked that lovers appear slightly ludicrous when we watch them soberly. What the lover needs in order to be capable of living in this world is to be reminded of the world lest he forget that it is governed not by love but by law.

Shakespeare uses the simplest symbols for indicating both the nature of love and its relation to law. Ferdinand and Miranda love each other at first sight. But the prince must do heavy and odious work before he wins Miranda, and his "sweet mistress" weeps before she gets her lover.

The reason which Prospero gives for forcing Ferdinand to pile up thousands of logs is a seemingly conventional one. Observing the delight of the lovers he says aside,

> They are both in either's pow'rs. But this swift business
> I must uneasy make, lest too light winning
> Make the prize light.

We would be mistaken, however, if we were to read into Prospero's harsh decision a fatherly desire to increase the value of his daughter. It is not mere delay, a test of time, but a trial by servitude which he demands. And while Ferdinand is laboring hard Prospero wishes that "heavens rain grace on that which breeds between" the lovers. Besides, even if Prospero respected merely a convention that was dear to Shakespeare's audience, we should still have to inquire into the meaning of this convention. Naturally, love is light-minded and a lover easily infatuated, whereas life in this world is not easy. A man should therefore prove that he knows not the whole of life to be love. Ultimately, the ground of the convention is identical with that of the service Ferdinand must render before he consummates his love.

The trial by servitude is imposed upon the man. Miranda, perhaps the gentlest creation of Shakespeare's mind, bears the burden of the world through Ferdinand. She says no word of reproof to her father, nor does she ever complain about him to her lover. She consoles Ferdinand:

> Be of comfort;
> My father's of a better nature, sir,
> Than he appears by speech.

Miranda, the woman, is made for love, and this is her whole world. Perhaps we understand in this connection also one of the most subtle symbols of the play. In the second scene of the first act, Prospero eventually reveals to Miranda the story of their past. It is a story of the world, filled with treachery, power and strange accidents. Miranda, at the end of the conversation, falls asleep. Her father says,

> Thou art inclin'd to sleep; 'tis a good dulness,
> And give it way; I know thou canst not choose.

If Miranda's sleepiness were merely to indicate Prospero's magic power, we would not be able to understand why he anxiously asks her twice if she is listening to his story. It seems probable that Miranda's sleepiness is meant to convey Shakespeare's idea that love is disinterested in history. Miranda falls asleep, not because Prospero induces her by magic means to close her eyes but because "she is inclined to sleep" when the world speaks.

In this sense the woman is a purer symbol of love than the man. The man loves and must live in this world. To him, life in the world becomes easier through love.

> The mistress which I serve quickens what's dead
> And makes my labours pleasures.

She does not have to serve in the world because through loving him she serves as her nature, which is made to love, demands.

XIII

A change of nature is a utopian wish on which order of the body politic cannot be built. Concord springs from love, but love which is nonpolitical exists within a political world. This means that lovers must learn how to live in this world. Also, love must be protected against the destructive passions in this world. As long as Calibans exist, even the most perfect love between Ferdinand and Miranda is secure only in its dependence on the law.

XIV

Thought and feeling, it has been said, are at one in great poetry. The poet, like the philosopher, looks at life with eyes both passionate and calm. His passion leads him to discover what his calmness enables him to endure.

Since the poet is not stirred by any desires to change this world, to make a world, as it were, he would irritate those who suffer and struggle, were it not for his pleasing art. Sufferings, injustice, agonies, the perishing gods of man, triumphant evil, and sublimity in anguish — all this is thrown onto the playground of fate at which the poet looks without horror or disgust, and without indignation. Indeed, he pays no less attention to the stark and the evil than to the lovely and the sweet. He sees what is and never pales.

The golden age, too, is an instance of sublimity in the anguish of this world. Ultimately, the two utopias which Shakespeare elucidates in *The Tempest*, Gonzalo's dream and the idea of perfect order, stem from the same root and must surrender to the same fate. Prospero returns from the island to Milano, to a world in which his magical power is of no avail; he discards this power. The world remains at it ever was, and yet poetically adorned by the magical restoration of justice and enriched by the prospect of Miranda's happiness. Is it possible that Shakespeare lets the curtain fall while we are still rejoicing and yet renounces in the face of death what he upheld against the mundane courtiers?

NOTES

1. Cf. W. C. Curry, "Sacerdotal Science in Shakespeare's *The Tempest*," in *Archiv für das Studium der Neueren Sprachen*, 1935, pp. 25–36 and 185–96.
2. On the relations of statesmen, philosopher and magician cf. Leo Strauss, "Maimuni's Lehre von der Prophetie und ihre Quellen," in *Le Monde Oriental*, vol. 28, 1934, pp. 99–139.

11

Simplicissimus, the Irreverent Man

Some great literary works enjoy immortal fame for reasons that have little to do with the deepest concern of their authors. *Don Quixote, Gulliver's Travels, Moby Dick* are books of this kind, and so, perhaps, are *Till Eulenspiegel* and *Alice in Wonderland*. These writings capture the imagination of young readers because great adventures never fail to enchant them. As they grow older they forget much that it is useful to remember, but not the knight of the sad countenance fighting windmills, or Eulenspiegel with his fool's cap laughing on an uphill climb in joyous anticipation of his descent; they always recall Gulliver tied by the Lilliputians and the elusive terrible white whale, and the Mad Hatter. But later in life some of them reread the books of their youth and then, perhaps, they suspect design in Eulenspiegel's folly and method in Don Quixote's madness; perhaps they discover that Ahab's whale hunt is a struggle with God and *Gulliver's Travels* a comment on a philosophical subject; and even Lewis Carroll's whimsies may then hold more than mere enchantment. Grimmelshausen's main work, *The Adventurous Simplicissimus*, belongs in this class of writings. Anyone who has read it in his youth will not forget Simplicius Simplicissimus and his adventures — some of them buoyantly roguish and profoundly comical, others cruel and obscene, a few of them deeply

First published in *Social Research*, Vol. 35, 1966. Reprinted by permission of *Social Research*.

moving, and some mysterious like dreams. But what lies behind the adventures?

The book was first published in 1669, twenty-one years after the conclusion of the Thirty Years' War, which provides the setting of the first five parts of the novel. In *Continuatio*, the last part, peace reigns, and so it does in the last two books of the Simplician cycle of novels, *The Enchanted Bird's-Nest*, Parts I and II, whereas the two other tales of the cycle, *Courage, the Adventuress* and *The Strange Skipinthe-field*, are also war books.[1]

Grimmelshausen published all but three of his works under a pseudonym, using no less than eight different anagrams of his name for that purpose.[2] Two of the books published under his real name were "serious" conventional novels, more or less satisfying the baroque taste for solemnity and learning. They are little read today and have indeed less literary merit than have other German novels of the period, especially those by Anton Ulrich, Duke of Brunswick, whom Goethe admired; but like Grimmelshausen's "serious" works, Anton Ulrich's novels today rest also respectfully buried in the graveyard of scholarship. All of Grimmelshausen's so-called Simplician writings, however, still are vibrantly alive; they seem to belong to folk literature. They deal with common or vulgar, and hence comical, people — soldiers, beggars, highwaymen, jugglers, camp followers — the kinds of people Grimmelshausen knew well. In the terrible war that brought the wolf packs back to once cultivated fields in Germany and decimated the population, he served first as a simple soldier and then as a regimental clerk. When peace finally came he remained a simple man, an innkeeper and bailiff in a small town not very far from Strasbourg. Never in his life did he mingle with the great captains of war and state. Nor did he keep much company with the rich in the city or with high dignitaries of the churches; none of the famous and learned authors of his time seems to have been a friend of his.

Illustrious ladies and gentlemen and their concerns, the heroic affairs of state and of love, can be found only in the serious, historical-political novel and in solemn baroque tragedy. To the extent that socially prominent characters appear at all in the Simplician tales their morals and manners are almost invariably satirized. Grimmelshausen said that his popular works dealt with "the low things" in life, and were written in "the Simplician style"; he distinguished that style from "the theological style" of sermons and other edifying prose. According to his own words, the Simplician style is a way of writing that hints at the truth through laughter. In this style the truth is not being told directly, and solemn statements may therefore be suspected of not being true. Those familiar with the old tradition of laughingly telling the truth know that this kind of writing is salutary and sweet: salutary, since it drives melancholy thoughts away, and sweet because it offers the bitter truth to us as a sugar-coated pill.[3] In short, those who read *The Adventurous Simplicissimus* are well advised to heed Grimmelshausen's warning: "It happens sometimes that . . . behind the printed words that deal with insignificant things something else is hidden which evades discovery by many a reader."[4]

First Impressions

What is it that is hidden in the book? Before suggesting an answer, it must be said that some of the impressions derived from a first reading of the work may be misleading as may also be some of the literary criticisms to which it has been subjected. Most critics now rightly agree that *The Adventurous Simplicissimus* is neither a "realistic" novel of the Thirty Years War nor a picaresque tale pure and simple, but most of them also hold the opinion that the truth of the book is the truth of the Gospel. As we shall see, this opinion is open to some doubt.

The Adventurous Simplicissimus is cast in autobiographical form, and various incidents in it reflect Grimmelshausen's own experiences in the Thirty Years War. The work is indeed one of the great books on war as a scourge of man;[5] the book can be compared to Jacques Callot's series of famous etchings, *Les misères de la guerre*. Both works abound with stark images of the ruin of town and countryside, the abject misery and unrestrained cruelty of soldiers and peasants alike, the degradation of men by sudden misfortune and windfalls of luck. Grimmelshausen presents all this as the story of a boy growing to manhood while caught in a maelstrom of violence, hunger, greed and corruption. But for all the knowledge he had of total war in the seventeenth century, he saw war as the extreme form of the human condition: in peacetime as well man remains warlike because of the terror he strikes and fears. "Reality" may be said to be "distorted" in Grimmelshausen's Simplician tales. Not only that which is sinful according to Christian teaching occupies a prominent place in them, but also the filthy, the rapacious in sex, and especially the scatological. By contrast, large areas in the canvas of life are left blank. What Grimmelshausen says about government and work is stated mainly in allegorical form; on love between man and woman he is silent; on family life he says very little. By contrast he waxes eloquent on popular

superstitions: the belief that some people are bulletproof, that possession of a mandrake root can bring wealth or a bird's nest can make its
owner invisible — on all this and the fear of the Devil, so widespread in
seventeenth-century Germany, Grimmelshausen is an invaluable
source of information, but a realist in the modern sense he was not.[6]

Nor is *Simplicissimus* a picaresque tale pure and simple. Grimmelshausen was influenced by Spanish models in the picaresque tradition
as well as by German satirists like Moscherosch, and perhaps more
than has been realized until recently by Charles Sorel's *Histoire Co-
mique de Francion*.[7] Grimmelshausen read many chap books of the
preceding centuries; as the autodidact he was he used compendia of
learning, contemporary complications of history, books on astrology
and a great deal more. These "sources" have been most painstakingly
investigated by several generations of scholars, and no end of the
research is in sight. But his main work does not treat us to a string of
self-contained adventures of a picaro, who throughout remains a solitary satirical figure without a moral history of his own. In *The Adventurous Simplicissimus* the picaresque form is modified by the introduction of secondary characters. Next to Simplicissimus himself, the two
most important persons in the novel are Heartsbrother, his friend, an
almost exemplary Christian, and Olivier, an unscrupulous highway-
man and murderer, who in his youth read Aretino in church. Simplicissimus encounters both men repeatedly in his life; he may be said to
occupy a middle position between them and thus between goodness
and evil. He fails to be as good a Christian as Heartsbrother, but
unlike Olivier, he is no devil in human form. Both Heartsbrother and
Olivier die, whereas Simplicissimus, armed with common sense, prudence and laughter, lives forever, like a legend. Taken as the story of a
moral struggle that is never completely won, *The Adventurous Simplicissimus* is structurally more closely knit than the usual picaresque
tale.

Many scholars hold that Grimmelshausen wanted to depict man's
struggle for salvation in this world of temptation and evil. They argue
that Simplicius, an innocent peasant boy, turns into a venturesome
young soldier who after a life full of error, folly, and sin finally learns
that peace of mind can be attained only through the renunciation of
pleasure and ambition, through remorse and trust in God.[8] Indeed,
Simplicissimus eventually confesses his sins and becomes a Catholic;
furthermore, after many fresh adventures he renounces the world
twice, once at the end of the fifth book and again toward the end of
the sixth book of the novel. Thus it seems clear beyond doubt that the

author of *The Adventurous Simplicissimus* was a devout Christian believer, and that the hidden truth of his popular writings is revealed not only in the solemn admonitions against sin and vice, to which the reader is treated whenever he has been made to laugh about them, but also in the ending of the tale.

Beyond doubt? Neither Grimmelshausen's life nor, upon close reading, his literary work stills all doubt. Grimmelshausen was born and reared a Protestant and turned Catholic most probably at the time of his marriage when he was twenty-eight years of age. His conversion does not necessarily reflect his religious belief for in his time many men changed their religion for practical reasons. It is true, his works contain very many solemn Christian admonitions, but they are inserted between comical accounts of folly and vice, told with admirable zest and undeniable relish. There are also many sharp attacks on priests and parsons alike. Nor was Grimmelshausen an admirer of the monastic life: he compared it with life in prison; if he admired anything it was the communistically organized life of the Hutterites, an Anabaptist, heretical sect. Furthermore, no less than three times in the Simplician cycle of novels are the diversity of the Christian churches and the existence of other religions adduced as reasons for not choosing any of them through conversion. Not only Simplicius but also a Jew argues slyly that salvation of the soul is too precious to be risked by a choice that might be wrong, since each belief claims to be the only one that is right.

If all of this limits the reader's religious comfort he is bound to get even more upset by the disagreement among Grimmelshausen's critics. For a long time the author was regarded as a Protestant writer, for example, by Jakob Grimm. More recently, the view has gained favor that he wrote from a Catholic standpoint.[9] But still other critics have detected irenical tendencies or even leanings toward Pelagianism in his work.[10] A few students have been unable to suppress their doubts that the serious Christian admonitions in his comical books, particularly in the last novels of the cycle, are to be taken seriously.[11] One Swiss scholar has recently referred to Grimmelshausen as a nihilist,[12] and no less than 130 years ago at least two German critics viewed *The Adventurous Simplicissimus* as a satire of Parzival.[13]

Dissimulation

In order to find the way to "the truth" let us begin by mentioning two of Grimmelshausen's own statements about his book. First, in one of the poems prefacing his conventional novel *Dietwalt und Amelinde* the author says that *The Adventurous Simplicissimus* describes the world in a way that gives nature its due.[14] Similarly, in the main novel itself Simplicissimus is called "a natural man," incidentally by a character suffering from religious delusions.[15] Sometimes, when a particular story might offend readers of refined taste, Grimmelshausen concludes with the apologetic explanation that he wants his story to be "complete." It seems that "incompleteness" meant to him not telling what he considered to be the whole truth about man's nature. Now he depicts man not only as a being that is tempted to commit evil, sinful acts, but also as an animal subject to the weakness and urges of all animals. Man must eat and drink and therefore vomits, passes water, breaks wind, and defecates. These natural body functions occupy a prominent place in all chap books and picaresque tales and in the realistic novels of the period. They occur in baroque comedy as well. All this is vulgar, like our own barracks humor, and a source of raucous laughter. To modern sensibilities, the literary treatment of the scatological is offensive, especially if used, as it is by Grimmelshausen — and by Bandello, Charles Sorel, and others before him — for depicting revenge by humiliation rather than by violence. Indeed, scatological incidents are the stuff of humiliation. They reveal the frailty of good manners; they shatter pride and dignity; they afford an opportunity for degrading intellectual pretentions; and they lengthen the terrible distance between man and God. And yet, different from human degradation by torture and violence, which have their origins in man's power over man, the weakness of man manifesting itself in his dependence on bodily needs is merely "vulgar." There is really no sound reason for feeling more revolted by accounts of such vulgarity than by accounts of torture, say those contained in Dante's *Inferno*.

Secondly, the preparatory poem in *Dietwalt und Amelinde* urges the reader to acquaint himself with *Simplicissimus* because this story can show when it is safe to speak, when it is necessary to be silent, and how important it is to be on one's guard in the company of the powerful. Nothing in this advertisement refers to the religious career of Simplicissimus. Surprisingly, Grimmelshausen does not speak of his work as though it could lead the reader to Christian piety but rather as if he held it to be a guide to worldly conduct.

In this connection, it should be noted that early in the novel Simplicius, the young ignorant boy, receives his first solemn instruction from a hermit (who later turns out to be his father). The pious man may be expected to admonish the young simpleton to love his neighbor, avoid temptation, and trust in God's mercy. Instead, he gives him this advice: know thyself; shun bad company; be steadfast. Surprisingly enough, there is nothing particularly Christian about these precepts: in baroque literature the "hermit" often is merely a mask for a "sage."

The Simplician world is corrupt and dangerous. He who wants to survive in it must dissemble, hide his true feelings, show false feelings, be evasive, and if need be, lie. As the following instances show, distrust, and dissimulation are as pervasive in Grimmelshausen's tales as they are in the serious novel of the period.

In his youth, Simplicius pretends to have lost his wits and plays a fool who tells his noble master and his distinguished guests the truth about their un-Christian behavior. But the boy is troubled, since he has not really lost his mind. At this point a good parson says to him: "You must not worry about that. The foolish world wants to be deceived. If you are still in possession of your wits, use them to your advantage. You must imagine that, like Phoenix, you have gone from unreason through fire to reason and thus have been reborn into a new human existence."[16] It is generally acknowledged that the symbol of the Phoenix and the image of rebirth through the acquisition of worldly knowledge are of great importance to an understanding of *The Adventurous Simplicissimus*. A picture of the Phoenix appears as the only illustration in the first edition of the work, taking the place of the long preface customary in serious baroque literature. The plate also contains a poem in which the parson's worldly advice, just cited, appears for the first time.

Simplicius treats this parson, too, with consummate dissimulation. When disagreeing with him, he adds, "I was smart enough not to say anything for if I am to confess the truth, by becoming a fool I became first of all prudent and more cautious in everything I said."[17] Dissimulation and the need for it stay with Simplicissimus throughout his life. Once, he reports that he feigns virtue in order to be loved more.[18] Later, when taken prisoner, he talks to the colonel under whose authority he lives "so cautiously that nobody could know his mind."[19] A Calvinist clergyman admonishes him not to fall prey to women, but the young lover hides his true heart behind clever lies.[20] When Simplicissimus meets the satanic Olivier, he calls him "brother," adding, "I called him that in order to be all the more protected from him."[21] Still later, Simplicissimus justifies his worldliness to Heartsbrother, his conscientious friend. "One must not provoke God," he says, "but come to terms with the times, and use the means that we cannot do without . . . St. Paul, the Apostle, too, . . . marvelously came to terms with his time and the customs in this world. . . . "[22] These examples can be multiplied from every book in the cycle. So can examples of distrust. The need for distrust and dissembling is well justified by a character in *The Strange Skipinthefield*: "He who is overwhelmed must accept the will and wishes of those in whose power he finds himself."[23]

Death

In the baroque period life was widely held to be a descent toward death. Poets rose to the height of their power when they lamented the transitoriness of human existence.

> Just as this light grows weak so in another day and year
> I, you, and what we have or see will disappear.[24]

So wrote Andreas Gryphius. The poets found ever new images of decay. The young lover pleaded for the favor of his beloved by reminding her that she soon would be ugly, old, and dead.

> Time will spare your beauty
> No more than the roses,

sang Weckherlin. And Logau:

> Your mouth, now coral glow,
> Will mold.
> Your hands will perish like the snow
> And you'll be old.

Disappointed lovers, like Hofmannswaldau, avenged themselves by lyrical descriptions of their sweethearts' unenjoyed beauty ruined by age. One observer explained this sombre cult this way: "When we consider the innumerable corpses which both raging pestilence and martial arms have piled up not only in our Germany but in almost all of Europe, then we must confess that our roses have been transformed into thorns, our lilies into nettles, our paradises into graveyards, nay, our whole being into a picture of death."[25]

Grimmelshausen was not quite so mournful as were these poets. Except for the moving descriptions of the death of the hermit he depicts misfortune and death quite factually without the investment of as much emotion as was later to be expended on descriptions of inclement weather in nineteenth-century novels. He reports the death of great military leaders, the fall of cities, and defeat in battle with the detachment of a chronicler who wastes few words on common events.

Rather than with death he appears preoccupied with change and transformation. Everything in nature and society, he felt, will soon be different from what it happens to be at present. To express this feeling he adopted from Hans Sachs, the sixteenth-century poet, the allegorical figure of *Baldanders* — Soon-different — a kind of popular goddess Fortuna who governs the world. He even arranged for a meeting between Simplicissimus and Soon-different in which the latter offers to teach the great fool the art of understanding the speech of inanimate objects. Soon-different does so by presenting to Simplicissimus a riddle in the form of apparent nonsense words, which the reader of the novel is expected to decipher himself. If he succeeds, instead of being consoled by a hint of God's wisdom, he is teased by another enigmatic message: "Why don't you imagine how all things fare, put this into the words of a discourse and believe that which resembles the truth; then you will have what your foolish curiosity desires."[26]

Grimmelshausen's seeming indifference toward disaster is most shocking when misfortune strikes the main characters of the narrative. For example, Simplicissimus mentions a battle in which "Count Götz lost his life and Heartsbrother his testicles; they were shot away; I got my share in the leg, but it was little more than a scratch. Then we returned to Vienna. . . . "[27] Heartsbrother, Simplicissimus' close friend, very soon thereafter becomes paralyzed. Simplicissimus dryly comments: "In this way, fortune changes unexpectedly. Shortly before Heartsbrother had decided to marry a young noblewoman . . . now he had to think of something else. For since he had lost that which he wanted to use in the production of offspring, and since he was threatened by his paralysis with a lingering illness, in which he needed good friends, he made his last will naming me as the only heir to his estate. . . . "[28] Thus, compassion for the suffering friend is smothered by onrushing fresh events and by the author's absorbing interest in the Change of Fortune.

If such a change crushes not your friend but an enemy you rejoice; you shake with laughter; and it should be noted that Grimmelshausen's candor in depicting this natural joy is censored by Christian ethics. Perhaps the most striking example is Simplicissimus' reaction to the death of his second wife. It is true, she is a spendthrift, a very bad housekeeper, a drunkard, and an adulteress to boot. Nevertheless, we might expect her death to assuage his hostile feelings. Oh, no! She dies unexpectedly, "which," says Simplicissimus, "so pleased my heart that I almost got sick from laughing."[29] The impact of this statement upon the reader is intensified by its explosive brevity, a literary technique of which Grimmelshausen was an unsurpassed master. Never did Grimmelshausen indicate any deep belief that after death man's soul lives on, possibly in heaven.

Friendship

In a life fraught with the ever-present danger of sudden disaster, only very few avenues of escape are open. In Grimmelshausen's world man is not in the position of, say, a seventeenth-century French nobleman who could, if he renounced his ambition, leave the court and join a salon in the city or return to his country estate. No woman ever enters a convent. Nor does Grimmelshausen regard the family as a place in which respite from the struggles and dangers of this world can be found. Love between man and woman offers no relief. What remains when the pretty or designing words of love are forgotten are lust, the fleeting satisfaction of animal appetites, subjugation, cruelty, abuse, disease, filth. Women are "animals with braids" or "veiled animals," and love very often is rape. Even the word "love" is rare. Instead, Grimmelshausen frequently uses an expression known from bird snaring: "*mit der Leimrute laufen*": "being in love" is "running about with twigs smeared with bird lime."

Two kinds of human bonds, however, offer some protection against disaster, that between an experienced older man, a preceptor, and a young man, following his guidance; and more importantly in many regards, that of true friendship between two men of equal age. Simplicius', the boy's, relation with the hermit, and later with a pastor in Hanau, then the young man's relation with the older Heartsbrother, and to a lesser extent even with the strange man who in his moments of madness thinks he is Jove: all these bonds are fashioned after the ancient image of an experienced guide who like Aeneas helps a curious novice to discover the world. The model of such a guide perhaps nearest to Grimmelshausen was Robertus in Moscherosch's main work.

Important as such tutorial ties are for Simplicius' education and survival, they do not have the weight of friendship. Grimmelshausen believed that nothing equaled it as a haven in this evil, hazardous world and as solace for the anguished soul of an active man. Only among friends is there no need for dissembling.

While heterosexual love in Grimmelshausen's world invariably enslaves the lover as well as the loved one, the friendship between the younger Heartsbrother and Simplicissimus breaks out of the haunted circle of lust and danger. Simplicius loves his friend "almost more than himself."[30] The two young men swear a solemn oath of "eternal brotherhood,"[31] pledging "never to abandon each other in good or bad fortune, in happiness or misery" and "to love each other until death."[32] Simplicissimus speaks of his affection for Heartsbrother almost like a modern romantic youth revealing the intoxicating effect of his infatuation with a girl. He mentions a "sweet" quarrel between himself and his friend; indeed, he says of himself and his friend that they were "drunk with love." And Simplicius finds simple and moving words about the death of his friend: "While I could not change it, it changed me." "I shunned all company and sought only solitude to follow my sad thoughts. . . . "[33] He knew that in all his life he would never again find a friend like him.

Paradoxically, for modern readers this exquisite emotion is marred by the sober standard with which Grimmelshausen and, presumably, his contemporary readers measured the worth of friendship: friends are friends if they are unselfish enough to share their possessions without regard to individual advantage and without fear of being robbed or murdered.

Grimmelshausen's literary critics have viewed Simplicissimus' friendship with Heartsbrother almost exclusively as an instrument of moral reform, but Heartsbrother's role as Simplicissimus' guide to Christian faith and morality is less impressive than it appears at first glance. To begin with, Simplicissimus reports that Heartsbrother's impaired health improves when he hears the news of Olivier's death. Since Heartsbrother has suffered much from the evil man, this is perhaps a natural, but certainly not a Christian, reaction. Next, the good Heartsbrother knows that Simplicissimus got rich by associating with Olivier, the robber and murderer. The money in his friend's possession is therefore tainted by heinous crimes. Simplicissimus himself says that one of the reasons why his friend first rejects his company on a pilgrimage and his offer of support is "revulsion" about the tainted money. But Heartsbrother never urges his friend to part with his illgotten wealth. Instead, he eventually accepts Simplicissimus' financial support as well as his company. Finally, when Simplicissimus later shows and offers to his friend the gold he has hidden on his person, Heartsbrother forgets all about the evil origin of the gold: he is overwhelmed by Simplicissimus' trust in him, and praises his friend for his lack of fear that he, the good and pious Christian, might rob him of the tainted money. Thus, Heartsbrother's praise of friendship appears like a subtle exercise in immorality. If we do not overlook this feature of the author's portrait of friendship, we are left with a startling choice. Either Grimmelshausen was a morally insensitive man in respect to friendship, or he wanted to render Heartsbrother's sterling character more natural and less incredible by providing it with a blemish; perhaps he believed that goodness can never reach the purity of evil.

Grimmelshausen's portrait of the relation between Simplicius and Heartsbrother presents a strange mixture of very ancient and startlingly modern traits of friendship. It brings to mind an observation in Lucian's dialogue on friendship that when life is fraught with dangers sworn brotherhood is "a necessary thing." But different from brotherhood among the ancient Scyths, to which Lucian refers, friendship in seventeenth-century Germany was hardly an institution vital for the functioning of the social order. No matter how important the bond between Simplicius and Heartsbrother is for weathering the storms of adversity, as an escape from the world of struggle, from public, political life, it adumbrates a later cult, that of private, intimate friendship among the romantics.[34]

Historically, sworn brotherhood is a pre-Christian, heathen institution, that flourished in societies in which man did not turn the other cheek, but avenged insults and slew his enemies without scruples, sometimes while they were asleep. In such societies, one did not love one's neighbor, nor were all men equal as sinners. In Christian teaching the friend is replaced by the neighbor, a sinner like yourself, and by God Himself as the only being capable of helping you. "He that feareth the Lord directeth his friendship aright; for as he is, so is his neighbor also."[35] In the seventeenth century, Christian moralists of all faiths sternly insisted on the religious error of placing reliance on any man, however beloved he might be.

For example, the Catholic Abraham a Sancta Clara, in order to exhort man not to place his trust in any human being, took him through the various stages of life—birth, youth, manhood, and old age—always asking, "Who's there?" and always offering the reply, "'A good friend,' says the guardian angel." At every age the guardian angel, and not any mortal, is the good friend.[36] Similarly, in 1657, the Protestant pastor Johann Balthasar Schupp in his book, *Der Freund in der Not* ("The Friend in Times of Affliction"), described the inconstancy of human affairs and repeatedly warned his son not to trust anyone, compatriot or stranger, nobleman or commoner, his own brother or his wife. "Do not rely on privileged people, on kings, princes, or other great masters," he said. "For they are men, and all men are liars." "When I ponder the course of human affairs, I see that one often is in greater danger among false friends than among true enemies." Schupp's teaching is more rigorous than that of Jesus Sirach. The German pastor despairs of finding any friend among men. The father's best advice to his son is not to trust any neighbor but "to see above all that you have God for a friend."[37] Grimmelshausen's portrait of friendship denies the soundness of such teaching.

Conversion and Renunciation

After many adventures as a soldier, as a kind of Robin Hood, as an obliging young man rendering amorous service to some ladies in Paris, as a quack, and in many other roles, Simplicissimus unexpectedly encounters a madman in a church who shocks him into awareness of his sinful conduct. He is overcome by fright, confesses, and becomes a Catholic. Curiously enough, this conversion has no effect on his life. Immediately following his religious shock, he turns to new rogueries as though nothing had happened, or rather, as though his conversion was but another adventure.

Finally, however, weary of his wasted life, he resolves to become a hermit. Again, this withdrawal from the world is not Grimmelshausen's answer to the question of how to find peace for the human soul, although most critics have so interpreted the author's intent. Having taken a most eloquent farewell from his sinful life, in words borrowed from Antonio de Guevara, a Spanish Catholic moralist, Simplicissimus concludes the Fifth Book with this comment on his new life as a hermit: "but whether I shall persevere in it, like my blessed father, remains to be seen."[38] These words are not Guevara's but Grimmelshausen's. Could the author have been more forthright? Could there be a clearer warning to read the remaining books of the cycle before drawing the conclusion that Guevara's famous "Adieu, World," the sonorous renunciation of mundane affairs, tells us something unequivocally important about Simplicissimus or Grimmelshausen? It appears that the author's intention still "remains to be seen."

In the first chapter of the next book Simplicissimus admits to "thousand-fold temptation" in the beautiful Black Forest where he lives as a hermit. Instead of fasting he enjoys his food. He delights in the noble sight of Strasbourg in the midst of the country below him. He can see the spire of its cathedral through a telescope that he has taken along, and at night, with the help of another instrument that magnifies sound, he listens to the barking of the dogs far away and to the stirring of the deer in the woods nearby. How this hermit loves the world! Indeed, soon he ceases to work and pray and resumes his life of worldly adventure.

Toward the end of the Sixth Book, however, we find him once more withdrawn from the world, this time not by an act of his own free will, but in consequence of a shipwreck. The chapters describing Simplicissimus' life on a remote island represents one of the first true Robinsonades in modern European literature. It struck André Gide's fancy and made him wonder whether Defoe had been familiar with it.[39] Grimmelshausen was inspired to incorporate the fantastic story in his novel by a satire, *The Isle of Pines*, published in London in 1668; its author was Henry Neville.

Neville described the aftermath of a shipwreck that had allegedly taken place in 1589. Five persons, George Pine, an accountant, the fourteen-year-old daughter of his principal and three maids, including a Negro girl, were washed ashore on an isle rich in fruit, fish and fowl, water, and palm wine. The good accountant had his pleasure first with one of the maids, then with the other, then with the daughter of his principal and finally with the Negro girl. When the captain of a Dutch ship landed on the deserted island seventy-eight years later the population had grown to 1789 persons. The tremendous success of Neville's satire in western Europe had little to do with popular interest in the idyllic rebirth of civilization on a faraway island. J. H. Scholte dryly remarked on the success of Neville's satire, "Simple souls probably liked the idyl of the Robinsonade. More sophisticated minds will have enjoyed the persiflage of the biblical notion of original mankind . . . 'Pines' stands almost too clearly as an anagram for 'penis.' It does not appear that all translators realized this realistic root of the story of population growth."[40] Probably Grimmelshausen was clearly aware of this allusion as was Dryden, in whose *The Kind Keeper* Pleasance says, "'Tis a likely proper fellow, and looks as he could people a new Isle of Pines."

Although Grimmelshausen stayed away from the theme of the natural growth of population, he made liberal use of Neville's satire in describing the island on which Simplicissimus finds himself stranded after his shipwreck. This fact alone might have cautioned the critics not to read too much religious meaning into his second withdrawal from the world. It is true that Simplicissimus adorns the island with wooden crosses and pious signs bearing quotations from the Scriptures, but compared with his adventures in the world that he has left all his activities on the island have an air of unreality and, indeed, of theatricality about them. As one critic has remarked, the hermitages of Simplicissimus exhaust themselves in "a pose affecting piety."[41] Furthermore, on his island Simplicius the hermit again leads anything but an ascetic life. The exotic food and drink which he enjoys make the reader's mouth water. Grimmelshausen had no illusions about it. In a later work he refers to the island as "Lubberland."[42]

After fifteen years of devout and comfortable life in his solitary paradise Simplicissimus is discovered by a Dutch captain who tries to persuade him to return to civilization. Simplicissimus declines. He paints a vivid picture of the sinful life that Europeans lead in peace time as well as in war. He contrasts the idyllic solitude of his island with the turmoils of the wicked world. But then he adds whimsically, with a twinkle in his eye, that everything else aside, were he to return from the island to Europe he might drown on the voyage. Apparently nothing is dearer to him than his life — a subject for despair but also for never-ending laughter.

In the later novels of the Simplician cycle Simplicissimus reappears merely as a minor figure. In *The Strange Skipinthefield*, after his return from the island he plays the unaccustomed role of a stern Christian who lives in peace with himself, his old foster parents and his illegitimate son. He urges his old comrade Skipinthefield, now a beggar and cripple seventy years of age, to abandon recklessness and swearing, and to prepare his soul for the hour of reckoning. The old rascal dies a Christian on Simplicissimus' farm. In this novel Simplicissimus is also eager to prove that his son is not the son of Courage, but of her maid: we learn that in his younger days Simplicissimus knew both of them at the same time. There are two other enigmatic incidents involving Simplicissimus. In one of them we see him in a marketplace making money by turning poor and sour wine into good wine. And in a most remarkable conversation Simplicissimus argues that man ought to weep about his sins rather than laugh about his folly, since the Scriptures do not report that Christ had ever laughed.* This lecture is immediately followed by a joke so obscene that Simplicissimus' listen-

---

*Grimmelshausen probably took this argument, directly or indirectly, from Thomas More. "In the thirteenth chapter of his *Dialogue of Comfort against Tribulation* More says: 'And for to prove that this life is no laughing time, but rather the time of weeping, we find that our saviour himself wept twice or thrice, but never find we that he laughed so much as once. I will not swear that he never did, but at least wise he left us no example of it. But, on the other side, he left us example of weeping.' More must have known that exactly the opposite is true of Plato's — or Xenophon's — Socrates: Socrates left us no example of weeping, but on the other side, he left us example of laughing. The relation of weeping and laughing is similar to that of tragedy and comedy. We may therefore say that the Socratic conversation and hence the Platonic dialogue is slightly more akin to comedy than to tragedy." Leo Strauss, *The City and Man*, Chicago, 1964, p. 61.

ers shake with laughter. The only man in all of Grimmelshausen's writings of whom it is pointedly said that he does not like to be laughed at, is Jove, the madman who plays God.

Grimmelshausen was a great satirist who made people laugh at human folly committed in a wretched and exhilarating world in which everything will soon be different. And God? On his island Simplicissimus calls him "a dark light," an expression which a learned critic has taken as proof of Grimmelshausen's leaning toward Cusanus and his doctrine that opposites coincide. But the profoundly equivocal "dark light" — *das finstere Licht* — cannot be compared with the contrary image of radiant light that ever since St. Augustine and Dionysius the Areopagite has been the symbol of God in Christian writing. "He who knoweth the truth knoweth that Light: and who knoweth it, knoweth eternity."[43] Grimmelshausen's "dark light" has nothing in common with Dante's Light Eternal that loves and smiles[44] or with Gryphius' image: "God, light dwelling in the light" — *Gott, der Licht in Licht wohnlafftig.*[45] Andreas Gryphius was a deeply religious man. Was Grimmelshausen? Was he a believer? Or was the hidden "truth" of his work that God is wrapped in darkness? He surely believed in the fickleness of fortune, in transformation, in chance. We cannot be certain that he believed in God. His genius, sustained by folklore and proverbs, created an image of himself which to this day has remained ambiguous: Simplicissimus, the most simple man, a fool who likes food and undiluted wine and adventure; a natural man pitting his wits against misfortune, bored by theological disputations, but always ready to tell a good story. He spoke the language of the common people, but for that was no less admired by duchesses like Sophie of Hanover, and philosophers like Leibniz. His heart was heavy from the cruelty of life, but lightened by folly and by the song of the nightingale. Grimmelshausen's laughter reverberates through the centuries — lusty, grim, and sometimes blasphemous.

Grimmelshausen explicitly said that anyone who failed to read all ten books of the Simplician cycle of novels could not hope to grasp the truth hidden in Simplicissimus. The last great novella of the cycle, and probably the last story the author ever wrote, almost certainly is a satire of the Christian belief in the immaculate conception of the Virgin Mary.[46]

NOTES

1. There is no complete translation into English of *The Adventurous Simplicissimus*. The edition published under this title by University of Nebraska Press, Lincoln,

1962, with a preface by Eric Bentley, is a reprint of a translation by A. T. S. Goodrick, originally published in London, 1912. It is not based on the critical edition of the German text of the first five books, edited by J. H. Scholte, Halle, 1938; 3rd ed. Tübingen, 1954, and of *Continuatio*, the sixth book, J. H. Scholte, ed., Halle, 1939. The translation by Walter Wallich, *The Adventures of a Simpleton*, London, 1962, omits even larger parts of the work. Even the best English rendition of the work, translated by Hellmuth Weissenborn and Lesley Macdonald, London, 1965, contains slight adaptations and deletions. The only other works of Grimmelshausen that are at present available in English can be found in H. J. C. von Grimmelshausen, *"Courage, the Adventuress"* and *"The False Messiah,"* Translation and Introduction by Hans Speier, Princeton, N.J., 1964; this is a complete translation of the second novel (the seventh book) in the Simplician cycle and of a novella to be found in chapters XII-XX of *The Enchanted Bird's-Nest*, part II, the last or tenth book of the cycle, published in 1675.

2. On Grimmelshausen's use of anagrams cf. Hans Speier, "A Woman Named Courage," *The Arts in Society*, ed. by Robert N. Wilson, Englewood Cliffs, N.J., 1964, pp. 193ff., esp. 214-18 and the literature cited there.

3. Cf. Hans Speier, "Grimmelshausen's Laughter," *Ancients and Moderns*, ed. by Joseph Cropsey, New York, 1964, esp. pp. 177-212.

4. *Grimmelshausens Simpliciana*, ed. by J. H. Scholte, Halle, 1943, p. 43.

5. "There is a great literature of war, and very much of it speaks poignantly today. The *Simplicissimus* may well be the most poignant book in all this literature because its war, alas, is our war, our *kind of* war." (Eric Bentley, in his preface to *The Adventurous Simplicissimus*, Lincoln, 1962, p. vi.)

6. This point was made first by Richard Alewyn, *Johann Beer, Studien zum Roman des 17 Jahrhunderts*, Leipzig, 1932, pp. 208ff.

7. Cf. especially Manfred Koschlig, "Das Lob des 'Francion' bei Grimmelshausen," *Jahrbuch der deutschen Schillergesellschaft*, 1, 1957, pp. 30-73; and Günther Weydt, "Don Quijote Teutsch," *Euphorion*, LI, 1957, pp. 250-70.

8. According to the esthetic counterpart of this view, Grimmelshausen moved from the old picaresque novel toward the modern novel of development, the first in German literature, adumbrating Goethe's *Wilhelm Meister*.

9. This view is very widely held by modern critics; cf., for example, J. H. Scholte, *Der Simplicissimus und sein Dichter*, Tübingen: 1950; James Hyde, "The Religious Thought of Johann Jacob Christoffel von Grimmelshausen as Expressed in the Simplicianische Schriften," unpublished dissertation, Indiana University, 1960; and Werner Welzig, *Beispielhafte Figuren Tor, Abenteurer und Einsiedler bei Grimmelshausen*, Graz and Cologne, 1963.

10. Irenical tendencies: Friedrich Gundolf, "Grimmelshausen und der Simplicissimus," *Vierteljahrsschrift für Literaturwissenschaft und Geistesgeschichte*, 1, 1923, p. 254; on Pelagianism: Paul Gutzwiller, *Der Narr bei Grimmelshausen*, Bern, 1959, p. 109.

11. Cf. Hans Ehrenzeller, *Studien zur Romanvorrede*, Bern, 1955, p. 78; and Hildegard Wichert, *Johann Balthasar Schupp and the Baroque Satire in Germany*, New York, 1952.

12. Paul Gutzwiller, op. cit., p. 108.

13. This view is usually attributed to George Gottfried Gervinus, *Geschichte der deutschen Dichtung* (1835-1842); cf. Carl Hammer, "'Simplicissimus' and the Literary Traditions," *Monatshefte*, (Wisconsin), Vol. XL, 1948, p. 461; it was also advanced by Theodor Echtermeyer, *Hallesche Jahrbücher*, 1838, p. 431.

14. Quoted by Manfred Koschlig, "'Edler Herr von Grimmelshausen,'" *Jahrbuch der deutschen Schillergesellschaft*, IV, 1960, p. 217.
15. *Grimmelshausens Simplicissimus Teutsch*, ed. by J. H. Scholte, Tübingen, 1954, hereafter cited as *Simplicissimus*, p. 210.
16. *Simplicissimus*, p. 114.
17. Op. cit., p. 115.
18. Op. cit., p. 207.
19. Op. cit., p. 260.
20. Op. cit., p. 264.
21. Op. cit., p. 337.
22. Op. cit., p. 375.
23. *Grimmelshausens Springinsfeld*, ed. by J. H. Scholte, Halle, 1928, p. 20.
24. Andreas Gryphius, *Werke*, ed. by Hermann Palm, Hildesheim, 1961, III, Sonnets IV, 3.
25. Quoted from Johann Peter Hallmann, *Leich-Reden* (1682) by Walter Benjamin, *Ursprung des deutschen Trauerspiels*, Berlin, 1928, p. 231.
26. Grimmelshausen, *Continuatio*, ed. by J. H. Scholte, Halle, 1939, p. 41.
27. *Simplicissimus*, p. 385.
28. Ibid.
29. Ibid., p. 404.
30. Op. cit., p. 374.
31. Op. cit., p. 158.
32. Op. cit., p. 164.
33. Op. cit., p. 394.
34. Grimmelshausen's most famous predecessor in substituting "modern" friendship as "une force inexplicable et fatale" for ancient, true and noble friendship was Montaigne; cf. *Essays* 1:27.
35. *Eccl.* VI:17.
36. Abraham a Sancta Clara, *Aus dem handschriftlichen Nachlass*, Akademie der Wissenschafter, Vienna, 1945, III, pp. 67–73.
37. Johann Balthasar Schupp, *Der Freund in der Not*, Halle, 1878, pp. 10, 12–48.
38. *Simplicissimus*, p. 463.
39. André Gide, *Journal, 1939–1949*, Paris, 1954, p. 69.
40. *Simpliciana*, ed. by J. H. Scholte, pp. xviii, xx.
41. Gutzwiller, op. cit., p. 70.
42. *Simpliciana*, p. 18.
43. St. Augustine, *Confessions*, book VII, chap. X.
44. Dante, *Paradiso*, XXXII:124–26.
45. Gryphius, Sonnets III, 3; op. cit., p. 99.
46. Translated into English under the title, *The False Messiah*. Cf. footnotes 1 and 3.

12

Courage, the Adventuress

On the title page of *Courage, the Adventuress*, Grimmelshausen indicates that in this novel the reader will find the account of a descending life. As a young woman Courage is the wife of a cavalry captain, then she marries a captain of foot soldiers, then a lieutenant, thereafter she becomes a sutler-woman, next the wife of a musketeer, and finally a gypsy.

Different from the heroes of the picaresque novel, who proceed from one adventure to the next without change in character, Courage does change under the influence of experience. In the early part of the novel she is not the evil woman she later turns into. To be sure, in part it is her native endowment that makes her a lustful creature, envious, greedy, and vindictive, but in part the evil in her emerges from senseless misfortune and in response to the cruelty of men.

Courage's exploits equal or excel those of men. In battle she is more valiant than her male companions, on marauding expeditions more daring, as a thief more resourceful and cunning. In most of her enterprises she is mistress, rather than helper; often she directs men to assist her. Her vitality is inexhaustible. When at the end of her career she has

Published in Hans Jacob Christoffel von Grimmelshausen, *"Courage, the Adventuress"* and *"The False Messiah,"* Translation and Introduction by Hans Speier. Copyright © 1964 by Princeton University Press. Excerpt from "Introduction" reprinted with the permission of Princeton University Press.

reached the status of an outcast, she remains a queen, if only of the gypsies, aged, but still beautiful in appearance, her spirit unbroken and her skill unrivaled.

Whenever she fights men, whether with her fists as a young girl, with sword and pistol in battle later, with a cudgel after one of her many wedding nights, with a knife in the woods, or with wit, false tears, and pretty words—she almost always wins. Almost without exception men who oppose her are beaten up or humiliated, taken prisoner, killed, duped, or exploited by her. Courage is as much an amazon as a harlot.

Indeed, she has many of the qualities of the heroines in the idealistic novels of the baroque era. Like them, she is a manlike, vigorous creature, a virago in the sense in which Pope still used this word:

> To arms, to arms the fierce virago cries
> And swift as lightening to combat flies.

The virago was the ideal of the Renaissance, fashioned after illustrious ancient models. Viragos appear not only in Ariosto's and Bojardo's heroic poetry, but also in life: women like Caterina Sforza—"prima donna d'Italia" to her contemporaries—or Isabella d'Este, the wife of Marchese Francesco Gonzaga, were admitted for both their beauty and their courage in meeting the formidable risks of their careers.[1] The third book of Castiglione's *Cortegiano* contains the portrait of the perfect lady at court and the Renaissance tribute to the civilizing influence that women exerted on men, but it also presents many great ladies in contemporary Italy, as well as in antiquity, who showed "virtue and prowess" in "the stormes of fortune."[2]

In the German idealistic novel of the seventeenth century, the Renaissance ideal is still potent: many heroines are amazons.[3] Even the middle-class Protestant, Andreas Heinrich Buchholtz, shows Valisca, his heroine, to be the equal of man in the fields of science and music as well as in battle. Disguised as a beautiful young man on a journey to Prague, she "does miracles" fighting off the highwaymen who assault her. At the Persian court, again in men's clothing, she shines in the arts of fencing and shooting with bow and arrow. She cruelly kills three Persian servants, defends her honor against the attack of a lover by thrusting her "bread knife" into his heart, and slays robbers with lightning speed. She fights gloriously as a general in battle, her beautiful hair falling down to her shoulders, a precious sword and a quiver of arrows at her side. In Buchholtz's novel, not only is Valisca a vigaro, but also Hercules himself has female qualities: for all his manliness, he is beautiful, like a young girl, dances daintily, and sometimes fights clad in the garb of an amazon.

Viragos appear also in the novels of D. C. von Lohenstein, who gave this description of Thusnelda through the eyes of Marbod, her lover: "The day before, Marbod had looked admiringly at Thusnelda only (!) as a woman, but this day he saw her on horseback as a valiant heroine. He had honored her as a half-divine being, now he was compelled to worship her as a goddess, for she sat astride her horse as a true amazon; in the race and in the shooting contest she did better than all, and she slew twice as much game as anyone else. For no stag was too swift for her, no bear too cruel, no lynx too terrible."[4]

Anton Ulrich's Aramena, too, at one time goes to the field leading a group of her female court attendants, "a marvellous host of the most beautiful ladies in the world." The amazon motif recedes in Anton Ulrich's second great novel, *Die Römische Oktavia*, as it does in H. A. von Zigler's *Asiatische Banise*, and Philipp von Zesen's novels. Johann Beer abandoned the heroic, idealistic mood and discovered new subjects of everyday life for literary treatment. But even in Beer's works amazons reappear, though with less bombast and fanfare. For example, in one of Beer's major works "a strange cavalier," his visor closed, suddenly enters the scene to help the noble friends who fight the villain and his evil companions. The stranger wounds and captures the wicked man, and when the friends, rejoicing about their victory, want to thank the stranger, he lifts his visor. Then, the friends all grow pale. They behold "the beautiful Amalia, disguised in knightly armor." Needless to say, beautiful Amalia is loved by one of the cavaliers whose valor she excelled so impressively in the fight.[5]

If the modern reader is amused by this theatrical display of heroism, just as he might be amused by the theatricality of the heroes and heroines in distress—when they pray with tears streaming down their cheeks or lift their eyes up to the Heavenly Father in martyrdom—he is in a mood which Grimmelshausen seems to have shared. For Courage is at least as much a caricature and mockery of the amazon to be found in the conventional baroque novel as she is a picaresque character. Her relation to the ideal virago resembles that of Don Quixote to the knightly code. Like the once much-admired ladies who populate the idealistic novel, Courage is an amazon, but she is a counterheroine. She displays the qualities of a wild virago, in the modern sense of that term, while still retaining all the physical features of the ideal: radiant beauty, physical prowess, intelligence, and manlike energy. Like the amazons in the conventional novel, she is indestructible in trial and misfortune. But in three respects she is a counterheroine.

First, despite her noble, if somewhat tainted, origin she moves in a socially undistinguished milieu, resembling in this regard all of Grimmelshausen's main characters. She is never at court, and when she meets an ambassador, spends some short time at a nobleman's castle, or lives for a while like a woman of means in town, it is for her sexual enjoyment and the amassing of a fortune.

Second, it is not virtue that is put to test after test in Courage's life, as in the conventional heroic career. If anything is tried, it is her ability to survive as a victim of a blind and impenetrable destiny. A plaything of senseless fate, which tosses her up and down in quick and violent motion, Courage is flung back and forth from the heights of prosperity to the depths of poverty, from health and beauty to disfiguring illness, from safety and comfort to hunger and humiliation. Pitting her wit and vitality against misfortune, she becomes in the end an outcast, because neither man nor woman can win in a world in which God is silent and which is more surely of the Devil than of God. But she survives and, like Simplicissimus, lives forever.

Finally, by all ordinary standards of Christian morality, which Grimmelshausen himself reasserts continuously, if only in the interstices of his tale, Courage is corrupt and wicked, whereas the heroines of the idealistic novel remain of untarnished virtue, no matter how often and how cruelly this virtue is put into thrilling jeopardy. Courage does not want to be virtuous. She has wild, unsatiable appetites for men and riches, but no conscience. Her moral character owes nothing either to religious teaching or to Descartes's theory of passion, but almost everything to Galen's views of the human temperament. "I cannot take out my gall," she says, "as the butcher turns the pig's stomach inside out to cleanse it." She is full of lust and avarice and envy, and most easily aroused to fierce anger; she is evil, although it should be stressed that she never inflicts pain on others without provocation. But she is natural, and this cannot be said of the heroines whose Christian conscience she in fact denies with every fiber of her existence.

Like Defoe's Mrs. Flanders, Grimmelshausen's Courage is a challenge to morality, but Moll Flanders belongs already to the age in which virtue began to be identified largely with chastity in women. She is a middle-class heroine. By contrast, Courage boldly calls virtue in the older, broader sense into question; in the account of her life she rocks even the Christian foundation of virtue. Moll Flanders has many children and finishes her dissolute life as a dowager, who has become respectable through remorse and wealth. Grimmelshausen created Courage barren, and he was aware of it. Childless, Courage is more of a man, as it were, without becoming any less desirable as a woman in the eyes of men. In the end, Courage prefers the life of a gypsy to that of a respectable widow, and so perhaps did Grimmelshausen. While Moll Flanders in her reckless life has only three principal sources of income — needlework, men as husbands and lovers, and theft — Courage adds to these booty in war, which she gains sword in hand. There is, of course, nothing manly about Mrs. Flanders, and the risks she takes lack grandeur.

The gulf separating Courage and Moll Flanders can perhaps best be shown by the involuntary, physical expression of their feelings. For all her wickedness Moll Flanders cries and blushes and faints hardly less often than her female, middle-class readers were prone to do. Her sickly femininity easily falls prey to lingering fevers when she receives adverse news. This woman, whom Defoe gives "that unmusical, harsh-sounding title of whore," weeps on every possible occasion, including the hour in which fear of being hanged overcomes her. Courage, too, weeps, especially in the early part of her career, but almost always in order to deceive men. She cries by design, her tears are a trick that never fails her. Only twice does Courage cry to express despair, the first time when she is among troops who are forced to surrender to the enemy and again after she has been utterly debased, humiliated, beaten, and cruelly abused many times by a mob of drunken, brutal officers and servants for several nights in succession. Courage never faints or blushes and yet, despite her vengefulness, her insatiable sexual appetite, and her excessive abandon, at the end of her enormous tale she appears to the reader as a radiantly beautiful woman of rare natural power, unquenchable zest for life, and inexhaustible vital resources. Courage is her just name in the extraordinary equivocation of meaning that Grimmelshausen in a master stroke of genius and humor bestowed upon it.

To the modern reader the name of Courage is most familiar from Bertolt Brecht's play, *Mother Courage and Her Children*. Anna Fierling is called Mother Courage because she meets all adversity and misfortune with ever new hope and resolution to make a miserable profit in her trade. She stands for all the downtrodden who believe that they have nothing but their own courage to lose.[6]

The meaning which Grimmelshausen attached to the name Courage is quite different. Courage is first introduced as a young girl under the

name of Libuschka. While dressed like a boy to escape rape she is
called Janco. As Janco she becomes a captain's servant and gets into a
fight with another boy at the sutler's. "When we were in the thick of
it," she says, "this fellow grabbed me between the legs, because he
wanted to get hold of my tool that I did not have." She prevails over
him. Later in his quarters the captain asks Janco, whom he still takes
for a boy, why she had beaten up her opponent so terribly. She replies,
"Because he tried to grasp my courage which no other man has ever
touched with his hand."[7] Then she confides in the young captain that
she is a girl who disguised herself as a boy merely to escape abuse by
the soldiers. She begs him to protect her honor, and he promises to do
so but to her delight does not keep his word.

When the captain understands the meaning of the word "courage,"
with which the girl had "so colorfully described the emblem of her
sex," he cannot help laughing at her and calls her Courage. Try as she
will to rid herself of that name it clings to her forever. The name
Courage, then, stands for what Grimmelshausen regarded as the physiological site of vitality, bravery, and godlessness.

Grimmelshausen's choice of Courage as a picaresque character for
one of his main works invites some speculation. Today, it is considered
unlikely that *Courage, the Adventuress* owes much to Francisco de
Ubeda's *Picara Justina* (1603), although Grimmelshausen may have
been familiar with the long-winded German translation of that work.
Ubeda's novel was an avowed imitation of *The Celestina* (1449)[8] and
other picaresque Spanish tales, whereas Grimmelshausen's *Courage,
the Adventuress*, like *The Celestina*, is a masterpiece in its own right.
Even if Grimmelshausen's work depended closely on *Picara Justina*,
however, the question would still remain why the author's imagination
was captured by a female picaro. Why did Grimmelshausen despite all
his ostensible contempt for love and women, create such an extraordinarily vivid picture of a manly woman whose beauty and vitality excelled the evil in her? No one who has read *Courage, the Adventuress*
will escape the conclusion that he was fascinated by Courage. He
admired her.[9] While condemning sex in all his writings, in this novel he
succeeded in presenting at the same time the portrait of an irresistible
woman, who reacts with lusty sexual abandon and revenge to terrible
abuse by men and yet remains human and attractive to the reader.

It is striking that both Simplicius and Courage, the tomboy, have
their first sexual experiences in homosexual situations. Later, Courage
repeatedly mentions her burning desire to wear man's clothing and to
be in every way like a man. Grimmelshausen himself had a keen inter-

est in hermaphrodites and in the changing of sex. References to hermaphrodites occur in several of his works. In his tale which deals with the birth of a false Jewish messiah the child turns out to be a girl. When the gullible Jews in Amsterdam believe that God may change this girl into a young man at the age of maturity, Grimmelshausen points out that it would be no miracle for a female child to develop male sex characteristics.[10]

It should also be noted that the only feelings of close attachment to another human being that Grimmelshausen ever describes are those prevailing between father and son and between two young men. In this respect, as a writer on friendship, Grimmelshausen is unique among the novelists of the seventeenth century. When he speaks of the friendship between Simplicissimus and Heartsbrother he finds words expressing deep emotion, but all his words on heterosexual love are detached or cynical and arouse either disgust or raucous laughter.

Finally, there is a most curious description of Skipinthefield in distress. Tortured by his love for Courage, Skipinthefield enters the woman's tent under the pretense of wanting a pot of wine. Grimmelshausen describes his appearance as seen through Courage's eyes as follows: "He looked so pale and disconsolate then as though he had just gotten a child without having or knowing its father, and without having either milk or meal-pap for it."[11] Along with everything else that has been said, this strangely ambiguous sentence might lend credence to the suggestion that Grimmelshausen had ambivalent feelings toward women and sex. Perhaps he felt even dimly anxious or uncertain about his own sexual wishes.

But these are speculations. There are few baroque authors who do not invite similar speculations. In many conventional baroque novels as in comedy and farce, disguise and confusion of the sexes are common. Homosexual allusions are far more prominent in Callot's engravings than in Grimmelshausen's Simplician writings, and other writers of the period, like Harsdörffer, were intrigued by hermaphrodites.

Leaving these speculations aside, it certainly was not Grimmelshausen's main intention in *Courage, the Adventuress* to parody the conventional literary motif of the amazon. While he succeeded in doing that, he had a still more important purpose in mind. He stated his intention clearly through the mouth of Courage in the grand opening chapter of the novel. The old whore explains that the sole purpose of her confession is to avenge herself on Simplicissimus. At the same time she laughs derisively at the idea that her monstrous confession might be taken as an act of penitence: her vengefulness involves not only Simplicissimus, but God himself. She defies both. The intensity of her feeling is conveyed by Grimmelshausen by a whole series of rogueries in which revenge is the main motive and with startling force, by Courage's observation that her heart is like her body: when hurt, it takes a long time to heal.*

Courage's soul is entirely untroubled by the dissolute life she has led. If she confesses anything it is her godlessness. She fears God as little as men. She loves life and is not afraid of death. Thoughts of punishment and damnation, of divine justice and hellfire, never curb her worldly passion. She loves money, but not her neighbors, and she says so. Her life is exuberantly evil. Nature has made her so, and neither the magistrate nor the priests, neither man nor God, are able to change it. By telling her story in order to avenge herself, she makes a mockery of the act of confession in the Christian sense.

Grimmelshausen's novel is cruder and coarser than Defoe's but, paradoxically, less lascivious. In *Moll Flanders* the most shocking episode is the marriage of the heroine to a man who unbeknownst to her is her brother. One of Mrs. Flanders' many children is the fruit of this incestuous relationship. But in the end her brother conveniently dies, giving Mrs. Flanders a chance at social respectability which she presumably deserves by her riches, her enterprising commercial talent, and by the confession and repentance of her sins in Newgate Prison. It is inconceivable that Grimmelshausen could have stopped to thrill his

---

*In many of his works Grimmelshausen's interest in revenge is so intense that one cannot help wondering whether he was himself a resentful and vengeful man. He had red hair, which according to a very old and widespread superstition was a sign of evil character. Since superstition holds especially the lower classes in its grip, it is likely that he was exposed to the full force of this prejudice in the army camps and taverns, the villages and the countryside where he spent most of his life. It is known that a colleague of his in the employ of the Schauenburg family derisively called him "the red steward" ("der rote Schaffner"). Grimmelshausen wrote a humorous pamphlet in fierce defense of red beards, "Der Bart-Krieg." Grimmelshausen's authorship of this pamphlet was proved only in 1940 by Manfred Koschlig, "Der Bart-Krieg — Ein Werk Grimmelshausen," *Neophilologus*, vol. xxiv, pp. 42ff. ("Der Bart Krieg" is included in *Simpliciana*, pp. 128-48). At least one perceptive literary historian, Walter Muschg (*Tragische Literaturgeschichte*, Bern, 1948, pp. 265-68) has suggested that Grimmelshausen must have regarded his red hair as a misfortune. Muschg mentions in this connection a number of writers who may have felt their physical deformity as a stigma; and he suggests that their work may have been influenced by the cripple's hatred of the healthy and by feelings fluctuating between "horror of themselves, extreme sensitivity and cynical conceit." He points out that "many great satirists and polemicists had such a stigma." Excluding from Muschg's list those writers who were repulsively ugly, there remain the cripples: Aesop, Thomas Murner, Scarron, Pope, Lichtenberg, Gottfried Keller, Kierkegaard. The name of Quevedo may be added: he was lame.

readers with the cheap pornography of inadvertent incest. For *The Enchanted Bird's-nest* Grimmelshausen borrowed from Bandello a shocking scatological story, in which a man takes revenge in the filthiest possible manner on his unfaithful wife, but the German author did not borrow from the Italian, as he could have, the story of an incestuous relationship, a tale that in plot and elegant execution far exceeds Defoe's prurient adventure.

The most shocking incidents in the life of Courage are not those in which refined tastes or affectations are offended, but those in which religious propriety is flaunted. The supreme instance is the extraordinary contract in which Courage makes a mockery of the sacrament of marriage. The musketeer who becomes her man under conditions stipulated in this contract must not only pledge submission to her in all affairs of the household, but also grant her the right to remain a whore, in order to get the phantom of a spouse. This perversion of Christian marriage results in the utter degradation of the musketeer to the status of a servant, thief, and mock husband. The woman whom he must treat as his wife insists on his own cuckoldom in the marriage contract. Moreover, Courage exercises her right to give him a name of her own choosing that marks him forever. The burlesque humor of this marriage arrangement cannot hide its fierce, shocking affront at the religious sanction of the relation between the sexes.

It is evident that Grimmelshausen was fully aware of the boldness of his conceit. He carefully prepared the reader for the incredible contract by dwelling first in detail upon the infatuation of the musketeer and the manner in which Courage cunningly exploits it for her purposes. In these passages of the book Grimmelshausen displays great power as a satirist of polite conversation. When the acceptance of the contract by the wretched musketeer is thus made credible, Grimmelshausen interrupts his narrative to issue a pious warning to "honest Christians" not to follow Courage's example!

Courage, the Adventuress, like all novels of the Simplician cycle, abounds with Christian warnings. They occur in prefaces and postscripts and as insertions in the main body of his tales. Since the use of such apologetic material is traditional among satirists[12] to justify their colorful depiction of that which is disapproved in society on moral, political, or religious grounds, Grimmelshausen's effort to dissociate himself by pious words from the evil he describes with so much gusto and humor should not distract the attention of the critical reader from the impious implications of his tales. In *Courage, the Adventuress* moral and religious protestations are made with particular insistence just prior to the description of the extraordinary marriage contract and in "The Author's Postscript" which concludes the novel. This Postscript is taken almost literally from *Piazza Universale* by Tomaso Garzoni and thus is written in borrowed prose like the sonorously Christian ending of the fifth book of *The Adventurous Simplicissimus*, which Grimmelshausen took verbatim from Guevara. As one critic put it, the curiosity of Grimmelshausen's reader "is legitimized by a moral superstructure which pacifies his conscience and thus leaves him free to enjoy pure adventure."[13] We may add that this superstructure protects the author from the wrath of censorious readers who lack his impious humor.

NOTES

1. Jacob Burckhardt, *Die Kultur der Renaissance in Italien*, 14th ed., ed. by Walter Goetz, Leipzig, 1925, p. 271.
2. Baldassare Castiglione, *The Book of the Courtier*, Done into English by Sir Thomas Hoby, anno 1561, Everyman's Library, p. 218.
3. For the following discussion cf. Antoine Claire Jungkunz, *Menschendarstellung im deutschen höfischen Roman des Barock*, Germanische Studien, no. 160, Berlin, 1937, pp. 42, 78–90, 189, 220.
4. Quoted in ibid., p. 88.
5. Johann Beer, *Kurtzweilige Sommer-Täge* (1683), ed. by Wolfgang Schmidt, Halle, 1958, p. 116.
6. Bertolt Brecht, *Mother Courage and Her Children: A Chronicle of the Thirty Years' War*, English version by Eric Bentley, New York. (Evergreen Book no. 372), 1963, pp. 75–76.
7. *Courage*, chap. 3. All main characters in the first eight books of the Simplician cycle of novels have significant names. Both Simplicissimus and Courage have many names, each appropriate to the respective stage of their careers. The meaning of this practice in Grimmelshausen's work has been commented upon by many modern critics. See, for example, Werner Welzig, *Beispielhafte Figuren. Tor, Abenteurer und Einsiedler bei Grimmelshausen*, Graz-Köln, 1963, pp. 42ff. On the question of significant names in general, see Franz Dornseiff. "Redende Namen," *Zeitschrift für Namenforschung*, 1940, vol. xvi, pp. 24ff. and 215ff.
8. An English edition of *Tragi-Comedia de Calisto y Melibar*, popularly known as *The Celestina* (after the character of the procuress in the play), has been prepared by Lesley Byrd Simpson, Berkeley and Los Angeles, 1955.
9. The point that Grimmelshausen admired Courage is also made by Siegfried Streller, *Grimmelshausens Simplicianische Schriften*, [East] Berlin, 1957, p. 195. Streller speaks of Grimmelshausen's "unconfessed sympathies for this hated and loved character" and refers to the magnificent description of Courage (then already sixty-six years old) by the Swiss clerk in *Grimmelshausens Springinsfeld*, ed. by J. H. Scholte, Halle, 1928, chap. 4.
10. *Bird's-nest II*, chap. 18. Cf. also the story of Aemilia who after twelve years of

marriage changes her sex and becomes Aemilius (*Ewigwährender Kalender*, ed. by Engelbert Hegaur, Munich, 1925, pp. 396–97).

11. "Er sahe so bleich und trostlos aus, als wann er kürzlich ein Kind bekommen und keinen Vatter, Mehl noch Milch darzu gehabt oder gewüsst hätte" (*Die Landstörzerin Courasche*, ed. by J. H. Scholte, Halle, 1923, chap. 15).

12. Hans Ehrenzeller, op. cit.

13. Hildegarde Wichert, op. cit., p. 140.

13

The Fool and
the Social Order

The Many Faces of the Fool

Paul Léautaud, a misanthrope clad in provocative rags, used to return
every night from his place of work to his house in the suburbs of Paris
to feed the animals in whose company he chose to live — at one time,
thirty-eight cats, twenty-two dogs, a goat, and a goose. There he wrote
in the course of many years the nineteen volumes of his diary, using a
steel pen by candlelight. Léautaud, who lived most of his life in the
twentieth century, was an eccentric. His behavior (unlike his diary)
offended no one of consequence.

Eccentrics are nonconformists, but as long as their unconventional
behavior does not disturb the peace, neither police nor neighbors
make life difficult for them. Exceptions occur in small towns where
privacy is less respected than it is in large cities. In confining circumstances gossip and censure of harmless dissenters provide thrills of
vicarious adventure and the comfort of vengeful righteousness. Even
so, it is generally true that eccentrics are not treated like thieves or
rebels, but rather as though they were simpletons falling lamentably
below the average in intelligence, foresight, and prudence. If they are
punished for their shortcomings, they rarely suffer anything more severe than social failure, perhaps isolation, and condescension or ridi-

From Hans Speier, *Force and Folly*, Cambridge, Mass., 1969. Copyright © 1969 by
M.I.T. Press. Reprinted by permission of M.I.T. Press.

cule. With these inconveniences the eccentric, like the simpleton, is usually permitted to go his way and make a fool of himself.

Except when smiling indulgently at a "foolish child," we speak today of "fools" and "folly" in a slightly pejorative sense. No longer do we hear the faintest echo of the bells which used to tingle on the fool's cap. Nor do we associate with the fool his traditional symbol, the stick that evolved from the wooden sword the comic actor used to brandish in antiquity.

The fool in the more colorful sense of the word once played a prominent role on the social scene. His heyday in art and literature was the period from the middle of the fifteenth to the middle of the seventeenth century. *The Praise of Folly* by Erasmus was published in 1511, in chronological time only a few years later than Sebastian Brant's *Ship of Fools*, from which it is removed in spirit almost as far as is reason from faith. Brant's book is a satirical condemnation of men in all walks of life for their failure to behave like good Christians. Brant, also an author of hymns, censured man for neglecting his true self-interest in salvation. He thought men were fools because of such neglect. Erasmus kept an ironic balance between Christian doctrine and the skeptical view of human nature that he owed to Lucian rather than to the Scriptures. He did not moralize. When Stultitia praised the follies of man it was clear enough that some fools were happy not because God loved them, but because they followed their natural inclinations. From the end of the period in which the fool was socially prominent, we have Velázquez' great paintings: "Aesop"; "Pernia," the buffoon of Philip IV: the so-called Don Juan of Austria and portraits of other physical "abnormities."[1] Velázquez' paintings remind us that fools throughout history have often been physically deformed or mentally defective.

But the history of the fool is by no means confined to two centuries. It extends back through the Middle Ages to antiquity and, more dimly, forward to our age. One of the famous mythical buffoons, Si-Djoha, who lived in the company of Timur Lenk, the conqueror, whom he entertained as a court jester, is proof of the fact that the popular imagination of the Arabs in the Middle Ages was no less preoccupied than was that of the Christians in the West with the juxtaposition of great folly and fearful power. One of the jests ascribed to Si-Djoha illustrates the point. His master, appalled by a glimpse he had caught of himself in a mirror, sobbed for two hours and so, dutifully or sympathetically, did his retinue. When the great man ceased weeping he noticed that Si-Djoha continued to sob. He explained to his astonished master, "If you saw yourself in the glass for a short moment and wept for two hours, is it surprising that I weep longer since I see you the whole day?"[2] Truly, only a fool speaks to a mighty man in this way, and such a fool may be a Christian as well as a Moslem, or, indeed, neither.

The more recent history of the fool is somewhat harder to trace. A learned student of folly has referred to Don Quixote as the last fool,[3] but then there is Dostoyevsky's *Idiot* and Jaroslav Hasek's *The Good Soldier Schweik*. Nor have the professional jesters completely vanished. There are the circus clowns for the children. There are comedians who pretend to be stupid so that their clever audiences will laugh. In every carnival, an atrophied off-shoot of the Saturnalia, we meet harlequins, whether they know something of the Commedia dell' Arte or not. And there are Will Rogers and Charlie Chaplin and Art Buchwald, none of them a Falstaff, but all of them distantly related to the great fools of the past.

It is not easy to describe the fool. It is a genus with many different species, and the most casual inspection of the historical records reveals changes, ambiguities, contradictions, and paradoxes in the way human folly has been described. Furthermore, however described, folly, too, seems to change her features with the observer's perspective, so that her true face eludes us. An evil woman like Goneril in *King Lear* says of those who respect authority and old age that they are foolish,[4] although in all her infamy she herself plays a role on what her father regards as "this great stage of fools."[5] Thus, unbeknownst to her, it is she who is foolish when viewed by someone who can remove the masks from the players on that stage. In general, to the fool the world is replete with folly, while the world considers the fool and not itself foolish.

The wilder paradoxes concerning folly originated in Christian rather than pre-Christian teaching. Their source is Paul, not Socrates. The latter was aware of the limits of his knowledge, but he never said that knowledge or the search for knowledge was folly. Nor did he urge the wise man to "become a fool that he may be wise."[6] Finally, Socrates never spoke of "the foolishness of God," as did Paul.[7]

The lower classes are less intelligent than the upper classes. In addressing primarily the lower classes, Jesus and his apostles endowed foolishness with great virtue, presenting it as a condition favored by God. The Christian fool, a sheep, follows the shepherd. As Erasmus put it through the mouth of Stultitia,

The Christian religion on the whole seems to have some kinship with folly, while it has none at all with wisdom. If you want proof of this, observe first that children, old people, women and fools take more delight than anyone else in holy and religious things; and that they are therefore ever nearest the altars, led no doubt solely by instinct. Next, you will notice that the founders of religion have prized simplicity exceedingly, and have been the bitterest foes of learning. Finally, no people seem to act more foolishly than those who have been truly possessed with Christian piety. They give away whatever is theirs; they overlook injuries, allow themselves to be cheated, make no distinction between friends and enemies, shun pleasure, and feast on hunger, vigils, tears, labors, and scorn. They disdain life, and utterly prefer death; in short, they seem to have become altogether indifferent to ordinary interests, quite as if their souls lived elsewhere and not in their bodies. What is this, if not to be mad?[8]

Every fool, whether he follows Christ or nature, whether his name is Eulenspiegel or King Lear, calls into question the moral order around him. The fool looks at the world with sad or merry detachment, if not with hidden contempt. He does not share the ambitions and aspirations of those who seek success and try to avoid failure. He does not obey the law, but instead always conjures up "another order of things," or a reversal of the existing order, or plain misrule.

According to Erasmus, "another order of things would suddenly arise" "if someone should unmask the actors in the middle of a scene on the stage and show their real faces to the audience."[9] Like Lucian before him and Shakespeare later, Erasmus likened life to "a kind of stage play through which men pass in various disguises."[10] The fool shows the world without disguises. He does so in various roles. As a satirist he is an "Undeceiver-General,"[11] who proves that the appearance of moral conduct is but a sham covering up an evil, sinful reality. As a tragic fool he speaks almost in riddles, yet still clearly enough to suggest that man receives no help from God. While the divine voice of thunder on the heath where King Lear is left in his agony is incomprehensible, the fool and King Lear, having turned fool himself, speak the truth:

FOOL: He that has a little tiny wit,
    With hey, ho, the wind and the rain,
    Must make content with his fortunes fit
    For the rain it raineth every day.
LEAR: True, my good boy.[12]

In his comic role, the fool is man undisguised, following his instincts, enjoying himself outside the pale of the social order. Through his antics and impudent speech he reminds those who observe the law that behind the masks of respectability lie the delights of nature. He, for one, has broken the shell of conventions that encrusts the natural life of the appetites. He loves life so much that he prefers discretion to valor, like Falstaff, and when buried, the ropes holding his coffin may break, so that, like Eulenspiegel, he remains standing upright in his grave.

We shall not pursue the subject of Christian folly nor, in particular, pay attention to the "holy fool," who avails himself of the fool's license for the sake of God and teaches His word through folly in parables.[13] Instead, we shall turn to the fools who follow their natural inclinations and care about preachers as little as about guardians of the law.

The Fool and Reality

Let us begin with the observation that a child may resemble a fool (as may a man who has drunk too much wine), especially by speaking the truth in circumstances in which the adult person soberly hides it or lies. The child crying out, while no one else dares to speak up, that the emperor is naked, does not act in defiance of authority and convention, but in ignorance of them. We rightly ascribe the child's affront to lack of experience and redouble our effort to teach him the ways of responsible adults. As yet, he does not know any better; only in time will he learn from his parents and teachers when it is proper to hide the truth and when it is prudent to lie. He will learn how to dissemble not only in order to avoid in adulthood the consequences of candor that will be painful to him, but also in order not to offend others by telling a truth that hurts them. For in the adult world, the truth may be hidden for many different reasons: fear, trickery, pride, guilt, awe, courtesy. The child is deficient in all these regards. In his ignorance he is reckless and discourteous. He has yet to learn when to feel guilty. Though not unselfish, he lacks intelligence in pursuing his ends, and while he may tremble in the dark, he is not awed by God's power.

The fool behaves like an untutored child. The fool is the man who does not lie; indeed, inability to lie is as good a criterion of folly as any. "You are incomparable," Radomski says to Prince Myshkin, "that is, a man who does not lie at every step and who, perhaps, never lies. . . . "[14] Similarly, Stultitia claims that she is not "two-tongued," and Falstaff that he is no "double-man," like the "wise" in this world.[15] By contrast, Gregory the Great observed polemically, "The wisdom of the world is, to conceal the truth of one's heart by trickery, to veil one's meaning in words, to make those things which are false appear to be true, to present the truth as falsehood."[16] Like the child, the fool speaks the truth and is permitted to do so because he is considered exempt from the responsibilities of other mortals who do lie, as everyone knows. Whatever he says can be discounted, if need be, and laughed at for its absurdity, or it may be taken in awe as something enigmatic and supernaturally inspired.

Ignorance or innocence which leads the child and the fool to violate the conventions of adult society may extend beyond the sphere of propriety to the perception of reality. A celebrated illustration of a fool's misconception of reality is to be found in Cervantes' *Don Quixote*. I am not referring to the general madness of the melancholy knight who mistakes windmills for villains and discovers great beauty in the ordinary face of a country wench, but specifically to a particular scene in the second part of the novel.[17] In this scene, Sancho Panza, himself a fool, indulges the spleen of his master, another kind of fool, by telling him that the three country girls approaching on their donkeys are illustrious ladies. Don Quixote, however, recognizes them for what they are, three ugly, peevish peasant maids. Thus, Sancho Panza, instead of asserting reality against his master's madness, as he usually does, plays a mad fool himself in order to indulge the spleen of his master, while Don Quixote for once seems to be free of his madness. But this reversal of roles turns out to be but an ingenious surprise that Cervantes springs on the reader in order to disclose the depth of the hidalgo's folly. Don Quixote kneels in front of the three girls, exclaiming in an exquisite bravura piece of chivalric eloquence that "some wicked enchanter spread clouds and cataracts over my eyes, changing, and to them only, thy peerless beauty into that of a poor rustic." Thus, the foolish knight recognizes reality for what it is, but instead of accepting it as such, avers that his senses are in error because he has been bewitched. After Dulcinea, who for contrast speaks the language of low comedy, has fallen off her donkey and jumped back on it like a tomboy, Don Quixote says to Sancho Panza, "See how I am persecuted by enchanters! Mark how far their malice extends, even to depriving me of the pleasure of seeing my mistress in her own proper form."[18]

On a less sophisticated level of folly we encounter simpler misconceptions of reality, for example, that of the child trying to grab the moon in his picture book, or the young fool in literature whose innocence and naïveté charm us: in German he is referred to as "*der reine Tor*," "the pure fool." Young Parzival, just taught by his mother that the difference between God and the Devil can be likened to that between light and darkness, encounters four knights in a forest. Not ever having seen a knight, but observing the shining armors, "the lad thought for sure that each one was a god."[19] Similarly, several centuries later, young Simplicius in Grimmelshausen's main novel is being raised in the house of a crude and ignorant peasant at the time of the Thirty Years War. The peasant warns him to beware of wolves when watching the sheep. When the boy, who has never seen either wolves or horses, meets some marauding soldiers on horseback, he thinks, in his folly, that each soldier and his horse are but one creature, a wolf.[20] It has been suggested that in telling this tale Grimmelshausen may have been influenced by the story of Parzival,[21] but while this may be so, it does not necessarily follow that the seventeenth-century satirist shared Wolfram's intention to depict the pure fool's closeness to God.[22]

Fools — Thieves — Confidence Men

When we turn from the folly of children to adult folly, we face a bewildering variety of fools: buffoons and jesters at court, harlequins improvising their repartee on the stage, and jugglers in the market-place; boys masked as bishops in church; slow-witted peasants and village idiots; physically stunted parasites, and entertainers of nimble wit or with a penchant for practical jokes, kept by lords and ladies for their amusement; mad men and epileptics, who in ages less enlightened than ours evoked awe since they were thought to be supernaturally inspired, like poets or prophets; etc.[23] Folly in literature is no less varied. All literary fools point to forms of foolishness in life. Whether they are the creation of an individual mind or, in myth and folklore, of collective imagination, they present reality transmuted and sublimated.

In life, as in literature, folly is either natural or studied. Man can be a fool because nature was niggardly when he was born, or he may be endowed with the gift of playing a fool for gain and fun. In literature, the fool and the license he enjoys, offer an opportunity for impudently critical comment on worldly and divine authorities.

Natural fools are men deficient in intelligence because of poor native endowment or because of inadequate education. In epochs in which the distinction between the subhuman and human element in society was drawn with less compunction than we are prone to feel in our age, with its well-advanced humanitarianism and technology, both the antics of the feebleminded, like those of the physically stunted, and the stupidity of the lower classes were a source of laughter. The more rigidly stratified and the less enlightened society is, the more it appears to men at the top that the unworthy, the ugly, and the comical are concentrated at the bottom. The Christian preference for the lowly lent poignancy to such discrimination, while it offered solace to the downtrodden by substituting, in Bertolt Brecht's cynical words from *Mahagonny*, "the just distribution of the other-worldly goods" for "the unjust distribution of worldly goods."

In light of the promise of life after death, the teaching that Christian folly was superior to worldly wisdom implied a radical criticism of the social order. Christian teaching tried to impose an ascetic discipline upon life prior to death. It presented the physical nature of man as corrupt and demanded that the pain that stems from the rule of men over men be cheerfully accepted like death.

Subsequently, the studied fool in literature was able to perform two major functions. First, by showing folly outwitting worldly wisdom, the fool could serve as an instrument of vicarious social revenge. If the privileged tended to associate low rank with the comical, it is not surprising that the underprivileged savored the pleasure of seeing the powerful and the wise subdued by a fool. Second, folly could become the advocate of nature against all order. The fool could insist, with cheerful irresponsibility or in a melancholy cast, on the merely conventional character of all discipline, whether such discipline claimed political or religious sanction. Since the fool had been endowed by Christian teaching with the special virtue of having access to the truth, the fool as a champion of nature could be used for throwing doubt not only upon worldly wisdom, but upon Christian teaching itself.

The literary paradigm of the triumph of folly over reason is to be found in the debates of a fifteenth century figure, the shrewd, misshapen peasant Marcolf, with wise King Solomon, whom he unfailingly outwits. Perhaps this contest was not only between the respectable, moral platitudes of a king and the common sense of a physically deformed rustic, but on a deeper level between divine reason and the power of an ugly, satanic mind. In any event, Marcolf's foolishness is both a parody and sarcastic refutation of Solomon's wisdom. At every stage of the contest the fool triumphs over the sage, the lout over the lord, turpitude over splendor. In order to win his case in this drama of social revenge, Marcolf frequently resorts to mischievous pranks. For example, once he gains entry to the palace by releasing a hare so that the King's watchdogs chase the hare instead of guarding the gate. In another episode, Solomon refuses to join Marcolf in his vilification of women. Marcolf predicts that the king will do so in due course. He then spreads the false rumor that Solomon has ordered each man to take seven wives, whereupon the women raise such a clamor that the king, like Marcolf, vents his spleen against them. Finally, the king, unable any longer to endure Marcolf's resourceful insults, angrily orders him to go out of sight: "let me never look you between the eyes again." Whereupon Marcolf crawls into an oven to lie there in such a posture that the king cannot see Marcolf's eyes, but only his backside. The coarseness of this insult is characteristic of the elementary revenge that throughout the history of the comical imagination nature delights in taking on nurture, *physis* on *nomos*, the bodily functions on the spiritual and — the underprivileged on those who are privileged. The king, so blatantly insulted by the lout, orders his servants to execute Marcolf, permitting him only to choose the tree from which he is to hang. The story ends, "So Marcolf and the servants travelled through the Valley of Hosaffat, and over the hill of Olivet, and from thence to Jericho, and over the River Jordan, and through all Arabia, and over the Grand Desert to the Red Sea, but they never found the tree on which Marcolf chose to be hanged."[24] As to King Solomon, he appeared as late as the eighteenth century, as a subject of laughter in Punch-and-Judy shows.[25] Later, Till Eulenspiegel and the antiheroes of the picaresque novel were to make fools of their adversaries by similar pranks.

No sphere of life is safe from the cheerful anarchism of the fool in literature. All conventions seem to be more vulnerable than they would be if all men were serious. The fool makes light of the meaning of words as well as of the social necessity of work, and of the distinction between mine and thine no less than of that between noble and base. Nor is the sacred exempt from the fool's laughter.

Consider the havoc the fool creates by his treatment of speech. Inadvertent rather than willful perversion of the conventional meaning of words occurs in medieval tales of the stupid peasant who gives foolish answers because he is unable to understand educated speech. The same device is used, however, by the studied fool, who outwits convention as a critic rather than violates it as an ignoramus. Thus, when Solomon says that he never again wants to look Marcolf between the eyes, and later that he be hanged from a tree of his choosing, the fool complies with the literal meaning of the commands, thereby defying the obvious sense that the king intended.

In the jest book *A Hundred Merry Tales* (1526), a penitent is enjoined by his confessor to say daily for his penance, "The Lamb of God have mercy on me." A year later he tells his confessor that he has done his penance, having said that morning and so daily, "The Sheep of God have mercy on me." It is twelve months since he has been enjoined to do penance, and the lamb, he avers, has become a sheep.[26] This is funny, but we cannot be quite sure whether it is funny because the penitent was stupid or because the sacred symbol of the Lamb has been ridiculed.

Similarly, Till Eulenspiegel executed orders given to him in their literal sense to the exasperation and detriment of the masters for whom he works. At night he sifts flour upon the earth of the garden since the baker who refused to give him a candle ordered him to sift "by the moonlight." While serving a tailor, he sews a seam under a barrel, because the master told him to sew so that nobody could see the seam. Another time he ruins the leather of a shoemaker by cutting all leather to fit the left foot, because he had not been told to use for a model "the last pair" of shoes, but merely "the last one," which Eulenspiegel willfully misunderstands to mean the last shoe. Once, being told to leave the house of a blacksmith, who overworks his servants, he knocks a hole in the roof from the inside and departs. From a hostess at an inn he demands payment after treating himself to a sumptuous dinner because she told him that he could eat and drink "for money." Again and again, he dupes and harms the conformists who behold the damage and can only say, like the shoemaker, "I meant not that," or "Ye do after my saying and not after my meaning."[27]

We still laugh about these stories, as people have done ever since they heard such jokes for the first time. Let us note that the good soldier Schweik often outwits his superior officers in World War I by availing himself of ambiguities of meaning in much the same way in which Marcolf duped King Solomon, and Eulenspiegel the tailor.

As to work, without which society crumbles, fools are known to shun it. Carefree and easy as they are, they like the fruits of labor, but not labor itself. All lower-class fools steal their food and drink always preferring wine to water and meat to bread. All picaros are thieves, revenging themselves on the stinginess of their masters or simply disrespecting private property. They are parasites taking what they need from the owners. Fools and picaros are natural consumers. They ridicule industry and thrift like all other traits of socially useful respectability. In one of José Rubén Romero's stories in *The Futile Life of Pito Perez* — the Mexican latecomer to the guild of picaros and an embittered fool — Pito takes charge of his uncle's store during his absence and sells his goods on credit "without recording any of the sales" in order not to become "addicted to the greedy, petty habits of businessmen." Pito, "drunk either because of the godly art of giving or because of the liquor" he is consuming "so devoutly and abundantly," merely watches "as those earthly goods disappear."[28]

The disrespect for the institution of private property that the fool displays by theft (or by not paying his debts or by willful destruction) brings to mind two other socially deviant types that have captured popular and literary imagination, the master thief and the confidence man. In some respects they resemble the fool.

As early as 1834 Søren Kierkegaard reflected upon the idea of a master thief; he abstracted it from the ventures commonly ascribed to different thieves in the tales of various nations. He pointed out that villainy and thievishness were by no means the only basic traits of the master thief. Instead, he also possessed admirable skills and was kind, amiable, and often generous, stealing from the rich to help the poor. "Often, we must think of him," Kierkegaard said, "as of a person that is discontented with reality and expresses his discontentment by infringing upon the rights of others, thereby seeking an opportunity for deriding, and quarreling with, the authorities." Comparing the master thief with the head of a band of robbers, Kierkegaard observed that the latter seeks relaxation from the dangers and drudgery of his profession in gay social abandon, whereas the master thief represents "something more profound, a certain melancholy trait, reserve, a dark view of the conditions of life, inner dissatisfaction."[29] Kierkegaard was of the opinion that the master thief resembled in certain respects Till Eulenspiegel, whom he regarded as the satyr of the North.[30] Indeed, the fool, too, is often melancholy at heart and, more than that, cruel and bitter. He, too, is a solitary figure rather than the member or head of a group. But the redistribution of values in favor of the poor, through which the generous master thief gains fame among the people, is no concern of the fool's. The fool is a natural anarchist, not a seeker of justice.

Nor does the confidence man right any wrongs. Though he usually operates on a grander scale than the master thief and excels him in fastidiousness, he, too, fills his pocket (whereas the fool fills his stomach). But he does share with the fool rather than the thief an outstanding ability to hoodwink other people. The confidence man exploits gullibility by misrepresentation and impersonation, his most astounding skill. Thomas Mann's Felix Krull exercises it while still a boy. He dissembles the symptoms of severe illness in order to stay away from school. He enjoys the applause of the crowd as another young Paganini, although he uses a bow greased with vaseline when pretending to play the violin in an orchestra. Similarly, before he is grown up he derives enjoyment from dressing up in various costumes, to represent a Roman flute player, a Spanish bullfighter, a youthful abbé, an Austrian officer, a German mountaineer, a Florentine dandy of the late middle ages, etc., looking in each disguise, "better and more natural than the last."[31] Like all fools, Felix Krull dislikes regular work, is fond of sleep, and believes that for him "the satisfaction of love is twice as sweet and twice as penetrating as with the average man."[32]

Anyone who has searched his heart or has read Thomas Mann's *Confessions of Felix Krull* is aware of the fact that a confidence man can make us laugh (so long as we do not become his victim). When laughing at him, we admire not only his incredible skill but also his success in exposing the foibles of society. Perhaps we secretly rejoice at the fact that those superior in wealth have been defrauded by one who is superior in intelligence and, by imposture, their equal in manners. At the same time we experience a feeling of reserve toward a man capable of impersonating others so perfectly as to throw doubt on his identity. We sense something pathological about the confidence man that is absent from the vitality of the fool and the dexterity of the master thief. If Kierkegaard was right in suggesting that the master thief takes a melancholy view of life, we have it on Thomas Mann's authority that the confidence man is depressed after his exploits.

Herman Melville, too, wrote a novel about an imposter who, like Felix Krull, is an expert impersonator; the subtitle of Melville's novel *The Confidence Man* is "His Masquerade." But Melville's confidence man is no fool. Thomas Mann made fun of the style of the old Goethe, of the German Novel of Education, and of the values of middle class civilization generally, depicted so vividly and with so much empathy in some of Mann's earlier works. Except for religion, Felix Krull plays havoc with nearly everything that is respectable in the society in which he moves. In contrast, Melville's primary concern was with gullibility and doubt. Many of Melville's images are emblematic, and there are innumerable allusions to the Scriptures in his work. A good case has been made that his confidence man personifies — God.[33]

Whereas Thomas Mann, in *Felix Krull*, satirized among other things the social convention of modern bourgeois society, Melville in *The Confidence Man* took issue with God and Christ. His was not a funny book. Early in the novel, an Ahab-like character, the skeptic with the wooden leg, by profession a customhouse officer like Melville, warns the passengers on the river boat *Fidèle* not to trust the confidence man. In his first disguise as a poor Negro, the latter tries to arouse and exploit feelings of charity among the passengers. A heated exchange ensues between a Methodist minister and the customhouse officer. The latter derides the "game of charity" which the imposter plays: "charity is one thing, and truth is another." The Methodist, a "resolute champion" of the "church militant," grabs the exasperating skeptic by the collar of his coat and shakes him furiously for scorning faith and charity and for "his evil heart of unbelief." It is with the help of the Methodist minister that the confidence man wins his contest with the skeptic, since enough gullible and charitable passengers are aboard the *Fidèle* for him to prevail. The skeptic exclaims in vain, "You fools . . . you flock of fools, under this captain of fools [the minister], on this ship of fools."[34]

On Sebastian Brant's *Ship of Fools*, too, all men are foolish, because in medieval perspective, all men are sinners and fail to conduct themselves as good Christians should, *sub specie aeternitatis*. Like Brant's ship, Melville's *Fidèle* transports men of all professions, ages, races, and nationalities. No doubt, the passengers represent mankind. Save for the skeptics, all of them are fools, but not because they are sinners, but because they are gullible victims of the malign impostor who seeks to gain their faith. In Melville's book, it is God who fools men. Or to put it less radically, Melville's *Confidence Man* is a fierce, though masked, attack on religion, while *Confessions of Felix Krull* merrily unmasks the pretensions of society.

Apart from disregarding the intended meaning of words and from preferring theft to work, the fool makes light of the moral order in many other ways. Order depends on law, and there can be no survival of the commonweal unless men with a sense of honor defend it. Men of honor are capable of choosing death in preference to the disgrace of cowardice or disloyalty. To the fool, however, the highest good is not honor, but life. If the fool is a knave in the eyes of honorable men, the latter are stupid in the eyes of the fool, because they do not seem to value life highly. The fool's indifference toward the honorable is most memorably expressed in Falstaff's "catechism" setting forth his belief that life is preferable to honor.

> What is honour? A word. What is that word honour? Air. A trim reckoning. Who hath it? he that died a'Wednesday. Does he feel it? No. Doth he hear it? No. It is insensible, then? Yea. To the dead. But will it not live with the living? No. Why? Detraction will not suffer it, therefore, I'll none of it: honour is a mere scutcheon, and so ends my catechism.[35]

In accordance with this catechism, Falstaff cunningly disgraces himself on the field of battle, first by playing dead, and then, in an extraordinarily bold mockery of honor, by wounding a dead enemy, the reckless and rash Hotspur. Finally Falstaff claims the distinction of having conquered Hotspur, trying to deprive Prince Hall, the true victor, of this honor. Before stabbing the dead man in the thigh, Falstaff repeats his credo:

> . . . to die is to be a counterfeit; for he is but the counterfeit of a man who hath not the life of man; but to counterfeit dying, when a man thereby liveth, is to be no counterfeit, but the true and perfect image of life indeed. The better part of valor is discretion; in the which better part I have saved my life.[36]

It is in this final scene that Falstaff transcends for the second time in the play the comic qualities of his ancient forebear, Plautus' *Miles Gloriosus*. The Latin soldier is vain and lecherous, a braggart who falls prey to the extravagant flattery of his slaves and to the roguery of a courtesan's feigned love for him. Falstaff has many similar traits, and "the fat rogue," "Sir John Paunch," a "sweet creature of bombast," is made a laughing stock by Prince Hal, who disabuses him to his face without restraint:

> Wherein is he good but to taste sack and drink it? Wherein neat and cleanly but to carve a capon and eat it? Wherein cunning but in craft? Wherein crafty but in villany? Wherein villanous but in all things? Wherein worthy but in nothing?[37]

But Falstaff is far more than a comic character. He denies order and the moral law; and if the sun is taken for the symbol of God, he challenges the divine order itself. In the first scene in which he appears he presents himself as a man not knowing "the time of day," a "squire of the night's body," a "gentleman of the shade," a "minion of the moon," not governed like the earth by the sun, but "as the sea is, by our noble and chaste mistress the moon, under whose countenance we steal."[38]

Shakespeare here echoed the saying to be found in Ecclesiasticus,[39] that a fool's discourse "changeth as the moon," and in the Latin of the Vulgate godliness is likened to the sun. As Erasmus had pointed out, "The moon is always understood to symbolize human nature, and the sun, the source of all light, to symbolize God."[40] In *Henry IV*, however, the sun is rather the symbol of noble majesty; the sun is associated with Prince Hal, the *cortegiano*,[41] who in the second part of the play inherits crown and scepter.

The last scene, then, in which Falstaff, the coward, pretends to be dead in order to save his life and then "rises" again to stab the corpse of Hotspur, provides more than comic relief: it shows the triumph of folly as a minion of the moon over a man who talked grandiloquently about honor. Were it not for Prince Hal, who knows that he, and not Falstaff, has conquered Hotspur, the scene would present natural disorder with the fool prevailing. In the second part of *Henry IV*, Falstaff comes to grief and dies. He must finally face the reckoning. Political order is reestablished by Prince Hal, in his youth himself given to folly, but now a noble ruler preventing the lasting triumph of folly.[42]

If the meaning of ordinary speech is twisted by fools, neither is God's word sacred to them. Religious doctrine and rites, nay, religion itself, may be drawn into the madness of folly. The fool values life, his life and this life, more than anything else, not excluding the blessings of eternal life. To him, the only thing that is certain about life after death is death itself. In pictorial representations of the medieval Dance of Death, the powerful and learned are treated like the humble, and Death often wears the cap and bells of the jester, fooling all living souls. Nor does the fool have edifying thoughts about the creation of gods and men. Concerning that creation, he believes, as Stultitia puts it, that "the job is done by that foolish, even ridiculous part which cannot be named without laughter."[43] To the fool, then, there is nothing miraculous about creation. In general, fools play off the world of the senses against speculation and spirituality. To the senses, the physical functions of the body are undeniably real, a source of natural, ungodly pleasure and pain and the fountainhead of knowledge about life and death—inferior to, but firmer than, theology. Such common sense always existed along with Christian faith and doctrine. It found expression in proverbs and, intermingled with pre-Christian superstition, in folk tales, in puns, the lowest form of humor, and in obscene jokes. The folk-fool and the picaro are never shocked by obscenity, and they do not hesitate to use it against theological speculation. Thus, the "trail of written remains" that the "ungodly" have left behind them "throughout the centuries"[44] includes "low" literature as well as the writings of ancient philosophers and historians which Melville's confidence man mentions: "the immorality of Ovid, Horace, Anacreon, and the rest, and the dangerous theology of Aeschylus and others . . . [and] views so injurious to human nature as in Thucidides, Juvenal, Lucian, but more particularly, Tacitus." The confidence man refers to such writings as "that mass of unsuspected heresy on every vital topic which for centuries must have simmered unsurmised in the heart of Christendom."[45]

The Fool as Social Critic

Many foolish pranks actually are crimes. Marcolf insults King Solomon. Eulenspiegel willfully damages the house of the blacksmith. Falstaff commits many unlawful acts. Simplicissimus steals sausages from a parson's smoke room: all picaros are thieves. Schweik steals dogs and is a malingerer, and although Pito Perez "never killed anyone" he knows quite a few jails "from personal experience." Fools never commit murder, but they do violate laws and conventions that we, as conformists, try to uphold. Why then do we laugh? Why are we amused by something that if done by anyone but a fool would endanger our way of life and make us turn to the authorities for protection?

Is it that the fool satisfies feelings of envy? In many of his pranks he makes sport of the possessions of others — whether material or otherwise — that the envious do not want to acquire but have a consuming desire to see destroyed. Is it for this reason that the notorious meanness and cruelty of many fools and picaros does not diminish their popularity? The master thief who robs the rich and is generous toward the poor appeals to some sense of justice that is absent in envy, because envy is no wish for the transfer of fame, fortune, or power from the haves to the have-nots: it merely wants the haves to become have-nots.[46]

It may be noted in passing that envy is a solitary passion. If we feel it, we try to hide it, whereas we like to profess our sense of justice. Thus, laughing about foolish pranks we may be happy that misfortune befell the fooled objects of envy and at the same time enjoy the release from the shamefulness of this feeling. But there is more than that to our laughter at folly. Envy remains within the social order, as it were, whereas in laughing at great fools we rejoice at their ingenious disrespect for the rules we are forced to live by.

The social order is a mold into which nature has been pressed with a crippling effect. The licentious fool disregards this order as though this was the easiest and most natural thing to do. In the process he not only exposes hypocrisy and dissimulation and pricks the bubble of pretension, but he also robs the social order of its claim to sanctity and permanence. The fool does so without pleading a cause; he is no rebel wanting to do away with rulers, nor does he seek to establish a better rule. He is simply unruly. He seems to make no sense, but he acts as though in the light of nature everything that we think makes sense is in fact nonsense. When laughing at the fool we share this carefree disregard of the rules that we sometimes wish, and almost never dare, to break. If we never felt that order fettered our natural appetites, we would not laugh, but punish the fool who indulges his appetites and permits us to indulge vicariously our own. Through laughter we become the fool's passive accomplices.

In some sense, then, the fool resembles the figure of the wild man to be found in almost every phase of Western civilization; as Papageno he still delights us, and those who do not like Mozart can turn to Tarzan for a wild man in our age. Richard Bernheimer defined the persistent psychological urge to which "the notion of the wild man must respond" "as the need to give external expression and symbolically valid form to the impulses of reckless physical self-assertion which are hidden in all of us, but are normally kept under control."[47] The fool, like the wild man, seems to live beyond the pale of the social order and to assert *physis* against *nomos*. But there is an important difference between the two figures. The wild man is a subhuman creature, dressed either in pastoral green, as in Pieter Brueghel's picture of the battle of Carnival and Lent, or in furs like an animal. In various folk customs and fairy tales, the bear is a substitute for, or a companion of, the wild man.[48]

Even the innocent child ignorantly growing up in the woods, like Parzival or Simplicius, has been related by Bernheimer to the lore of the wild man rather than to that of the pure fool; but this can be done only by neglecting the career of the pure fool, in the light of which innocence is a necessary precondition of his rare perfection in maturity. Something childlike is in fact forever preserved in Parzival, as in all great fools.[49]

A fool never resorts to brute force in acts of physical self-assertion. Never does he abduct a maiden, as the wild man does. Fools outwit rather than outclub civilized men, and socially they are not creatures of the woods, but of the court or the town. They are not subhuman, related to demons and beasts; they are not wilder than ordinary men. They excel by confronting civilized life with foolishly truthful reflection rather than with brute force.

The fool lifts constraints, invalidates social values, and upsets the social order. His triumph is complete when folly manages to reverse the social order for a while. In the Roman Saturnalia the slaves became masters of the house, and in the medieval Festival of Fools, buffoonery and obscenity were put into the service of burlesquing Christian worship and morality. According to a letter written in 1445 by Charles VII, King of France, the Bishop of Troyes, his loyal councilor, had complained that although in 1431 the Council of Basel had

> expressly forbidden to ministers and attendants of the Church to participate in a certain mockery and scandalous festival that is called the Festival of Fools, which is usual during the Christmas octave and holidays in not a few churches, cathedrals, and other chapter-houses, wherein said churchmen commit irreverences and mockeries toward God the Creator and His holy and divine services, to the grievous discredit and disrepute of the ecclesiastical calling at large, nevertheless, said churchmen in all churches and holy places during divine service, as well as outside, continue to utter great insolences, mockeries, and irreverences, with public spectacle and masquerades, using indecent attire unbecoming their state and profession, such as the raiment and garb of clowns, soldiers, and other similar occupations, some wearing female raiment, masks, false faces. . . . [50]

The Festival of Fools can be traced back to the ninth century, when Byzantine courtiers made fun of the divine mysteries. Not much later, on certain days, Western vicars and subdeacons began to mock the Magnificat at Vespers and even the Mass in the cathedral towns of France. For several centuries the Festival of Fools served as a safety valve for releasing the tensions imposed by church discipline. As a doctor of Auxerre explained it, "wine barrels break if their bungholes are not occasionally opened to let in the air, and the clergy being 'nothing but old wine-casks badly put together would certainly burst if the wine of wisdom were allowed to boil by continued devotion to the Divine Service.'"[51] Despite repeated prohibitions, the mad and impious excesses of the Festival of Fools, recognized at the time as a relic of pagan rites,[52] died out only in the sixteenth century.

The Festivals had their secular counterpart in the fool societies that flourished in the towns, law courts, and universities of Europe from the fifteenth century to the end of the seventeenth century. The most famous of them, the *Enfants-sans-souci*, with young carefree and poor Parisians as members, was led by an annually elected *Prince-des-Sots* (to whom François Villon made a bequest). The fool society of Dijon had hundreds of members in the middle of the sixteenth century, most of them drawn from the third estate, but others also from the nobility and the clergy. While the Festival of Fools offered an opportunity for temporary reversals of the ecclesiastical order and of moral judgments, the fool societies with their *Princes-des-Sots* and *Mères-Sottes* were more permanent, legally recognized institutions dedicated to scandal, music, and satire. The members of these fool societies wore the traditional garments of imbeciles so that they could not be blamed for social and moral criticisms they advanced under the traditional license of folly. Different from both the village fool and the court fool, different also from the ecclesiastical fools, the fool societies were urban institutions, that sprang up in conjunction with the growth of towns and guilds and with the spread of secular education in the late Middle Ages.

It is perhaps not quite correct to say that the rulers of the fool societies were the middlemen "who conveyed the cap and bells from the shaven heads of the half-witted into the creative imagination of the philosopher, the satirist, and the comic poet."[53] Certainly, philosophers and satirists had known, long before the rise of fool societies, that it is possible and prudent to say the truth laughingly. Erasmus, to whom the sage-fool owes so much, studied ancient literature as well as the Scriptures. He was familiar with both Lucian and the northern mysticism of the *devotio moderna*. Without such learning the sophisticated irony of Stultitia would not have been possible.[54] Finally, not only the imagination of the comic poet but that of the tragic poet as well created great fools.

King Lear is the most eminent example of the foolish reversal of political order as a means of presenting the truth about the human condition in a profoundly melancholy cast. On the heath, Lear is deprived of reason as well as majesty. He has become a fool akin to the jester in his company. The King is destitute, like the beggar he meets, and in agony, like Gloucester, the great blinded lord, led by the beggar. Lear's prayer to "sweet heaven" that he may be spared madness has met with no answer except that the voice of God can be heard as thunder; but thunder is void of meaning. Lear, the outcast, has become a fool of inspired madness. In addressing Gloucester he says:

> . . . thy name is Gloucester.
> Thou must be patient; we came crying hither . . .

And his words are reinforced by Edgar:

> Men must endure
> Their going hence, even as their coming hither.[55]

When the political order is completely reversed, it is the tragic fool who recognizes the truth: patience, endurance, resignation, rather than salvation, are man's lot. As Enid Welsford put it, "Patience, here, seems to imply an unflinching, clear-sighted, recognition of the fact of pain, and the complete abandonment of any claim to justice or gratitude either from Gods or men."[56] Lear is a "fool of fortune," not of God.

The Fool and Modernity

As an important figure on the social scene, the fool could not withstand modernity. The claims of modern science and the spread of Enlightenment lumped the sage-fool in literature with other pale and somewhat embarrassing achievements of the past — pale, because no fool ever promised future glories to man, as did science; embarrassing, because science is serious and folly is not. Modern man credits scientific knowledge with the power to subdue nature, hopes to extend human life ever more and to bring about an affluent, just, and peaceful social order. He does not hesitate to speak of the abolition of war, of human engineering, or of social inventions, and he is concerned with sharpening his sight when forecasting political "futures."

The fool would have included all these hopes and preoccupations in a catalog of human follies. While asserting *physis* against *nomos*, no fool ever believed that nature could be conquered by man, and those who used to laugh about folly did not dream of it either. Modern enlightened man retaliated by discarding the fool's comments on human affairs as fatuous nonsense. Enlightened man scorns the classical fool. In Nicholas Breton's words, he is but "the shame of nature, the trouble of wit, the charge of charity, and the loss of liberality."[57]

We still speak of folly and fools, but in literature as in everyday speech, "fools" and "folly" have been attenuated in meaning, and sapped of deeper significance. With a few exceptions — Charlie Chaplin among them — fools now satisfy tastes unaccustomed to excellence. The obscenities that the old fool indulged in are still abroad, but they have been lifted from richer textures of life and literature and relegated to the barracks, to cheap picture postcards (as George Orwell has shown[58]), and to similar forms of lowbrow *l'art pour l'art*. In life we treat a fool like an eccentric and we would indeed be eccentrics ourselves were we to believe that in madness (not caused by drugs) man is inspired.

Let me conclude these comments by observing, foolishly perhaps, that in our time, the role of the Undeceiver-General is played by the psychoanalyst, and that many sad fools have become his patients. By the same token, the fool societies of our time are composed of "hippies," while the descendant of the court fool is a professional comedian appearing on the television screen, telling jokes that more often than not originated in the mind of a ghostwriter not sage enough to play the fool and not sad or bold enough to plumb the depth of irreverent humor.

NOTES

1. Cf. E. Tietze-Conrat, *Dwarfs and Jesters in Art*, New York, 1957.
2. Quoted by Enid Welsford, *The Fool. His Social and Literary History*, New York, 1935, p. 30. *The Jests of Si-Djoha* is an anonymous collection of anecdotes about an unhistorical figure "known to us only by a reference in a tenth century work." The jests reached the West first by word of mouth.
3. Walter Kaiser, *Praisers of Folly*, Cambridge, 1964, pp. 277ff.
4. Shakespeare, *King Lear*, IV.2.50–62.
5. Shakespeare, *King Lear*, IV.6.188.
6. I Corinthians, III:18.
7. I Corinthians, I:25.
8. Erasmus, *The Praise of Folly*, translated by Leonard F. Dean, New York, 1946, p. 127.
9. Erasmus, op. cit., p. 66
10. Ibid.
11. Francisco de Quevedo, *Visions*, translated by Sir Roger L'Estrange, Fontwell Sussex, 1963, pp. 69ff.
12. Shakespeare, *King Lear*, III.2.74–78.
13. Cf. the important study of St. Simeon and St. Andreas by Erich Bens, "Heilige Narrheit," *Kyrios*, vol. 3, 1938.
14. Dostoyevsky, *The Idiot*, III, chap. 4.
15. Cf. Walter Kaiser, op. cit., pp. 222–23.
16. Migne, *Patrologia Latina*, vol. 75, col. 947, quoted by Barbara Swain, *Fools and Folly during the Middle Ages and the Renaissance*, New York, 1932, pp. 198–99 n32.
17. Cf. Erich Auerbach, *Mimesis*, Garden City, 1957, chap. 14.
18. Cervantes, *Don Quixote*, translated by Charles Jarvis, New York, n.d., part II, chap. 10, pp. 439–40.
19. Wolfram von Eschenbach, *Parzival*, 120, translated by Helen M. Mustard and Charles E. Passage, New York, 1961, p. 68.
20. *Grimmelshausens Simplicissimus Teutsch*, ed. by J. H. Scholte, Tübingen, 1954, vol. I, chap. 3, p. 16.
21. The first critic to suggest in considerable detail that *Parzival* had influenced *Simplicissimus* was Theodor Echtermeyer, *Hallesche Jahrbücher* (1838), p. 431, but Echtermeyer viewed *Simplicissimus* as a satire of *Parzival*, whereas Werner Welzig, *Beispielhafte Figuren. Tor, Abenteurer und Einsiedler bei Grimmelshausen*, Graz

and Cologne, 1963, considers the young Simplicius as well as Parzival to be a "pure (Christian) fool."

22. Cf. Paul Gutzwiller, *Der Narr bei Grimmelshausen*, Bern, 1959.

23. Cf. T. K. Oesterreich, *Possession, Demoniacal and Other*, English translation, New York, 1930; and E. R. Dodds, *The Greeks and the Irrational*, Berkeley and Los Angeles, 1951, chap. 3.

24. Quoted by Enid Welsford, op. cit., p. 37.

25. Barbara Swain, op. cit., p. 34.

26. *A Hundred Merry Tales and Other English Jestbooks of the Fifteenth and Sixteenth Centuries*, ed. by P. M. Zall, Lincoln, Nebr., 1963, 67th Tale, p. 124.

27. In the English version, "Howleglas," 1528, op. cit., pp. 198–99.

28. José Rubén Romero, *The Futile Life of Pito Perez*, translated by William O. Cord, Englewood Cliffs, N.J., 1967.

29. Søren Kierkegaard, *Die Tagebücher*, translated by Theodor Haecker, Innsbruck, 1923, pp. 4–6 (diary entry under date of September 11, 1834).

30. Op. cit., March 16, 1835, p. 10.

31. Thomas Mann, *Confessions of Felix Krull, Confidence Man*, translated by Denver Lindley, New York, 1955, paperback edition, 1963, pp. 19–20.

32. Op. cit., p. 41.

33. Lawrence Thompson, *Melville's Quarrel with God*, Princeton, N.J., 1952.

34. Herman Melville, *The Confidence-Man: His Masquerade*, New York, 1949, pp. 23–26.

35. I *Henry IV*, V.1.136–43.

36. I *Henry IV*, V.4.116–22.

37. I *Henry IV*, II.4.507–12.

38. I *Henry IV*, I.2.31–33.

39. Ecclesiasticus, XXVII.12.

40. Erasmus, op. cit., p. 118.

41. On Prince Hal as a perfect courtier in Castiglione's sense, cf. E. M. W. Tillyard, *Shakespeare's History Plays,* (New York, 1946, pp. 276–81.

42. E. M. W. Tillyard, op. cit., pp. 264ff.; Walter Kaiser, op. cit., pp. 195ff.

43. Erasmus, op. cit., p. 49.

44. Barbara Swain in commenting upon the creed of the ungodly in the *Book of Wisdom*, op. cit., p. 47.

45. Herman Melville, op. cit., p. 39.

46. Cf. Helmut Schoeck, *Der Neid. Eine Theorie der Gesellschaft*, Freiburg-München, 1966.

47. Richard Bernheimer, *Wild Men in the Middle Ages*, A Study in Art, Sentiment, and Demonology, Cambridge, Mass., 1952, p. 3.

48. Richard Bernheimer, who thoroughly discusses this aspect of the wild man, overlooked Grimmelshausen's fairy tale, "Der erste Bernhäuter," later included (with adaptations) in Grimm's collection of fairy tales.

49. In Dostoyevsky's *Idiot* several characters remark that Prince Myshkin is a child and will still be a child when he reaches high age.

50. Quoted by Vilfredo Pareto, *The Mind and Society*, New York, 1935, vol. I, sect. 737, p. 446. Cf. also Barbara Swain, op. cit., chaps 4 and 5; Enid Welsford, op. cit., chap. 9.

51. Quoted by Enid Welsford, op. cit., p. 202.

52. E. K. Chambers, *The Medieval Stage*, Oxford, 1903, vol. 1, p. 292 n2.

53. Enid Welsford, op. cit., p. 217.

54. Cf. Walter Kaiser, op. cit., pp. 1–100.

55. Shakespeare, *King Lear*, IV.6.182 and V.3.9–100.

56. Enid Welsford, op. cit., p. 266.

57. Nicholas Breton, "The Good and the Bad, *Archaica*, 2 vols., ed. by Sir E. Brydges, London, 1815, vol. 1, p. 24, quoted by Barbara Swain, op. cit., p. 185.

58. George Orwell, "The Art of Donald McGill," *A Collection of Essays*, Garden City, N.Y., 1941, pp. 111ff.

14

The Truth in Hell:
Maurice Joly and *The Protocols of the Wise Men of Zion*

I

In an autobiographical account, published in 1870, Maurice Joly told the story of how he came to write his *Dialogue aux Enfers entre Machiavel et Montesquieu*. He was scandalized by Napoleon III's domestic and foreign policies. After Napoleon had usurped imperial power, his regime became repressive and corrupt, and his foreign policies involved the country in many wars. Joly was fiercely critical of the emperor's despotism and his vainglorious ventures abroad. Searching for an appropriate disguise that would enable him to hoodwink the censors when attacking the emperor publicly, he recalled the *Dialogues sur le commerce des blés* by the Abbé Ferdinando Galiani (1770), in which this friend of Holbach's and Mme d'Epinay's had departed souls wittily discuss tariffs and trade in grain. "While walking on the terrace along the river near Pont Royal in bad weather" Joly happened upon the idea of a fictional conversation between Montesquieu and Machiavelli in Hades. "It is Machiavelli who represents the policy of force as opposed to Montesquieu who will represent the policy of justice; and Machiavelli will be Napoleon III, who himself would describe his abominable policies."[1]

Commenting upon contemporary events in the form of such a con-

This essay originally appeared in the fall 1977 issue, of *Polity*, vol. 10, no. 1. Reprinted by permission.

versation rendered by Joly's attack more elegant and dramatic, but hardly less obvious. The time-honored literary device would have been too thin a veil to conceal his thought even from censors less experienced than the police in the Second Empire.

The *Dialogue in Hell between Machiavelli and Montesquieu or Machiavelli's Policies in the Nineteenth Century* was published anonymously in French at Brussels in 1864. Copies of the book, smuggled across the border for distribution in France, were seized by the French police, and its author was easily identified. Joly was arrested and held for several months until the court pronounced sentence on April 25, 1865. The newspaper *Le Droit* published a lengthy excerpt from the decision:

> In a dialogue between Machiavelli and Montesquieu the author begins by opposing the political principles developed in the writings of these famous men, then establishes a general thesis that the dreadful despotism taught by Machiavelli in his treatise, *The Prince*, has succeeded, by artifice and evil ways, in imposing itself on modern society. . . . The author charges the French government with having, through shameful means, hypocritical ways, and perfidious contrivances, led the public astray, degraded the character of the nation, and corrupted its morals. . . . For these reasons Maurice Joly, having committed the crime of inciting hatred and contempt against the Government, is sentenced to fifteen months imprisonment, 300 francs fine, and confiscation of the copies of the *Dialogue in Hell*.[2]

Joly's account of 1870 did not do full justice to his intellectual achievement, for he had done more than set forth Napoleon's misrule, the resort to a plebiscite in order to legitimize his coup d'état, the corruption of parliament and the courts, the perversion of the freedom of the press, the fraudulent handling of public finances, the ubiquitous employment of political informers, the Saint-Simonean policy of public works, the cynical use of all available symbolic means of power, and the distraction of public attention from domestic affairs by waging wars. Concealing his indignation Joly exposed all this with chilling detachment. But it should not be overlooked that in the preface to the *Dialogue in Hell* he claimed that his book was a serious undertaking and neither a lampoon nor a political pamphlet. Like all serious writings, he said, it ought to be read slowly.

The very first sentence of Joly's preface claims that the work contains fancies applicable to *all* governments, and early in the conversation Machiavelli protests to his adversary that Machiavellism is older than Machiavelli. It seems to follow that Machiavelli cannot be regarded as the architect of Machiavellism nor can Napoleon III be held solely responsible for his despotic regime. Indeed, in the plebiscite of December 21, 1851, more than 90 percent of about 8 million French voters had legitimized his rule.[3] Joly's book deals with the legacy of the French Revolution inherited by modern industrial society and perverted by a modern caesar. It is for this reason that all serious students of his book have commented not only upon Joly's intellectual brilliance, which matches his moral passion, but also upon his startling foresight, which anticipates political developments in the twentieth century.

Maurice Joly was born of Catholic parents in 1821. His father, married to an Italian woman, was councilor-general of the Jura. Maurice Joly studied law. After serving as secretary to Princess Mathilde, a cousin of Napoleon III, he became a barrister in Paris and published several political and literary studies of advocates under the title *Le Barreau de Paris*.

After his release from prison in 1867 Joly was denounced by the defenders of the Empire and treated with reserve by the Republicans. Perhaps his friends did not consider him politically adroit enough, or he may have offended them by his uncompromising sternness, which moralists sometimes do. In any event, his failure to excuse the people for their support of the emperor must have alienated him from radicals.

While the emperor was still in power, Joly embarked upon a new venture as editor of the journal *Le Palais*, but this activity ended in a duel with his principal collaborator. After the collapse of the Empire, in October 1870, Joly sought to obtain a government post through Jules Grévy, who was to become president of the National Assembly in 1871. He failed and joined the radical resistance under the leadership of Louis Auguste Blanqui and Louis Charles Delescluze. In November, he was arrested again and freed only a few months later by the Council of War. Joly considered himself at that time a "revolutionary," but he opposed communism.

In 1872, he was offered an important position on the journal *La Liberté*. In 1878, before Jules Grévy succeeded General MacMahon a president of the Republic, Joly attacked Grévy in public. Thereupon not only Gambetta but whatever supporters or friends Joly still had turned against him. The list of public figures Joly had attacked in his life is long indeed and comprises persons of very different political persuasion: Napoleon III, Victor Hugo, Gambetta, Grévy. In addition, he had many feuds in his professional life. He was a lonely man, devoted to moral principles and apparently never forgave anyone who did not live up to his standards. Perhaps his keen insight into politics and society was sharpened by a passionate desire to remain pure and morally inviolate. If so, he paid with his life for his rigor. On July 16, 1878, he shot himself. He left the manuscript of a novel, *Les Affamés*, dealing with French society of his time.

II

Joly sympathized with Montesquieu's views on liberty, but through Machiavelli refuted Montesquieu's belief in progress toward the perfection of man and his social order. In the *Dialogue* Montesquieu holds that institutional inventions of the modern enlightened age have erected a bulwark against repressive political forces of the past. To the extent that the principles of enlightenment have spread in Europe and the principles of modern political science become known, law has replaced force in theory as well as practice. Machiavelli counters with what he regards as an "eternal truth": Man's "evil instinct" is more potent than are his good intentions, and force, fear, and greed hold sway over him. Montesquieu contends that his teaching has promoted order and liberty; Machiavelli replies with the charge that by giving the nations the right to choose their political institutions, Montesquieu had introduced "the infinite era of revolutions." According to Joly's Machiavelli, the people lack the virtues which must sustain a liberal social order; they live instead "without God and faith," dedicated to the pursuit of their subjective interests and of a high standard of living. Furthermore, they easily turn from their admiration of a powerful man to violent rebellion, unless they are manipulated without moral squeamishness. Thus despotism can save the great modern states from revolution and anarchy.

While Joly was a liberal, his pessimistic view of the corruptibility of the masses matched his moral condemnation of the unscrupulous use of force and cunning in ruling them. Joly was no democrat. Like many other nineteenth-century European liberals he had the fear of Jacobinism in his bones. His *Dialogue in Hell* reverberates with distrust not only of plebiscitarian despotism but also of the "novel ideas" of Napoleon I, the "testamentary executor of the Revolution" of 1789. As such Prince Napoleon-Louis Bonaparte, the later emperor, had characterized Napoleon I, his uncle, in a political manifesto published as early as 1839. Trying to capitalize on the growing legend of Napoleon I, the nephew had depicted him as the founder of peace in Europe, serving the idea of a solid European association, and as the harbinger of domestic freedom and order. Prince Napoleon-Louis Bonaparte had claimed that the interests of the sovereign and the people were identical. "The Napoleonic idea," he had written, "is by no means an idea of war, but a social industrial, commercial, humanitarian idea." If Machiavelli in Joly's *Dialogue* sometimes appears to speak of the Nazi regime when satirizing the statecraft of Napoleon III, it may be observed in passing that this manifesto of 1839 adumbrates appeals and claims made by totalitarian leaders in twentieth-century politics. As one of the liberals, whose political perception was bounded neither by a blind faith in progress nor by the Napoleon-worship of the French bourgeoisie, Joly foresaw a great deal of the future because he stood between the political fronts, perceiving the hazards of popular sovereignty as well as abuse of power by social engineers. In looking at France under Napoleon III he detected political forces that can be activated at any time in modern society. They result from the interplay of egalitarianism as an ideology with the increasing efficiency in all spheres of life — whether in the modes of peacetime production or the methods of destruction in war, whether in the techniques of communication or the technology employed in the invasion of privacy.

Joly did not peer into the future but looked piercingly at the political and social forces of his time. Or to put it more precisely, only Montesquieu in the *Dialogue* viewed political life in historical perspective, whereas Machiavelli discovered unchanging political principles in contemporary conditions. Montesquieu's delusion about progress in human affairs is predicated, moreover, on his *ignorance* of the present. In the netherworld he has learned what has been happening on earth only until the year 1847, whereas Machiavelli's information is up to date, so that, ironically enough, Montesquieu's historical view is faulted by lack of information on the latest happenings of a few years, whereas Machiavelli's unhistorical view, which does not really need this information, is vindicated by it. In this regard, Joly is in the good company of political philosophers prior to the rise of positivism and historicism. While critics have often pointed out that Joly's sympathies are on the side of Montesquieu, it would be more correct to stress that in the *Dialogue* he shared Montesquieu's moral preferences but regarded Machiavelli's knowledge of politics as superior to that of his adversary. The explanation of Joly's power of prediction, then, can be reduced to the paradox that, strictly speaking, his foresight was insight.

This paradox also applies to Joly's contribution in the field of mass communication. At first glance, it is quite extraordinary that seventy years prior to the rise of Hitler and Goebbels and long before the emergence of the electronic media Joly described in considerable detail the political manipulation of public opinion, which we associate today with totalitarianism. Nobody who studies political propaganda in the twentieth century can afford to neglect its most eminent nineteenth-century analyst. Considerably more can be learned about Hitler's propaganda techniques from Joly's two dialogues about censorship and the management of public opinion than from the famous passages dealing with this subject in Hitler's *Mein Kampf*. Interestingly enough, there are a few close parallels, for example, the importance both Hitler and Joly's Machiavelli attribute to the spoken word in swaying the masses or the power both attribute to the news media in creating and destroying what we now term public "images." But the early analyst of modern propaganda techniques was more articulate, specific, and incisive than were its latter day practitioners. Again, this paradox will startle the historian more than the political philosopher. It ought to caution the contemporary reader whose personal experience includes modern totalitarianism not to underestimate the analytical power of a mind familiar only with a prototype of this historical phenomenon.

Joly's insight into the politics of modern mass communication could have been buttressed by a more detailed description of the interplay between power and economic gain in the Second Empire. For example, DeMorny, a half-brother of the emperor, invested 100,000 francs in a journalistic enterprise and sold his interest later for a half a million. Another newspaper felt obliged to protest that it was not involved in speculations on the stock exchange. Similarly, it was true enough, as Joly mentioned, that the emperor spent regularly as well as on special occasions large sums of money to buy journalistic services and that he gave honorific positions in his government and decorations to obliging press servants. Joly did not mention, however, that quite apart from Napoleon's techniques it was sometimes difficult to decide whether the lucrativeness of journalism or enthusiasm for causes believed to be righteous drew some of the most distinguished minds of the nation to writing for newspapers: men like Ernest Renan, Hippolyte Taine, Alexandre Dumas, Théophile Gautier, Prosper Mérimée.

In contrast to his novel *Les Affamés*, Joly's *Dialogue aux Enfers* does not focus on the sociological analysis of the conditions of life prevailing at the time of Napoleon III. The *Dialogue* is a political work concerned with the anatomy of power. Nor did Joly buttress, as he might well have done, his findings by comparative studies. When Joly wrote his book, neither press censorship nor the use of domestic and foreign newspapers by the government was a uniquely French phenomenon. After 1848, Prokesch-Osten, the Austrian ambassador in Berlin, took up contact with the press of the opposition and furnished it with material. He was careless enough to let his drafts fall into the hands of the Prussian authorities. Bismarck, who despised public opinion, when it criticized him, had highly paid talented henchmen, like Lothar Bucher and Moritz Busch, write for the press and influence it according to his instructions.[4] While the French emperor had even fewer scruples than Bismarck in using the news media for his political ends, he was by no means the only European statesman to manipulate public opinion at the time Joly wrote his book. Maurice Joly did not need the comparative method to make his point. He established for a span of time far exceeding that of his life and for many countries other than France the precariousness of liberty in modern society.

III

If Maurice Joly did not receive during his life the recognition which his intellectual achievements deserved, posterity has treated him more capriciously than any other writer of distinction. His *Dialogue in Hell* became the source of the most momentous fraud in the history of political propaganda. In many lands across Europe it was plagiarized by opportunists, common criminals, terrorists, police agents, paranoid priests, and reactionary fanatics. Many of Machiavelli's observations in Joly's book about the practices and principles of statecraft in the Second Empire were attributed by the plagiarists to a fictitious group of Jewish leaders plotting the corruption of the prevailing political and moral order so as to bring about Jewish world domination. Some of the liberal ideas of Montesquieu were also exploited by the forgers in order to document alleged stratagems of the Jews in their efforts to enfeeble their victims' will and ability to resist.

The history of this notorious case of plagiarism began in 1868 when a German writer published a novel *To Sedan* under the pseudonym Sir John Retcliffe. His true name was Hermann Goedsche. After having been dishonorably discharged, at age 34, as a petty official of the Prussian Postal Service, he became a staff member of a conservative newspaper, the *Preussische Kreutz Zeitung*, and a popular author of sensational fiction. His novel *To Sedan* contains the weird story, "The Jewish Cemetery in Prague," in which the heads of the twelve

Jewish tribes keep a centennial appointment in the presence of Satan to report on their plans for the enslavement of the world. The speeches of the Jewish leaders deal with topics discussed and ideas propounded by Machiavelli in Joly's book.

It is not known for a fact that Goedsche read one of the rare copies of the first edition of the *Dialogue in Hell.* Nor is it certain that he knew French. It would have been easy for him, however, to obtain access to Joly's book through the first German translation published anonymously by Otto Wigand at Leipzig in 1865.[5]

The sinister proposals made by the twelve fictional Jewish leaders at the cemetery in Prague were consolidated in a single pronouncement which became known among anti-Semites everywhere as *The Rabbi's Speech.* It was printed many times, beginning in the 1870's, in France, Germany, Russia, Austria, and later in other countries as well, always with the claim that the speech was not fiction but fact. The Rabbi soon acquired a name, and it was stated that he had revealed actual secret plans of Jewish leaders to corrupt the world and seize power. Joly's analysis of existing conditions in the Second Empire had been turned into an evil design of the future. *The Rabbi's Speech* helped in provoking the pogrom at Kishinev in Bessarabia in 1903. In this century it became intertwined with the crowning forgery, *The Protocols of the Elders of Zion,* many editions of which also contain *The Rabbi's Speech.*[6] The *Protocols* consist of a series of fabricated minutes of an alleged council meeting of Jewish leaders discussing their ruthless and cunning measures to reach the goal of world domination.

The framework for the *Protocols* — a meeting of a council of elders — was perhaps set by Osman Bey in his book *World Conquest by the Jews.* The author of this fantasy was of Jewish origin; his real name was Millinger. Before trying to make a living through anti-Semitic writings he had been an international swindler with a history of several arrests.[7]

The fabricators of the *Protocols* wrote in French and drew inspiration also from writings in the French anti-Semitic tradition, in particular *La France Juive* (1886) by Edouard Drumont, who in turn had plagiarized Gougenot des Mourreaux's *Le Juif, le judaïsme et la judaïsation des peuples chrétiens* (1869) and *La Franc-Maçonnerie, Synagogue de Satan* (1893) by Msgr. Meurin, archbishop of Port-Louis, Mauritius. The main source of the plagiarists, however, was Joly's *Dialogue in Hell.* "In all, over 160 passages in the Protocols, totaling two-fifths of the entire text, are clearly based on passages in Joly; in nine of the chapters the borrowings amount to more than half the text, in some they amount to three-quarters, in one (Protocol VII) to almost the entire text."[8]

Although the first version of the *Protocols* seems to have been fabricated in French at the time of the Dreyfus affair, probably in 1897, the form in which the forgery was launched upon its career throughout the world appeared as an insertion in the third edition of a Russian book by the eccentric priest Sergey Nilus, *The Great and the Small*, published in 1905. In a conversation with Count A. M. du Chayla, a Frenchman who spent many years in Russia and had accepted the orthodox faith, Nilus referred to the *Protocols* as "the charter of the Kingdom of Anti-Christ."[9] No doubt, Nilus believed that the Jews were secretly at work to enslave and inherit the world. Nilus was a former landowner, who after the loss of his fortune abroad had turned from a believer in anarchism and Nietzschean teachings into a priest in the orthodox church; as such he continued to reject modern civilization. A mystic with worldly ambitions, his mind bordering on madness, he lived with three women, one of whom was a former court lady who maintained his ménage.

The *Protocols* became a worldwide best seller after 1917. The Bolshevik Revolution, the collapse of the Austro-Hungarian Empire, and the defeat of Germany in the First World War left the West with shattered political institutions and disrupted traditions, with dashed hopes among the vanquished and an appetite of the victors for sweeter fruits of victory than history granted them. War propaganda had fomented national self-righteousness and hatred of others. The political and economic upheavals of the struggle and its aftermath created fear and resentment of other nations and social classes. The results were intellectual disorientation, moral weakness, slackened restraints of the forces destroying civility, an atmosphere of civil war that seemed to engulf the international community. In these circumstances, the *Protocols* offered a conspiratorial theory of history to those who could not, or would not, cope with the vicissitudes of life and an appealing invitation to hatred and aggression. They enabled large masses to blame innocent victims that were nearer at hand than enlightenment or courage: the Jews and their "tools," liberals, freemasons, socialists, communists, and unpopular statesmen. The Nazis in Germany and, in the thirties, Nazi organizations abroad, were most active in using the *Protocols* to foment anti-Semitism throughout the world. At the trial of Ernst Techow, the driver of the car from which two young assassins fired the shots that killed Walter Rathenau, the German foreign minister, on June 24, 1922, the following exchange occurred. "President (of the Court): Rathenau is supposed to have confessed that he was himself one of the three hundred Elders of Zion. The three hundred Elders of Zion come from a pamphlet. Have you read it? Techow: Yes."[10] In Germany, the forgery became required reading in the schools. But had it not been for latent hostility everywhere, it would not have been possible for the *Protocols* to become, in this century, the most widely read book next to the Bible. Today, it is available in any language: Russian, English, Polish, Portuguese, Norwegian, Spanish, Japanese, Flemish, Latvian, Dutch, Rumanian, Czech, Walloon, Arabic, Bulgarian, Chinese, Yugoslav, Greek. And new editions are still being published.

In the United States, the *Protocols* were launched in full in New York and Boston and, in 1920, by Henry Ford's newspaper, *The Dearborn Independent*. This last edition, prepared by a German, August Müller, and a Russian refugee, Boris Bracol, was republished as a book under the title, *The International Jew*, which in Norman Cohn's opinion did more than any other publication to make the *Protocols* world famous. Although Henry Ford eventually disclaimed all responsibility for the book in 1927, it was translated into sixteen languages and still advertised in Germany at the beginning of the Second World War. Hitler sported a photograph of "Heinrich Ford" in his study for many years.

Thus Joly's ideas became effective in history by way of a monstrous distortion. Joly's concern with liberty was perverted beyond recognition. Against his will and unbeknownst to him his words helped to incite persecution of liberal reformers in Czarist Russia. He exposed political repression in his homeland, and half a century later his words helped reactionary White Russians abroad to foment hatred of the Bolshevik leaders. Like Montesquieu in the *Dialogue in Hell*, Joly hoped that constitutional government would ensure civil order and restrain violence in the streets, yet his book became instrumental in instigating pogroms culminating in the mass murders of 5 to 6 million Jews by the Nazis.

IV

The *Protocols* contain many obvious discrepancies. In addition, the various editors have given conflicting accounts of both the alleged authorship and the ways in which the text had allegedly come to light. Today, it is hard to understand that it should have been necessary to prove painstakingly that the *Protocols* were put together by literary counterfeiters. And yet, tracing the history and the precise nature of the forgery took years of effort by many publicists, historians, and lawyers.

The American diplomat Hermann Bernstein in his book *The History of a Lie*, published in February 1921, was the first to trace the content of the *Protocols* to Goedsche's tale, *The Jewish Cemetery in Prague*. Bernstein also showed the transformation of the speeches by Jewish leaders in that short story into *The Rabbi's Speech*.

At about the same time, Philip Graves, a British correspondent in Istambul, acquired by chance a rare copy of the first edition of the *Dialogue aux Enfers* from a White Russian émigré. Graves was the first to notice that many passages in this obscure book coincided with statements in the *Protocols*. In August 1921, he published a series of three articles in *The Times* exposing the plagiarism. It was a jolt to many that had been duped by the forgery. Only a year earlier two English language editions of the *Protocols* had been published, one under the title *The Jewish Peril*. *The Morning Post* had endorsed the main theme in a series of articles; the *Spectator*, in its issue of May 15, 1920, had considered the *Protocols* "brilliant in (their) moral perversity and intellectual depravity." A *Times* editorial of May 8, 1920 had raised the question, "Have we by straining every fibre of our national body escaped a 'Pax Germanica' only to fall into a 'Pax Judaica'?" It advocated an investigation of the charges! Now that Graves had uncovered the forgery *The Times* stood up for the truth endorsing Graves's findings in an editorial.

The next major step in tracing the history of the forgery was taken in 1934–1935 in Bern when Swiss Jews brought a law suit against two Swiss Nazis charging them with violating the Bern law against *Schundliteratur*, that is, worthless and improper literature, by circulating the *Protocols*. The trial, which attracted international attention, was remarkable for the array of distinguished witnesses—including Baron du Chalay, Philip Graves, Paul Milyukov, S. G. Svatikov, Boris Nikolaevsky, and Vladimir Burtsev—all of whom denied the authenticity of the *Protocols*. The defendants did not meet this issue, but argued their case on narrow legal grounds trying to prove that the *Protocols* were not "improper" according to Swiss law.[11] Two of the Russian witnesses gave testimony pointing to the involvement of Pyotr Ivanovich Rachkovsky in the forgery.

Rachkovsky, like Goedsche in Germany, had started out as a minor civil servant. In 1879 he avoided banishment to Siberia by joining the ranks of the secret police that had arrested him. He had a spectacular career. From 1894 to 1903, he was the head of the Okhrana outside Russia, and in 1905 he became assistant director of the police in Russia. Rachkovsky's career abounds with ingenious political intrigues and accomplished forgeries. He was responsible for the arrest of many Russian liberals and radicals in Russia and abroad, for pogroms in his country, for assassinations by his men of politicians standing in his way, for various bomb plots and other acts of violence perpetrated by his agents and attributed to political opponents he wanted to destroy. He was a reactionary, a ruthless anti-Semite, and the founder of a terrorist organization in his homeland.

The Bern trial established once more beyond doubt that the *Protocols* were a fabrication based to a large extent on Joly's *Dialogue aux Enfers*, but it did not ascertain beyond doubt the identity of the original forger or forgers. Most recent research supports the views of Boris Nikolaevsky, expressed in a personal communication to Norman Cohn, and of Henri Rollin in *L'Apocalypse de notre temps* to the effect that the *Dialogue aux Enfers* was first used for polemical purposes against the Russian minister of finance, Count Sergei Witte, by a Russian expatriate, named Elie de Cyon (Ilya Tsion). He was of Jewish origin, and his published writings testify to the fact that he was not an anti-Semite. But he plagiarized Joly's book in writing a political satire against Witte. Witte introduced the gold standard in Russia and by promoting the modernization of Russian industry and transportation set forces into motion that led to the Revolution of 1905. Upon orders from Witte, the Okhrana burglarized de Cyon's villa in Switzerland and obtained his unpublished manuscript attacking the Russian minister. According to Norman Cohn, "All in all, the most likely hypothesis is that Joly's satire on Napoleon III was transformed by de Cyon into a satire on Witte which was then transformed under Rachkovky's guidance into the *Protocols of the Elders of Zion*. There is also good reason for thinking that Rachkovsky had some contact either with Nilus or with Nilus's copy of the *Protocols*."[12]

V

In histories of political thought Joly's *Dialogue in Hell* has generally been overlooked. Historians who know the work as the most important source of the *Protocols* have used it to prove plagiarism: many studies contain page after page of parallel columns from the two publications in order to demonstrate the extent of the fabrication. In this procedure, Joly's originality has been lost sight of, although Norman

Cohn, who refers to Joly's book as a "pamphlet" — as does the *Grande Encyclopédie* — and consistently misquotes its title, acknowledges Joly's brilliance. Even the dates of Joly's birth and death vary widely in the literature.[13]

On the other end of the spectrum are admirers who deny that Joly wrote the *Dialogue in Hell* for any specific political purpose — despite the author's own explicit statement to the contrary. As though satirical skill and polemical fervor diminish intellectual merit, Hans Leisegang shut his eyes to Joly's polemical intent. He considers the *Dialogue in Hell* an elegantly written masterpiece of modern political philosophy and compares its importance for understanding the history of European politics with that of Dostoevsky's chapter "The Grand Inquisitor" in *The Brothers Karamazov* for understanding the history of Christianity.

The fair appraisal of Joly's contribution to political thought lies somewhere between these two extreme views: the polemic against Napoleon III is at the same time a masterful statement on the preservation of despotic political power in modern industrialized society. Precisely for this reason, Joly's book gave a shock of recognition to generations of readers living under very different political conditions. Each of them felt that the *Dialogue in Hell* stated the principles of statecraft practiced by the regime they knew best from bitter personal experience. In 1864, the French printer whom Joly tried to persuade that his manuscript was the translation of a work by an English author, named McPherson, recognized Napoleon III at the end of the third dialogue. He refused to continue the printing. The German philosopher Hans Leisegang, who translated Joly's book when Hitler was ruling Germany, quoted in his introduction one of Machiavelli's predictions, which he thought had come true in the present. The latest French edition of the *Dialogue aux Enfers* was published in 1968. In the preface, Jean-François Revel ascribed to Joly "a prophetic view" of the manipulation of public opinion by modern governments referring in particular to DeGaulle's use of the electronic media. And who can read Joly today without thinking of contemporary American political scandals as apt illustrations of Machiavelli's teaching in Joly's book? Nor is the bitter freshness of the *Dialogue* confined to the discussion of public opinion and its manipulation. Much of what Joly had to say about the secret police, the invasion of privacy by informers, political apathy, the abuse of the courts for political ends, the debasement of patriotic rhetoric, the corruption of moral standards in modern political life, the cult of personality — much of this applies to Bismarck's

Prussia, Hitler's Germany, Stalin's Russia, and other illiberal modern regimes, as well as to Napoleon III's despotism.

Ironically enough, the only trait of modern totalitarianism which Joly did not foresee was precisely that which his book — perverted by forgers — helped so much to promote: genocidal anti-Semitism. In very many other respects, however, the work invites reflection on the lesson it holds for the fashionable concern with "futurology." The contemporary reader may be led to compare the power of Joly's foresight with that of Alexis de Tocqueville or Jacob Burckhardt and his satirical sharpness with that of George Orwell's *1984*. How was it possible then for a French liberal lawyer in the sixties of the past century to have such keenly predictive powers? Joly's method was neither that of extrapolation, as in predicting future developments from statistical data showing past trends, nor that of an historicist philosophy, such as Marxism. Instead, it was derived from certain firmly held views of human nature in combination with very close, analytical observation of the political scene. Sensitized by his liberal predilections to the hazards of liberty in the industrialized society of nineteenth-century France, he described Bonapartism as though it was a prototype of twentieth-century totalitarianism.

NOTES

1. Quoted in Herman Bernstein, *The Truth About "The Protocols of Zion,"* New York, 1935, pp. 16–17.
2. Ibid.
3. The margin of electoral support of Napoleon dropped steadily during the Emperor's reign from 6.9 million in 1851 to 4.8 million in 1857, 3.3 million in 1863 and 1.1 million in 1869. Cf. S. C. Burchell, *Imperial Masquerade: The Paris of Napoleon III*, New York, 1971, pp. 36 and 345.
4. For a comparison of Napoleon III's and Bismarck's manipulation of public opinion, cf. Wilhelm Bauer, *Die öffentliche Meinung in der Weltgeschichte*, Wildpark-Potsdam, 1929, pp. 326–47.
5. The existence of this translation has been widely overlooked in the literature. Even Hans Leisegang in the preface to his own, excellent modern translation of Joly's book into German (*Gespräche in der Unterwelt zwischen Machiavelli und Montesquieu; oder Der Machiavellismus im XIX. Jahrhundert*, Hamburg, 1948) does not mention the first translation of 1865. Hans Barth does, in his valuable essay, "Maurice Joly, der plebiszitäre Cäsarismus und die 'Protokolle der Weisen von Zion,'" *Neue Zürcher Zeitung*, March 31, 1962.
6. For English translations of "The Jewish Cemetery in Prague," "The Rabbi's Speech," and *The Protocols of the Elders of Zion*, cf. Exhibits C, D, and E in Herman Bernstein, *The Truth About 'The Protocols'*.

7. On Osman Bey, cf. Walther Laqueur, *Russia and Germany*, Boston and Toronto, 1965, p. 96.
8. Norman Cohn, *Warrant for Genocide*, New York, 1969, pp. 74–75. Cohn's book contains the most recent scholarly research on *The Protocols of the Elders of Zion*.
9. Quoted by Cohn, *Warrant for Genocide*, p. 91.
10. Quoted by Cohn, *Warrant for Genocide*, p. 146.
11. For a description of the Bern Trial, cf. John S. Curtiss, *An Appraisal of the Protocols of Zion*, New York, 1942, chap. 5.
12. Cohn, *Warrant for Genocide*, pp. 106–07.
13. The article on Joly in *Grande Encyclopédie*, Hans Leisegang, *Gespräche in der Unterwelt*, and Hans Barth, "Maurice Joly," state that Maurice Joly lived from 1821 to 1878. Herman Bernstein gives the dates 1831–1878. Norman Cohn, *Warrant for Genocide*, has 1829–79. Finally, Henri Rollin, in his "Avant-Propos" to Maurice Joly, *Dialogue aux Enfers entre Machiavel et Montesquieu*, published in the Collection "Liberté de l'esprit," dirigée par Raymond Aron, Paris, 1968, states that Joly was born in 1829 and died on July 17, 1877.

PART FOUR

The Present and the Future

15

The Mills of Death

Bad Homburg, November 14, 1945*

Yesterday I went to Frankfurt in the evening where we had a test showing of the first film about concentration camps ever presented to Germans in a movie house. The Oberbürgermeister ("chief mayor"), the heads of the political parties, a number of licensed newspaper editors, a Protestant minister, a few ladies from the Office for Displaced Persons, etc., all were present upon special invitation. The invited Germans were asked to leave the theater inconspicuously after the film had run in order to attend a discussion with us in the back room of a restaurant. I was the leader of the discussion.

The picture had been screened first, a few days ago, to ICD (Information Control Division, of U.S. Military Government in Germany) personnel here in Bad Homburg, and it was then decided to have a few test showings. A few American soldiers were placed in the audience to listen in on conversations, etc., while the invited guests, seated on the balcony, were the only Germans who knew that they were attending a test showing.

The film is called *Die Todesmühlen* ("The Mills of Death"). It shows

*Letter to Lisa Speier, the author's wife.

Reprinted with permission from Hans Speier, *From the Ashes of Disgrace: A Journal from Germany, 1945-1955*, Amherst, 1981. Copyright © 1981 by the University of Massachusetts Press.

the conditions in the concentration camps when they were liberated by the Americans;[1] Eisenhower visiting them; the people of Weimar visiting them; corpses, emaciated bodies, buckets full of gold teeth broken out of the mouths of the victims, gas chambers, and all the horrors we are now familiar with. All pictures were selected from Allied military photographs taken on the spot, with a special German commentary written for the German edition. Toward the end of the film, you see thousands of Nazis from Nuremberg Parteitag meetings, while the commentator says, "You remember I was there, you were there. . . . " It ends, as it begins, with a procession of people carrying white wooden crosses.

The film is almost unbearably powerful, because it is factual without any attempt to preach or to arouse and express hatred or pity — far better than the atrocity pictures or newsreels (Russian or American) I saw in New York.

I had been going to Frankfurt in a jeep. It was dark and we had lost our way, with ruins and gaping holes all around us. Finally, with the help of German policemen and civilians (who are unfailingly courteous, by the way), we found the theater in a dark street mainly by spotting a row of jeeps and military cars all half-parked on the sidewalk.

When the title *Die Todesmühlen* appeared on the screen (after a very poor newsreel, American-made), I noticed that I was trembling. The documentary lasts for twenty minutes. Not one person walked out. The audience sighed audibly at the worst scenes of horror. It laughed sarcastically once when a German officer hesitated to visit the dungeons and was complimented into them (gently) by a GI.

Now a word about the discussion. Everybody talked freely and without any fear. I had several votes taken. Should this film be shown? (The question was asked after prolonged discussion.) Unanimous Yes. (At the ICD showing, we had been doubtful about the advisability of showing the film to Germans.) Should it be shown now or in connection with the war crimes trial? Or after the winter, when people will be less concerned with food and fuel? Answer: As soon as possible (again, unanimous). Should it be shown to children (which some of us had wanted to do)? Answer: Unanimous No. One woman said softly: "Children are always innocent." Everybody, with the exception of the pastor, favored *compulsory* attendance. "Anyone who cannot prove that he has seen this film should not get his food ration cards." We had to point out that we would not have enough theaters to pursue that policy.

Among the discussants were three former inmates of concentration camps. One of them claimed he had been present when some of the pictures were taken. Two of them were Communists. One of them attacked the mayor for something that had nothing to do with the film, and was quite irritated when I asked him to speak about the film. He then attacked the military government for its "policy," that is, for not showing what happened *inside* the camps prior to their liberation (as though we could have done it without staging the scenes); for not mentioning in the commentary that many of the people shown in the film fought against Hitler before they were imprisoned, and continued to fight inside, and so on. The Communists were most vocal and often quite articulate. They definitely dominated the scene.

The minister pointed out that the brutality and horror we had just seen were not merely political matters. When the most pitiable remnants of what were once healthy people were shown, the commentator had said, "And these were once God's children." "When you forget," the minister said, "that men are God's children, then you have reached the end." Strangely, he did not appear to preach. "It started before the Nazis got into power, and it can happen wherever men lost sight of God." Of course, you would expect a minister to speak like that. Nevertheless, it sounded definitely relevant. It was free of hatred. And in the circumstances in which it was said, it assumed more meaning than it might have when you read it.

I wonder whether there is a genuine new religiosity in Germany today. I have no doubt that some people turn to religion or did so during the war (just as Englishmen were reported during the bombing to have developed a lively interest in astrology). You find a faint suggestion of it even in some newspapers these days. For example, the *Rhein-Neckar Zeitung* in Heidelberg, of which I have read all issues from the first to the last page, gives you this impression, although it does not contain any sermons. It carries poems by Matthias Claudius (*all* papers publish poetry, old aphorisms, essays, etc., in *every* issue!), and an article by Alfred Weber titled, *Orientierung und Aufgabe* ("Orientation and Task") in which you read:

> We saw ourselves shrouded in a darkening that had overcome us and we faced the transformation of man by spiritual forces, the like of which we no longer knew. We were confronted with decisions about these forces. And we felt that we could reach these decisions to save our souls only if we evoked contravening, also objectively existing—let us not hesitate to dub them (however cautiously)—*divine* forces of light and entrust ourselves to them. . . .

Now, Alfred Weber was anything but a preacher when I knew him. (Incidentally, even he resorts to mystification when talking about the Nazi regime: "transformation of man by spiritual forces . . . ," and so on. Neither was man transformed in any sense, nor were the forces at work of a spiritual kind!)

During the discussion of the film, which lasted about two hours, a few subtle suggestions were made indicating, to me at least, that misery does not necessarily blunt the mind or darken the heart beyond hope. And everybody listened patiently, even to his political adversary: they were all united in a sense, although it would be wrong to say that nobody was affected by the totalitarian way of thinking. Some of them definitely were (in the way they talked about "the Germans"). All of them, as I said, wanted people to be *forced* to see the film. Finally, all of them may have felt the need to prove where they stood by aggressive anti-Nazism—a symptom of the difficulty any German has today in finding his moral bearing, in using his freedom, in proving his worth—particularly when Americans are watching him; or a sign of understandable self-consciousness in the presence of American uniforms on the other side of the table. The self-consciousness, however, was not shown overtly, except by the protests, "I was in these camps!" and toward the very end, by the question that an elderly woman asked. She said, quietly, "May I ask *you* a question? When this film is shown abroad, it will deepen the hostility against the Germans, will it not?" A Communist snapped back, "Of course, it will." I replied, "I believe it as difficult to know the reactions to this film abroad as it is to be sure about the German reaction to it. If it were easy, we would not have needed this discussion. Everything depends on the people who see it, their past experience, their beliefs, their ability to grieve."

NOTE

1. See Report of the Joint Congressional Committee, "Atrocities and Other Conditions in Concentration Camps in Germany," Washington, D.C., 1945.

16

Firestorms

May 13, 1952

Londoners during the blitz experienced the horror of fire, death, and destruction, which American civilians were spared. The Germans were subjected to far more powerful area bombing than the British and were exposed to firestorms in several cities, including Hamburg, Kassel, and Dresden. Firestorms were the disasters in Europe most closely resembling the consequences of atomic attack in Japan. Not long ago, a woman about forty-five years of age, who had been in Hamburg during the war, told me while preparing supper for her family that she would commit suicide rather than try to survive another war.

In the meantime, I have talked to several experts in and outside of the Ministry of the Interior concerned with planning civil defense. This is an activity which — prior to the complete legalization of German rearmament — is, strictly speaking, a violation of Control Council Law no. 23 prohibiting German air defense. One official I talked to was a former general, an intelligent and likable man, with a great deal of experience in passive air defense in World War II. As he told me, "The problem of air defense, if fully understood, is quite simple. A large-scale attack on a city from the air causes a catastrophe on the ground. Civil air defense cannot prevent it; it begins after the catastro-

Reprinted from Hans Speier, *From the Ashes of Disgrace: A Journal from Germany, 1945-1955*. Amherst, 1981. Copyright © 1981 by the University of Massachusetts Press.

phe has occurred. Help can come only from outside areas that have not been subjected to attack. The notion that the fire brigades of your own city can rush in to help is nonsense; the equipment will burn. (He saw this happen.) The first thing about civil defense is, therefore, not organization, but protection; that is, air raid shelters and reinforced cellars (which were blown up in Germany after the war by order of the occupation authorities). In addition, people must know how to protect themselves until help can come from the outside. Nowadays, there is too much preoccupation with organization and too little with protection; apparently this is so also in your country."

Then the general spoke about the firestorms, but he did not dwell on the scenes of horror described in the literature: suffocation in the shelters, people burning like torches, their feet sunk in the molten pavement. He spoke of something else. In a toneless voice he said, "The storm is so strong, it tears the clothes off so that in the face of death, the people are—naked!" To the general this was unsurpassed human degradation and horror, and it left an indelible mark of anxiety in his heart: people in the street swaying in a storm of fire, undressed before they die. I was silent. After the shadow of doomsday had passed, he continued. He said that the air attacks did not win the war and the morale of the people was not adversely affected by them, nor was production until the last phase of the war. All this is correct.

Later I thought of political decisions that degraded human beings in a measure comparable to that caused by a firestorm. Jews were sent naked to the ovens to be gassed, and participants in the abortive attempt to kill and overthrow Hitler on July 20, 1944, were hanged on piano wire—naked. Such was the fate of Admiral Canaris.

17

"Reeducation"—
the U.S. Policy

I

It may be doubted whether anyone in a position to make policy decisions on the future of Germany during the Second World War considered in much detail and with any sense of urgency the project of reeducating the Germans after the war.

If grand strategy embodies both military and political decisions, the United States may be said not to have had a grand strategy during the war. American foreign policy helped solve military problems. It served the immediate military cause of defeating the Axis as quickly as possible and at the least possible human sacrifice, but it was not devised with a view to establishing such international political conditions *after* the war as would favor the pursuit of American national interests.

When decisions had to be made which required weighing political against military objectives, military needs tipped the scale. Illustrations abound, viz., the agreement with Darlan, the way in which Lend-Lease aid was extended to the Soviet Union, the momentous decisions not to invade Europe through the Balkans but across the Channel by way of France, the treatment of Badoglio and the Italian king, the policy toward Poland.

Written in 1947 and published in Hans Speier, *Social Order and the Risks of War*, New York, 1952. Copyright © 1952 by George W. Stewart, Publisher, Inc. First M.I.T. Press paperback edition March 1969. Reprinted by permission of M.I.T. Press.

In all these cases, important military considerations of great urgency were permitted to obscure political vision. In retrospect, one could be tempted to regard this subservience of foreign policy to military warfare, which was reflected in the relatively weak position of the Department of State, as militarism by default, were it not for the fact that a predominantly political determination of grand strategy would probably have prolonged the war and increased its human cost.

Since the war was a war of coalition, maintaining and strengthening the alliance at any price became an overriding principle of American policy. This principle weakened American foreign policy in the long run, but American military success which helped doom the Axis concealed this weakness. At the time, the Axis propagandists were untiring to point out the inevitability of conflict among the United Nations, particularly between the Soviet Union and the United States, with Great Britain losing its status as a ranking world power. It was, of course, of vital importance to keep the alliance against the common enemy intact.

In the face of the common danger to national survival, the conflict between communism and capitalism seemed to lose significance in the West and was, moreover, minimized with the argument that the historical development of both the Soviet Union and the Western capitalists countries had brought about a lessening of the original differences in political and economic systems. Any analysis of the strategic interests of the great powers after the war in military security was strictly taboo in the public utterances of Allied statesmen. Nor was there any incisive public discussion of the historical record of wartime coalitions after victory, which would have had a sobering influence on political thinking. The future of international relations was considered without reference to historical experience but with much hope. Men of good will were confident that the United Nations could develop into a peacetime instrument of international cooperation among the great powers.

A realistic estimate of the chances for continued peace in view of the probable distribution of international power after Germany's defeat would have been not only impolitic but also unpopular, because it would have been tantamount to disregarding the international distribution of morality that prevailed at the time. Germany and the Axis were the villains and the Allied powers were the heroes. Millions were expected to die and kill for the triumph of decency over international immorality. In these circumstances, a cool appraisal of international politics beyond the accepted notions of the moral worth of nations would have appeared as rank cynicism, as heresy, or it would, at the very least, have dangerously confused the moral issue of the war.

Since German foreign policy had achieved the impossible by uniting Soviet Russia and the Western powers, it appeared desirable to the leaders of the coalition, whenever they met, to express their determination to continue their common effort in the future. With Germany as the common enemy, the future of Europe could be amicably discussed as long as the goal of rendering Germany impotent was taken as the springboard for reaching agreement. Finally, Germany's disregard for international treaties, her exploitation of the countries her armies had overrun, and her practice of exterminating powerless minorities had thrown the moral issue of the war so sharply into relief that the destruction of Germany as a world power appeared to many as the essential guarantee of peace in the future.

Thus, American policy toward Germany was initially conceived in military and moral terms rather than as a political issue; in relation to current experience rather than with foresight of developments in the postwar era; with an image of Germany as the common enemy of civilized mankind rather than as one of the areas in the world in which the struggle for the balance of power among the wartime allies would be resumed, and least of all as a land where the population would be subjected to a large-scale experiment in education.

II

At the same time, men interested in ethics and education talked about the reeducation of the German people with the zeal and political naiveté of missionaries. Here was an important peace aim in Europe. The future seemed safe if only the German people could be brought to realize their past sins and the wickedness of any future design to break the peace once more. It was conceded that the need for rendering the Germans incapable of renewed aggression might take precedence over the wish to teach them repentance for past crimes and unwillingness to commit new ones in the future. The desire to reform, however, inspired more enthusiasm than the prudent policy of disarmament.

The discussion of reeducation in the United States grew partly out of moral condemnation. It appeared that the Nazi regime could not have maintained itself in power and inflicted so much suffering on the world if it had not been for the popular support which the German people had given it. Yet the concern with reeducation stemmed per-

haps not only from indignation at German aggressiveness and atrocities, but also from the moral discomfort which civilized people feel
when they resort to violence.

In total war, more than in any type of restricted war, there is a need
for understanding the momentous events as a moral drama. The enemy's cause is evil, and every individual member of the enemy nation
seems to share in it. One's own cause appears good regardless of the
fact that the very business of war requires the use of means which,
taken as such, are cruel in nature. Hence, with the need for righteousness there arise conflicts between the devotion to one's own cause and
the doubt that the means of serving it are as good as the cause;
between the urge to condemn the enemy nation and the feeling, if not
the knowledge, that not all of its members can be equally guilty. While
these conflicts impair the comfort of righteousness, the advocacy of
reeducation serves, in a subtle sense, to restore it. It enhances the
moral self-respect of the educator. By changing the "enemy" into a
"pupil," the "conqueror" becomes a "teacher," a role which strengthens
the conscience at a time when it experiences stress.

Conquerors who love to conquer do not think of reeducation. They
loot, destroy, and rejoice. In modern civilization, war becomes a mirror of man in which he sees a terrible face. It is understandable that he
wishes to see the face of the enemy. Reeducation is an attempt to
smash the mirror, because the enemy's face remains human despite all
talk about the enemy's inhuman nature.

Strong moral convictions, however, lead to neglect of time and circumstances, since good and evil are not subject to change. And yet,
regard for time and circumstances are of the essence of politics, as they
inevitably affect whatever relevance certain good or evil actions assume
for taking or justifying a particular political course. Nazi Germany, as
a living menace, presented the same moral problem yesterday which
she presents today as a haunting memory. Politically, however, there is
a difference between Germany to be conquered and Germany vanquished. A peculiarly modern type of man, usually referred to as a
"moralist," tends to overlook this difference.

The idea of reeducation grew out of the division of the world into
good and evil nations, with the good nations united to conquer evil.
Shortly after their victory, however, the conquerors illustrated the
meaning of disunity with startling rapidity and unmistakable clarity.
This development alone would have sufficed to cut the roots of reeducation. As Mr. Byrnes put it in his Stuttgart address of September 6,
1946, "So far as many vital questions are concerned, the Control

Council is neither governing Germany nor allowing Germany to govern itself."

It became evident that there was no universally accepted understanding of democracy, freedom and peace, of good and evil in international relations. To the Germans it could but appear that there existed only zonal definitions of the values for which the victors had waged war. Political reality was at variance with the ideals of the reeducators. It developed into a struggle for power in Europe with the zones of Germany as pawns, and the whole of Germany as a possible stake, in the struggle. It is almost inevitable that to any German with political sense the idea of the United Nations was compromised by the very fact that the victors failed to reach agreement on what to do with Germany.

III

Strictly speaking, the term "reeducation" is meaningless. If it is true that one is either educated or not, one cannot possibly be reeducated. It would certainly be erroneous to contend that the Germans once were "educated" for tyranny and war, and should now, or in the future, be "educated" for tolerance and peace. Such a contention would suggest that the goal of political education can be set and reset by whatever regime happens to be in power. Thus, the very word "reeducation" introduces a relativistic element into the ideas of education. It is preferable to distinguish clearly between indoctrination, terror, and propaganda — methods of human management employed by totalitarian governments and falsely equated by them with education — and democratic methods of free information and education. It is beyond the scope of this discussion, but of some interest, to consider how far the very popularity of the term "reeducation" indicates inroads which totalitarian practices and the so-called philosophies which underly them have made upon political opinions in contemporary democracies. In any event, it was almost inevitable that some Germans after the defeat of their country should insolently remark that "reeducation" reminded them of the "retraining" (*Umschulung*) to which the Nazis had so ignominiously subjected their opponents.

The term "reeducation" cannot be found in any official statement of American policy made during the war; nor is it contained in the Potsdam Agreement, released on August 2, 1945. The only official pronouncement which came close to a pledge of reeducating the Germans was made by President Truman in his report on the Berlin Conference to Congress on August 9, 1945. He said, "We are going to do what we can to make Germany over into a decent nation. . . . "

Only in August 1946, the "Long-Range Policy Statement on German Reeducation" was made public in the United States and in the American Zone of Germany. It had been drafted by a small group of American educators on May 28 and 29, 1945. It was approved, in a slightly revised version, only a whole year later by the State-War-Navy Coordinating Committee, and then, another few months later, it was published. No other occupying power has ever published a similar policy statement on German "reeducation."

The doctrine reflected in this statement conflicted with that governing American policy toward Germany (although this conflict was concealed), until in July 1947 a new directive to General Clay was issued replacing the so-called Joint Chiefs of Staff Directive 1067, of April 1945, many statements of which had in substance been adopted in the Potsdam Agreement. The new directive was issued in response to the change in American foreign policy toward Germany and Europe, respectively, which was announced by Secretary of State Byrnes in Stuttgart, on September 6, 1946, and by Secretary of State Marshall at Harvard on June 5, 1947.

Chairman of the group of advisers who drew up the policy statement on German reeducation was Archibald MacLeish, then assistant secretary of state. Before the war came to an end, MacLeish used to attend the weekly meetings of the Planning Board of the Office of War Information. He made a pointed remark in one of these meetings on American policy toward Germany. Either we mean what we say when we talk about reeducating the Germans, he said, or we do not. If we do, reeducation should be the governing principle of all our policies toward Germany, including those governing economic and political measures. If we do not seriously mean what we say, we might just as well abandon the idea of reeducation. With this remark, MacLeish did poetic justice to the problem, but he failed to see at the time that there was no chance whatever for reeducation to be taken that seriously by the makers of American policy — or for that matter by the policy-makers of any other nation at war with Germany. Power, and security guaranteed by power, have more practical significance than education in international affairs.

The Potsdam Agreement was not conceived as a directive for the reeducation of Germans, but as an instrument for carrying out the Yalta Declaration of February 11, 1945, that is, for the destruction of German militarism and National Socialism in order to insure by means more tangible than education that Germany will "never again be able to disturb the peace of the world." The forces that occupied Germany came as conquerors with the idea that the vanquished foe must be disabled to rise again or to cause any trouble to them while they were there. They did not come as reeducators.

One by one, great and small powers had aligned themselves against Germany and united in defense against her aggression after September 1939. None of them had previously made any effort to educate or reeducate the Germans. In the years 1933 to 1939, when the national socialists terrorized only their German opponents, and were technically at peace with the outside world, there had been no outcry from the outside world for denazification. It would be unrealistic to assume that the victors should have engaged in democratizing Germany after the war for any reason other than their own self-interest.

While the prevalence of this self-interest in Allied policies toward Germany appears to be clear enough, there is some reluctance to admit it plainly and to deny that the victors are committed to any moral or political reform in Germany purely for the sake of improving German moral and political conduct. It requires, nevertheless, only a minimum of political realism to face this fact, and such realism can serve as a wholesome antidote against excessive belief in a moral mission of victors, while it will, at the same time, reduce any utopian schemes of "reeducation" to more manageable proportions and more modest expectations.

The group of university presidents and professors which the State Department assembled to design a long-range policy of reeducation was not so bold as to suggest that reeducation should be the supreme goal of our policies toward Germany. They chose a language less irritating to the practical men who were to approve the statement and its publication. They said, "The reeducation of the German people can be effective only as it is an integral part of a comprehensive program for their rehabilitation. The cultural and moral reeducation of the nation must, therefore, be related to policies calculated to restore the stability of a peaceful German economy and to hold out hope for the ultimate recovery of national unity and self-respect."

Thus, MacLeish's insistence on the overriding importance of "reeducation" had been softened to the proposal that Germany should be rehabilitated on the basis of a comprehensive program of which reeducation should be an integral part. But even this proposal conflicted with American political and economic policies as well as the measures of U.S. Military Government, because neither JCS 1067 nor the Potsdam Agreement were primarily concerned with German rehabilitation.

JCS 1067 stated that chaos and suffering were "inevitable" in Germany and that "it should be brought home to the Germans" that this was so in consequence of Germany's ruthless warfare and the fanatical Nazi resistance. This language reappeared in the Potsdam Agreement. The economic provisions of JCS 1067 were not related to the minimum requirements of German consumption according to any conceivable standard of nutrition; nor were they derived from the requirements of a plan for economic recovery of Europe after the war and the contribution which Germany might be able to make to it. Instead, they referred to international security and to the requirements of safety of the occupation forces. Under the heading, "German Standard of Living," the Directive to the Military Governor read: "You will estimate requirements of supplies necessary to prevent starvation or widespread disease or such civil unrest as would endanger the occupying forces."

While according to the Potsdam Agreement the German people were to be given "the opportunity to prepare for the eventual reconstruction of their life on a democratic and peaceful basis," it was by no means acknowledged or recognized that the "reeducation" of the Germans could be effective only if the stability of a peaceful German economy were restored.

IV

It was only in the directive of July 11, 1947, to General Clay that a constructive American policy toward Germany was stated more fully and related to broader policy aims. The directive said, "As a positive program requiring urgent action, the United States Government seeks the creation of those political, economic and moral conditions in Germany which will contribute most to a suitable and prosperous Europe." Thus, Germany was no longer regarded merely as a potential aggressor and as a country in which the security of the occupation forces remained the guiding policy principle, but as a part of Europe: the policy toward Germany was to be determined in relation to the objective which the United States hoped to attain in Europe as a whole.

In the meantime, however, two years of occupation had passed in which American foreign policy toward Germany was pursued by the American representatives at the quadripartite authority in Berlin on the basis of JCS 1067.

JCS 1067 had set forth policies on Germany "in its initial postdefeat period." As such it was "not intended to be an ultimate statement of policies concerning the treatment of Germany in the postwar world." In fact, there was no "ultimate statement of policies."

Furthermore, both the Potsdam Declaration and JCS 1067 were rather specific on the restrictions to be imposed in order to demilitarize, denazify and disarm Germany, whereas the absence of such specific language regarding reconstructive measures to be taken by the Military Governor required a great deal of discretion and initiative on his part. This freedom of action was not unwelcome to him.

American military bureaucracy in Berlin had inherited the distribution of initiative and responsibility between Washington and "the field," which had prevailed during the Second World War. Washington used to give orders to the generals in command of American forces overseas in the broadest possible terms, since it was felt that more detailed directives of how to wage the war might stifle both the initiative and the sense of responsibility of the theater commanders and would almost certainly disable them to deal promptly with any exigencies that might arise. It was the responsibility of the generals to implement these general orders as they saw fit, and in this way the war had been won. American Military Government in Germany inherited not only personnel from SHAEF, but also wartime relationships with the government in Washington. The distribution of initiative and responsibility remained essentially unchanged. The political tasks of governing the American zone in Germany and of bargaining with the Allies in the Allied Control Authority, however, were enterprises quite different from battles and invasions. Much freedom on the part of the Military Governor now meant freedom from detailed policy directives from Washington as to how to win the peace and how to deal with the Germans. The momentum of the administrative arrangement regarding channels and interrelationships among U.S. bureaucratic establishments proved to be stronger than the reasons for altering a wartime arrangement in view of changed functions and tasks. Besides, it is not certain that a different arrangement approaching more closely the British administrative pattern would have helped, since the State Department was not quick and resolute in taking action and lacked political foresight.

While the general outline of the American reorientation effort in Germany was thus drawn up, in JCS 1067, mainly as a moral qualification of the restrictive measures to be applied to Germany, the execution of the basic directive was influenced by forces over which Washington had little or no control. The situation was aggravated by the fact that Washington itself was slow to reexamine the wartime basis of its policy toward the common enemy and may perhaps be said to have been somewhat influenced by the slowly ebbing anti-German and pro-Russian currents of public sentiment in the United States which had developed during the war.

Also, while the function of the political advisor in Germany, who represented the Department of State, was so understood and exercised as not to curtail the power of the military, the influence of the War Department in Washington on formulation of German policy was comparatively strong. Basic policies were discussed in the State-War-Navy Coordinating Committee, where the representative of the War Department may be surmised to have considered General Clay's opinions as extremely important, especially when they differed from views held in the Department of State.

V

The Office of Military Government was in a strong position not only in Berlin but also in Washington because it was able to influence the size and distribution of the funds in the budget of the War Department which the Congress was asked to appropriate for occupation purposes. This influence in part accounts for the feeble effort — measured in dollars and cents — which the United States government made in the field of education. There has been a tendency to keep down expenditures for educational purposes, because expenditures for other purposes, such as food, appeared more palatable to the Congress. General Clay himself once pointed out at a press conference that one cannot teach democracy on an empty stomach. He did not point out that one cannot teach anything without text books and the paper necessary for printing them. To observers intensely interested in reeducation, it could appear as if the empty stomachs of the Germans were considered a good reason for not worrying much about their education. The work done by American military government in the field of education has been less impressive as well as less expensive than that of other occupying powers.

Illustrations abound. The U.S. Education Mission, a group of American educators visiting Germany at the invitation of the State and War Departments during the summer of 1946 for a month in order to study the German educational system, reported that the staff of the Education and Religious Affairs Branch of Military Government "should be double its present size if a thorough job is to be done." At the time, there were fifty-five Americans employed in the Branch to serve in the German territory under American occupation. Assistant Secretary of State William Benton, in transmitting the report of the Mission to the Secretary of State, commented on the recommendation to double the staff: "If this does not suffice we should be prepared to go further." The War Department, the Office of Military Government, and the Congress did not heed the recommendation, and the educational personnel of OMGUS remained about one quarter of the corresponding staff in the small French Zone.

Similar conditions prevailed in the field of publication. In the spring of 1947, one million new text books had been published in the American Zone, whereas the Russians had published seven times, the French four times as many. As to radio broadcasts to Germany originating abroad, the German language desk of the International Broadcasting Division of the Department of State consisted of six people, including secretaries, after the congressional curtailment of the budget of the State Department Information Program for the fiscal year 1948. In the corresponding operation at London, the British Broadcasting Corporation employed more than 100 persons. While many people in the United States were alarmed by Soviet propaganda in Central Europe, the "Voice of America" in the occupied areas had been smothered to a mere whisper.

On occasions which did not require the expenditure of large funds, the American military authorities showed less enterprise than the representatives of other occupation powers. For example, in June 1947, a conference was held in Munich at which foreign spokesmen addressed German youth. The conference aroused considerable interest in Germany, because it was the first time that an attempt was made to break down the cultural isolation of German youth from the outside world. Writers and university professors of many lands attended the conference and addressed the audience. France, England, Switzerland, Holland, and other countries were represented. There were even speeches by Chinese and Egyptian guests. France sent André Gide, among others; England, Mr. Brailsford, in addition to the official representatives of their military governments. The United States was represented by two employees of the American military government in Berlin who lectured and cited figures; no American of international repute was present.

The doctrine of American military government which served to justify the extreme economy and continual cutbacks of personnel in the fields of public information and education was a simple one. Democracy could not be imposed upon the Germans by the conquerors. Reeducation would fail unless it was largely the work of those elements in German society which had not been infected by the Nazi spirit. The Germans were to exert themselves under the leadership of anti-Nazis and true democrats in their midst to build their own political future. This doctrine had been incorporated in the Long-Range Policy Statement on German Reeducation, and nobody will quarrel with it who has reflected on the magnitude and feasibility of the task confronting the reeducators.

There can be little doubt, however, that the doctrine was used not only for justifying extreme economy but also for disparaging the educational tasks faced by the military government.

If any final evidence were needed for the low priority assigned to education among the occupation tasks, it could be found in the rank within military government of the office that concerned itself with education. Education was but a section placed somewhere in a branch of an unrelated functional division of public health.

In the early days when preparations were made for the structure of the American occupation, the persons planning the educational work were shifted, moreover, from one place in the organization to another. Harold Zink, in his study of American military government in Germany, said of those days, "One hardly knew from day to day exactly where to find the education planners." He also mentioned "the niggardly support" which education was given; it "never received the recognition that Legal, Finance, Economic Affairs, and other no more important fields received."

By contrast, the control of the mass media of public information — press; radio; magazine and book publications; film, theater and music — was organized as a separate office, which had grown out of the Psychological Warfare Division of SHAEF. Public information thus enjoyed a higher ranking than education, but it suffered from three major shortcomings — all of which could be foreseen at an early date and could have easily been avoided. First, public information remained organizationally separate from the Education and Religious Affairs Branch so that plans and activities in these related fields were not properly coordinated. Secondly, it remained somewhat aloof from the rest of the military government structure, because it was not an independent division of an equal plane with other functional divisions but an "office" that had been established after the original plan of placing public information under American civilian control had been thwarted by the general in charge of Psychological Warfare at SHAEF. Thirdly, the basic orientation in that office was not primarily derived from familiarity with the German scene and a clear understanding of the tasks of reorientation but was, to a considerable extent, the outgrowth of psychological warfare against the Germans.

In these circumstances, it is not surprising that the Office of Information Control distinguished itself by its careful screening of politically suitable Germans for information jobs but was far surpassed by its French and Russian colleagues in matters related to cultural policy.

There are few human activities which are less susceptible to planning by civilians — let alone military officers — than the creation of ideas. The books which stir the minds and conscience of men are not written upon order or by instigation of government authorities. The government can coin gold but not make it. It can organize, promote, exploit and suppress talent but cannot breed it, and it usually does best by simply respecting it. Nor can it promote ideas which it does not have.

The effort to show American motion pictures to the Germans has, on the whole, done very little to undo the harm done by Goebbels: at best, one erroneous notion of American life was replaced by another which was less vicious but perhaps even more baffling to the Germans. For several years, no attempt approaching in scope that of the French or the Russians or even that of the British was made in the American Zone to bring German intellectual leaders, artists, writers and musicians in contact with outstanding Americans who shared their interests and equaled or surpassed their talent.

Goebbels had tried everything he could to strengthen the European prejudice in Germany that the United States is a culturally backward country. American military government did not reread Goebbels. To judge from its cultural policy, it seemed to hope that the Germans had forgotten him.

VI

In considering the question as to how successful reeducation has been in Germany, it need hardly be pointed out that no simple answer can be given. The question clearly pertains not only to the effect of public information and education after Germany's defeat. It rather requires an appraisal of Allied policies at large — political, economic, and otherwise — their interrelations and their effect upon German life. Certain observations of the political and intellectual climate in post-Hitler Germany, however, may throw some light on the answer and particularly on the merit of the doctrine that the Germans should reeducate themselves.

When Germany was first occupied many observers of the German scene noticed the prevalence of political apathy among the population. It was often pointed out that this apathy was the result of the shocks of bombing and defeat and of the occupation. The rapid development of political institutions after the war should not be regarded as a sign of political vitality on the part of the Germans; it was a sign of General Clay's impatience. When the development of political attitudes is examined, it rather appears that constitutions, political parties and elections notwithstanding, apathy has remained widespread. In October 1945, it was found in a survey that more than 70 percent of the population in the American Zone claimed to be "not interested" in politics. With the authorization of political parties and local elections, the interest in politics rose until, in June 1946, the proportion of those who claimed to be uninterested in politics dropped below 50 percent. In August and September of 1946, however, it had risen again to about 65 percent.

A particularly striking illustration of widespread indifference toward important political events was the popular vote cast for the adoption of the constitutions in the three Länder, Würtemberg-Baden (November 24, 1946), Bavaria (December 1, 1946), and Hesse (December 1, 1946), in the American Zone. Nowhere did the vote in favor of the constitutions amount to more than half the electorate. At the time when the constitutions were voted on, elections were also held for the legislative assemblies in these three Länder. Participation in the assembly elections amounted to 76.7 percent in Bavaria and 73.4 percent in Hesse. Voting strength on the constitutions was considerably lower. The adoption of the new basic democratic constitutions did not stir the interest of the Germans in politics.

It is interesting to note that the elections in the Soviet Zone in 1946 did not reflect this indifference toward politics which can be observed in the Western zones. In the October 1946 election participation was 90 percent as over again 79.5 percent in the community elections of September 1946. Characteristically, the increase in total voting strength in October went entirely to the conservative parties, whereas the Socialist Unity Party, the German instrument of the Soviet occupation authorities, lost votes both in absolute numbers and in relation to the opposing parties. What appeared as a growing interest in politics must therefore be attributed to increasing disapproval of the Soviet occupation policies, a result which it is intriguing to compare with the corresponding relative gain of communist votes in the latest British elections. It is possible that the longer the occupation lasts, without giving to the Germans hope of the gradual improvement of their lot, the platforms of the various political parties will become less important than their relation to the occupation authorities in the respective zones. A vote for the Communist ticket in the Western zones may not necessarily mean a vote for communism, but rather a vote against the military authorities, just as a vote for the right-wing parties in the Soviet Zone may merely express opposition to Soviet policies there.

German indifference toward politics may possibly conceal fear of, or contempt for, political activities in Germany. This is suggested by the outcome of two polls held in 1946 and in 1947, in which a cross-section of the population in the American Zone and in Berlin was asked whether or not they would like their sons to choose a political career. In both polls, the overwhelming majority answered in the negative. While it is likely that this negativism is related to the fact that Germany is an occupied country, the increase in the number of negative responses found in the more recent poll indicates failure rather than success of the reorientation effort. In 1947, only 12 percent of the respondents answered the question with "Yes." Politics as a career seems to be unpopular in post-Hitler Germany.

VII

Reeducation aims at radical changes in attitudes and conduct, but such changes can not be brought about merely in school and through the media of public information. Attitudes are shaped by experiences in the home, on the street, at the place of work as well as by formal schooling or by reading the newspapers. Face-to-face contacts with members of the occupation forces, for example, provide the people with more effective illustrations of the character of foreign lands than do radio broadcasts or magazine articles. Particularly in a situation in which the belief in all ideas is undermined and words meet with a distrust that has been engendered by their long-continued abuse for propaganda purposes, examples matter more than precepts.

Planning political reeducation means comprehensive social planning not only of the political institutions, but also of the nonpolitical institutions which bear upon the formation of political attitudes. Philosophers and statesmen who thought about the most desirable political order and about ways of realizing it by institutional changes have never neglected the family, because it is as children that we are first introduced to the kind of conduct which adults regard as proper. Similarly, religion has always been recognized as important in shaping the attitudes of both adults and children toward authority and politically important activities. Any effort to change the moral and political climate of a community requires the cooperation of the church, or else its exclusion from matters affecting the political aims of education. Social planning can be obviated by passive resistance or active obstruction; it is difficult to reconcile planning with freedom. It requires coordination, central direction, supervision, and, in the extreme case, coercion of all institutions which contribute toward the formation of political attitudes and help to set the pattern of community life, although the immediate concerns of these institutions need not be with politics.

Similarly, there is little hope of effecting trenchant changes in the political outlook of a nation in circumstances of economic misery and uncertainty. Since an economic crisis taxes the resilience of well-established democratic institutions, it is unrealistic to expect enthusiasm for new democratic institutions to grow along with economic despair about the future. Life is departmentalized only in the minds of administrators and analysts. Political planners must recognize its integration.

If social planning is comprehensive and radical its execution requires a redistribution of power at the beginning rather than at the end of the process. In other words, radical social planning presupposes either a revolution, in which the planners gain power to deal with resistance and obstruction against their plans, or a defeat in total war so that the conqueror can divest controlling groups among the vanquished nation of their power.

Yet the assumption of political and military power by a conqueror does not automatically dislodge all the leading groups in the defeated nation from their positions of power. In particular, it does not automatically dislodge the leading groups and individuals controlling administration, the economic process and the cultural life of that nation. Defeat in total war effects a change in the distribution of power in the conquered land, which, in a sense, is *more* radical than that brought about by a social revolution, because supreme control passes to a foreign conqueror rather than to a domestic counterelite. In another sense, however, such change is *less* radical than a domestic upheaval if the defeat is not followed by a domestic social revolution or by radical measures of the conqueror which provide a substitute for revolution. Neither of these changes occurred in Western Germany.

Obviously, the attitudes toward both revolutionary measures and social planning in Germany vary among the occupation authorities of the four victorious nations. These attitudes are determined by the political traditions at home and by the national interests of the respective powers.

The domestic political traditions which influenced Soviet policy in Germany promoted rather than stifled radical institutional changes in the Soviet Zone. In fact, the only considerations which could possibly arrest such changes were not inspired by any respect for civil rights and basic liberties, but exclusively by the overriding interests of the Soviet Union, for example in reparations, or in control of as large a part of German territory as possible through German political and social organizations under Soviet direction. Soviet occupation policy has been characterized by radical changes in German institutions, vigorous support of communist or communist-dominated organizations and institutions of all types, by creating conditions of precariousness and insecurity for all other organizations and institutions, and by encouraging their denunciation as "fascist" or "reactionary" whenever such attacks have appeared expedient.

For example, Soviet authorities instituted a radical school reform as early as September 1946. To the Soviet authorities the aims of educational reform are clearly political in nature, and since in the Soviet view political change must be buttressed by social change in order to last, the school reform, like the land reform, aims at a transformation of both the social class system and the promotion of communist political activities and opinions.

The universities no longer are a monopoly of the middle and upper classes; instead, the percentage of students who come from the working classes (and from parents who are members of the Socialist Unity Party) has strikingly risen. Contrary to developments in the Western Zones, the universities have not been allowed to restore their autonomy. Soviet authorities exercise administrative control through the Central Administration for People's Education.

Similarly, income and social status which used to bar the children of the poor from secondary education have been removed: talent, and the political affiliation of the parents, rather than socioeconomic status have been made the basis of admission to secondary schools. On the level of elementary education a unified school (*Einheitsschule*) has been established; private and denominational schools have ceased to exist.

France has been interested in weakening Germany's power permanently and in every respect by increasing her own power at Germany's expense. Having been the victim of aggression by her German neighbor quite frequently and having experienced occupation by the forces of the vanquished foe herself, France does not understand reeducation as a task of laying the foundation for a strongly democratic Germany. Her efforts are focused instead on discouraging among the Germans in the French Zone any interest in centralization of German political power and in fostering proFrench sentiment. If the French have cared less about denazification than the Americans, this may be attributed to the paradox that they do not put much trust in the anti-Nazis either, as long as their strongest loyalty is toward Germany. At the same time, the French have realized more clearly than any other occupation power that the Germans stand in awe of "culture." Thus, the French have exerted themselves in attempts to win over intellectuals and artists. The French have never underestimated their own cultural heritage and regard it as the best conceivable foundation of a civilized life. Thus, they are more interested in teaching German children French than in teaching German adults to appreciate the blessings of equal educational opportunities.

The French authorities exercise more control over the educational institutions in their zone than do the American or British military governments. The reform of secondary education in the French Zone was imposed in August 1946 against the will of the Germans, whose own plan was disregarded. By contrast, American military government did nothing to curb the Catholic influence upon education in Bavaria. Cultural freedom in Bavaria today is in a more precarious state than it was under the Kaiser prior to the First World War.

American advocates of reeducation had overlooked the plain fact that the Western democracies would be unwilling to embark upon a policy of radical social planning in Germany. Such a radical policy would have violated the American traditions of free enterprise and the American respect for efficiency and the middle classes. There was as little inclination on the part of the American officials to undertake or tolerate a revolution in Germany as there was evidence of any revolutionary inclination on the part of the Germans. It appeared democratic and practical not to make any basic social change. The institution of the family was indeed shaken by war, economic misery and occupation, probably more violently than Americans realized at home; but this had not happened in pursuit of a policy. The churches, anxious to prove their anti-Nazi record, which had not been without blemishes, were respectable organizations with powerful international backing.

Private property? It would have been undemocratic if Americans had advocated socialization and so they did indeed not do so. In short, no radical reeducation could possibly be undertaken in the American Zone.

The advocates of reeducation, however, remained convinced that democracy, like peace, is the natural choice of men free to pursue their happiness. The paradox of the American philosophy of reeducation became apparent: the German people had been held responsible for National Socialism and were now expected to be anxious to embrace democracy. To this end, it was merely necessary to eliminate and control National Socialist and militarist institutions, personnel and ideas. Since the military authorities had rebuilt the bridges destroyed during the war and had prevented the outbreak of epidemics afterwards, it was assumed they could also prevent the spreading of those ideas which had once proved so disastrously infectious.

American policy did not seriously face the fact that the strengthening of democracy in Germany could not be achieved without the most active help to the noncommunist left. The representatives of the noncommunist left were socially less acceptable to the top layer of U.S. personnel in Germany than some of the rightist Germans who spoke English more fluently, believed in the value of private initiative, and had been good administrators. Social democracy in Germany was given far less support even by the British Labor Government than the German communists received from the Soviet Union. Few Americans at home realized that German Social Democrats fought communism in postwar Germany before U.S. policy turned anti-Soviet, and that they did so without any noticeable encouragement by American officials. Again, it would have been undemocratic to help one party more than another.

The story of the American reeducation effort is but an anecdote in the larger context of U.S. foreign policy in Europe. The lessons to be learned from it do not lie in the field of education or public information. They pertain to a moral dilemma created by victory in total war and to the futility of teachers telling generals and businessmen what they should do. Finally, they pertain to the speed with which the modern moral temper can turn from indignation to indifference.

18

Karl Jaspers on the Future of Germany

In the early thirties many refugees from Germany discovered to their dismay that their views of Hitler were not taken too seriously. Abhorrence of the Nazi regime was expected of them, but opposition to appeasement policies in the West was another matter. The warnings of refugees that in the absence of early counteraction Hitler would remain in power until he had lost the war he was certain to start were often attributed to refugee prejudices or to ignorance. Some Western economists predicted that Germany would be bankrupt long before Hitler was ready for war. Prior to the invasion of Poland in September 1939, many exiles from Germany felt like premature anti-Nazis in their host countries.

At that time, Karl Jaspers was not a premature anti-Nazi abroad. He was silenced at home. As professor of philosophy at Heidelberg University, he could not longer teach, perhaps because his wife was Jewish. He had to confine himself to reading and writing. Nobody who knew the man and his work ever believed that he hailed or supported the Nazis, as Martin Heidegger and many other German professors had done. It generally was taken for granted that he silently condemned them. Some German intellectuals who had left their country, including some former colleagues and students of Jaspers, never-

Originally published in the *Bulletin of the Atomic Scientists*, December 1968. Reprinted by permission of the *Bulletin of the Atomic Scientists*.

theless were disappointed by the fact that he had remained in Germany. Indeed, almost all institutions of higher learning anywhere in the world would have considered it a privilege to receive Jaspers as an exile. Merely by leaving Germany in 1933 he would have contributed to the public condemnation of the regime, and he would have done so in a manner befitting a philosopher devoted to the contemplative rather than the active life. For reasons that are not known to me, Karl Jaspers stayed in Germany. His decision to remain cannot have been an easy one. Often in the twelve years of Nazi rule his moral endurance must have been heavily taxed.

For reasons also unknown to me, Jaspers left Germany — some time after Hitler's fall. He went to Basel, although he retained his German citizenship. It is possible that personal circumstances in his life as well as his Protestant upbringing and what he calls his philosophical faith contributed to his vehemence when he could again speak freely — after Hitler's suicide and Germany's defeat. In his first public address, delivered in August 1945, Jaspers bared his heart in agony. "When the Jews were taken away in transports," he said, "we did not go into the streets to shout until we, too, were destroyed. . . . Being still alive, that is our guilt." It was embarrassing to witness such public contrition about having been neither a hero nor a martyr, but it was not the time to argue that a philosopher need not be either.

A little earlier, on June 28, 1945, Konrad Adenauer, who had been imprisoned by the Nazis, wrote a memorandum to the British occupation authorities in which he set forth the argument that the exclusion of all members of the Nazi Party from every activity might drive them into the arms of a new National Socialist movement. Later, in his *Memoirs*, he wrote "I am certainly not for letting National Socialists, who have burdened themselves with heavy guilt, run about free. But I know about the weakness of human nature, and anyone who has ever lived in a police state understands how much courage is required of a man who resists the government, and how much he thereby imperils himself and his family. I think each case must be considered individually. Heroism is not an everyday occurrence." Of course, it is as little an everyday occurrence as is self-inflicted martyrdom. This is not to say that Adenauer's political level-headedness and his Catholic understanding of human nature were sufficient reasons for the employment of Nazis and Nazi supporters in politically prominent positions. Such employment was practically unnecessary and morally unjustifiable. Jaspers and others have rightly criticized the first Chancellor of the Federal Republic for tolerating former Nazis in his entourage.

Since 1945, Jaspers has written a number of books and essays and has given many interviews to magazines on subjects of political importance. He now always speaks in ringing tones, proclaiming to his countrymen apodictically the moral standards which they failed to meet under Hitler and which in his opinion they still do not meet. Free from Nazi or Communist suppression and censorship, Jaspers has become one of the severest critics of political life in the Federal Republic. He has written on collective guilt and responsibility, on peace and the nuclear problem and on the moral and political shortcomings of West German postwar policies.

No one concerned with postwar Germany should neglect Jaspers' political writings. Among other things, he has urged the adoption of a German policy of detente toward East Europe that was frowned upon in Bonn for many years. Only recently Bonn's views have begun to change; it is yet too early to say whether for better or worse.

According to Jaspers, West Germany is pervaded by deep lies. "Perhaps they can all be grouped around a single one: that the Germans were never really Nazis. That an incomprehensible fate delivered them into the hands of a wicked criminal. That at bottom . . . they always remained as decent, peaceloving, and truthful, as they had been previously and are today." This was not written in 1945, but twenty years later. Perhaps the voice of Professor Karl Jaspers is so indignant because he could not speak for so many years when Hitler ruled his country. His writings do not offer any insights into the weakness of human nature in Germany under Hitler. The great moralist will help the reader to condemn evil, should he be in need of such help, but not to understand the evils of cowardice, of compromise and fear, of indolence and opportunism, of self-delusion and accommodation. Thus, anyone who wants to understand Nazism and the Nazi heritage ought to read Jaspers, but he must supplement his study with other books. Nor should he overlook the fact that Jaspers's views on present-day Germany partake of that heritage; they are conscientious reactions to Hitler's policies and to the behavior of "the Germans" in the Nazi era, but they are myopic on Germany's position in the struggle for power in the postwar world.

Parliamentary Analysis

The most valuable piece of work done by Karl Jaspers as a political writer on German affairs is his analysis of the Parliamentary debates in Bonn, on a statute of limitation for Nazi crimes. This is a specific, empirical study of the thinking of German parliamentarians. Jaspers read the Bundestag record for March 10 and 25, 1965, as carefully as a philosopher studies a philosophical text, or a psychiatrist the case history of his patient. Jaspers believes that there can be no statute of limitation for genocide. Such crime must be punished. He shows the German Bundestag deputies to be men who are jurists juggling provisions of the law but forgetful of justice, phrase-makers skilled in the use of subterfuge, sophists, little men. Only once or twice, in discussing the contributions by the Social Democratic deputies Jahn and Arndt, does Jaspers admit that these men at least came close to facing the moral issue at hand.

Jaspers's analysis was originally published in 1966 as the second part of his book *Wohin treibt die Bundesrepublik?* It is regrettable that the American edition of this volume, published in 1967 under the title *The Future of Germany*, contains only the third part of the original volume, brought up to date and enlarged by passages from another German full-length book by Jaspers written in reply to his critics. The translator has struggled to render the original German into readable English. His occasional failures are not always his own fault: Jaspers writes too much, and sometimes his statements border on triteness. For example, in talking about skills vs. *kultur*, a favorite concept of German philosophy, he says: "To acquire skills, people must first have the will to be part of mankind's great march, to help form and develop the realities that make up our existence. . . . To acquire culture, a people must first have the pedagologically animated will to find in culture its own infinite common bond." On "grand designs": "'Grand designs,' patterns of the history of mankind and of certain sequences, make sense at particular times, but they are drawn up in different forms, none of which can be the one that is valid." On education: "'Educate our youth!' goes the cry. Politicians cultivate the young politically. They spend money for schools, large sums of it, yet not enough." On force, "reality" and freedom: "Force, reality, and freedom never coincide in lasting harmony. Politically things remain in flux. . . . Political thinking takes knowledge. Political education means book learning as well." Such writing, while mildly irritating, should not detract from the importance of Jaspers's book.

Taking the Consequences

Rejecting the notion of collective guilt in its simplistic form, Jaspers has always insisted that all Germans — whether they were once Nazis or not, and regardless of whether they were men or children or yet unborn in the Nazi era — are obligated to accept the consequences of Germany's defeat. In particular, they ought to accept the destruction of Bismarck's Reich as something final, an outcome of Germany's aggressive war. According to Jaspers, the territories east of the OderNeisse Line under Polish rule are lost forever, as are the eastern territories annexed by the Soviet Union. Any hedging based on the Potsdam Agreement and on oft-repeated Western policy declarations supporting reunification is both unrealistic and pernicious. West German insistence on the reunification of Germany is precisely what the communists say it is: endangering the peace by concealed aggression, or as Jaspers put it, "a camouflaged will to violence." This is rather harsh. It is also simplistic because it fails to discriminate between, say, Adenauer and von Studnitz, the right-wing nationalist. And it leaves open the politically important question of what the present power of German nationalism would be if sometime in the past twenty years a federal government had meekly or bravely accepted once and for all the division of Germany.

For many years, Jaspers has argued that the restoration of freedom in East Germany is more important than the reunification of the two Germanys. While one may well agree with him on this point in principle, there remains the question of how the Germans living under Ulbricht's regime can become free. Jaspers suggests that they may eventually travel the road of the Czechs (written prior to August, 1968) and the Slovaks — and the Poles!

Jaspers does not deny that the Ulbricht regime is a product of Soviet force rather than an expression of the will of the people. But he insists, quite rightly, that the Federal Republic, too, is the creation of foreign powers and cannot be regarded as the creation of men who freed themselves of a tyrant in order to give themselves a democratic constitution. The Germans did not liberate themselves. They were conquered. Nor did the Western conquerors favor the Social Democratic Party, which had a better record of resisting the Nazis than did its political competitors. In the Bundestag of 1953, 31 percent of the Socialist Deputies had been imprisoned or thrown into concentration camps by the Nazis. Nine percent had emigrated from Hitler's Germany. The corresponding figures for the Christian Democrats were five and 0.4 percent. When the Federal Republic was established, the West German political parties were resurrected from the ashes of the Weimar Republic, including those parties that had supported Hitler's dictatorship.

The origin of the Federal Republic however, is itself no indictment of German democracy. Whether or not the new republic is a viable democracy is a question of its structure, not of its origin. Jaspers realizes this, but looking at the Federal Republic he is deeply pessimistic about its political prospects. Apparently, he fails to see any symptoms of political health in postwar Germany, even for example, in the successful integration into the social order of millions of Germans expelled from territories now under communist rule. Jaspers, the moralist, does not attempt to assess the weight of what is good, bad, and indifferent in German political life. He strikes no balance.

As a liberal, Jaspers is impatient with bureaucratic organizations. Political party machines are bureaucratic organizations everywhere, and, according to Jaspers, they have established an oligarchical rule in West Germany. Parliament does not exercise its political function of controlling the government, nor do the people really participate in a democratic process. Consequently, the danger to which the Federal Republic is exposed is the rise of a new dictatorship by the machinations of the party oligarchs. In another context, Jaspers mentions also the danger that the Bundeswehr may establish a *military* dictatorship in West Germany. The road to dictatorship, Jaspers argues, leads from the formation of a grand coalition government to the acceptance of emergency legislation enabling the government to stifle and abolish what is left of democracy by the arbitrary use of force. He does not foresee the success of a neo-Nazi movement, nor does he comment at all on the perils of left-wing extremists. He fights the Bundestag deputies of all parties.

These alarmist views seem to me grossly slanted. They can be held only when massive political factors operating in the Federal Republic are disregarded: the presence of foreign troops on German territory, the decentralized, anti-Prussian, federal structure of West Germany, the power of the trade unions, the loss of prestige and political status of the officers' corps, the widespread contempt for politicians, the equally widespread popularity of intellectuals who criticize the government.

Kiesinger's Position

The American edition of Jaspers's book contains an appendix (taken from the German sequel to *Wohin treibt die Bundesrepublik?*) in which Georg Kiesinger's ascension to the chancellorship of the Federal Republic in December 1966 is treated as another indication of the moral inadequacy of postwar German politics. Jaspers is sharp and bitter in commenting on this event, not only because he is alarmed by the virtual elimination of parliamentary opposition through the formation of a grand coalition government, but also because Kiesinger once was a Nazi. Indeed, Kiesinger's two predecessors, Adenauer and Erhard, had political records in the Hitler era that were compatible with holding high office in post-Hitler Germany. Kiesinger lacked this qualification, and the German politicians who accepted him as chancellor were naive not to regard his chancellorship as a potential liability in Germany's domestic and international affairs.

Kiesinger joined the Nazi Party early in 1933. Much ink has been uselessly spilled over the trivial issue of whether or not his job in the Foreign Office under Hitler was politically important. In the meantime, instead of remaining silent on his past, the chancellor has testified as a witness in a Nazi war crimes trial. On July 4, 1968, he declared that he had joined the Nazi Party neither out of conviction nor out of opportunism. One wonders anew why he did join. It is true, he became a Nazi prior to the mass murder of foreign Jews, but not before it was known to every German above the age of, say, 14, that the Nazi Party was a party of fanatics and brutes. Hitler had set forth his views in a book and had hailed the Nazi murder of a Polish citizen. Goering had promised the storm troopers a "night of the long knives," that is, freedom from police interference with their terror and violence. German communists, Social Democrats, Jews, Pacificists, liberals, intellectuals were vilified, arrested, and tortured in Germany. I remember that early in 1933 in Berlin, where Kiesinger lived and made his decision to become a Nazi, all this was known to everyone except children.

According to his testimony, Kiesinger, as a member of the Nazi Party, eventually noticed that German Jews were arrested and removed to a destination which, he claims, no "official" information helped him to identify. He assumed that Jews were shipped off to work in "munitions factories," since they were "unacceptable for military service." He said that when fewer people wearing the Star of David, thus marking them as Jews in public, were to be seen in the streets, he realized that "something ugly" was happening. Had Kiesinger's sensibility not been offended earlier by the official requirement that Jews had to wear the Star of David?

Anti-Semitism

Today, when leading Jews in Poland and the Soviet Union deny or minimize the existence of anti-Semitism in these communist countries, it may seem pedantic to mention a remote phase in the career of the present German chancellor. Nor was he a murderous Nazi. It has been claimed that during the war he was denounced to the security police for having used his official position in the Foreign Office to obstruct German anti-Semitic propaganda to the United States. Anyone who ever studied German English-language broadcasts during the war will be aware of the fact that he was not very successful. But he may have tried, because in the later years of his Nazi career he came to regard Goebbels's propaganda as ugly. All this does not matter. What does matter is this: in 1966 the German Bundestag failed to select as Chancellor of the post-Nazi German Republic a man who had not been associated in any way with the Nazi Party; and in mid-1968, Kiesinger considered it politically useful to encourage other Germans to share with him a sense of indifference about his personal Nazi past. Perhaps Kiesinger thought that by this puzzling performance he could regain some votes for his party from the right-wing extremists or create additional difficulties for the politically ailing Social Democratic Party by increasing left-wing resentment of its role in Kiesinger's government.

In any event, Jaspers's sense of moral outrage at the fact that Kiesinger was chosen to be Erhard's successor is understandable enough. And yet, Jaspers's passion interferes with his political judgment. He should not have remained silent on the fact that Kiesinger's government is a motley collection of men comprising not only former Nazis, but men with very different political pasts. Willy Brandt, the vice-chancellor is a former, active anti-Nazi. Not so many years ago, some of his present colleagues in the government contested his political qualifications for high office on the grounds that he had been a refugee fighting Germany during the war. Another member of Kiesinger's cabinet left Adenauer's government protesting German rearmament. Still another is a former communist. The principal victim in the so-called Spiegel Affair, which led to Franz Josef Strauss's resignation as Minister of Defense, now occupies a high government position, along with Strauss, who became Minister of Finance. Thus, in speaking about the current German government it is somewhat beside the point that the Chancellor once was a member of the Nazi Party. It would be more to the point to examine the implications and consequences of the fact that the present grand coalition government is composed of men who generally do not attribute importance to their own and each other's past moral and political convictions — a phenomenon not confined to the Federal Republic.

Present Policy

Paradoxically, it has been under Kiesinger that Bonn's policy toward communist Europe has moved in a direction which Jaspers, among

other German writers, must welcome. Bonn, for all practical purposes, has abandoned the Hallstein Doctrine, according to which the
Federal Republic would break off diplomatic relations with any government that recognized the communist East German regime. Ulbricht
has adopted a Hallstein Doctrine in reverse. The new German policy of
detente includes many concessions to the Ulbricht regime that were not
and could not have been granted two or three years ago. Only a grand
coalition government could violate the tabus which were set in the
Adenauer period with the help of Germany's allies.

Today, those who fail to heed Jaspers's advice on West Germany's
Eastern policy no longer sit in Bonn. The policy of reconciliation is
opposed in Moscow, East Berlin, and Warsaw.

Jaspers's concern with the dangers of emergency legislation in West
Germany is very intense. He has opposed it with a fear and passion
that were kindled in 1933 when the German Reichstag enabled Hitler
to establish his dictatorship. Various drafts of the emergency legislation have been debated and changed for the last ten years in West
Germany. Jaspers has made no effort to examine these changes. Nor
has he compared the provisions of the emergency legislation in the
Federal Republic with those existing in other democracies, like Switzerland, Canada, the United States, or Great Britain. Had he done so, he
would have found that in various respects emergency powers in West
Germany are less sweeping than those other democracies have found
acceptable.

In the interest of peace and German security, Jaspers is pro-Ameri-
can. He praises even Adenauer for entrusting the security of the Federal Republic to American deterrence. At the same time, Jaspers supports a condominium of the United States and the Soviet Union,
primarily in order to prevent the proliferation of nuclear weapons. In
Germany, Jaspers's book was criticized because, among other things,
it contains some extravagant views on the nuclear disarmament of
Communist China. Jaspers recommended that the United States and
the Soviet Union should jointly urge Britain, France, and China to
give up their nuclear weapons. Britain and France, Jaspers surmised,
would comply. But what about China? Well, if everything else failed,
the superpowers should jointly destroy China's nuclear installations
and arsenals after due warning to the local populations to evacuate the
target sites. Thus, at this point, the moralist turns into a crusader,
sword in hand. In the sequel to *Wohin treibt die Bundesrepublik?*
Jaspers defended his thoughts on the Chinese peril and how to meet it
by telling his German critics that he had not advocated unilateral

action against China, nor a preemptive strike prior to the use of diplomatic pressure.

The Future of Germany contains many other comments on world affairs ranging from de Gaulle to J. F. Kennedy and the Warren Report, and from the war in Vietnam to the race problem in the United States. All of these comments are outspoken, but few of them are more than journalistic in character.

The Future of Germany is a serious, though unbalanced book, reminding those who have forgotten the past that "any madness seems as possible today as ever."

19

The Chances for Peace

Statesmen frequently declare that they want to preserve peace. Such declarations are both popular and useful. For one thing, we associate peace with life and the expectation that tomorrow's calamities will not be worse than the misfortunes we survived yesterday. For another, existing international conflicts appear less disturbing to us when we are not urged to view them in the light of national interests but hear that men who deal full time with the conflicts want to resolve them amicably. Clearly, professions of peace are preferable to warnings that war is inevitable or imminent, as we have heard them in recent times primarily from Chinese and Arab leaders.

Of course, when statesmen and diplomats publicly talk of peace or war they usually have certain political objectives in mind, so it would be naive to consider their pronouncements to be the historical or philosophical truth. It takes at least two to make peace, but only one to disturb it. Often in the past declarations of peace did not halt the outbreak of war, and sometimes talk of peace has been rhetoric that statesmen indulged in to deceive others or themselves.

In a book about Napoleon published in 1839 Prince Louis Bonaparte declared that it had been his uncle's admirable aim to bring peace

Opening address of an international conference held at Bad Godesberg, Germany, on June 20–21, 1974, in honor of Gustav Heinemann, President of the Federal Republic of Germany, on the theme "Is Peace Possible? Can We Plan for Peace?" Published in *Social Research*, 1975. Reprinted with permission of *Social Research*.

and unity to Europe. Later, as Napoleon III, the nephew embarked upon policies characterized by Saint-Simonianism, repression, and frequent resort to war. Neville Chamberlain proclaimed "peace in our time" after reaching an agreement with Hitler in Munich; the invasion of Poland was not far off. Throughout the period of the so-called cold war, the leaders of communist nations claimed to speak and act in the interest of peace-loving people everywhere, but they rejected the Baruch Plan and they denounced the Marshall Plan. Under John F. Kennedy, "peace as a process" became an oft-repeated slogan; the President insisted on it, among other things, in order to disabuse people of the notion that peace had been firmly established by the beginnings of détente with the Soviet Union so that costly security efforts could be relaxed. Lately, we have heard a great deal in the United States about "peace with honor," the "structure of a lasting peace," and, with reference to China, even about "the long march toward peace." Brezhnev, on his part, and the Soviet press welcome the recognition of existing boundaries in Europe as the foundation of peace.

Peace Not Indivisible

As the era of negotiation allegedly has replaced that of confrontation, and as "relaxation of tension," "peaceful coexistence," "détente," and "renunciation of force" have become favored terms in the political vocabulary, peace research has become fashionable in Western academic circles. Some now hold it to be more respectable than research on war and to be different from, if not morally superior to, the study of international relations.

In this paper, I shall first present my view that a generalized conception of peace is not very helpful in understanding the problems with which this conference is concerned. There are many different kinds of war and peace. Unless we specify more exactly what we are talking about, our talk will be empty.

I shall start with the observation that peace is not indivisible. At least four reasons can be adduced to support this proposition.

First, as Hobbes observed, the climate in the relations between states is not confined to the extremes of foul and fair weather. There are many kinds of weather, that is, many kinds of war and peace. Just as not all wars are total wars, so not all peaceful relations represent a state of full harmony of interests or perfect concord. Relations between states may be regarded as a continuum bounded by the extremes of total peace and total war. Peace itself is a continuum ranging from total peace to the point of severe crisis that marks the transition to war. Put differently, it is possible and useful to apply the notion of escalation not only to the means of violence when a limited war develops into total war but to international conflict as such, which can be more or less intense in times of peace. This means that but for the marginal, utopian, and lifeless condition of perfect concord, peace includes international conflict — more or less severe, more or less easily resolved, and representing risks of varying magnitude that resort to war will occur. Similarly, domestic peace includes domestic conflict of all sorts short of civil war. Peace is not indivisible because the peaceful relations that exist in various parts of the globe involve conflicts of different magnitude and intensity.

Second, just as we distinguish between localized and global war, so we must recognize that peace has a territorial dimension. There may be areas of war within larger areas of peace. A war may be extremely intense — when measured by the number of casualties in relation to the total population — and yet be confined to a certain locale, so that, as in the case of a tornado, devastation may be terribly intense at the center while large surrounding areas are not affected.

A notable case in point was the war between Paraguay on the one hand and Brazil, Argentina, and Uruguay on the other; it lasted from 1864 to 1870. In those few years, the total population of Paraguay was reduced from 525,000 to 221,000, with only one tenth of the survivors being men. Clearly, this was war catastrophically total, but neither its impact on world peace at the time nor its long-range consequences for international relations were as momentous as the wars against Denmark, Austria, and France waged for German unification at about the same time. And these three wars taken together were relatively less bloody than was the fighting that decimated the population of Paraguay.

The third reason why peace is not indivisible is extremely painful to contemplate and perhaps for this reason frequently neglected. We regard peace around us as more important than peace elsewhere. Faraway war disturbs us less than war nearby, just as a quarrel in our family upsets us more than a case of wife-beating down the street. Is it too harsh to suggest that, generally speaking, the magnitude of bloodletting in the aftermath of decolonization in Africa and Asia since the end of the Second World War has remained a matter of indifference in Europe and America; or if this *is* too harsh, a matter of lesser concern than, say, the uprising in East Germany in 1953, the invasion of Hungary in 1956, of Czechoslovakia in 1968, not to mention the wars in Vietnam and the war in Korea? Yet measured in numbers of people killed, the record demands a different assessment. An effort to count the fatalities in Asia and Africa in the twenty-two years from 1945 to 1967, when Europe was virtually at peace, came up with the estimate of 7.5 million deaths.[1] By this time, the figure is likely to exceed 10 million dead. The count until 1967 includes 2 million killed during the partitioning of India and the creation of Pakistan; 500,000 Sudanese blacks killed (until 1967 only!) in their war against the ruling Sudanese Arabs; 200,000 Watusi and Bahutu mutually killed in the breakup of Burundi and Rwanda; 150,000 Kurds killed in warring against the Iraqis; 100,000 Nagas, Mizos, and Ahams killed in Assam in their efforts to separate from India; 100,000 minority people killed in fighting the ruling Burmese in Burma; 100,000 Chinese killed by Indonesians.

If we were to include in our search for peace local, far-away wars of this kind, clearly our discussion would be considerably extended beyond the limits within which Western considerations of "a lasting peace" are usually conducted. Nor is it possible to discuss the subject with the facile and surprisingly vulgar-Marxist expectation that continued or increased economic aid to the new states will bring peace to them.

Thus one of the reasons why peace is not indivisible may be termed a matter of political perception. We pay considerably more attention to our own domestic and international security problems than to bloody conflicts that occur far away. Nor is this ethnocentric orientation confined to matters of war. All nations tend to consider their own immediate interests of paramount importance. They often do so at considerable long-range risk to themselves and, of course, without moral qualms. Recent illustrations include the disjointed responses of NATO governments to the October War in the Middle East and to the economic warfare against countries dependent on oil imports.

The final reason why peace is not indivisible resides in the modern technology of destruction. We fear certain types of war more than others. In the period between the two world wars, it was the devastation of the cities by air attack, outlined at the time by General Giulio Douhet, and the use of poison gas as a personnel weapon, which terrified the West. In the crisis of 1938, when Czechoslovakia was dismembered, the U.S. War Department was "besieged with requests from towns all over the country, including some far inland, for antiaircraft protection."[2] Poison gas was not used in World War II, as it was after World War I by Italy against the Ethiopians and more recently by Egypt in Yemen. And contrary to Douhet's predictions, the awesome devastation of cities from the air did not suffice to achieve victory in World War II. But now we live in the age of nuclear and missile technologies, so when we hope for peace we fear above all, at least in the West, *nuclear* war.

Feelings of dread and intense indignation at new weapons have been common phenomena throughout history from the invention of gunpowder to the building of dreadnoughts, from the first feeble use of air power in the form of observation balloons in the eighteenth century to the invention of submersible ships. Unfortunately, these feelings have very rarely led to restraint in war. Instead, as science and technology have spectacularly improved our standard of living, they have also potently pushed the corresponding means of destruction to higher levels of efficiency. But this time civilization itself appears to have reached the crossroads: nuclear war, the experts tell us, would mean the end of civilization, and the laymen trust that it will not break out, or erroneously think that it cannot possibly occur.

What we may refer to as "nuclear peace" is very widely and rightly regarded as something much more important than the avoidance of "conventional war." It is probably no exaggeration to say that the Cuban missile crisis or the confrontation of Soviet and American tanks in Berlin after the erection of the Wall caused more apprehension in the Western nations than did most of the many conventional wars in the rest of the world that have occurred since the end of World War II. Fear of nuclear war also inspired the American efforts to conclude the treaty that is to prevent the proliferation of nuclear weapons among nuclear have-not powers. To Senator Robert Kennedy no domestic issue and no armed conflict abroad equaled in urgency and importance that of erecting a safeguard in the form of an international treaty against the further spread of nuclear technology. On the floor of the Senate, he made a truly astounding statement on October 13, 1965, about the problem of nonproliferation. He said:

> *I do not care* what progress we make, whether it be in education or poverty or housing, or even in South East Asia, in our relations with Laos and Vietnam, or in the Middle East; if we do not find an answer to this problem, *nothing else means anything.*[3]

Total War

The most urgent task of a policy for peace is the avoidance of the "most total" war, if I may use that phrase—that is, of global, nuclear war. Reducing the incidence of limited, localized, or far-away war is, by comparison at least, a less urgent task. It becomes more urgent, however, to the extent that limited, localized, or far-away wars may develop into nuclear war. The probability of escalation is never zero, but in certain wars it is evidently higher than in others. For example, war in the Middle East is more dangerous in this regard than an armed conflict in South America or Central Africa. By the same token, political conflict involving West and East Germany is potentially more dangerous than one between Canada and the United States.

The trouble with this proposition, which seems to be almost a truism, is the different meaning it assumes depending on the national vantage point from which it is viewed. From a global point of view a violent conflict may appear local and limited while in the experience of the population living and dying in the delimited locale it is well-nigh total. This statement hardly needs amplification, particularly in the center of Europe where it has long been understood and often resented that any limited World War III would in all likelihood be a total war for Europeans. After the war people would be unable to tell the elation of victory from the grief of defeat. A conventional global war may well be won in the end after the loss of a campaign at the beginning, but unlike earlier times, an ill-fated campaign in a future limited world war—in which the use of nuclear warheads was restricted by size, target, or in some other way—might well involve not the provisional loss of a province but the devastation of a country or indeed of several countries. I recall hearing this observation for the first time shortly after the formation of NATO in a conversation with the late General von Sodenstern. He added a comment to the effect that this prospect would not readily be accepted in Europe.

To cite another illustration, in an interesting essay titled "Does War Have a Future?"[4] Professor Louis J. Halle has recently come to the conclusion, which I regard as controversial, that "the time has probably gone, perhaps forever, when the formal resort to war . . . was an accepted practice among organized societies" and that "except for the acute danger entailed in the sudden internal collapse of some power . . . the day of general wars, directly involving great powers on both sides, may also be past." To reach the first conclusion, Professor Halle makes light of the wars in Africa and Asia that have occurred so frequently since 1945 and have taken such an appalling toll. He comments on the war of 1972 between India and Pakistan over the secession of what had been East Pakistan by saying, in parentheses, that "it may be considered at least a peripheral case, for it concerned the settlement of an unworkable arrangement in the provisions made for the succession of a colonial empire that had been dissolved in the crucible of World War II."

Now wars usually do not break out over workable arrangements, nor are unworkable political arrangements in the wake of a war by any means uncommon. Even from the viewpoint of the victorious Indians the enormous cost of the relatively short war and the influx of 10 million refugees from Bangladesh made this minor war of 1972 a disaster, particularly if added to the economic consequences of the subsequent droughts and the suffering caused by the recent increase in the oil bill from 20 to 50 percent of India's export earnings. Thus again, from a global point of view or from far away, a war may appear as an exception on the fringes of world peace, while to the more than 500 million people directly involved it is a major calamity. Hence it ought to be with a sense of proportion and more than a touch of melancholy that we agree to regard the control of limited or localized war as a relatively unimportant task.

The circumstances in which total war—that is, war involving the depletion of nuclear arsenals—may develop cannot, of course, be foreseen. And there is little sense in assuming that insight into the outbreak and course of such a war can be gained by way of war games and sophisticated calculations. Elsewhere I have called attention to the fact that in 1780 the Prince of Ligne proposed the opening of an international War Academy in the belief that by studying and teaching military science with topography and geometry providing the basic analytical tools it would be possible to abolish war.[5] War would be recognized as so calculable an enterprise that no reasonable man would want to wage it in the knowledge that he would lose. By present standards, the Prince of Ligne's optimism was unsophisticated. In order to sustain it he had neither research teams of experts nor computers at his disposal. But we who do use "think tanks" and computers should, if anything, be less optimistic than the Prince was. For the most frightful war, nuclear war, which we must study in order to avoid it or to control its development, is a war without historical precedent. The experts who study nuclear war are literally studying irreality. Unable to learn from history—and usually unwilling to try—they must establish and proceed on assumptions. Nevertheless, such studies of defense analysts do contribute to the search for peace in a few principal ways.

First, they result in critical evaluations of existing or preferred defense postures on the basis of specified assumptions and assessments of probabilities. This is a more intelligent procedure than recommending defense expenditures on grounds of political preference. If we grant that an adversary may disturb the peace by the use of overwhelming force or pervert the value of peace by successful nuclear blackmail, deterrence is an important safeguard of peace, and an analytical effort that helps to shape an adequate deterrent posture is a contribution to peace.

Second, such studies consider scenarios of nuclear war and inquire into sophisticated weapons systems and strategies with the object of maximizing the likelihood of intrawar deterrence. Efforts in this regard are based on the assumption that tacit or explicit agreements with the adversary are possible during the war which will prevent escalation of the conflict to a full-scale nuclear holocaust. Restraint, for example, in the selection of certain targets or the use of certain weapons may be mutually advantageous. Personally, I am quite skeptical about many of the assumptions regarding "signals," "pauses" in which to arrive at tacit or explicit agreements, and, generally, the possibility of reaching rational decisions under conditions of unprecedented confusion and stress. It is true, however, that restraint in the use of violence is a phenomenon well known from past conventional wars at virtually all levels of technological development.

Third, such studies impress upon us the so-called irrationality of general nuclear war. They teach us that as long as the risks of an unsuccessful surprise attack are staggeringly high, it is counterproductive to embark upon nuclear war, since it will end in catastrophe. Responsible studies of nuclear war increase the awareness of the unprecedented calamity its occurrence would constitute for combatants and noncombatants alike, for neutral as well as belligerent states, and possibly even for unborn generations. To the extent that this awesome understanding does not entail a process of unilateral renunciation of power favoring the state with the stronger will, a peace of submission may be avoided and the way to the search for a worthier peace may remain open.

Finally, then, analysts of the historically unprecedented nuclear war can attempt to state reasonable priorities for political efforts to establish a balance of terror on a lower technological level by means of arms control and disarmament agreements.

Belittling such analytical and political contributions would be about as foolish as turning against the research and cure of certain types of cancer for the reason that modern medicine is unable to prevent and cure all forms of the disease.

It remains a fact, however, that many so-called experts on nuclear war have little use for history. Perhaps they disdain the goddess Fortuna, and almost certainly they are disturbed by the disorderliness of the human condition. And yet history and the humanities can offer us important insights. Above all, it is possible to assert quite confidently that unrestricted wars are not the result of technology but of unmitigated hatred and horror of the enemy.

Wars tend to be unrestricted especially when the enemy is viewed as a threatening incarnation of evil or as something subhuman — vermin, dogs, snakes, beasts of prey. Such total wars, in which the enemy is satanized or monsterized and is felt to pose a horrible, existential threat, occur in preliterate societies, on very low levels of technology, as well as at more advanced stages of human development. In such conflicts, the enemy can never be bargained with. Nor is it the object to defeat him. He must be destroyed. The aim is not to gain an advantage over him, be it in territory, human or natural resources, privilege, power, or standard of living; the aim is rather to wipe him off the face of the earth.

Now wars in which few, if any, restrictions are placed on the use of violence, on cruelty, fanatical rage, and on horror felt and inflicted, occur under certain typical conditions. I shall not describe and illustrate them in detail, but confine myself to saying that total warfare tends to occur in racial wars, in wars of religion (so-called holy wars), in "ideological wars," to use de Jomini's term, and in class or civil wars. Unrestricted warfare also occurs in violent attempts at liberation from foreign rule, particularly when the subdued population disposes only of grossly inferior weapons and is driven to magnify its power by terror. The technologically superior enemy, in turn, feels justified to lift all restraint in striking back. Guerrilla war, therefore, is characteristically merciless and, unless it ends in exhaustion, may rage until the last opponent is killed. Perhaps the most extraordinary account of guerrilla warfare in its pristine form, comparable in grandeur to Tolstoy's *War and Peace*, is Euclides da Cunha's *Rebellion in the Backlands*, telling the incredible story of the resistance offered by religiously inspired, semibarbaric natives against Brazilian government forces in 1896–97.

Any possibility of compromise and hence of restriction of violence tends to diminish when in such ethnic and cultural clashes one side has a monopoly of superior weapons and is not interested in exploiting the manpower of the defeated enemy. As Adam Smith observed in 1776, "In ancient times the opulent and civilized found it difficult to defend themselves against the poor and barbarous nations. In modern times the poor and barbarous find it difficult to defend themselves against the opulent and civilized."

Compared to the orgies of cruelty, death, and destruction to be found in the total wars of history at all levels of technology, limited war contains elements of civilization — the observance of conventional and legal rules, political and economic reasoning, conscience. Or, simply, limited war contains an element of peace. Again, the specific conditions giving rise to limited wars can be stated in detail, and it would be an appropriate subject for peace research to do so more systemically and more fully than has been done in the past. It must be noted that if under present conditions war does break out, preventing such a war from turning nuclear means keeping the war limited and preserving an element of peace.

Having given the analytical futurologists of thermonuclear war their due, let us now list a few simple historical or humanistic reservations with which their rational efforts must be treated.

1. Fear of violent retaliation to the use of violence deters war only if the aggressor calculates that he will suffer defeat in the end. Since the aggressor may miscalculate, however, and since the attacked — motivated by honor or outrage or simply hoping for an unforeseeable turn of events — may fight against all odds, the fear of war is no firm, reliable bulwark against its outbreak or its escalation.

2. Nor is the calculated prediction of the human and material costs of war a firm, reliable safeguard of peace, no matter how staggering and awe-inspiring these predictions are. This is so because man is capable of recklessness and self-destruction. To repeat, while rational deliberations and calculations, which increase the fear of war and its consequences, help to preserve the peace, we cannot be so assured as to turn away from the problem of war in our time.

3. The control of escalation in a grave political crisis may be easier for dictatorial regimes than for democratic ones, since the former are less subject to pressure by public opinion.

4. In a grave political crisis established bureaucratic procedures may be suspended in favor of action by small, secretive bodies of decision-makers, created ad hoc, or indeed by the supreme decision-maker assuming responsibility for the smallest detail. (Incidentally, in view of this phenomenon, exemplified by Churchill in World War II and John F. Kennedy during the Berlin and Cuban missile crises, it is necessary to qualify Max Weber's teaching that modern life is inexorably engulfed by ever-increasing bureaucratization.)

5. Several serious confrontations of the nuclear superpowers were resolved peacefully — for example, in Berlin, in Cuba, and to a lesser extent, in the Arab-Israeli war of October 1973. Similarly, limited wars involving a nuclear power in the period following World War II — for

example, in Korea and Vietnam — did not lead to the employment of nuclear weapons. This record holds no firm promise that such restraint will necessarily be exercised in comparable future situations.

6. If history is any guide, the most nightmarish scenario of future armed conflict would be an engagement of nuclear powers in which differences in political ideology were exacerbated by racial antagonisms.

7. I do not think it likely, however, that sometime in the future the advanced countries may be subjected to nuclear blackmail and sabotage by terrorists acting for desperately starving millions of the Third World. This specter has recently been conjured up by Professor Heilbroner. In my view, increased violence in the large areas of despair is more likely to occur than terrorist warfare against the outside world. Nor do I consider it probable that the advanced countries would react meekly, should they be so challenged. Their response to the economic-warfare measures against the oil-importing countries of the world provides no precedent for response to international nuclear terror. Finally, I do not think that attempts at such terror could count on Soviet support, since the risks would be infinitely greater than have been the risks of supporting the oil embargo.

8. At the time when the Soviet leaders were still under the spell of Stalin's doctrine that socialism would emerge victoriously from the inevitable clash between so-called imperialist and socialist powers, Western leaders advocating détente hoped that in time the Soviet leaders might understand that there could be no victor in nuclear war. That is to say, the great hope of détente policy in the West was that, in time, the Soviet leaders might prove to be capable of learning the truth about nuclear war despite their adherence to party doctrine. Khrushchev did indeed sanction this revision of Stalin's reckless and unenlightened teaching on war. Today, it is only the Chinese school of communist ideology that still adheres to the doctrine of the inevitability of war between imperialism and socialism. Nor has the world received word from the Chinese as yet on the irrationality of nuclear war. Neither the pedagogy of détente nor the influence of conscience-stricken students of nuclear weapons has thus far had any moderating influence on the Chinese doctrine. And in this case it is likely that Russians rather than Americans would have to be the educators, but the Russians are not likely to perform that role. Of course, this doctrinal intransigence need not have any influence on policy. Just as Chinese foreign policy has been remarkably cautious despite its aggressive rhetoric, so the Chinese may exercise restraint in a major war, should they be

embroiled in it. One would feel more comfortable, however, if the mounting body of professional opinion on the catastrophic consequences of nuclear war contained contributions from China.

9. As to disarmament agreements, the historical record prior to World War II does not encourage optimism for the future. But perhaps the outcome of SALT II or SALT III will break the historical pattern and set a new precedent. The consequences of failure would be much more ominous than past failures ever were.

Deterrence

Neither the work of the defense analysts nor the qualifying observations that an historical orientation may suggest provide very powerful reassurance for peace. On the whole, fear and caution seem to pervade responsible discourse on the chances for peace. And deterrence, itself inspired by caution and fear, emerges as a continued need.

We must add that deterrence may fail not only because of unforeseeable qualitative and quantitative changes in the balance of strategic power but also by virtue of its continued success. Prolonged avoidance of nuclear war may undermine the domestic and Allied consensus without which the defense policy of the West will be enfeebled. Those who deny the need for deterrence may be encouraged to spread the idea that the adversary's intentions have always been peaceful and that those who insist on guarding the ramparts of peace are obsessed with war — erroneously, neurotically, or maliciously. This paradoxical result of successful deterrence may be reinforced by clamor for disengagement, isolationism, or neutralism and by demands that the government correct shortcomings of its domestic policy. Since deterrence works upon the mind and is a matter of will as well as capability, domestic denials of the need for deterrents are in fact antideterrents.

In Western Europe, such antideterrent moods have been deepened not only by prosperity at home, the Sino-Soviet conflict, and Soviet interest in Western technology and trade, but also by two other specific developments: the success of West German *Ostpolitik* and the shift in Soviet pressure from Central Europe to the Middle East and the Mediterranean. Nobody will deny that *Ostpolitik* has been a contribution to peace, whether or not he may be inclined to argue that the price paid for it has been too high. Massive Soviet support of Arab military and economic warfare and the Soviet naval buildup in the Mediterranean may be viewed as an attempt to outflank NATO after direct political attacks and threats were unproductive. In addition, these Soviet efforts were probably prompted by logistical considerations of Soviet policy toward countries bordering on the Indian Ocean. While all direct political assaults on the Western alliance failed in the past, the October War of 1973 in conjunction with the Arab oil embargo succeeded in shaking Allied solidarity more severely than any other Soviet initiative. In Europe, the October War was perhaps considered a faraway war, while in the United States at least some observers were concerned lest the war escalate into something worse than Vietnam and more dangerous to world peace than the Cuban missile crisis.[6]

Clearly, this is a matter of judgment and controversy, as is the whole broad topic of my talk. I am glad that others at this conference will speak and probably submit different views for your and my benefit.[7]

Let me say in conclusion that I know of only one major contribution coming from the Soviet Union that has broken out of the circle of deterrence, fear, and caution in which the chances for peace are otherwise confined. This is Andrei D. Sakharov's "Thoughts on Progress, Peaceful Co-existence and Intellectual Freedom" of 1968, to the effect that the nuclear powers must join in an effort to attack common problems that transcend their rivalry and face mankind. But Sakharov is a critic of the Soviet regime.

NOTES

1. Robert D. Crane, "Postwar Ethnic Cultural Conflicts: Some Quantitative and Other Considerations," manuscript, Hudson Institute, New York, 1968, cited by Harold R. Isaaks, "Changing Arenas and Identities in World Affairs," in Harold D. Lasswell, Daniel Lerner, and Hans Speier, eds., *Propaganda and Communication in World History*, Honolulu, vol. 3, 1980, p. 423, n. 1.
2. The New York *Times*, October 23, 1938.
3. *Congressional Record*, 89th Congress, October 13, 1965, p. 25900; emphasis added. For a discussion of this statement, see Hans Speier, *Force and Folly*, Cambridge, 1969, pp. 126ff.
4. *Foreign Affairs*, LII, October 1973, pp. 28–34.
5. See p. 81.
6. Cf. Eugene V. Rostow, "America, Europe and the Middle East," *Commentary*, LIII, February 1974, pp. 40–55.
7. I regret especially that my selective treatment does not include a discussion of Harold D. Lasswell's notion of "the expectation of violence" introduced into the literature more than forty years ago.

Index